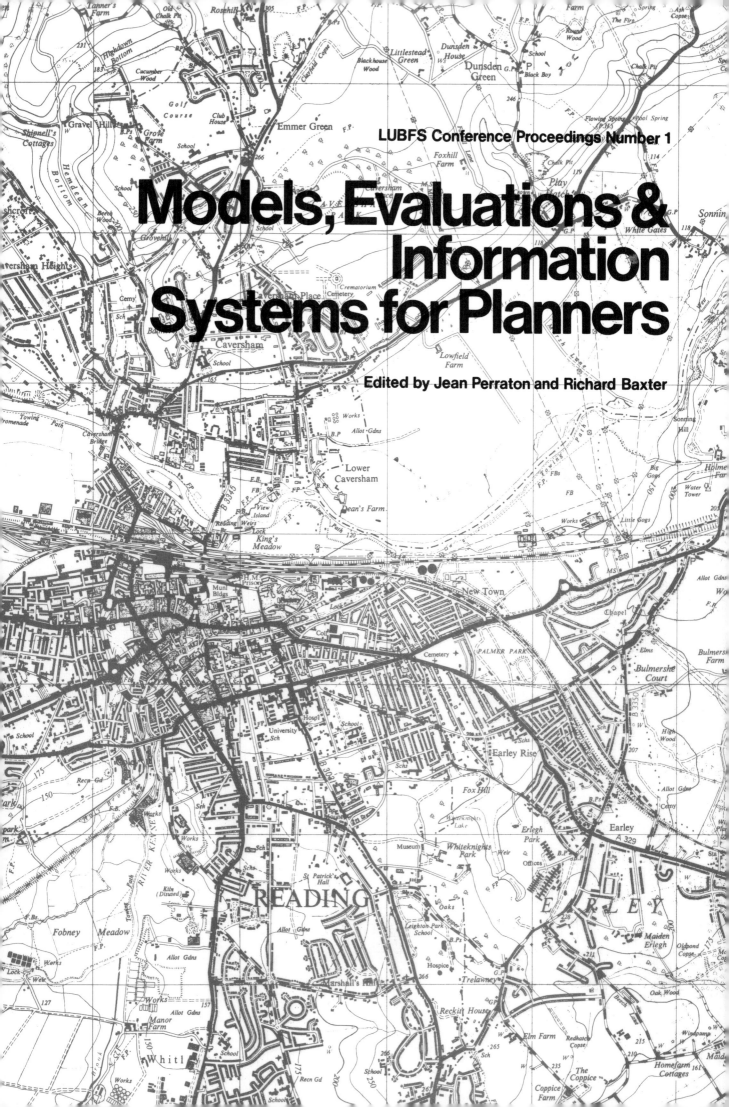

LUBFS Conference Proceedings Number 1

Models, Evaluations & Information Systems for Planners

Edited by Jean Perraton and Richard Baxter

Models, Evaluations &
Information
Systems for Planners

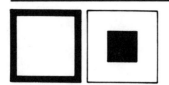

Land Use and Built Form Studies

University of Cambridge Department of Architecture

LUBFS Conference Proceedings Number 1

Models, Evaluations & Information Systems for Planners

Edited by Jean Perraton and Richard Baxter

MTP Construction
1974

ISBN 0 85200102 9

Published in 1974 by
MTP Construction
Medical and Technical Publishing Company Limited
P.O. Box 55,
Lancaster, England.

Reprinted in 1976 by
The Construction Press Limited,
Lunesdale House,
Hornby Lancaster LA2 8NB

Editorial

The Urban Systems Group at the Centre for Land Use and Built Form Studies has been engaged in urban research since 1967. Increasingly it was felt that the techniques developed were potentially of use to planners. Hence, the first LUBFS conference was arranged to help disseminate more widely some of the work and the ideas of people at the centre, and of people doing closely related work at other centres.

The conference took place at Pembroke College, Cambridge, on July 3 to 7, 1972. The scope and content of the conference, including the selection of contributors, was arranged by Richard Baxter of the Centre, but the conference administration was carried out by Applied Research of Cambridge Limited on behalf of the Centre.

This collection of papers covers the more formal proceedings of the first three days of the conference. The last two days were devoted to more informal seminars and computer demonstrations. No attempt has been made to include or summarise the discussions between papers. Since the speakers were not asked to submit formal papers in advance, the papers published here are mainly edited versions of the taped transcripts of the proceedings. In most cases, this editing was done initially by the speakers concerned; in a few cases it was left entirely to the discretion of the editor. In other cases, a re-written or shortened version of the original paper, submitted after the conference, was used. This accounts for a certain lack of uniformity in style and length.

The subject matter of the conference falls into three main groups. After two introductory papers, the major part of the proceedings are devoted to papers covering the development of urban models, how they work, and how they have begun to be applied in British planning. A smaller section touches, somewhat unevenly, upon problems of evaluation in planning, and the use of models for evaluative rather than predictive purposes. The final section deals with problems of data collection and management, many of which are raised in the course of developing urban models.

The reader will no doubt note a certain euphoria - often found among pioneers of new techniques - but he will also find considerable divergences of opinion about the scope and limitations of urban models, about the best way to approach evaluation or the building of an information system. These differences, one suspects, spring partly from the fact that researchers have only just begun to think hard about how to apply such techniques and procedures to urban planning, and partly from the contrast between the necessarily simple abstract representation of the world embodied in the model, and the complexity of the reality that planners have to grapple with.

Contents

Part 1

Introductory papers

The relationship between planning and research

Brian McLoughlin

One does not begin a conference such as this by plunging straight
into subjects like maximum entropy and doubly-constrained gravity
models. It is necessary to make a more gradual approach, setting
the scene for what is to come.

The substance of the papers which follow lies in the context of
the relationship between planning and research. It is an open
question whether it is better to know a great deal about one side
of this relationship and perhaps have a sympathy and understanding
of the other or to have some lesser knowledge of both.

Please bear in mind that, for my part, I know a little about planning,
a little about research, have practised a little of each but am
really an expert on neither.

Recent growth of planning practice and research

The fact that conferences like this take place at all is not in the least
surprising to those of you who are younger than I am - and I suppose that
is the majority of you - but to people of my age and brought up in planning
schools in my generation, planning research was almost laughable. It was
non-existent. Since 1967 or thereabouts we have seen a great upsurge in
the volume of research from virtually nothing to something which is still
almost laughable when compared with, say, medical research and other forms
of research funded by government. Equally it is fair to say that we are
seeing a vast expansion in the amount of planning that goes on in Britain
now. I am being a little insular for I am not talking about the growth of
planning in the developing economies; that is well documented and well
understood, and all the reasons for that great upsurge in planning activity
have been well spelled out by pundits. Huge risks are undertaken by modern
governments and private investors and colossal time lags require even greater
and greater ability to foretell or to will the future. But I think in Britain
we are witnessing through local government reform, through the transformation
of local authority management structures and (as far as physical planning
is concerned) through the inception of the 1968 and 1971 Town and Country
Planning Acts, a sort of intellectual revolution lying behind it which does
suggest a great increase in the amount of planning however general or specific
a meaning you want to put on that. So the burden of this introduction is
to discuss the relationship between two rapidly growing fields. One is the
field of government-funded social-science-based research into urban, regional
and other forms of planning. That is growing very rapidly. So too are all
the kinds of planning at which it is directed, which sustains it and requires
it.

It is not in the least surprising that with two such rapidly-growing areas, there should be a great deal of uncertainty. Think, for example, of medical research – how very long-established this is and what a huge intellectual and practical tradition it has inherited. Consider also the operational end of medicine in all its forms – general practice, hospital service, specialist medicine, social service medicine – all of which are very well established. Of course ideas and medical practice are changing but if we think of the relationship between the practice of medicine and medical research, we would not be surprised to find it relatively clearly defined. We would find that people have fairly clear roles to play, and know more or less what to expect of each other, when to be disappointed and when to rejoice at certain strengths, weaknesses, successes and failures which arise within that huge relationship. This is by no means the case in the field of planning and its related research activity. Can I take the two things separately first of all? First I shall say a few words about planning – rather personal words – then something about research and then try and bring them together.

The expanding scope of planning

Of the two, I would guess that planning is by far the more volatile area. Traditionally, planning was regarded as a technical activity largely within local government with neutral political values. To many people that political neutrality is surprising when one thinks of its clear social welfare origins in the late nineteenth and early twentieth century movements of reform and legislation. Planning, it seems, started off quite clearly as a radical social welfare movement but it became institutionalised and quite quickly profession-alised, and professionalised between about 1900 and 1920 meant that it came to be seen as essentially a technical design activity with neutral political values. The 1950's development plan, based on the 1947 Planning Act, expanded the concern of planning from fairly straightforward land use and physical design to the mid-1960's post-Buchanan land use and transport plan. Now I think it is clear that we are trying to expand it yet again into the 1970s' structure plan. As we do so, it is becoming evident within the planning profession, and not only there, that planning is not simply a technical service related to a single department of government or local government, but a very important aspect of the total process of governing, managing and deciding about processes and actions within towns and regions. It may be that this is a sign of our having come a full circle in about seventy years by a curious helical route back to the social welfare aims of the original planning movement before it became institutionalised and professionalised. Of course, like all helical processes, we have <u>not</u> got back to quite the same place as we started, but it does seem clear, that in the transition from the early fifties to the early seventies we have moved a very very long way from the land use/physical design type of statutory document to a very broad (some would say an alarmingly, ambiguously broad) structure plan, which may or may not have got us back to the original social welfare aims of planning in Britain.

Now, planning is not to be found by looking at one particular point within government. There is not only one place where planning is done, nor is it necessarily confined to the formal organs of government. If I borrow a colleague's turn of phrase, planning is a principle or style of management and can occur at several places. First, it can occur at the level of corporate management of all the services and activities of local government. Secondly, it can occur at the level of specific services or programmes: the educational, social and transport services. All these specific services, and some even more homely than these – the dustbin collection service – need planning.

Then again, we can look at particular geographical sub-areas of a local authority's area and say that all of the services together in that small geographical area (not only for the town as a whole) need to be planned. Planning can also occur in quite different ways, some of them fairly novel. It can occur through the medium of public participation; it can occur as 'counter-planning' in which a distinct conflict mode is developed between a group and the formal organs of government. There are other sorts of planning too: community planning and inter-authority planning. The need for the latter arises when we make a mess of local government reform (as perhaps we are going to do) so that the new counties may not always cover complete local labour markets and local housing markets. So there are inter-departmental or inter-agency plans.

In studying the planning process – the process of "strategic choice" – Friend and Jessop (1969) identified something called the 'governmental system', acting on behalf of, acting on and responding to, and directing the 'community system'. It may be useful when we are thinking about planning and research to look at the field to which planning research is directed, as being a coupled pair of systems – the governmental or planning system on one hand and the community or urban system on the other. Of course neither of them is a monolithic block; there is not a community and a governing body. There are many different agencies and many different initiatives taking place within the governmental planning system with very complex interactions and very many different initiatives and problems within the community together with their interactions. When we couple these two together we get a very complex scene indeed and no simple-minded approach is likely to get very far. It does not mean deliberately striving for abstract complexity but it does make anyone pause who thinks there are simple problems to be defined and which are susceptible to simple techniques.

The nature of social research

Following that inadequate sketch of the growth of planning in governmental systems, can I turn to research. Research is of course a process in or an aspect of the knowledge industry. It is the 'upstream' end of the knowledge industry, the growing point; at least that is true of basic fundamental research. There are 'downstream' aspects of research, and these are found in development and in application. But perhaps the sort of research you will hear most about will either be fundamental research or be fairly close to the fundamental end.

The techniques of the research worker, and his intellectual traditions, have been most fully developed in the natural sciences. But the current methods of the natural sciences have derived mostly from the study of relatively closed systems. That is, they can be fairly well isolated from interaction with the observer. The classical requirement that experiments should be repeatable by others is usually quite simple to arrange. The social sciences have no comparable well-developed techniques, and they deal almost exclusively with open systems on which the investigator interacts freely whether he is studying individuals or whole communities, whether he is studying a governmental process and trying to test a theoretical model of that process, or whether he is doing empirical work. In a sense then, all social science research is action research, especially when the results are published. To publish the results of your research in the social sciences is often – though perhaps with time-lags and perhaps with 'noise' in the communications system – to influence the very subject of your research. When Norman Dennis (1970) published his book about aspects of planning and decision-making in Sunderland, I think that it is fair to say that the system which

5

he was researching - that is the Sunderland Corporation and its relationships with the community of Sunderland - would be distinctly modified by his book. One outcome was that Mr. Dennis is now <u>Councillor</u> Dennis of Sunderland County Borough Council, which I think is rather nice! If you state your research findings on urban poverty or you publish your forecasts of, say, car ownership and traffic congestion, you affect people's attitudes and values.

All social science research therefore lies in a political arena. It is something which people like Friend and Jessop know only too well because the very sort of research they were doing was research into the decision-making process. They were looking at that realm in which there is a very blurred distinction between the role of chief officers or a management board in local government and the elected members (in that case of the Coventry City Council). Younger research workers would do well to bear in mind that when they are studying the processes of government planning they are entering into a political arena and observing political decision-making. The field of urban and regional planning, which we are interested in, is essentially a political process rather than a technical service.

Relationship between planning and research

If I turn now to the relationship between planning and research, certain things seem to follow. This is a relationship between two sorts of activity which are both more or less directly related to the making, implementation, review and revision of public policies. The realm in which those policies are made and revised, for example the corporate management level, probably corresponds to Dainton's 'strategic research', whilst the implementation level can use 'tactical research' results. (Council for Scientific Policy, 1968.) Some of the strategic research could well be done 'in house', that is within local government R. & D. units, whilst better programmes of action, better tactical choices depend very largely on the direct application or the development or extension of existing research findings. What Dainton called 'basic research' probably could not and should not take place in local government itself but in various kinds of specialised research institutions.

If we look at government - and I am using that term generically to mean government <u>and</u> local government - as an hierarchical continuum from the setting of broadest goals down to specific actions and from general ideas about redistributive justice right through to a specific building programme or a rent rebate scheme, it may help to clarify this relationship between planning and research. I am asking you to conceive of a continuing process in government which extends from the broadest kinds of value judgement and political choice, right down to the most specific action which directly impinges on the community at the 'sharp end'.

That sharp end is the implementation end; it is the world of the child care officer, the school teacher, the development control case-worker, the housing architect, the people who actually deliver that kind of service, the agencies in which they work, the problems which they face as the deliverers of services. Those people and that field can, I think, have a fairly clear and direct relationship with the downstream end of research; that is, with the development and application end of research. They have specific problems for which very often fairly specific research results are available. When they are not, then a fairly specific research request can usually be directed either to in-house research workers or to a research-and-development agency. The sort of thing I have in mind is the kind of work which has been done over the years by people like the Building Research Station, to help with improved construction and design standards, improved materials, and performance specifications in public housing, or in the Road Research Laboratory on the problems of developing certain kinds of pavement and surveying techniques; these are 'sharp end' problems. This is not a question of transportation policy, this is a question of how to build this specific road across this kind of soil, where a policy decision about roads has been taken in some other place, at some other time.

Under those circumstances a fairly direct face-to-face kind of communication can be developed between the public servant and his opposite number in a research agency. Sometimes, if his information systems are working properly, the research worker can say "Fine. I will look at the results which are already available for you. We will write you a letter and have a meeting, and tell you what research has already been done." Also the researcher may identify that there is no readily available research but he could either say "We can do the investigation here" or "I know where it can be done, but it is not here, it will be somewhere else and the person you want to speak to is Dr. So-and-so". So at this sharp end of government, where the planning process ends in decisions and actions, we can expect and we should pursue, these very direct relationships between the public official, his client communities and the research worker.

Let us now look at the other end, the 'blunt' or fuzzy end of the continuum, the realm of political choice. Take, for example, the realm of goal setting for structure plans. What should be the objectives for a particular structure plan? Ought we to go for redistributive goals? Are we trying to direct more resources to the poorer members in the community, or are we making a structure plan which more or less keeps things working the way they are now, and improves things in various areas?

This essentially political debate cannot be entirely the province of members nor entirely the province of senior officers. It depends upon a very complex on-going relationship between the senior officers in government, their political opposite numbers and the community. The sort of problems which are thrown up by setting goals for a structure plan have very indirect, very complex and very elusive relationships with research work. In the first place, it is extremely difficult to pin down precisely what the problem is. This is not a problem of finding a certain kind of material with a sheer stress resistance of so much. It is not a problem of getting a certain kind of concrete mix to be supported on soil with a certain bearing pressure. It is not to get a certain kind of paint which will stand certain weathering characteristics on the east coast of Great Britain in January. These are specific problems of the sharp end of the public service which are susceptible to clear definition and can be transmitted unambiguously to a research worker.

One simply cannot adopt the same relationship to a research worker when considering a problem of setting goals in a structure plan. Nor are there always a lot of results from social science, political science, administrative theory and local government research lying around which are easily trans-latable, easily adaptable and easily applicable to those kinds of problems. The time lags which exist between those sorts of problems being identified by the public service or the researcher and the results filtering through to practice in the policy realm of local government can be very considerable. If you go along to the Road Research Laboratory with a specific problem about a material, they should be able to tell you that, in view of the vast amount of knowledge which exists about this kind of problem, and considering the amount of resources which can be devoted, the manpower, the skills, the young research workers and the middle management that can be put on to the job, that you should have some sort of an answer within eighteen months to two years. It should be readily understandable how to apply that answer within another six months to a year, and the whole situation could be transformed, at the outside, within five years. But when problems arise in public life about new modes of planning, whether one means structure planning or corporate planning, and management in local government, the relevant research results may have to wait ten, fifteen or twenty years before they start to affect the corporate policy-making process in local government.

This complexity with its time-lags and indirectness means that those who look for results from research workers to help with the problems at the blunt end, at the fuzzy origins of policies, goals and objectives, must not expect that there will be a lot of immediately useful results lying around already. Even if there are, like good books on local government management structures or splendid theoretical works in political science, they should not expect that it will be easy to translate these research results directly into practice. For their part research workers should not expect government to jump into action immediately they have delivered themselves of a brilliant review of the literature on "some aspects of departmentalism in certain kinds of bureaucracies". It may take years and years and years of filtering, of reading, of debate, of teaching in graduate schools or INLOGOV before the whole thing begins to make any sort of limited mark in the public service. The reverse relationship is equally true. It may be a very long time before you can clearly identify your policy problem in local government and translate that into terms which would interest certain kinds of research workers. You simply cannot go out and buy this sort of a research worker. They are not queueing up to study the problems of setting goals in structure plans, whereas there may be very many more people who know an awful lot about reinforced concrete design.

Conclusions

Can I mention one or two other things by way of conclusion, and make what I hope is a practical suggestion? The first practical suggestion is a bit of a 'con' really, because I am going to say what has already started to happen.

Because there are so many more people concerned with planning in its various guises and meanings in the public service and so many more research workers who are becoming interested in those problems, it seems that the number of relationships between those sort of planners and those sort of researchers is on the increase. I myself am one example of the relationship between local government structure planning and the research end of the knowledge industry. If there are so many more relationships arising, we can expect an increase in the number of problems which arise in managing research. We have so far lacked some sort of 'code of practice' which would help, for example, people in senior and middle management posts in local government when they are approached by research workers wanting to study what they are doing. The research workers will want to publish the results if they are publishable, and the local government officials will quite rightly want to know what sort of formal relationship they should have with such research workers. Who is paying for this research? Is the authority being asked to pay and, if not, what relationship will it have with those who are sponsoring the research project? The local authority may be acting as a sort of catalyst - somebody else may be paying for the research, and the chap on the other side of the desk is wanting to do the research. Where does the public official stand? He has to be accountable to the community and to his colleagues in various ways.

There are problems for the research worker too. Quite rightly, he wants to be able to publish what he, and his intellectual 'peer group' regard as being useful and valid results. He does not want to be told that he must not say such and such because it might embarrass an alderman, or it might make the Dimshire County Council look rather foolish when the results are published. We have lots of precedents for this but these precedents have usually been hammered out one at a time as one-off situations. It would be of great practical help if all concerned in this growing set of relationships could turn somewhere for, at least, some basis for a code of practice.

I told you this was a con, because the Centre for Environmental Studies (CES) has been chairing a working group representative of research interests, public service professions, government departments and local authorities to this very end, and we hope to publish it soon.

Secondly, I think all of us on both sides of this interface between the researcher and planner could be more clearly aware of just how much we may already know about certain kinds of urban system problems and just how much the research industry may already have churned out, which is of immediate practical use. There must be a lot of research work which can be applied fairly directly, no doubt with some development effort, but can yield useful results in a fairly short space of time. There are many examples of this. There is a fine example in the work of part of the centre for Land Use and Built Form Studies in Cambridge, which offers a service of advice to government, local government, and other people, based on established research findings and which does some development work as well. The Planning Research Advisory Group, the tie-up between the Local Government Operational Research Unit and the Centre for Environmental Studies, is another example.

Thirdly, there is the inevitable plea for more research. Everyone has his own favourite. My own plea for more research would, I think, not yield immediately useful results. It would be an example of the sort of work where we may have to wait some considerable time before we begin to see real impacts in the field itself, in the field of community and its government. I am talking about research into certain kinds of "markets" which have so far been ignored or seriously underplayed – such things as housing market performance, intra-urban employment markets, markets in education, training and the acquisition of skill, and access to skill in education. All of this is urban systems research; finding out in rather an analytical way, and not necessarily directly related to how policies are made or how the governmental system works, how the urban and regional systems work.

Lastly, and above all, a huge research effort is needed to improve knowledge of the governmental and political systems. We should study, for example, the relationships between local and central government as they evolve and change. We are now going to be saddled with two tiers of a reformed local government system and a whole set of complex relationships there. What could we learn – what lessons can be learnt already from over seven years of two-tier metropolitan government in Greater London? What lessons are there for Greater Manchester, Merseyside, West and South Yorkshire, or Tyneside from seven years of two-tier relationships in the London Metropolitan Area? What problems are there of inter-agency working in government? That is not just inter-departmental relationships within local authorities but between them and the new water authorities, between passenger transport authorities and their successors, between the regional health authorities and one or two tiers of local government. How do these things really work? How do policies get formulated when aspects of a whole problem, as seen by the consumers, must be tackled within many different agencies. How do policies get translated into action under those

circumstances? How does professionalism affect the way services are
delivered in the public service? Does it matter, and if so how does it
matter, that virtually all educational policy is formulated, reviewed and
put into application by professional teachers rather than anybody else
who knows anything at all about children, their families and their environment? Can we leave physical planning entirely to physical planners?
What is the relationship between the various things separately called
community action, public participation, public enquiries and parts of the
information and intelligence systems in local government? Are these things
quite distinct? Or should they be conceived and practised as aspects of
a larger democratic process?

These are all examples, simply that and no more; certainly not a list of
research imperatives. These are examples of what I mean by the general
imperative for planning research workers to understand the way governmental
systems which are directed to urban and regional problems, actually work.

I hope that I have said enough to persuade you that it is not true to say
that relationships between planning and research are always complicated and
difficult and nebulous. Neither is it true to say there are usually simple
and clear-cut relationships between urban-regional problems and research.
There are both. What seems to me to be important is to define which end
of the whole governmental system one is talking about, and the level of
planning problem to which it is directed. There are different kinds of
research, some of which can be immediately applied with results which are
immediately useful to certain kinds of problems and others where research
interest either does not exist or is just coming into being, and whose
results and whose effects on the whole process of planning in government
may take a very long time indeed to show any results. Sometimes they may
show no results at all.

Quantifying the environment

Lionel March

In this paper I shall touch only lightly on certain ideas in
information theory, since further emphasis might prove more confusing
than useful. The main discussion will concern some aspects of
quantifying environmental situations which we have been looking into
at the Centre for Land Use and Built Form Studies.

A scientific view of the world

I think the first thing to mention is that our view of the world – that is to
say, our collective view, apart from our individual view – is constantly
changing. Our individual view is one which we gain through our experiences
in our day to day lives, and we probably make adjustments as certain things
occur during the course of our life, which would suggest the world is other
than we originally thought it was. Obviously, the very simple decision-making
things that we do every day are dependent on how we view the world outside, how
we see it structured, how we expect it to respond when we act on it in a part-
cular way. It is very important from a planning point of view that this is a
collective matter and not something done by a private individual, i.e. the
planner as a private individual. We would hope very much that planning is
something collective, and it makes use of collective knowledge about the world
and not merely the prejudice of the individual planner, acting upon the world
at that particular moment.

So we look to science for a model of this situation, because science is where
we find the slow evolution of a collective view of the world out there. We
would not, I think, look to artists or to literature for this because, on the
whole, artists and novelists present a more individual view of the world,
tempered of course by the scientific knowledge of the period in which they
live. So it is mainly to a scientific view that we are going to look.

Earlier this century it was said that Einstein changed our view of the world,
the cosmology, through his theories of relativity. At the same time, artists
were changing our way of looking at and perceiving things: people like the
Cubists and the Futurists were doing this, and a man like Gideon could write
about this in what has become a classic book for architects and for planners –
Space, Time and Architecture. He tried to show there how a changing scientific
view influenced the artistic, architectural and planning views of the world.
He tried then to describe how modern planning theories were influenced by
changes in scientific viewpoints.

That is the first thing I want to say, and when I come on to discussing one or two emerging ideas from information theory, I do so because in my opinion this particular development is certainly important, and probably a good deal more important than what Einstein did at the beginning of the century. I think it will colour and influence the way we, as planners, act upon the world.

Data collection rests upon theory

The next point I want to take up is that the data, the things that we collect from out there about this world, are essentially theory-laden. In other words, we cannot just simply act as a garbage bin and let data drop into it higgledy-piggledly because it is out there. In fact we collect it intentionally, and behind those intentions are theories about how the world is constructed. I can give you one example of this from literature. Edgar Allen Poe wrote a very good short story in the 19th century, called 'The Spectacles', in which he, an anti-hero, falls in love with somebody in a box in an opera theatre. He has a theory that the person he sees in the box is the most beautiful woman in Paris, and also that he is going to marry her. So, every piece of data that he collects during the course of the short story actually appears to confirm this theory. He can see no reason why it should not. The result is that he marries his grandmother. It is a beautifully told story, and there is a great warning, to both scientific investigators and planners, that we do have theories, we do think the world is going to go the way we imagine it, and very often the sort of information we collect will be precisely that which apparently confirms our opinions rather than tests them.

It is extremely important, therefore, that data collection for planning should not be seen as an end in itself. It needs to be accompanied by a very strong and vigorous research effort to develop theory and to develop this collective view of the urban world. If that is not done then we shall, with the new technologies now available to us, end up collecting more and more data about the world out there; our machines will turn into garbage bins, lots of people will be processing it and pushing it through this way and that way, and we will be swamped by the amount of information coming in to us, but also very ineffective in doing anything about the urban world which we are really concerned with. It is, therefore, extremely important that theory develops in parallel with the potential for collecting data and information.

Encoding our information

The main point that I want to bring out in this paper, though, is that out in the urban world we have a collection, an ensemble, of situations which we are looking at. Someone - an authority, an individual, a planner - has to bring in this information and to encode it in some kind of language. He cannot just bring the outside world into his room, so he has got to make a code of it, a representation of that world. The traditional forms, if you look at planning, have been the map, the written report, and tables. I think these are the main forms in which the outside world is encapsulated and recorded, and you use these forms to communicate to other people, to committees, to other planners, and to developers. I am going to argue that they are rather clumsy forms in certain respects. They are very good in many ways, but not so good for representing the urban world as a system, where the elements are interrelated, as opposed to a collection of unrelated items or elements. A map certainly can show the elements of land use or rateable values or population density or incidence of certain kinds of diseases, but it is very difficult to deduce the connections between them from a map. Traditionally this has been attempted through statistical techniques: to develop ways of looking at the inter-relationships between different elements, and to comprehend them, to show which elements are strongly related and which are weakly related.

The advances, I think, now being made in research, and to some extent in practice, suggest that we will now be able to look at the urban world as a system, as something that does work altogether, taking elements and relationships together in one go. How do we represent such a complex organisation? The answer that most of us would put forward at the moment - it may not be the only answer but certainly the one that we would put forward - would be through some form of computer representation. The computer, in fact, is able to represent urban systems, both the elements and the relationships, and to work as a dynamic picture of the world rather than the static picture given by a map, a table or a report. The map can be made in a machine to change, to give up, new information, to represent changing relationships, and to give some kind of picture of changes over time. The tables, too, can do this inside the machine. You can interrogate them, and you can find out a great deal of information from them in ways which you cannot from the static representations that we have been using so far.

One of the main problems, though, if we start out now with the urban world as a source of information, is what do we collect, because there is so much. I have said before that we are likely to collect that information which accords with our theories. We reckon it would be useful information because we could use it with our theories to give us certain predictions or understanding using the theory. So we are probably going to select on the basis of theories that we have. The theory could be extremely crude. It could simply be some-thing like: accidents are more likely to occur at crossroads. So, we collect some information about crossroads. That is a very crude theory, but it is one which could initiate our first look at the world and influence the sort of information that we collect.

If we can get over that problem of what we are going to collect - and I will come back to that a bit later on - then there is the problem of encoding the information for parts of the system. A lot of information obviously can be encoded purely quantitatively. We can say how many square feet of floor space there are in a certain building, which is just a continuous system of rational numbers. You can choose any one and that will give you the answer. Other collections of data will be like the number of storey heights; these will be integers or some sort: one, two, three, four, five. Other pieces of information may be rather different in nature; for example, which sex: male or female. Already we are beginning to move away from the quantities simply as, say, 322.4, which might be the floor area of a certain space. Then, moving on from that type of information, we get on to the question of relationships themselves: such as these children are the offspring of these parents. This is a relation-ship, which we might also have to record.

In an information system, if I have read some of the literature correctly, we would need to have a way of representing variables which include more or less numerical data, which we would operate in a fairly straightforward algebraic way; as well as non-numerical pieces of information such as male and female, which some people call tags, and finally the relationships between them. There are ways of encoding each type of information. Clearly the first one can be encoded straightforwardly in a more or less algebraic way. The other two types will probably call upon a form of encoding which is essentially isomorphic, or similar in form to set theory and developments of set theory. To some extent there will need to be developments of set theory in order to accommodate a lot of the things we want to do. Standard, classic set theory is very limiting and much of the information that we want to handle has much more structure than traditional set theory will permit; we want to hold on to that structure and not lose it. There are new developments in set theory, at a fairly high level, tackling these kinds of problems.

After we have encoded the world in these sorts of ways, we would want to transmit this picture to a machine. There are changing technologies for transmission and some of these are better than others. The transmission goes via some sort of channel to a receiver. The channels themselves are going to limit the amount of information we can pass through, this may mean that we will lose information. Certainly, even in the traditional form of map, table and report, there is likely to be quite considerable loss of information as these things are communicated from their original authors to the committees. Also a lot of ambiguities arise, and a lot of problems that planners meet in committees are probably due to this kind of problem. We have to think about who receives these encoded messages about the outside world. Increasingly, we have got to think about the fact that the general public will also want to be in on the picture and not just the planners, and so the form in which we finally receive these pictures will have to be ones which ordinary, reasonably intelligent people can understand and appreciate. All these are major problems and each one is, in a sense, something which has to be dealt with and looked at separately.

Some problems in dealing with systems

To go back to the question of the source: the urban system. We look at it – and we assume we have now got some theories to help us look at it – and we select certain elements of interest. We do a survey to seek certain pieces of information. We also know that there are certain relationships that hold between some of these pieces of information, and we want to see how these are changing or how they are developing from the last time we surveyed this information.

There are several problems. We can expect that all elements in the urban system are probably related to all other elements in some way, but mostly these relationships will be extremely weak. There will be some obvious relationships and these may appear to be very strong. There may be a certain danger that, in studying an urban system as if it were a set of elements with fairly strong relationships between them, we may be overlooking a large number of weak relationships between elements which may have more effect than a few strong ones. Certainly in urban research the first thing we try to do is to pick up the most obvious relationships and build models around the strong ones. But, I think, we are always aware that there may be a lot of contingent factors at work on the system which make it difficult for us to say how much influence is due to the relationships which we have picked out, and how much to the minor relationships, which we have not considered and studied.

Another problem in looking at the urban system arises from the fact that we are trying to control it. We are looking not only as a scientist might look at a natural system, but we are also looking at a system which we are interfering with, and the effects of our controls are also something that we are trying to observe. It is a very tricky problem, this one, which control engineers in particular are very concerned with. How can you look at a system state, and appreciate the effect of your own controls on that state as it moves forward, as well as taking into account the contingent factors, the things that you really do not know about but you know exist and do have an influence on the system? This is a problem that planners, too, must become more concerned about. It is, in fact, also a development from communication and information theory: the idea that you have a system which you can act on and can change, and yet at the same time you do not know all about it and you are interested in investigating the way that that works.

Research which changes our view of the world

The next point on the question of collecting information concerns the way in which research and theory building can help in looking at the world. I can give an example from a piece of work done by one of our people, using mainly micro-economic theory, to look into housing demand (Apps 1971). The traditional forms of housing models usually divide housing into categories. They make each house a sort of urban unit: a detached house, a bungalow, a semi-detached house, a type of flat, or a terraced house. In other words, each of the items out there is given a name. There are a number of difficulties which emerge when you try to do an economic study on this basis. There are also difficulties which emerge when you even think fairly simply about the problem. One of these is that we tend to associate certain groups of people with, say, detached houses or semi-detached houses in suburban situations, but we also find the same kind of people go into central cities to buy up old, somewhat decaying, 19th century industrial cottages, which they renovate and turn into something highly desirable. It is very difficult, on the traditional theory, to see why it is that a person who apparently would normally want to buy a semi-detached or detached house in the suburbs is prepared to come into the central city and buy the sort of house that one would expect to be associated with a different group of consumers.

A similar sort of problem arose in trying to study the automobile industry in the United States when each car, each product, was given a different name. The economists imagined that they had to go along with this, and as they were calling each car by its name, every time a new car came on the market they really could not predict how people would respond to it. All they knew was that a certain sort of car was sold this way and a certain sort of car was sold that way. Traditional theory tended to break down, and in the 1950s, the psychologists moved in on the field and said it was all due to sex. They claimed that the sexual image of a motor car totally explained the sales, and that it was nonsense to talk about the efficiency or good steering, because it was really a question of colour, shape, internal decoration and so on.

Economists seemed to give way on this one for some time, until, I think, the early 60's when various papers challenged this way of looking at the world. If we simply accept that all these things have different names and so treat each one as a separate item, when we get a new item we cannot say anything about it. So if we have a new form of housing we get a new name for it, say, a town house, and we add this to our list of names, we cannot say anything about how the market is likely to operate. The way in which the economists get over this is to say it is much easier in a highly developed technology to consider the characteristics of housing, and not simply names. So, we want to look at a number of important, relevant characteristics. In the case of the motor car, they were the size of the vehicle, handling and steering, the engine, repair record, and the price. These five characteristics, when different values were given to them, not only described perfectly about 40 or 50 vehicles actually being put on to the market, but they also described adequately the behaviour of the market.

Now there were a lot of other factors that the economists could have taken into account. Here, then, theory would begin to suggest the sort of characteristics that the people in the car industry should be looking at when they are considering putting on a new product. If they think about these characteristics and can show that they have improved – or that you can get more of them at a lower price – then the product is likely to be fairly effective in the market, given that most of the other things are up to scratch. The point is, these seem to be the significant variables which make a difference, providing everything else is pretty well as expected.

In the case of the housing market, Patricia Apps, who did this study, looked at a whole series of variables. Instead of talking about semi-detached and bungalows, which are still talked about in a lot of planning literature, she looked at the variables. She found that a few variables were able to describe a large variety of housing forms. This could be very valuable because the amount of information you have got to collect on those variables is perhaps less than the amount of information you would need to collect if you took every type of house separately.

She then tried to match these variables, the physical attributes of the world out there, with the response of the public to them, or, in other words, the preference structure of the people acting in the housing market. She had to test how these variables influenced the prices by looking at the way the market was behaving, and thereby to discover the **preferences** of people, in different socio-economic groups, to different characteristics of housing. What I am really trying to get across here is that having done this it emerges that there are certain important pieces of information about the housing market which are very much more important than a lot of things we go on collecting. For instance, much of the data the Census collects about housing, such as the condition of toilets, are not so important as a lot of other things.

Secondly, there is another thing that came out of this study which is relevant at this particular moment, with house prices shooting up and planners being attacked for having created the situation of land shortages, etc. But, none of these things seemed to be very important compared to the subsidy system and the tax structure. Patricia Apps predicted, by projecting forward her own work, that about now we would be in a hell of a mess, entirely due to the tax system and the subsidy structure and very little to do with the supply of housing or land. These factors, not the purely physical factors, were dominating the behaviour of the housing system.

The point of this is that research itself does influence the way we look at the world. That piece of research has changed the way that I would look at the housing market. The planner faced with housing shortages, and being asked to do something about it, ought to be able to make use of that kind of research in trying do decide what information he is going to collect and how he is going to use it.

Thirdly, it may be that such research can demonstrate that the problem is not where most people think it is. This is typical of any kind of scientific advance. We imagine the world operates in a particular way because of our particular individual experiences. But, as we introduce more and more controls, overlapping controls from different systems, not only the planning system but the economic world outside, the tax structures and things like that, these overlap and play on one another in very unpredictable ways. Very serious mistakes could be made if we ignore this kind of interplay.

This is the nature of the urban world that we are looking at. It is very complex, and there are a large number of systems meshing together and playing together. It is because of this, I believe, that only a systems approach and only a much more sophisticated representation of that world, will make it possible for us both to understand it through research and to control it in our planning.

To conclude, I want to mention one piece of work that we did on a very simple control system, on the control of bulk in large buildings, particularly office buildings. This is relevant to the discussion on office buildings in London at the moment. We explored, using a very simple model of office buildings and bulk, two post-war planning aims: to get large sites for comprehensive development on the one hand, and to control bulk and floor space on the other. We found that if one takes a very simple geometric model, these aims contradict one another. In other words, it might well have been possible to have got large scale comprehensive development with large open spaces if we had not been quite so heavy-handed about bulk control. Indeed, if there had been a developer rule allowing proportionally more bulk the larger the site, then we might have got not only more large-scale redevelopment, and fewer isolated point blocks, but also more humane environments. The development on large sites would not necessarily have appeared bulky, whereas in fact the legislation seems to have driven the bulk on to small sites, where it appears bulky.

This is another example of the need to look not only at the world out there but also at the control systems which we are implementing, and the influence which they will have on the world that we are observing.

System modelling and planning

Michael Batty

In this paper, I am going to attempt to review the role of urban modelling in the plan-making process. I will introduce certain definitions of terms such as 'model' and 'system' which might help in developing a coherent view of modelling in planning. However, I do not claim to have any definitive view of model-building in planning, but I do have some ideas of how models can help planners to plan. But firstly, I want to look briefly at the development of models during the last decade, and at the major changes in thought which have occurred both in planning and also in the subjects connected with investigating cities.

The development of models

Over the last decade, for all sorts of reasons, many of which have already been explained by Brian McLoughlin and Lionel March, people have felt the need for a more scientific, more rigorous, less subjective, view of cities, and a more scientific method or approach to planning cities. So, in a sense, any view of models in planning must be accompanied by a very brief review of the recent history of theory and model-building. I want to make, right from the start, the distinction between cities and planning, for I think that such a distinction is very important and it has already arisen in previous lectures. Brian McLoughlin, for example, talked about the distinction between planning and research which is very similar to the distinction between planning and research into cities.

If we look at the changes in knowledge about cities, then we can discern parallel changes in subjects like geography. The development of quantitative geography from about 1958 onwards has had an all-embracing effect on the sort of research which I am going to be talking about in this paper. The same can be said for subjects such as urban economics or the application of economic ideas to urban phenomena. Again, the same can be said about transport economics and transport modelling.

I think the important thing to note about these subjects, which deal with cities primarily from the point of view of cities as statistical phenomena, is that there has been no development of a conscious or explicit systems approach. We really have to look to the other side of the coin, that is the planning side of the coin, to begin to see the areas in which there has been an explicit development of the so-called 'systems approach'. This is not to say that there is no systems approach in urban research; it is just that the traditional disciplines which have been involved in such research had already developed a natural implicit systems approach in their research philosophies. If we look at physical planning, we can discern a swing away from the traditional idea of planning in terms of controlling the physical environment to a much wider view of planning concerned with socio-economic activity; and today, planning is concerned with an even wider view of urban government in general. In all of these developments one can see that planning is being looked at in terms of management, and it is, I think, essentially in response to this kind of view of planning that the systems approach has been developed.

I think, also, that you can see similar trends in other disciplines which, in many respects, deal with the same kind of phenomena and have similar kinds of research philosophies. For example, if you look at sociology, politics or anthropology during the last decade you find that people have been concerned with the systems approach and it is not unusual to find books called 'A systems approach to sociology', 'A systems approach to politics' and so on. In one sense, the systems approach is only implicit in geography. You have tended to get books which have been concerned with systematic analysis rather than the systems approach per se, although recently, I note, there has been a book published called 'A systems approach to physical geography' (Chorley and Kennedy 1971), which is the exception to prove the rule, I suppose.

Basic texts of the systems approach in planning (McLoughlin 1969, Chadwick 1971) set the context for any further discussion of the systems approach, but they also set the context for any discussion of modelling. It is also important in such discussion, to distinguish between research into cities and research into planning. In this particular paper, I am concerned with the relationship between both, and with the gulf between research into cities, as systems, and research into plan-making.

This gulf is probably due to the particular subjects involved. If, for example, a person is motivated by a desire to build models which are suitable for solving planning problems, or if he perceives a need to be more scientific about solving such problems, then he probably gets involved in very fine, very detailed, modelling problems which are strictly speaking not concerned with planning. He would be involved in treating the problem from a mathematical and from a statistical viewpoint. He would also be concerned with factors like computer technology. And, if the problem were to be studied in any serious way, or in any long-term way, then it is inevitable that there would be more emphasis on the problems which are not strictly associated with planning. The model-builder, for example, would be concerned with analysis in urban geography and urban economics. The present obsession by model-builders on such problems is not due to the fact that people doing research into urban systems are unwilling to think about these things in a planning context. There is the major difficulty of trying to bridge this gap between the kinds of issues one has to be concerned about when building a model, and the kinds of issues to which that model must eventually be focussed. I think in everything I am going to say in this paper, this dilemma will be recognised.

On mathematical model-building

With this in mind, what I want to do is to talk about how I see the use of mathematical models in a planning context. As used here, a mathematical model is a simplified symbolic representation of some natural or artificial phenomenon. Today one reads in various journals that everything is called a model, just as everything, I suppose, in geography twenty years ago was called a theory. In this context, the definition of the term 'model' is narrower in that such models are mathematical. Clearly, if we want to talk about other models then we have to widen the definition, but the models I am concerned about here are strictly speaking symbolic and come out of the research which stems largely from traditions in urban economics and urban geography.

Brian McLoughlin, in his paper earlier, made a very personal plea for particular areas for planning research. I will make my plea now. I think that this gulf between modelling and between planning can only be tackled if we develop what is truly planning research. In one sense, what we will be talking about in this paper and in later papers can be discussed without mentioning the word 'planning', for one can discuss planning in an entirely separate way. I do not believe that modelling is, strictly speaking, planning research. Planning research is about planning, whether from a political or technical point of view, and we have very little planning research in this country although we have a lot of lip service to it. There is a very useful book called 'The Sciences of the Artificial' by Herbert A. Simon (1969) which deals with this very problem – the contrast between artificial sciences and natural sciences. I think that only when we begin to do research in this area will we really begin to see how models can be used in planning. Then we will find the limitations of such models within the planning process.

As I said at the beginning of this paper, I cannot give you a completely coherent view; all I can give you are some impressions about how models have been and can be used in planning. In any discussion of this subject we are plagued by the problem which affects all of us, whether we are researchers or practitioners; the problem is that whenever we get new ideas, we tend to be very euphoric about these ideas and we tend to be very unselective. Mathematical model-building like the systems approach should be absorbed into planning in a much less volatile sort of way.

Classifications of models

To discuss models in planning and to reinforce the distinction between cities and planning, I have got to introduce some rather pertinent sorts of definition and classification of the kinds of models which we will be discussing in this paper.

There is a fundamental distinction between what are called 'descriptive models' and what are called 'predictive models', and these terms are self-explanatory. There is a further distinction between behavioural models and normative models. By 'behavioural' I mean models which represent existing patterns of behaviour in an urban or a regional system. By normative models, I mean models which imply some kind of value judgement as to what should happen rather than what actually does happen. In a sense, all these distinctions between descriptive, predictive, behavioural and normative can be summarised by the division into non-optimising models and optimising models.

In this paper, we are concerned essentially with non-optimising models – behavioural models and descriptive models. In later papers, I note that some of my colleagues may be talking about evaluation models whose role is self-evident in the planning process. This is not to say that the kinds of models discussed here, descriptive or behavioural, cannot be used in any predictive context. Quite the reverse; and I am going to talk about how descriptive models and behavioural models can be used in a predictive context.

Before the actual structure of such models is developed, there is a technical classification of models which is useful. We can define models in terms of the kind of mathematics which are used. For example, there is linear mathematics and non-linear mathematics, and as these terms suggest, linear mathematics deal with relationships between variables which vary in some linear way, and non-linear with relationships which vary in a non-linear way. We can also make a distinction between solution procedures – between analytic models and simulating models. Analytic models have direct and standard solution procedures, whereas simulation models have indirect solution procedures.

There is also a distinction in terms of comprehensiveness, between general models and partial models. Most of the models which we will be discussing are essentially general models; that is, they deal or tend to deal with two or more sub-systems in an urban system. For example, we probably will not be dealing explicitly or in any great depth with shopping models or transport models. The kinds of models we will be dealing with are syntheses or integrations of the transport model, the shopping model, the residential location model, and so on.

In terms of substantive content, it is important to think about the actual phenomena pertaining to the system being modelled. We are dealing now with an urban system or a regional system, and I think we can define three major classes into which models can be placed. We can define models in terms of the actual space which is modelled, into a town or into a region, and we will be seeing examples of this distinction between town and region in later papers. We can also define models in terms of how the time dimension is treated, whether the model is a static representation of the reality, or whether it is dynamic in that reality is modelled over a period of time. A very important aspect of this classification is the fact that we have static models which tend to represent one cross-section of time, but planning is a dynamic activity involving time and the future. We could say that there is a big conceptual rift between the models we have which describe the city as it exists, and models which would be most useful for planning.

The third possible classification concerns the 'level of aggregation'. Strictly speaking, aggregation can refer to any of these particular classes. We could refer to spatial aggregation or temporal aggregation. The conventional use of the term relates to the aggregation of the variables which are being modelled. Population, for example, might be dis-aggregated into a series of classes or income groups; housing might be broken down or dis-aggregated into a series of types, for example, by size or by socio-economic group of the occupants.

Most of the models being used at present are essentially descriptive. They are essentially non-linear because urban phenomena vary in a non-linear way; for example, exponential growth of population. They tend to be analytic, although people argue over this and say such models are simulation models. With analytic models we are able to get solutions to the model directly, rather than through trial and error, although this can be very much a matter of degree. They tend to be general rather than partial. They deal both with towns and regions. They are static, and they are largely aggregative.

The diagram in Figure 1 shows a simple way of classifying models. This figure extracts two of the main dimensions or classifications of models which were mentioned previously – the linear and non-linear dimension, which is essentially a technical one, and the optimising and non-optimising dimension, which is essentially one of content or how the model is being used. Evaluation models tend to optimise certain variables in the system whereas a model which is built of the present reality tends to be non-optimising. This is not always completely true, for there are examples of optimising models which attempt to measure what happens at the present time; for example, the Penn Jersey-Herbert-Stevens (Herbert and Stevens 1960) model of the housing market worked on the premise that people optimise some criterion of rent-paying ability; in other words people live in the best houses they could afford, which is part of the present reality.

Figure 1 gives a crude idea of the kinds of model which have been built in the United States, Western Europe, and in this country. Most models are essentially non-optimising or descriptive, and non-linear, and these are the kinds of models we are talking about here. We do not have many linear, non-optimising models although there are examples which I will point to later. There are very few optimising models of any type. If we have decided that mathematical models are to be used within a planning context, then it seems to me that what we really need to be building are models which are essentially optimising, because in planning we are trying to optimise, or maximise, some general welfare function. The fact that we are not doing this shows that there is a major problem in designing such models: I think that this will become clear in later papers. By linear optimising models, I mean models which use some kind of resource allocation mechanism like linear programming. There are very few, if any, non-linear optimising models for these models tend to involve rather complicated techniques like non-linear programming.

The model-building process

We can distinguish between two major aspects of model design or development, and this reflects the difference between cities and planning again. We can think of the model-building process as being constructed in three basic stages: first, there is the theoretical model design itself, which is clearly the first preoccupation of the model builder, or planner. Questions such as, what kind of model is suitable for particular problems, are the subjects of this stage. There is a second stage which is called calibration, or statistical estimation. Any theory, if it is to be of general value, must not pertain to any particular situation; it must be of general applicability. The process of calibration or estimation is essentially concerned with trying to fit a particular theory or mathematical version of the theory (model) to a particular situation. It corresponds in some respects with the scientist's idea of experiment, which follows and tests scientific hypotheses. There is a cyclical process involving model design followed by calibration. We can, if we wish, discuss this sort of process quite separately from the concept of planning. I will show later some applications in this country, which have been accomplished outside the plan-making process.

When one has fitted the model (estimated its parameters), and is satisfied that this model is acceptable in a wider sense in terms of its function, one can attempt to use it in some kind of planning problem. This assumes, of course, that the model has been initially designed for use in a predictive way.

At this point it is important to note that descriptive, non-optimising, non-linear models will predict on the basis of existing structures or existing patterns of behaviour. There is really no getting away from this, for most of the descriptive models we have tend to predict past trends. People may argue with me about this, but my own impression is that the parameters of the model which reflect the model's structure, reinforce existing trends. If it is a static model, then many elements of the present situation will be present in the future anyway, and in the short term a projection of trends of existing behaviour may be acceptable. One can begin to modify the model

	LINEAR	NON-LINEAR
NON-OPTIMISING	CHAPIN (Greensboro') HILL (EMPIRIC-Boston) LAKSHMANAN (Baltimore, Connecticut) (10+)	SEIDMAN (PennJersey) LOWRY (Pittsburgh) GARIN-LOWRY (see Figure 2) LATHROP-HAMBURG (New York State) ROBINSON (San Francisco) (35+)
OPTIMISING	HERBERT & STEVENS (Penn Jersey) BEN SHAHAR (?) SCHLAGER (South West Wisconsin) (5+)	?

Only the main examples are listed here. The numbers in each cell show the <u>minimum</u> no. of applications of each class of model.

Figure 1   A simple method for the classification of models

by building constraints on optimality into it, criteria which the model must satisfy. Then the role of the model begins to change from a descriptive model towards an optimising kind of model.

The development of models in Britain

I feel the best way to discuss the successes and failures of models used in a planning context is to show where they have been built and to talk about how they have been used.

In Figure 2 a map of Great Britain is shown with each model application marked. Perhaps it is significant to note the lack of modelling ventures in Scotland and Ireland — most of the modelling ventures are in England. Most of these modelling ventures will be explained later in more detail. This diagram distinguishes between the regions or towns to which these models have been applied.

Three of the models shown are rather different from the rest, and I will outline these to begin with. The North-West model, the Wrexham model, and the Leicester model are based on different structures from the rest of the models. In a later paper Marcial Echenique demonstrates that most of the models which have been built in this country are of one standard kind, based on Lowry's model or its derivatives, and there are very good reasons for this. The point I want to make is that most of these models have not been built from the point of view of research, and this is really very significant. Most of the people who have been involved in building these models have related their ventures to some kind of planning activity. It might only be a passive kind of interest in planning, but it has been there all the same. We have not, for example, had people solely in geography departments or economics departments concerned with building models of the city or models of the region for their own sake. There are different kinds of models which are built in economics departments, like input-output models, but those do not really concern us now

The North-West model was built by Ian Masser in the Department of Civic Design in the University of Liverpool. This particular model is very much out of tradition of modelling in Britain for it is a linear model and it is based on standard econometric research. The Wrexham model is dealt with by Tony Houghton in a later paper. The Leicestershire model is based on work by Brian McLoughlin, reported in the Leicester and Leicestershire Sub-regional Planning Study (1969). This model, although based upon the formulation of the classic Lowry model, is not strictly speaking a computer model of the type we are talking about. Although it focusses on the same major relationships it is a manual simulation, and consequently it is considerably less integrated than any of the other computer models.

The first class of models has been constructed by Land Use and Built Form Studies here in Cambridge. Most of these models have been applied to particular town situations; the main model is applied to the town of Reading, and there are a number of other applications which simulate the form of new towns, such as Stevenage, Milton Keynes, and Hook. There is also a model of Cambridge and one of Luton. Now, I know the intention was not to use these models in relation to any particular planning problem, apart from hypothetical ones, so what I have done is to divide the planning applications of these models into hypothetical applications, which might have been used by a particular researcher, and planning applications in practice.

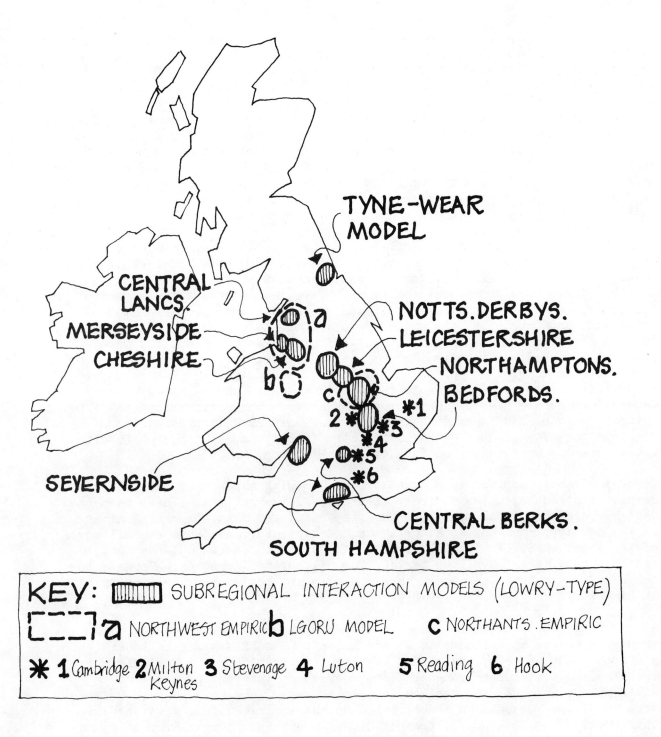

Figure 2   Sub-regional and town scale models in Britain

Applications in practice include those where a planning authority has
actually used the results in some indirect or direct way, or where there
has been a local authority sponsor. In Figure 3, a table of such applications
has been drawn up. It is clear that the researchers at Land Use and Built
Form have produced planning output in terms of hypothetical problems, apart
from the Luton exercise which has been applied in consultation with the Local
Authority.

In the case of CES, the researchers have been much more concerned with the
application of these tools in a planning context than many of the other
research groups, and this has been done largely by the Planning Research
Applications Group (PRAG). The Cheshire model which CES have developed is
well-known, and this model has been applied to the Ellesmere Port Structure
Plan. I do not know whether or not it is actually being used in any explicit
context at present, although this is something I want to return to - whether
or not we should use models as demonstration tools, or whether or not we
should use the outputs of them in practice. PRAG is also concerned with
modelling the Monmouth, Northampton, Gloucester and Peterborough areas, and
as Figure 3 shows, all these exercises have been sponsored by local
authorities.

A number of applications at the sub-regional scale have been developed by
members of the Urban Systems Research Unit at Reading. The Bedfordshire
model, for example, was built for a planning authority in practice and
although there were demonstrations of using the model to test the impact of
Milton Keynes new town, for example, and the Third London Airports at
Cublington and Thurleigh, the actual results were not, as far as I can gather,
used in any practical situation. This was very largely because the model-
builders left halfway through the project to do research, which tends to be
a characteristic of a lot of these projects. The Central Lancashire model
was not sponsored by a local authority, but we tested the impact of the
Central Lancashire new town on surrounding areas. The Nottinghamshire-
Derbyshire model was an example where the tool was used to predict the
consequences of a series of alternative structure plans, at a coarse level,
and this was sponsored by the Sub-Regional Planning Unit.

Several of these applications have to be taken with a pinch of salt, because
despite statements to the contrary these models may not really have been used.
Central Berkshire is an example. This is one of the fastest growing areas
in the country: the new M4 Motorway has just opened, and there are all sorts
of pertinent kinds of planning problems which these models could be used to
test. None of them have been tested, for all sorts of reasons. Perhaps the
basic reason is that the researchers are more interested in modelling than
in planning.

A number of models have been used in student projects. We are engaged in
such an exercise in Northampton at the moment. The PRAG group is looking
at Northampton as well, and we are both semi-sponsored by the East Midlands
Technical Unit at Loughborough. We have built an interesting model of
Northampton, which I will mention in a later paper, and we also have a linear
version of the Northampton model, based on the empiric model, developed by
Dave Foot. This is a useful project because we have a couple of models working
side by side so we can get direct comparisons between the two models.

I can list the other models very quickly: there is the Tyne-Wear model
which is not very widely known, but this is basically a sub-regional model
built by Colin Buchanan and Partners for the Tyne-Wear plan. This model is to

AGENCY	TOWN – REGION	PLANNING APP.		LOCAL AUTHOR-ITY SPONSOR
		Hypothet	Actual	
LAND-USE AND BUILT FORM – CAMBRIDGE U.	READING STEVENAGE HOOK MILTON K. * CAMBRIDGE LUTON	Evaluation Study	Structure Plan	NONE INFORMAL LIASON
CENTRE FOR ENVIRONMENTAL STUDIES & PRAG	CHESHIRE MONMOUTH EAST MIDLANDS		Structure Plans	INFORMAL CONS. FORMAL CONSULTATION
URBAN SYSTEMS RESEARCH UNIT, READING UNIV.	CENTRAL * LANCS NOTTS. DERBY BEDFORDS. CENTRAL BERKS NORTHANTS. *	Impacts Motorway Impacts Alternatives	Alternatives Impacts	NONE FORMAL CONS. FORMAL CONS. NONE INFORMAL CONSULTATION
CIVIC DESIGN, LIVERPOOL UNIV.	MERSEYS.* NORTH WEST REG.	Alternatives		NONE
BUCHANAN	TYNE-WEAR		Structure	FORMAL CONS.
SOUTH HANTS	SOUTHAMPT.		Structure	FORMAL CONS.
LONDON UN.	BRISTOL	Alternat.		INFORMAL CONS.
LEICESTER	LEICESTER		Alternat.	FORMAL CONS.

✳ MEANS MODELS ALSO USED IN EDUCATION

Figure 3 Practical and theoretical applications of urban models in Britain

evaluate a series of structure plans. It is worth examining because it appears to be very successfully used in the sense that the model was built very quickly (in a matter of three months or so) and was calibrated and used to predict the effects of a series of structure plans for that particular region.

The Merseyside model and the North-West empiric model built by Ian Masser, have had no direct planning applications as far as I know. At this point I must say that the authors of these models know a lot more than I do about them, so some of what I am describing may be wrong. The Severnside model was built by Turner and Williams at University College and was used to evaluate a series of structure plans. It has had a rather interesting history in that Bristol County Borough actually sponsored the model informally, although I understand that the results were never actually used in practice. The South Hampshire model and the Leicestershire model were both used in practice, and as you are probably aware they were sponsored by the relevant authorities.

I think the most important point to digest from Figure 3 is the fact that of the eighteen models completed, only six were actually used in any kind of planning context. Eight of those models were in fact sponsored by Local Authorities; there are two models, the Bedfordshire and Severnside models, sponsored by local authorities which were not actually used. These models were built but never used. It is hard to know what to make of such apparent failures. One can be very bitter and say that planners have been reluctant to follow up such exercises. On the other hand, if you compare this with the American experience, I think there is a great deal of hope. Certainly if you look at the last couple of years, most of the models which have been built by PRAG and by the centre for Land Use and Built Form are being used in an explicit planning context, and this is clearly what is required.

The point I want to make is that improvements to such models can never come if modelling is just an exercise in design and calibration. One needs to project with these models by trying to find out how sensitive they are in the context of evaluating structure plans, evaluating impacts and so on. From the point of view of prediction, one can go back to re-design the model in a cyclical way. There is not only a link from testing in an academic environment; there is also a link from the predictive side of modelling, in which the task is to find out how bad the projections are, and how they cut across one's intuitive insights into what the future should be. These factors are extremely useful in the quest to design better models.

Models in the technical planning process

By way of a conclusion I will say something about how such models fit into the planning process. Now when one talks about the planning process, one is on very dangerous ground these days. When I was trained in planning, the planning process meant the technical process of plan design, starting from survey going through to analysis, synthesis, evaluation, and implementation. Today the planning process, as for example defined by Friend and Jessop (1969), is a much wider process. I want to talk about modelling not in relation to this wider process of planning but in relation to the narrower technical process of plan-making.

I will define the technical plan-making process as a problem-solving process carried out by a team of technical experts, so in one sense I am taking the politics or the wider role of management in a long-term sense out of this. The technical process can be carried out on a fairly short time scale; I think this is important. If we start talking about 20 years or so then clearly this technical process can occur many, many times. So we are really talking about something which can be carried out at the minimum, I suspect, in probably about two or three weeks, at a very coarse level, to a maximum of two or three years.

Another decision I have made is that I am not going to discuss modelling in the context of implementation or monitoring. There is a lot talked about how we could use models to monitor things. However, I am rather sceptical about the use of models in any kind of monitoring situation. I think that the models can best be seen in relation to this rather narrow technical process which can be divided into two major parts: one concerned with the present and one with the future. Interpreting the present with glimpses of the future is a matter of problem-definition, the assembling of data, the problem of defining goals or criteria to be satisfied. These are the first stages in the plan-making process.

The other side of the planning process can be described as a view of the future with glimpses of the present, and this involves the role of design in a very general sense: the design of alternative strategies, alternative structures, the testing or modelling of the implications of these structures, and some kind of evaluation process involving the concept of choice.

The role of models in this process is very hard to decide. At the beginning of the paper I said I would give you no coherent view and I mean this. Models fit somewhere in the middle of the process and such tools can both help with understanding what is going on and also help with predicting the future. Various articles on this subject (some of them my own, I think) suggest that models can be used for testing alternative strategies, impact analysis and evaluation. They identify the use of the model with different stages in the planning process. Now I do not think the correspondence of models with these stages is exactly right. I think models can be used throughout the process to structure intuition. I agree they can be used to do these standard things, but I do not think that you would use different models (certainly we have not used different models) to test alternative strategies or to test the impact of large developments like new towns or airports.

I think that the model has a fairly neutral existence in the planning process. I do not mean to suggest that any of the things which have been said about the use of models in terms of impact analysis and other things are necessarily wrong. It is just that these models can be used in many different ways, and this is their real value. They can be used to structure any part of the planning process, but I would suspect that you cannot easily slot such models into the different stages in the process. What one has got to do is to try to design a planning process around certain models. This is essential because the model, or the theory inherent in the model, must clearly structure what you are going to do, the data that you are going to collect, and the kind of design procedure which you can engage in.

To conclude I must give a personal opinion of models in planning. Increasingly we have this debate as to how to use the model. Is the model just a tool for enhancing our understanding, or is it something more? Is it a means for actually predicting results which we can use in a very precise way? I think that the argument about the use of models must focus on whether we use models as demonstration tools, or whether, to take an extreme example, three-zone problems on the backs of envelopes and the knowledge gained from such exercises is sufficient, or whether we need the full-blown mathematical modelling which was a big feature of the land use-transport studies in the States.

We have got to take a middle line on this. Clearly such ventures have to be matched against the resources available. If one does not have a great deal of money and a great deal of expertise, it might be better, rather than not use models at all, to think about modelling as an aid to understanding the urban system. For this it may be sufficient to just play around with the equations and with models on three-zone hypothetical examples. On the other hand, some full-blooded modelling procedures are inevitable if one is to structure the plan-making process around them.

Part 2

Urban and regional modelling

History of regional and urban models

Marcial Echenique

Introduction

The purpose of this paper is to trace the theoretical basis of present-day urban and regional models. To this effect, I will distinguish between a model, which I define as a representation of a system based on some kind of theory, and a theory which tries to give an explanation of why things occur. This distinction is not always clear, because the kind of theories which a model is based on are usually verbal explanations and not formal. Because of this difficulty I will call this area 'theoretical approaches' rather than theories as such, in the sense that they are not completely and formally structured.

Most of us believe that urban and regional models are fairly recent things. As a matter of fact, the fundamental ideas upon which urban and regional models are based are more than a century old. What is new is the application to real planning and decision making. This has come about as a consequence of the introduction of high-speed electronic computers which provide the necessary capacity for handling large amounts of statistical information.

It is true that most of the models are conceptually simple. What is difficult is the amount of work needed to solve one of these equations. For example, a typical model of a town of a hundred zones would take, perhaps, many years to solve manually, while a fast computer will take a couple of minutes.

If we look at the operational models developed here and in America, we find that in spite of differences in detail there is considerable unity in their theoretical basis. I think I could class most of these models as belonging to three families: the first one is what can be called the micro-economic or behaviouristic approach; the second one can be called a macro-approach or social physics; and finally, I lump all the rest together as a simulation approach. We will look at the main differences between these approaches and trace the historical development of these ideas.

This paper will be structured in the following way. First I will look at the economic approaches and the most significant contributions to them; they are Von Thunen (1826), Weber (1909), Christaller (1933), Losch (1954) and Alonso (1964). As an example of operational models of this kind I will briefly look at the Penn-Jersey transportation model and the San Francisco urban renewal model. Secondly, I will review the social physics approach, starting with Carey (1858) in the 19th century and ending with Lowry (1964). I will review two operational models as examples of this approach: the Chicago area transportation study model, which is not very interesting theoretically, but is important as the first operational model (1959) and the Lowry model and its derivatives. I will not go into detail on the Lowry model because other contributors will be reviewing developments of that model in later chapters.

The simulation approach will not be reviewed because its major exponent, the Forrester Model (1969), will be discussed by Cordey-Hayes. Finally, I hope to draw some conclusions from this brief exposition.

Micro-economic or behaviourist approach

This approach dates back to the originators of classical economics. The fundamental concept behind this approach is that the world can be understood through the mechanism of an economic market, composed of producers and consumers working within a system of perfect competition. The behaviour of these actors as producers or consumers can be explained as a product of their seeking to maximise their utility, which in the crudest way is interpreted as seeking to obtain the maximum profit, or sometimes to minimise their costs. They are called rational economic men. The label 'behaviouristic', in the sense that Skinner uses it, is right, because men are motivated by a system of punishment and reward - in this case economic punishment and economic reward.

The linking of the economic theory with spatial theory is done through a very important variable - the concept of transport cost. Travel or transport cost is considered in addition to the conventional factors of production, and introduces the spatial dimension into the urban models.

The idea of maximisation of utility lends itself to mathematical programming. The typical case would be linear programming, because we can maximise a function subject to certain constraints, either to minimise transport costs or maximise profit. A good review of the problems of linear programming techniques was made by Stevens (1967).

Von Thunen's agricultural location model

The earliest attempt to formalise this kind of location theory was made by Von Thunen (1826). In his book <u>The Isolated State</u> he explained the first definite economic model of agricultural location. Von Thunen's main concern was to explain the location of types of agriculture. He put forward a very simple model of the world, consisting of one city and its surrounding region. All the agricultural products are sold in this single centre. The isolated state is, in this initial exposition, a featureless plain with transport costs which increase radially from the centre of the town.

Von Thunen is concerned to explain two things: first, what type of crop will be cultivated at different distances from the town centre, and second, what kind of rent the producer will pay to the landlord to use this particular location. I will just put forward the first equation that he uses, which I think contains most of the important elements of this kind of approach.

$$R_{ij} = E_i \left(P_i - C_i - r_i t_j \right) \tag{1}$$

where R_{ij} = bid rent of crop i at distance j from market

E_i = yield per acre of crop i

P_i = demand price per unit crop i at the market

C_i = production cost per unit crop i

r_i = transport cost per unit distance per unit crop i

t_j = distance at location j

If we analyse the equation (1) we can plot for every type of crop i the rent that it can pay at distance j from the market (see Figure 1), knowing the demand price, P_i; cost of production, C_i; cost of transport, r_i, and the fertility, E_i, of the crop i.

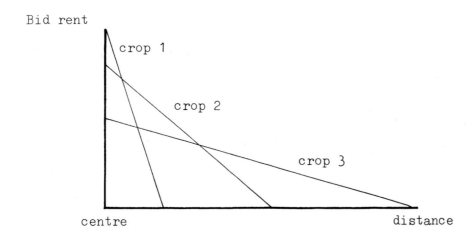

Figure 1   Von Thunen's agricultural location

Here we have two things, a locational model and a rent model. Within a certain distance from the centre a particular crop will outbid the others; in a second area another crop will outbid the others, and so on. Therefore the pattern of land uses or location of crops will be concentric. In this case the most intensive use of land will be near the centre, and the rent or land values will decrease outwards.

The same idea has been taken further in an urban situation. The crop types can be equated with urban activities, i.e. service or retail office use, low income residential, and commuter belt using less intensive land.

Von Thunen goes further and introduces some changes in the main concept; for example, he introduces a river along which the transport costs are much cheaper, and therefore the pattern of land use extends in that line of less or equal cost. Later, Losch (1954) expanded the basic Von Thunen model to take into account more elaborate problems and Dunn (1954) uses it to predict patterns of agricultural development, especially in the United States.

Weber's industrial location model

The other type of approach in economic theory is a model of industrial location by Weber (1909). The main difference between Von Thunen and Weber is that the actor, in this case an industrialist, is considered as a dimensionless point in space; that is to say, he does not consume land. Therefore the problem of out-bidding another user does not occur. He presents the basic model from which

most of the further developments stem. The problem is to explain the location
of a firm in a featureless plain. One firm is to be located, requiring two
inputs (which are fixed) of raw material and selling its output to the one
market. This has been called the classical Weber triangle. It is assumed here
that the maximisation of utility is equal to transport cost minimisation. Therefore if we know the cost of transport of the raw material to the firm, and the
finished product to the market, we will be able to find the least cost location
and that will be the location of the factory (see Figure 2).

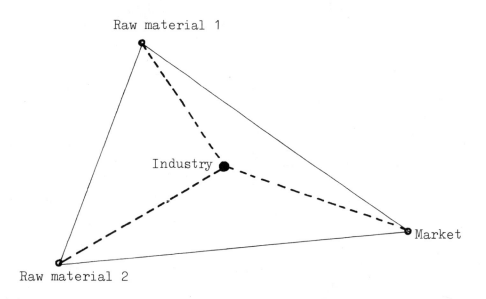

Figure 2   Weber's triangle

Actually, this kind of problem does not have analytical solution. An analogue
solution has been implemented. Mathematical programming also is used. But
one solution is the one in which you make holes in a table and you put weights
representing the cost of transport, and then using a string you find the location
of the factory. The weights representing transport costs will pull the factory
to an equilibrium point.

Christaller and Losch's services location model

The other type of model based on economic theory is a development of Christaller's
central place theory (1933) by Losch. Again, the same basic assumption of a
featureless plain is developed as in most of the previous locational theories.
Christaller was concerned with the location of settlement and villages, but we
can also use his model to consider retail or service location. It emerges from
this model that there is a minimum population needed to support a good or a
service; that the distribution of the population or consumers of this service
or good determines the size of the market area of that service. If, for example,
all the consumers are distributed homogeneously, as in the case of an agricultural
society, then the spacing of settlement will also be homogeneously or uniformly
distributed. Then centres can be classified into hierarchical groups according
to the type of service and size of the market area. Each higher order contains

the lowest order service. The free entry of business in a perfect competition, produces a trade area of nested hexagons because it comes to be the closest to the ideal of the circle. It can be interpreted in economic terms. If the population is distributed homogeneously throughout the plain, there is an increase in the demand for a particular good near the centre because of cost decreases to it; the demand curve drops away with distance from the centre. This is a circular market area but as you try to pack circles into a homogeneous plain the best form comes to be the hexagon.

Alonso's residential location

Finally, I will come very briefly to the last one of the economic theory approaches, which is Alonso's location theory (1964). Alonso's contribution is a development of the Von Thunen model. He also used the bid rent function – which means that some residential groups can outbid others – and he used space as in the Von Thunen model. Therefore you can equate crops with people in this case. The pattern of land use results from the same process as in the Von Thunen model. In the case of residential location, a particular resident with a fixed income has two basic decisions to make: How much money will he spend on all other goods apart from transport or housing, and where will he locate? As he moves further away from the centre he will have less money to spend on housing, and if you fix two of these variables the third can be calculated. The solution then is found by different methods but I think the best one that he has produced recently is a mathematical programming type solution.

I do not think it necessary to go further at this point into this kind of approach, but I would like to summarise the main ideas. As I said, the man we are considering here is a perfect, rational man, and rationality is defined in terms of maximising utility. The assumption of this approach is that there is a market of perfect competition. If there were not perfect competition, that is to say monopoly, the patterns would be different. Secondly, it assumes that people have perfect information about the system in order to make the right decisions. We know this is not the case. Thirdly, some of the authors of this approach believe that the optimization approach also produces the best solution, in other words that the world should be like this; it is a normative rather than just an explanatory model. But, as Joan Robinson, the economist, has put it, utility is a metaphysical concept of impregnable circularity (Robinson 1962). People buy commodities because these commodities give them satisfaction, but the only way this satisfaction can be shown, at least in economic terms, is the fact that people buy the commodities. Therefore you have not got a chance to break that circle.

In spite of all these criticisms, it is still the one model which offers a consistent explanation of why things occur. Most of the other models are not very powerful in terms of explanation.

Two operational models based on the economic approach

I will now review very briefly two kinds of operational models which emerge from this kind of approach. The first one is the Penn-Jersey Transportation Model. This was originally formulated as a device for the Pennsylvania-Jersey Transportation Study. Although the model was eventually abandoned by that Study in favour of other approaches, its development was resumed at the Institute for Environmental Studies, University of Pennsylvania. Originally the model was very ambitious. It included all activities and their distribution, to be simulated over a set time period in such a way that their distribution was to be sensitive to changes in the regional totals and to changes in the transportation network. Because of severe difficulties of data requirement and conceptual difficulties as well, all non-residential activities were dropped and treated exogenously, that is, outside the framework of the model, and the development of the model concentrated on the simulation of residential location. This model was developed mainly by Herbert and Stevens (1960). It follows very closely the conceptual framework of Alonso. The data required for the model is very large and requires an inventory of households classified by income, patterns of consumption preference, and of daily movement. The sites were to be located and classified by size, type and quality of structure, location characteristics and neighbourhood amenities. Each site has a cost of transport calculated to all other destinations, reflecting the patterns of daily movement, which means that if you are located at a particular zone your cost of transport to services and to work will be a given cost.

The problem is formulated in a linear programming fashion:

$$\text{Maximise } z = \Sigma_k \, \Sigma_i \, \Sigma_h \, x_{ih}^k \, (b_{ih} - c_{ih}^k) \qquad (2)$$

subject to

$$\Sigma_i \, \Sigma_h \, s_{ih} \, x_{ih}^k \leqslant L^k$$

$$\Sigma_k \, \Sigma_h \, x_{ih}^k = N_i$$

and all $x_{ih}^k \geqslant 0$

where x_{ih}^k = households of group i using residential accommodation type h in zone k

b_{ih} = residential budget of household of group i using residential accommodation type h

c_{ih}^k = cost to a household of group i using residential accommodation type h in zone k

s_{ih} = land for household group i using residential accommodation type h

L^k = total land in zone k

N_i = total number of households of group i

The connotations here are that if you maximise everyone's rent-paying ability you will have the perfect system. They tried to demonstrate that this solution produced the least cost location as well.

This was a model subject to a set of constraints. These were that you cannot get more land than is available in a zone; you cannot locate more than a given number of a particular group, and so on, and the result should be positive or zero but never negative. The problem, in fact, proved to be extremely difficult in spite of the simplicity of the formulation. The main problem which came about concerned assessing the required preference structure - what housing types each group wants. There was also the problem that because the distribution was in two-year increments, during a particular period of time they only considered new increments of population without taking into consideration the previously located increment. This is unrealistic, because you can always redevelop a particular site to higher densities. It also required a fantastic amount of a priori knowledge to run this kind of model. One needed to know where the services, shops, schools, etc., were located to calculate transport requirement, workplaces, preference structures, and so on. In fact, the model has never been able to simulate the real world successfully. However, it is still very interesting as the first one which tried to use classical economic theory to explain the urban system.

A second model, which continued more or less the same tradition but in a different way, is the San Francisco model of the housing market in 1965. This model was developed by Robinson, Wolfe and Barringer (1965) for the city and county of San Francisco, to assist them in the analysis of planning urban renewal. There were three main purposes of the model: first, to identify and assess the impact of alternative long-range strategies and programmes for renewal and development of the city; second, to serve as an on-going tool for the city government, to permit city officials to keep the community renewal programme going and to review goals; and third, to identify key statistical symptomatic indicators which should be maintained by the appropriate public agency, so that they could monitor the rate and direction of changes affecting the city and take the appropriate responsive action.

The model, then, tries to be an ambitious simulation of the housing market, simulating the demand for housing space and the supply of the space. Once the model was working various planning programmes could be tested. They did not use linear programming methods here, but a set of algorithms, or computer rules. In essence, then, the operation of the model consists of matching various potential users of space to types of existing spaces. The population of San Francisco was classified into households by type, number of members in the household, race, income, occupation and rent-paying ability. This amounted to about 150 groups of people. Projections were made exogenously by independent forecast to predict the number in each group at two-year intervals. You can imagine the kind of problems to predict 150 groups at two-year intervals! Each household has attached to it a preference list defined by the type of housing they would like to have, its location and the amount they can pay to rent or buy. The residential floor space is classified in 1100 possible types, combined by type of housing, number of rooms, condition, tenure and rent or value together with location characteristics. The model assigns household types to housing types and this process depends on the rent-paying ability of the group and on the space characteristics. If the rent-paying ability is greater than the space - which could occur if there are increases in the number of the users, increased wages, or changes in the supply of stock due to deterioration rate - a process of simulation of residential development starts. This process ensures a change in the supply of floor space – more space or renewal – if the gains from the change are sufficient; that is, if the cost of the change is less than the future profit.

According to the authors, this model was extremely successful in reproducing what was going on in San Francisco. While it was in the hands of the consultants the model seemed to work satisfactorily, but when it was handed to the Corporation the whole thing stopped. The reasons given were the difficulties of data gathering, making projections for all the groups and training enough planners within the Corporation to run and interpret the results of the model.

The two examples of the economic base approach that I have described have not been a success. This is unfortunate because, in some senses, it is the most consistent theoretical approach which we have had.

The social physics approach

Now I will review briefly the social physics approach. This approach, in contrast to the previous one, looks at the urban phenomena in aggregate. It is no longer important to discover the motivation behind the actions of individuals; interest is focused on the behaviour of the mass – the aggregate of individual actions. The origin of this approach is in 17th century thinkers. The extraordinary progress of physics, mathematics and mechanics during the 17th century called forth an effort to interpret social phenomena in the same way that mechanics has so successfully interpreted physical phenomena. Some of these thinkers believed that the same laws which ruled matter – the physical world – should apply to the social world. Others used it only as an analogy for formulating precise descriptions of social phenomena. The social physics approach is based mainly upon analogy, and this is a valid scientific tool. As the philosopher, Hesse (1963), said, provided you use the analogy correctly it could be used as data for a new model. Analogies are based on a very simple idea, that if certain things have some attributes they may have others. Therefore you can use a theory which explains one phenomenon in the real world to help explain others. A well known example is the use of the theory of sound as an analogy for explaining the theory of light. This has been the typical pattern in the scientific world. But what is important is that eventually you need to drop the analogy, and the model explaining the phenomenon should be able to stand or fall in its own right.

First, I shall review the origins of social physics. The term 'social physics' was introduced by George Berkeley in the 18th century in his theory of moral attraction and social stability. He used the concept of physical gravitation as an analogue to explain social attraction. Other writers of the 18th and the beginning of the 19th century used the same ideas, like Saint-Simon and Charles Fourier. But the most important contribution in this field in the 19th century was by H.C. Carey (1858) who believed that "the law which governed matter in all its forms, whether that of coal, clay, iron, pebbles, stone, trees, oxen, horses or men, is the same". In his book Principles of Social Science he formulated the gravity model stating that "gravitation is here in human society as everywhere else in the material world, in the direct ratio of the mass of cities and inverse ratio of the distance". You can see that we have moved very little from that point!

In spite of the numerous criticisms of sociologists against what they call the 'mechanistic school', this approach continued to flourish during the later part of the 19th century and the 20th century. The sociologist Sorokin (1928) says about Carey's theory: "Cities do not attract the human molecule in direct ratio to the mass or inverse ratio to the distance. Any statistician who would predict the rate of growth or of the increase in the size of the city on this basis, on the basis of this law, will be doomed to failure." Maybe he is right about growth, but I am sure that Sorokin would be amazed at the number of models developed on this same idea: for example, migration, transport, residential and service location models.

We can grasp intuitively the basis of this analogy. If we can see some type of interaction such as, for example, traffic flows between cities, we can see that if distance were not to play a role in the decision to travel – that is to say, if travel were instantaneous and costless one could expect that the probability of traffic flows between pairs of cities would be proportional to their size, to the mass. As we know, distances impose a cost, an effort, and therefore the probability of travel decreases with the increase in the distance (see Equation 3).

$$T_{ij} = k \frac{P_i P_j}{d_{ij}^2} \qquad (3)$$

where T_{ij} = traffic between city i and j

k = constant

$P_i P_j$ = population at places i and j

d_{ij} = distance between i and j

But it goes a bit further than that. This is explaining interaction, but it can be used equally well as a locational model. If we know the distribution of the origin i we may be able to predict the location of the desgination j based on some kind of attraction function. For example, if we know the location of employment we may be able to predict the location of residence based on a concept of the distance and some kind of attraction. Or, if we know the location of the origins of consumers we may predict the location of services.

Until a very short time ago there was no proof that this kind of model would work in human society. It seems to work, according to empirical evidence, but there was no a priori or theoretical reason why it should do so.

Migration models

Carrothers (1956) and Olsson (1965) have reviewed the development of these concepts. Ravenstein (1885) formulated the first model of migration, following the analogy by Carey. He described another kind of interaction between cities, the migration from place i to place j. His model assumes that migration from city i to city j is a function of the population of the destination (the size of the mass) and inversely proportional to the distance between the two cities. The most complete analogy is made by Zipf (1946):

$$M_{ij} = k \frac{P_i P_j}{d_{ij}^2} \qquad (4)$$

where M_{ij} = migration between place i and j

k = constant

$P_i P_j$ = population of place i and j

d_{ij} = distance between i and j

Many other people developed variations of the same fundamental concept, and this has been reviewed by Willis (1968). The Lowry migration model (1966) also derives from the same approach. It retains the same concept of gravitation, but the origins and destinations are weighted and it includes unemployment rate and wage levels. Fundamentally, however, it is the same concept. This kind of model has been used in America to predict inter-regional flows and also in England by Masser (1970).

Retail location models

The second line of research in this social-physics approach includes retail location models. Reilly (1931) developed the first retail location model. He formulated a law of retail gravitation in which he stated that two centres attract trade from an intermediate place, approximately in direct proportion to the size of the centre and in inverse proportion to the square of the distance from the centre. He was not trying to predict the location of a shopping centre but the flows of people from certain origins to a given destination. His interest was in the delineation of market areas, or service centres. You can see that from this point it is a very short step to predict a potential for the location of a given centre. Thus, we have 'potential models' which predict the potential of a particular zone to attract consumers.

Huff (1962) extended the formulation to consider many centres. But, the best known model is the Lakshmanan and Hansen market potential model (1965), which treats explicitly the flows of money between one origin and a destination.

$$S_{ij} = P_i \, G_i \, \frac{A_j^{\alpha} \, d_{ij}^{-\beta}}{\Sigma_j \, A_j^{\alpha} \, d_{ij}^{-\beta}} \qquad (5)$$

where S_{ij} = flow of money between place i and centre j

P_i = population of place i

G_i = mean expenditure per person in place i

A_j = attraction of place j

d_{ij} = distance between i and j

$\alpha \, \beta$ = parameters

These models have been used in many places to predict the sales level in shopping centres in this country and in America. The retail floor space in a particular zone was used as the attraction. You could use the existing floor space in retail shopping to produce an attraction function.

From the same model you can also predict the location of service employees with a little modification (see Echenique et al. 1969ᴄ, 1970).

Cordey–Hayes (1968) has made an excellent review of these and similar models, including the intervening opportunity model.

Residential location models

Another kind of model which we ought to talk about is the residential location model. Perhaps the earliest reference to residential location is Clark's 'Law of Density' (Clark 1951). He described the distribution of residential densities from the centre of a town as an exponential which decays with distance.

$$D_j = A \exp(-\beta d_j) \tag{6}$$

where D_j = residential density at place j

A = constant

d_j = distance to the town centre

β = parameter

But the first model to predict residential development was the Hansen accessibility model (Hansen 1959). He stated that the accessibility at point 1 to a particular type of activity at area 2, say employment, is directly proportional to the size of the activity at area 2 and inversely proportional to some function of the distance separating point 1 from area 2. It is the gravity concept again. He used it to predict the level of residential development in a particular zone.

The same concept is used by Lowry (1964) in his model of a metropolis. He located residential population around a work place in proportion to the potential of the accessibility to employment.

$$P_j = k u \Sigma_i E_i d_{ij}^{-\beta} \tag{7}$$

where P_j = population living in place j

k = constant for normalisation

u = labour participation rate

E_i = employment at place i

d_{ij} = distance between i and j

β = parameter

Extensions of the same idea have been used by Batty (1969) and by the Urban Systems Study at LUBFS (see Echenique et al. 1969c), not as a potential model but dealing with actual trips between work and residence.

$$R_{ij} = \frac{E_i \, F_j \, \exp(-\beta c_{ij})}{\sum_j F_j \, \exp(-\beta c_{ij})} \qquad\qquad (8)$$

where R_{ij} = journey from work place i to residential place j

E_i = employment at place i

F_j = residential floor space at place j

c_{ij} = cost of travel between i and j

β = parameter

Developments of this model, including the disaggregation of the population into income groups and the floor space into housing types and rent have been proposed by Wilson (1970).

Finally, within this approach, we have other kinds of models. We have been dealing with location of activity sub-models, residential, migration, transport flows, and so on. But this approach has also been used for locating infrastructure, the amount of space for roads (Owens 1968), and we have also developed a floorspace model in Cambridge (see Echenique 1968), based on the same idea of potential for development. Therefore, you can combine all these models to produce a more comprehensive model.

Two examples of social physics

Now I will look at two examples of operational models of this approach. The first model which I will talk about very briefly is the Chicago Area Transportation Study model (CATS). The interesting point about this model is that it was the first operational model of an urban system, developed in Chicago to predict transport flows. It was an attempt to predict the development levels of all activities in each zone of the city. As Lowry (1967) put it, it has a very crude structure and 'ad hoc' judgements are introduced within the process which they call "staff judgements". The model distinguishes six land uses – residential, commercial, manufacturing, transport, public building and open space. The process starts by designating land for public open space, shopping and commercial use. A model is not used for this; this information is just fed based upon "staff judgement". Then, the residential land and industrial land use (density of development) is predicted using a Hansen-type accessibility model. Density is a function of accessibility to existing employment or to the town centre. Once you know the level of density you can transform this into population, and adjust the number for distribution of the total (predicted exogenously), and the land use for public building and transportation is assigned by applying rates or norms according to density. Having checked the totals against the independent projection, a transport model is run to calculate the flows between one zone and another. As I understand it, this model has been in operation nearly eleven years or more, to predict traffic flows and residential development and industrial development.

The second model which I will review is the Lowry model, because we will hear so much about it in the remaining sessions. The Lowry model was developed in Pittsburgh by I.R. Lowry in 1962-63, but it was published after Lowry had moved to the Rand Corporation (Lowry 1964). This model has tremendous influence in America and I think the rest of the world because it has very simple basic ideas,

and is, in some ways, very elegant. It is easier to collect data for it and
much easier to understand than the CATS model. The Lowry structure - the only
thing that is left from the original Lowry model because all the rest is more
or less completely outdated - is based on the concept that if we can define
the basic employment, we can predict the location of population, which in turn
enables us to predict the location of services (retailing, schools, and so on),
that is, the employment dependent on the distribution of the population. These
services generate more employment, which requires more population to be located
(see Figure 3).

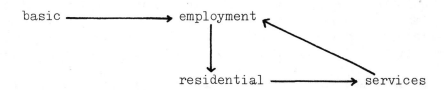

Figure 3   The Lowry structure

The equations that Lowry used are much more complicated and not very good,
especially for the location of services. He used a kind of quadratic equation
to predict three levels of services, like metropolitan, district and neighbourhood levels.

I think the next model, the Garin-Lowry model, which introduces two new
variations, is no longer a 'potential' model, distributing population as a
function of the potential to the accessibility of employment, but it distributes
actual trips from work places to residential places. Given then the basic
employment, the residential population generated by this employment is distributed
according to a journey to work function, which is the kind of model which I
described previously, from place i to zone j. This gives a population distribution, and also distribution of trips which you can allocate to the network. Then
you have another model, journeys from home to service. Again you can describe
this as actual trips from zone i to zone j, which in turn generate more
employment which is again distributed, and so on. It was an important improvement to treat this kind of relationship as flows between one place and another
place. In this way you integrate transport with land use models.

Models which derive from the Lowry model have been reviewed recently by Goldner
(1971); Mike Batty (1972c) has also done a fairly comprehensive review of these
models. The popularity of this model has been tremendous. In this country,
Wilson has improved most of the equations; Eric Cripps applied a version of
the model in Bedfordshire in 1968; Mike Batty also applied another version of
the model in Lancashire and North Derbyshire. Here in Cambridge we have mainly
used the model for spatial distribution within a town, rather than on a regional
scale, for Cambridge, Reading, Stevenage and so on. The Centre for Environmental
Studies has some experience of running this kind of model in Cheshire. You will
be hearing about these applications in later papers. Goldner in America has
used the model to predict the level of development in San Francisco. The same
model has also been applied in Ljubljana, Yugoslavia. We have also used it in
Chile, and developed a model of Caracas, Venezuela, with a different kind of
structure but similar in content.

The problems of this model are different from previous models. The theoretical basis of these models is not convincing. It is not very clear why phenomena seem to conform to the relationships described in the model, and this makes its predictive value uncertain. Although we can grasp intuitively how this kind of thing works, there is no formal demonstration of why this model should hold true. There is, however, now some indication of why this kind of thing seems to work. Wilson (1967) derived the same kind of basic formulation from another analogy in physics, in the field of statistical mechanics, and since then it has become clear from the work of Jaynes, Tribus and Wilson that the reason why these things happen to fit reality is that you can demonstrate that it is the best assumption we can make based on the kind of information we have. This can be demonstrated with reference to information theory; in other words, with a given level of information which we can make explicit, we can derive the most probable distribution of the system. This has been called the Maximum Entropy Estimate.

I still think there is a legitimate doubt about this model, which comes from the fact that we are not really explaining anything, or very little. We are just making the outcome consistent with our information. Therefore if we have, for example, the information about a mean trip length we can include that and find the most probable distribution which includes that constraint. But this mean trip length is an outcome of a problem; it is not the reason why people are distributed in that fashion. In other words, there is very little theoretical explanation of why these things occur. Therefore, while this kind of model has been the most successful in reproducing reality, and has been very easy to use in an operational context, it is a weak predictive tool.

Conclusion

Most of the audience must wonder, after the criticism of both the micro- and macro-approach, what is the use of attempting to build models? The first approach while presenting a more consistent explanation of the behaviour of people, has been rendered useless, up to now, by operational difficulties. In the second approach, the ease of operation has demonstrated usefulness in practice, but because of lack of theory, severe questions are posed about its predictive power.

I think this situation imposes a challenge to theoretitians and academics but for the real world planners a dilemma exists. If we follow the pattern of the natural sciences, we should continue to use deficient models, aware of their shortcomings, until a better model comes about.

Contemporary thoughts on urban models

Martyn Cordey-Hayes

This lecture outlines three urban modelling styles, namely comparative static, recursive and dynamic simulation, and makes an assessment of the strengths and limitations of these approaches with particular reference to their usefulness in the planning process. Here only a synoptic description of the three modelling approaches is given, a fuller description of the use of the models is given in recent papers by Massey and Cordey-Hayes (1971) and Cordey-Hayes (1972).

Comparative statics

An example of a comparative static model is one which attempts to analyse the repercussions of alternative arrangements of transportation networks, land development regulations and public service facilities on the distribution of population. A comparative static model of this type assumes that the spatial distribution of population is determined by the number and accessibility of jobs in neighbouring zones, supplemented by indices for the intrinsic attraction of a zone for residential location and by constraints on population density. The model is summarised in Figure 1.

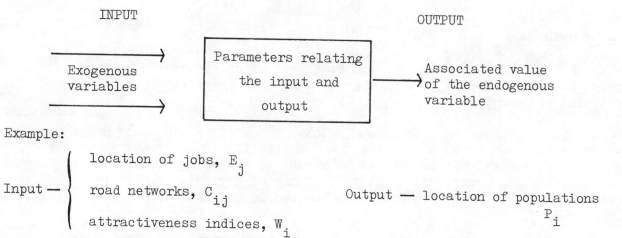

Example:

$$\text{Input} - \begin{cases} \text{location of jobs, } E_j \\ \text{road networks, } C_{ij} \\ \text{attractiveness indices, } W_i \end{cases} \qquad \text{Output} - \text{location of populations} \\ P_i$$

Relationships defined by the experimentally determined parameter β

i.e. $P_i = A_i \sum_j E_j W_i f(C_{ij})$

where $A_i = \dfrac{1}{\sum_i W_i \exp(\beta C_{ij})}$

Figure 1   Summary of a comparative static model

Essentially, it is assumed that the variables 'intrinsic attractiveness' and 'job accessibility' can be used to circumscribe the housing market to provide a rough perspective of an equilibrium distribution of population at a coarse geographic scale. They are equilibrium models in the sense that, given the level and geographical distribution of employment and road networks, the model generates the associated population distribution. Equilibrium assumes that there exists a balance or stability between the above inputs and outputs and that a 'prediction' merely involves the specification of the inputs at the assigned point in time. All uses of the model then involve examining the output implications of changes made to the inputs.

The models are essentially atemporal because they do not consider the process of moving from one situation to another and because the length of time required for the system to adjust to the new inputs remains unspecified. But it is often assumed, at least implicitly, that the response to the changed value of an input appears at the same instant as the stimulus (changed input). However, there always exists a time lag between the stimulus and response, which is variously referred to as the relaxation, reaction or response time. This time lag is particularly important if it is greater in duration than the time scale over which it is wished to observe the response. In the above models the time lag is, for example, the interval required for the population to adjust to the changed job distribution. This gives serious limitations (that are rarely observed) for both conditional forecasts and for the calibration of comparative static models.

The presence of a time lag means that one or more other variables intervene in the process which is therefore more complex than represented in the model. One approach to the improvement of such models is to break down the structure of the 'black box' given in Figure 1 and attempt to represent the organisation and mutual couplings within the process of population re-adjustment. This is essentially the approach adopted in recursive models.

Recursive methods

Although similar to the methods of comparative statics, recursive methods do recognise the existence of time lags and aim at the description of the development process through time.

The development process is broken down into a number of finite steps and the step length (or resolution time) is assumed implicitly to be greater than the response time required for the output to adjust to the changed inputs. Growth (or change) is then considered in steps by means of periodic changes in the exogenous variables. The approach is summarised in Figure 2.

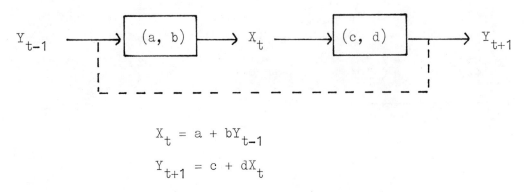

$$X_t = a + bY_{t-1}$$

$$Y_{t+1} = c + dX_t$$

Figure 2   A recursive description

As in comparative statics, endogenous variables are related to exogenous variables by constant parameters, but reaction times can be made explicit and the method aims at a more complete description of "how" change occurs. A simple example of a recursive approach to residential re-distribution is to break down the process into two sub-problems and firstly to identify which households move and then to consider where (Butler et al. 1969). The new residential distribution is used to assess which families move in the next time period. The residential location model of Kain, currently being developed in the States, appears to be a sophisticated model of this kind. My interpretation of this model is given schematically below.

i   Identify which households move

Some of these will be moves caused by new household formation. Some moves will be related to a job change. The majority are moves due to changes in life cycle - the need for a bigger or smaller house with changing family size.

ii   Where

(a)   Allocate these 'movers' to a particular housing sub-market
(b)   Allocate to a zone (but this spatial allocation comes after the supply considerations given below).

iii Supply side: for each sub-market

(a)   Estimate house construction by zone
(b)   Allow for existing housing stock to age
(c)   Estimate housing improvement.

iv   Price mechanism

Compare supply and demand for each sub-market calculated in (ii) and (iii) above.

v   Spatial allocation

Spatial allocation, by linear programming, to minimise a house price and travel cost function.

This housing market model is a logical way of alleviating some of the limitations of the simpler residential locations described above (section 1). But the difficulties of designing and implementing a model of this type should not be underestimated. It is a major research and development exercise requiring perhaps eight researchers for three to five years.

Dynamic simulation models

The objective of simulation models in urban planning is to be able to conduct policy experiments through simulating and comparing the repercussions of alternative courses of action. Simulation models aim to provide an explicit means of exploring and displaying the consequences of alternative strategies for the growth and change of the urban environment.

Attempts at dynamic simulation of urban processes (for example Forrester 1969 and Hamilton et al. 1969) are much more strongly structured on an ability to make forecasts than the recursive and comparative static methods. A formal prediction in time involves a statement of the initial conditions combined with an equation of 'motion' for the development process. Equations of 'motion' translate information from one time to another by considering the rate of change of a variable. Dynamic simulation requires that these

formal equations of motion be known. Often plausible hypotheses for these
can be made: for example, that the rate of change of population due to
migration within a region depends on the relative levels of unemployment
in that region and all other regions. But very few rigorous tests of such
hypotheses have been made and there is a complete ignorance of any time lags
involved. A dynamic simulation model comprises a dozen or more simple
hypotheses of the above sort in which the rate of change of one variable
is related to other variables at a previous time period. As an integrated
set of differential equations they form a comprehensive dynamic simulation
model. But unlike similar problems in engineering the equations of motion
are unknown; there are no equivalents of Ohm's law or Newton's laws which
form the basis of many simulation models in engineering. Each plausible
relationship may contain a 50 per cent error (and possibly much more) and
as a result of compounding these errors the simulations are of limited use
for conditional forecasting. Thus the numerical projections obtained from
the dynamic simulation of urban processes are of doubtful value, particularly
when dealing with simulations up to thirty years ahead. But the strength
of such models lies in their explicit exploration of how urban and regional
systems work and how they may react to the implementation of various planning
policies.

These views are partly based on a testing and modifications made to
Forrester's model 'Urban dynamics'. These results are described in a recent
paper (Cordey-Hayes 1972), in which the following main conclusions are
drawn:

i   Forrester's results do not follow from counter intuitive systems
    behaviour, but follow from the particular structure of his model, and
    from his evaluative criteria. In essence, the model is considered a
    novel way of expressing his subjective views.

ii Modifications to the equation system give rise to markedly different
    values for his evaluative measures, and there is scarcely sufficient
    understanding of urban processes to specify these equations adequately.

iii Despite these criticisms, the methodology is considered a potentially
    useful approach (particularly as a contextual framework for more
    specific subsystem studies). This is provided that the work is accom-
    panied by a serious programme of experimental research devoted to the
    formal understanding of urban growth processes (essentially the experi-
    mental deduction of the equations of motion).

The use of models in British planning: applications in Monmouthshire and Peterborough

Richard Barras

This paper is split into three sections. Firstly, there is a brief outline of an approach to the practical application of models in planning that has been developed at the Centre for Environmental Studies and subsequently in the Planning Research Applications Group. Secondly, there is a discussion of two applications projects: one with Monmouthshire County Council, and the second with Peterborough Development Corporation. Finally, some general conclusions about the application of models in the planning process are drawn.

The development and application of models

The whole process of model-building and application can be characterized as a continuum:

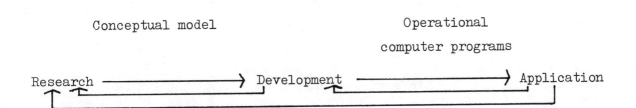

Different institutions and different projects operate at different points on this continuum. Thus the joint project between the CES and Cheshire County Council, which initiated this whole approach, spanned research and development. It took the conceptual model framework first developed by Lowry, improved its design and eventually produced an operational computer package. Several theoretical improvements were made to the model, but the principal focus was on questions of operational design, and some of these will be mentioned when discussing specific applications. (For a full description of the Cheshire exercise see Barras et al. 1971).

Following the completion of this exercise we received several enquiries from planning departments interested in using the model. This implies a move across the spectrum to the area of application, using models that have been developed to the operational stage and that have further been tried and tested in practical situations so that their uses and limitations are understood. It was felt that this could best be achieved by a separate applications-oriented institution, rather than within the Centre whose function should remain that of research and development. Consequently the Planning Research Applications Group was set up as a joint exercise between the CES and the Local Government Operations Research Unit in Reading. The aim of this Group is to act as a two-way channel: introducing new techniques into the planning process as they emerge from research and development projects, while at the same time providing the feedback to research, so that the problems of practical planning can act as a stimulus to new research ideas. Thus, by linking research, development and application, as an integrated process, it is hoped that the introduction of modelling techniques into planning can proceed more effectively than has sometimes been the case with the earlier generation of transport models. There, questions of operational design have sometimes been given insufficient attention when trying to implement conceptually very sophisticated models.

The approach being adopted in the Applications Group can be illustrated by briefly describing two projects on which we are currently engaged.

Application in Monmouthshire

The objectives of the Monmouthshire project were two-fold. Firstly, the County Council were engaged in a land-use transportation study with consultants that was to provide inputs to the on-going structure plan work. When we were brought into the study, the initial strategy-generation phase had already been completed and they had developed four strategies to be tested and elaborated using the Lowry model. In addition to the specific task of testing these alternatives, prior to the selection of a preferred strategy, the second aspect of our role was a general educative one: to introduce the modelling techniques into the planning department, teach the planners how to understand and use them and eventually to make them operational on the authority's own computer. In this way the model was to be useful beyond the immediate needs of their strategy testing work; it was to be integrated into the on-going planning process for future work on monitoring and updating the structure plan.

There have been three phases to the project. The first, concerned with testing the original set of strategies, took approximately six man months of professional time for the staff of the authority. Monmouthshire had responsibility for the design of the system and data collection, while the operational computer runs were carried out on the Applications Group's computer in Reading. During this first phase two professional planners from the authority were trained in the understanding and use of both the model and the computer programs. Following the testing of these original strategies the planners went through a second cycle of strategy generation, revising the original strategies in the light of the results of the first testing phase. This has led to a second phase of strategy testing, in which the local planners are formulating and setting up all the model runs themselves, using the Applications Group merely as a bureau service. The third phase will involve transferring our programs on to their new computer when it has been installed. After that they will be able to carry on using the model without any further help from us.

In order to describe the way in which the model can be used in this type of strategy-testing exercise it is necessary just to recapitulate on what others have said about the operation of this type of model, putting emphasis on the main inputs that can be used as policy testing variables. Models of the Lowry type take as input a spatial distribution of basic employment and from this they generate distributions of population and service employment. Both allocation processes are based upon generalized measures of accessibility modified by the relative suitability of different zones for the location of residential and service activity.

From this outline of the principles of the model, four main inputs can be distinguished: the location of basic industry, the transportation network, the zonal area available for residential development and the location of service centres. These four inputs provide the policy variables by which strategies can be expressed, and the model will produce the population and service activity distributions as outputs by which the effects of strategies can be compared. The use of each of these main inputs in the Monmouthshire study can be briefly outlined:

i   Location of basic employment. This was a key factor in Monmouthshire. While the total number of jobs in the area may not be changing radically, there are major changes occurring in the location patterns of employment, reflecting the changing industrial base, and this is what the model is concerned with. The employment pattern was formerly more dispersed, based upon traditional mining activity in scattered settlements in the Valleys. It is now concentrating into fewer, larger centres: principally in Newport, in the large Spencer steelworks on the coast and in the new town of Cwmbran. The strategies we examined were principally concerned with alternative ways in which the employment pattern may continue to change and develop in the future.

ii   Transportation networks. These are the basis for the accessibility measures used in the allocation mechanisms in the model. Since the first phase of the project was part of a major land-use/transportation study, alternative future transportation networks for the area had already been prepared. These could therefore easily be incorporated into the alternatives tested.

iii   Area for residential development. The land area available for residential development in each zone is an important input to the model in determining the allocation of residential activity. Apart from physical constraints on development, this measure can be treated as a policy variable through which the application of planning constraints can be expressed. It allows the exploration of alternative strategies both for constraining development around urban areas and for the release of land for new residential areas. In Monmouthshire the only significant constraints that were being applied were around Newport, while alternative locations for substantial new development were being considered in other parts of the area.

iv   Location of service centres. This was not such a significant factor as the other three in this study (see the comments on Peterborough for a study that concentrates on the service sector).

With an interaction model of this type the design of the spatial system is a vital part of the study. When developing this model for Cheshire a two-level spatial system was built up, and this has become the basis for subsequent applications of the model. At the subregional scale the study area as a whole can be treated as a single system that can be partitioned into several subsystems. These subsystems correspond to subareas within the study area that can be identified according to several criteria. They are based on the self-contained journey-to-work areas that typically can be defined in any multi-nodal subregion. However, such subsystems also often show distinct characteristics in terms of economic structure, such as activity rates, that further differentiate them. With the spatial system developed for this model it is possible to model the interactions within each subarea in fine detail and to model aggregate interactions between subareas. Not only does this considerably ease computational problems in dealing with large systems, allowing urban areas to be handled in more detail than has previously been possible with models at this scale, but it also emphasizes the overall structure of an area more clearly.

In Monmouthshire the study area was divided into six such subareas. There was one subarea around Newport, the largest town in the county; the Valleys were divided into two, and there were three rural subareas around Chepstow, Monmouth and Abergavenny. The degree of closure, in terms of journey to work, for these six subareas varied between 70% and 85%, and the main inter-action between them was fairly accurately modelled because the inter-subarea approximation corresponded reasonably well with the pattern of major linkages in the actual transportation network.

As a final point, the calibration of the model should be mentioned. The data that had been collected for the Land Use/Transportation study enabled us to calibrate against base year trip matrices rather than aggregated zonal distributions, and this is a considerable advantage since the calibra-tion is far more sensitive when using trip matrices or even mean trip lengths. The fits obtained when calibrating against trips were reasonable, considering that the matrices were rather sparse, varying between 0.7 and 0.9.

Application in Peterborough

It has been our intention to extend the basic set of programs developed for the Cheshire model to form a flexible package that can be used for various types of spatial interaction modelling. The first stage in this process was to adapt the existing programs in order to produce a hierarchical shopping model. This is currently being applied in a joint project with Peterborough Development Corporation.

Peterborough is undergoing a major expansion and the object of our study was to study future shopping patterns in the town and its surrounding subregion. Major expansion is planned both for town centre shopping facilities and for a ring of new suburban centres around the town. Particular emphasis in the study is being placed on two aspects: on the relationship between Peterborough and competing subregional centres such as Nottingham, Leicester and Cambridge, and secondly on the relationship between the development of the town centre and of the surrounding suburban centres.

For this study the model has been split into two sectors, for convenience and durable goods, and the hierarchical spatial system already described for the Monmouthshire study has been adapted so that each sector in the shopping model can be modelled using a different spatial system appropriate to the structure of that particular sector. Thus, durable goods are modelled over the subregion as a whole using a 'rectangular' interaction pattern involving nearly two hundred expenditure zones interacting with about 25 durable goods shopping centres. Convenience goods sales are modelled at a second level in the system, with the subregion split into nine market areas corresponding to the main local centres in the subregion, with one larger market area around Peterborough itself and a ring of smaller market areas around it. There are aggregate interactions between market areas, and fine zone interactions within them. It is intended to build in a mechanism such that there will also be an interaction between durable and convenience sales trips.

The approach being adopted in the study is to make a set of upper and lower limit forecasts for inputs, such as zonal populations and expenditure rates. Then we use the model to test alternative combinations of these forecasts against alternative development strategies expressed in terms of floorspace totals for the expanded town centre and for the new suburban centres. Thus the interaction between demand (expenditure by zone) and supply at each shopping centre, under varying conditions, can be compared through the allocation mechanisms in the model.

Some general conclusions on the application of models in the planning process

There seem to be broadly three main ways in which spatial interaction models of the type described above can be used within the operational planning process. But it must be stressed that, however they are used, they can only remain one small part of the much wider and more complex normative process in which planners are engaged.

i   In the early stages of the structure planning process the exercise of setting up one of these models and running it to try and reproduce the existing situation can lead to significant insights into the structure of an area and how it functions. This can be characterized as the early understanding phase of the process.

ii   Secondly, as part of the cyclical process of strategy generation and evaluation, these models can be used to test and elaborate alternative strategies. This was the purpose of the first part of the Monmouthshire study.

iii   Thirdly, such models can function as part of the on-going monitoring and updating process that must continue after the structure plan has been prepared. They can be used both to test the impact of major new developments, or to monitor the cumulative effects of several incremental changes. With this type of use it is particularly necessary to establish the model system within the local authority, so that the planners themselves can run the model as they wish. This is the objective of the third phase of the Monmouthshire study, when our programs are being transferred on to their own computer.

An essential part of any joint project of the type being undertaken by the Applications Group is the educative one. It is most important to ensure that the planners fully understand both the uses and the limitations of the techniques and that they are able to interpret model results sensibly. This is the only way that models are going to be introduced effectively into the planning process.

There are several operational problems with the type of joint studies we are undertaking. Since the emphasis is on low cost projects they are by necessity constrained by tight schedules, and if anything goes wrong at some crucial point in the study the timetable can be seriously affected. Some local authorities have small computers and this can present another problem when trying to transfer programs, but this problem is likely to diminish as authorities acquire the new generation of large machines.

Finally, perhaps the most important problem is that of data availability, since the quality of data is critical in determining the success of any modelling study, particularly during the calibration stage. The data needs of these models are not excessive and much of this data is of the strategic type that should in any case be collected as part of a structure plan exercise, whether using models or not.

The use of models in British planning: applications in Bedfordshire and the Reading sub-region

Erlet Cater

This paper will examine how urban development models can help the planner formulate his structure plans in the light of the more stringent requirements of the 1968 Town and Country Planning Act, and then will illustrate this theme by specific reference to two studies in Bedfordshire and one in the Reading subregion.

Forecasting and analytical tasks in structure planning

Firstly, let us look at the forecasting and analytical requirements of structure planning. The requirements of the 1968 Town and Country Planning Act changed the approach of urban and sub-regional planning from that of a fragmented topic-oriented one, where the development plan was regarded as a series of development projects, to a comprehensive systematic approach. The Structure Plan, as envisaged in the 1968 Act, is to be regarded as a depiction of the state of the urban system at a particular point in a given path through time. The requirements for flexibility are such that the plan should be modified to account for the dynamics of cities and city regions.

One must distinguish between the different emphasis necessitated in the approaches of county authorities and urban authorities. County or sub-regional authorities will be planning for inter-connecting systems of towns or cities, whereas urban authorities will be concerned with the interactions and relation-ships within the cities themselves as systems. Eric Cripps (1968) distinguishes between the two levels of structure planning and points to the different considerations involved.

At the county or sub-regional level the planner needs to understand the nature of urban hierarchies, the structure of urban hinterlands, how towns and cities interact together and the strength of these interactions and interdependencies. He will be concerned with where people live in relation to their work place or to service centres, and the trips they make. The planner at this level is concerned more with the macro-location of people, jobs and services and he will want to have an idea of how this will change over time, and indeed how this change will be affected by, and will affect, his plans and policies.

Cripps identifies three major classes of policy variables which are relevant at the county or sub-regional level, all of which are controllable by local or central government. Aside from the normal constraints on resources, these are as follows:

i   Major unique locators. These include new towns, town development schemes, major research establishments, nuclear power stations and airports. We will see how models have validity in examining the impact of these types of unique locators.

ii   Major transport networks, such as new motorways.

iii   Policy constraints. These can cover a wide range of subjects such as greenbelts, areas of high agricultural quality and areas of outstanding natural beauty.

Any one of these, or any mix of them, can have a considerable impact on the system of interactions and the location of activities that the planner is considering at the county or sub-regional level. The designation of a new or over-spill town, for example, has the effect of shifting a settlement up several stages in the urban hierarchy. The location of a new airport brings in its train a whole line of associated expansion and employment opportunities, which in turn induce considerably changed settlement and interaction patterns. The planner's problem, then, is to attempt to evaluate alternative policies where he can, on the one hand, influence the locational implications of such variables or, on the other hand, where his policies will affect the locational implications but not necessarily alter them. He will have to continually bear in mind the desirable distribution of population and employment in his area and the associated problem of adequate accessibility.

At the urban structure level the planner needs to be aware of the micro-implications of his policies. At this finer level of detail the control is more direct and will cover such fields as housing and transportation policy. To be able to apply policies at this level implies a more detailed understanding of urban activity systems; specifically, the spatial structure of the housing and labour markets and the relationship between them. In order to have an adequate understanding of the behaviour of the urban population in terms of job and house choice, at the urban structure level, it is essential that descriptions of urban structure include the sub-divisions and attributes of population, jobs, trips and houses and so on. The considerations, therefore, at this level are not purely locational and they imply a much more disaggregated analysis. The data requirements at this level of dis-aggregation are considerably more demanding.

It can be seen, then, that structure planning at both the county or sub-regional level and the urban level present a somewhat formidable requirement for the adequate understanding of the way the systems work, the relationships between the components and the way they interact.

The use of models

How, then, can urban development models help us towards this understanding? Urban development models have a considerable analytical value, and therefore contribute towards better planning decisions. By abstracting from reality the principal activities and interactions involved, they enable the planner to assess the implications of alternative policy decisions.

Firstly, let us examine the application to the planning problem at the county or sub-regional level. This, as we have already stated, resolves itself into how best to describe the present structure of the sub-region and to show how this will change in the future. The complex web of inter-relationships that face a planner when he begins to consider the problems involved is daunting enough in itself, and it is easy to see why the problem was resolved into a set of isolated compartments before the development of better analytical techniques such as urban development models. Not only does the planner have to attempt to understand the inter-relationships involved, but he needs to examine the implications of alternative policies and constraints and also be able to examine the impact of possible major disturbances in the sub-regional system.

The value of urban development models in this sphere lies in the fact that
they attempt to reproduce mathematically the main components in a sub-regional
system, they describe them in terms of population and employment and the
interaction between them, both spatially and functionally.

It is probably best to examine briefly the general nature of the Lowry model
in order to see how it can perform an analytical role as an aid to decision-
making at this level. In spatial terms, the Lowry model assumes that the
size and distribution of population is related to the size and distribution
of employment by trips between zones of work and zones of residence. It
assumes that the growth of population depends mainly on the growth of employment in the basic sector in the sub-region, and the growth in service industry,
in turn, is dependent on the growth of population.

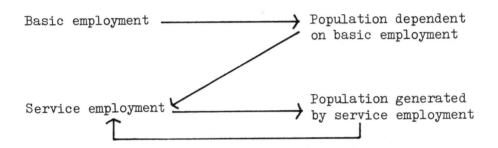

Basic employment gives rise to the population dependent on basic employment,
which gives rise to service employment, which in turn generates further
population. This is an iterative process so that the population generated
then gives rise to further service employment and so on, until the system
closes.

In the Lowry model the initial input of basic employment is located to
residence zones by a residential location sub-model (Figure 1). This
residential location sub-model has been the subject of considerable refinement by Alan Wilson and we have been applying this refined version to
Reading sub-region. When the disaggregated residential location model, as
applied at Reading, is referred to later in this paper it is necessary to
appreciate that it describes only the residential sub-system.

The intervening role of the planner can be introduced into the model in
terms of constraints. Apart from its value for monitoring change in the
system, the model can be used as an aid to the generation and evaluation
of alternative plans by plugging in alternative inputs. It is this latter
use in impact analysis that I will presently examine with reference to
the work done by Cripps and Foot on the impact of Milton Keynes and of the
third London airport in the Bedfordshire region.

Firstly, however, let us draw attention to the utility of urban development
models at the level of urban structure plans. We mentioned previously that
at this level the planner is more concerned with the micro-analytical implications of fluctuations, say, in the labour market, in housing policy, or in
changes in interaction and trip-making patterns due to network changes. I
will attempt to illustrate the analytical role of urban development models
with specific reference to Wilson's disaggregated residential location model,
which we have been applying at Reading.

In order to formulate and apply policies at the urban structure level, a
much more detailed understanding of urban activity systems is needed. Not
only are we interested in the net locational effects but also in examining

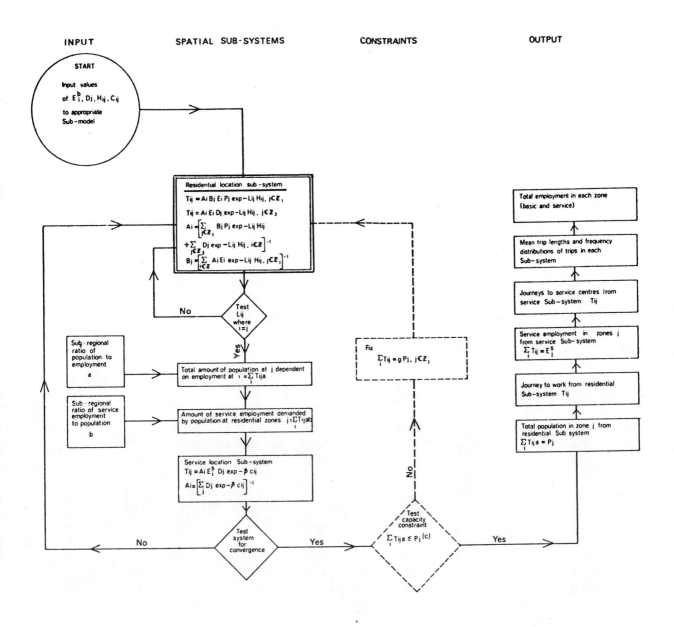

Figure 1   The setting of the Residential location sub-model in the overall
framework of the Lowry model (Cripps and Foot 1969).

the attributes of population, employment and so on in far more detail, to try to formulate some hypothesis as to how different groups behave, mould and are moulded by the city structure. Consequently, as I mentioned earlier, we are interested in population differentiated by such attributes as social class, age, sex, income groups, employment by type and wage, trips by mode and purpose, houses by type, size, price and so on.

The disaggregated residential location model attempts to reproduce the complexity of the system at this level by dividing population into socio-economic or income groups, houses by type, and jobs by wage-group, as well as considering their spatial distribution. The model also introduces a budget term, which is interesting in itself because it attempts to reproduce the micro-economic concept of the trade-off between house prices and the cost of travel in residential location decisions.

Applications in Bedfordshire

To illustrate further the use of urban development models as analytical tools in decision-making, let us go on to examine the actual application of the two models I have mentioned. Firstly, Cripps and Foot (1969) used their version of the Lowry model in Bedfordshire to study the existing and possible future population and employment structure of the county. Their application of the model examined the long-term future impact of major changes in activies in the sub-region, and in particular examined the possible future impact of the development of the new town of Milton Keynes and the third London airport. (These can be classed as major unique locators as mentioned previously.) By using as an input the anticipated change of basic employment in Milton Keynes, which incidentally accounted for 30% of the total anticipated change in basic employment in the entire sub-region up to 1996, the locational impact throughout the system could be assessed, particularly in terms of the location of homes and jobs, and in the changing pattern of journeys to work and to shop.

There is a clear difference between the actual flows in 1966 from work to home in the Bedfordshire sub-region (Figure 2) and the predicted flows using the model for 1996, which show the considerable impact of Milton Keynes on the system (Figure 3). The predicted flows illustrated are unconstrained in fact, but Cripps and Foot also ran the model constrained; that is, they put a limit to the amount of basic employment input and the resulting population.

In examining the urbanisation impact of the third London airport on two of the sites proposed by the Roskill Commission in Bedfordshire, namely Thurleigh and Cublington, a similar process was involved. The model was used to assess the impact of a major change in the number of basic jobs due to the intro-duction of the airport, and its effect, in terms of activity change and inter-urban journeys, on the spatial structure of the sub-region. The model, therefore, allows for different assumptions to be made about major inputs, such as the level of basic employment, and is of value in impact analysis of this kind. It has further application insofar as particular planning policies can be fed back to constrain the model.

Applications in Reading

We move now to the work that we have done at Reading using the disaggregated residential location model proposed by Wilson. This model has considerable

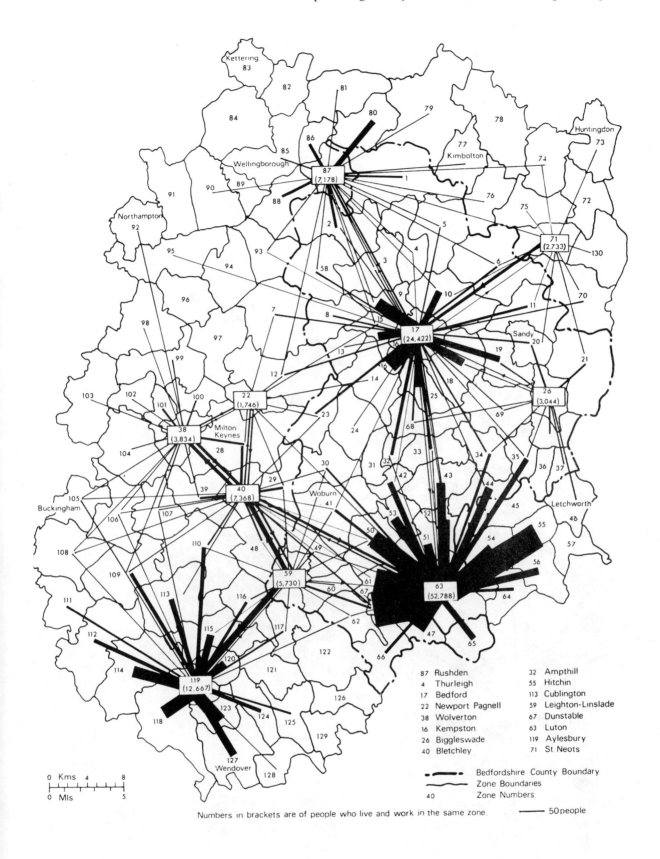

87	Rushden	32	Ampthill
4	Thurleigh	55	Hitchin
17	Bedford	113	Cublington
22	Newport Pagnell	59	Leighton-Linslade
38	Wolverton	67	Dunstable
16	Kempston	63	Luton
26	Biggleswade	119	Aylesbury
40	Bletchley	71	St Neots

— ·· — Bedfordshire County Boundary
——— Zone Boundaries
40 Zone Numbers

Numbers in brackets are of people who live and work in the same zone. ——— 50 people

Figure 2   Desire line diagram of spatial interaction and journeys from work to home. Actual flows (1966) for a selection of towns in the Bedfordshire sub-region (Cripps and Foot 1969).

61

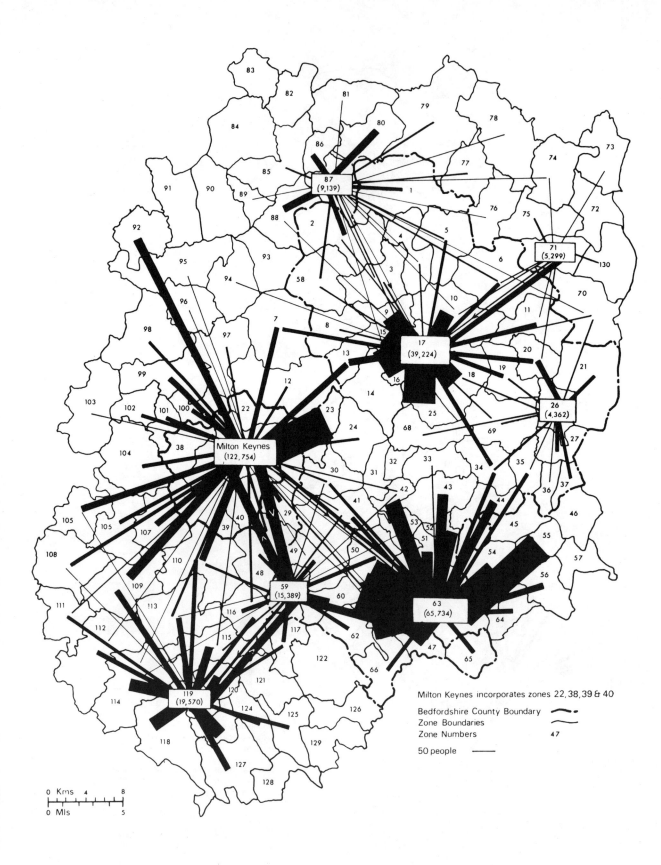

Figure 3   Desire line diagram of spatial interactions. "Unconstrained" predicted flows from work to home (1996) for a selection of towns in the Bedfordshire sub-region (Cripps and Foot 1969).

analytical utility; in addition to disaggregating the inputs of the more elementary residential location models relying on the gravity concept (such as the residential location sub-model of the Lowry model already mentioned) to allow for a disaggregation by wage-group and house-type, it also introduces a budget term which acts as an additional constraint in locating workers to homes. The budget term takes into account the differing prices of houses by location and balances against these the proportion of income available to different wage groups to spend on housing after travel costs have been deducted.

The equation is as follows:

$$T_{ij}kw = Ai^{W} Ei^{W} Hj^{k} \exp(-\beta^{W}cij) \exp\left[-\mu^{W}\left[pj^{k} - q^{W}(w - cij^{1})\right]^{2}\right]$$

where

$$Ai^{W} = \frac{1}{\sum_{j}\sum_{k} Hj^{k} \exp(-\beta^{W}cij) \exp\left[-\mu^{W}\left[pj^{k} - q^{W}(w - cij^{1})\right]^{2}\right]}$$

$T_{ij}kw$ = the number of workers in income group w who work in employment zone i and live in residential zone j in a house type k.

Hj^{k} = the number of houses in residence zone j of type k.

Ei^{W} = the number of jobs in employment zone i by income group w.

k = a size/tenure type classification of housing (5 groups combining size and tenure).

w = 'income' groups. In this case it describes an aggregation of the standard socio-economic groups into the three broad groups of professional, white collar and blue collar.

cij = travel time in minutes from workplace zone to residence zone.

Pj^{k} = price of a house type k in residence zone j.

q^{W} = the average percentage of income spent on housing, after travel costs have been deducted, by a person wage group w.

cij^{1} = out-of-pocket costs of travel incurred by an individual travelling from i to j.

β^{W} = usual travel parameter controlling trip length.

μ^{W} = parameter controlling the distribution of the "budget term".

By using this model it is possible to predict the number of houses by type demanded at zone of residence (j) as an outcome of the allocation of workers by wage-type, from zone of work place (i). In an urban planning context, given the inputs of the employment distribution by wage group, the travel times or costs on the transport network, and a knowledge of the prevailing market house prices, it will be possible to forecast the location of demand for quantities of houses of different types. In fact, the model can be manipulated to give different outputs, according to the inputs. This model has considerable potential in assessing the detailed implication of the location of jobs by type, and houses by price and type.

The model can also be used to test the impact of a major change in the network on residential location which will obviously affect the value of c_{ij} and c_{ij}^1. It is being used to assess the impact of the M4 on the Reading sub-region. The model can yield various outputs of considerable interest; for example, the predicted journey flows before and after the introduction of the motorway, and the predicted distribution of house prices by type and zone. This latter analysis will be of particular interest as it will reveal what areas are likely to be the most attractive in terms of accessibility, taking into account at the same time the distribution of the housing types and the element of choice introduced through the budget term.

The development of models such as this, which are quite demanding on data, is not without its difficulties, however, and we had to make certain assumptions, especially regarding wage-groups and income. The results from running the 23-zone model in the Reading sub-region (Figure 4) can best be illustrated by an examination of the diagram.

Figure 5 is a plot between the actual work trips for professional workers from the 1966 sample centres, and the predicted work trips from the model. The R^2 value is quite high here, and it improves for white-collar and blue-collar workers (Figures 6 and 7). It is of interest to notice that intra-zonal trips fit more closely the regression line than the inter-zonal trips.

Figure 8 shows the difference between the actual and predicted flows from one central zone (Abbey) in Reading to all other outlying zones. It can be seen that the model predicts reasonably well, especially for the smaller flows, but in certain cases it does tend to over-predict or under-predict. Similar patterns are displayed for the white-collar and blue-collar flows (shown in Figures 9 and 10).

Figure 11 shows the actual and the predicted trip distributions from residence to work place, by the different socio-economic groups, for an urban zone. We can see that the model does not predict this type of distribution too badly. Figure 12 shows the results for what we call a suburban/rural zone. It is not quite so rural as the next zone. It does not predict quite so well; for example, in the 5-10 minute range for professional workers it seriously overpredicts. Figure 13 shows the results for Mortimer, a rural/suburban zone. Again, they are not quite so good. The model therefore tended to predict best for the central zone.

Figures 14 to 16 show how the model allocated the different socio-economic groups to house types. For professional workers it tended to over-predict in the public rented sector and to under-predict in the owner-occupied small sector. For the white-collar workers the model predicted a lot better, whilst for blue-collar workers it tended to under-predict in the private-rented good category, especially in the outer zones.

On the whole, at face value the model appears to have reproduced existing patterns quite successfully. But the calibrated values of the parameters derived by using Mike Batty's programs gave a negative value for μ for both professional and white-collar workers. This is clearly inconsistent with the hypothesis suggested by the budget term, and means that in fact the greater the difference between the price of the house type k in a residence zone j, and the average available expenditure on housing (after travel costs have been deducted) by w wage-group, the more attractive is the k-type house and the residential zone j to this household type. This is clearly inconsistent with the hypothesis.

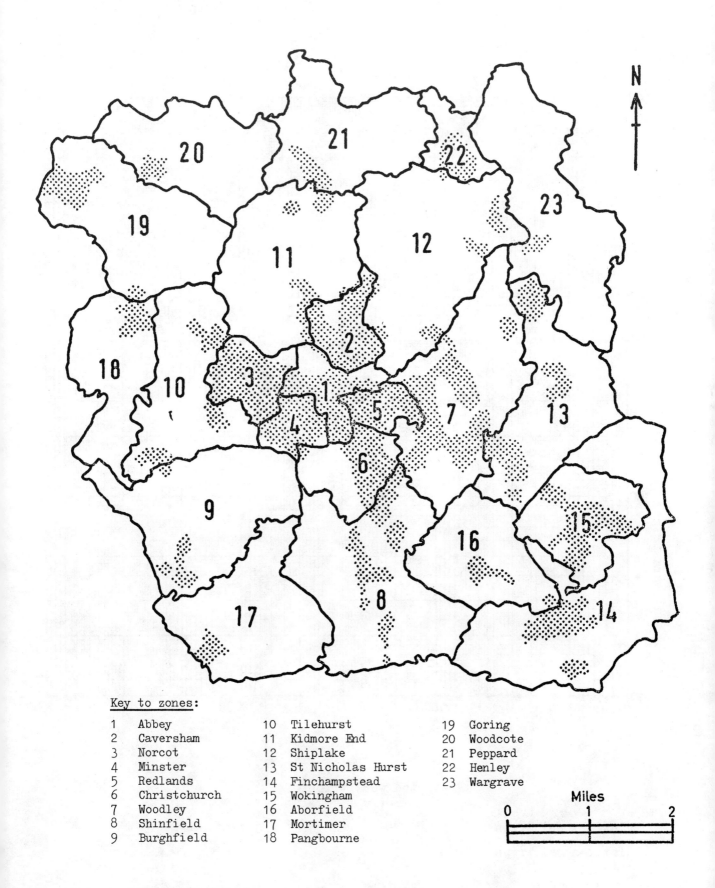

Key to zones:

1	Abbey	10	Tilehurst	19	Goring
2	Caversham	11	Kidmore End	20	Woodcote
3	Norcot	12	Shiplake	21	Peppard
4	Minster	13	St Nicholas Hurst	22	Henley
5	Redlands	14	Finchampstead	23	Wargrave
6	Christchurch	15	Wokingham		
7	Woodley	16	Aborfield		
8	Shinfield	17	Mortimer		
9	Burghfield	18	Pangbourne		

Figure 4   The 23 zone Reading sub-region

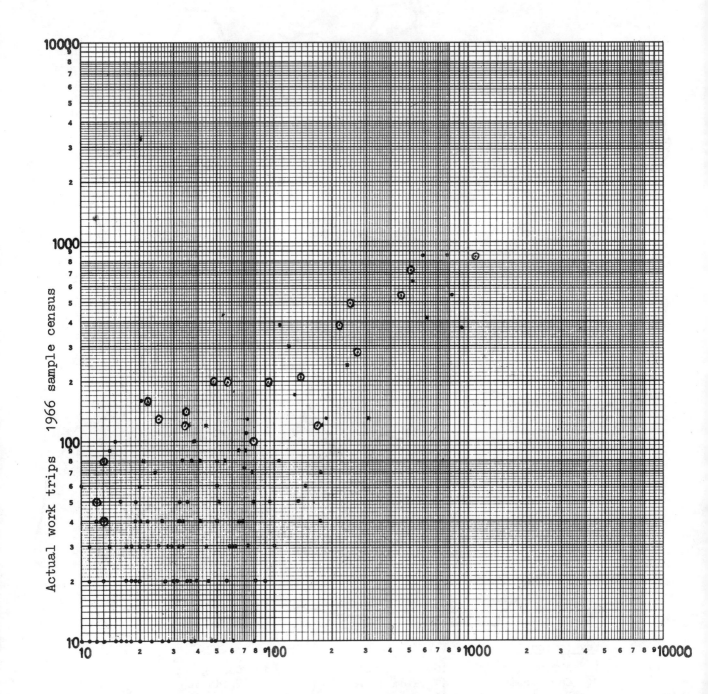

Predicted work trips

◉ Intra-zonal trips $R^2 = 0.7751$

• Inter-zonal trips

Figure 5   Professional work trips in the 23 zone Reading sub-region

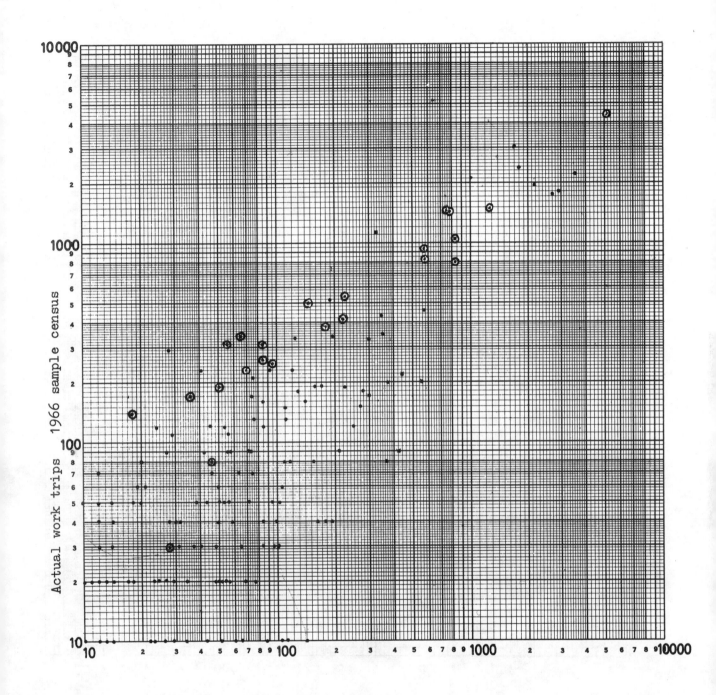

Predicted work trips

⊙ Intra–zonal trips

$R^2 = 0.8518$

. Inter–zonal trips

Figure 6   White–collar work trips in the 23 zone Reading sub–region

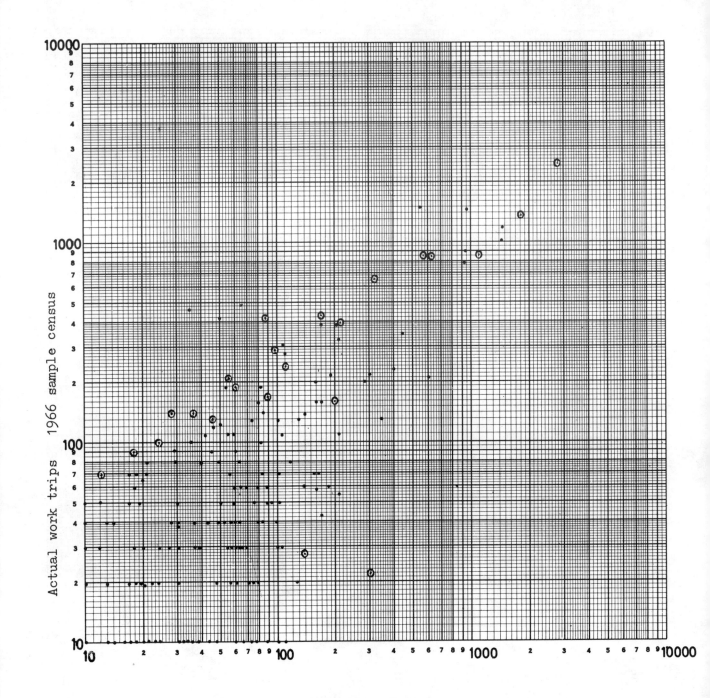

Predicted work trips

⊙ Intra-zonal trips

• Inter-zonal trips

$R^2 = 0.8950$

Figure 7   Blue-collar work trips in the 23 zone Reading sub-region

In subsequent work on the model, therefore, we have pursued different directions to try to ascertain the sensitivity of the μ parameter to different data inputs. If, for example, the proportion q^W is raised, μ tends to go positive. This indicates that there is some sensitivity to the data in the budget term.

The model has also been run for the 64 wards and parishes comprising this sub-region, thus disaggregating it still further areally, but this still resulted in a negative value for the parameter and, generally speaking, the fits have not been quite so good. A weighting was then introduced to scale-down the house prices in the budget term, to bring them more in line with the available income to spend on housing after travel costs have been deducted. This scaling down of prices was suggested after the summation of all the house prices, over all zones in the region, was revealed to be considerably greater than the total available income to spend on housing. The two components of the budget term obviously did not balance to start with.

This scaling down of prices is quite consistent theoretically insofar as the 1966 house prices which were used in this model reflect only the state of the market at that instant, and are not representative of earlier years when the majority of households being modelled in the system were actually entering the market.

Clearly, the operational application of this model in the practical planning sense will depend on the availability of a suitably disaggregated data base, but it has considerable value as an aid to the understanding of the under-lying relationships in the spatial organisation of housing markets, recognising as it does that there are several sub-markets. It is dangerous to claim too much in the way of predictive ability of the urban development models described. However, as analytical tools they unquestionably provide the planner with more information about the interface between himself and the system he is planning than he would usually have in a more conventional approach to the preparation of a structure plan.

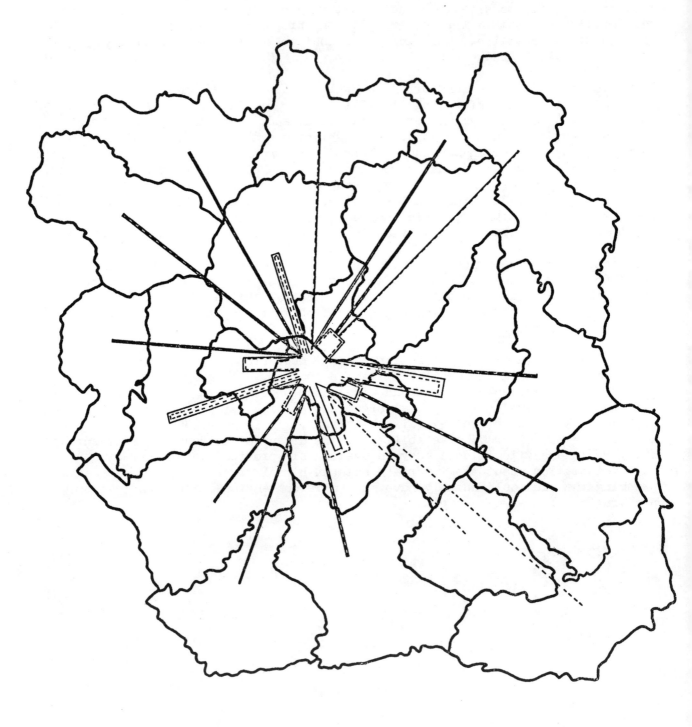

Predicted   Actual

500 trips

1000 trips

Intra-zonal flows in Abbey:

Actual   830
Predicted   1089

Figure 8   Actual and predicted flows from Abbey zone to zones of residence –
professional.

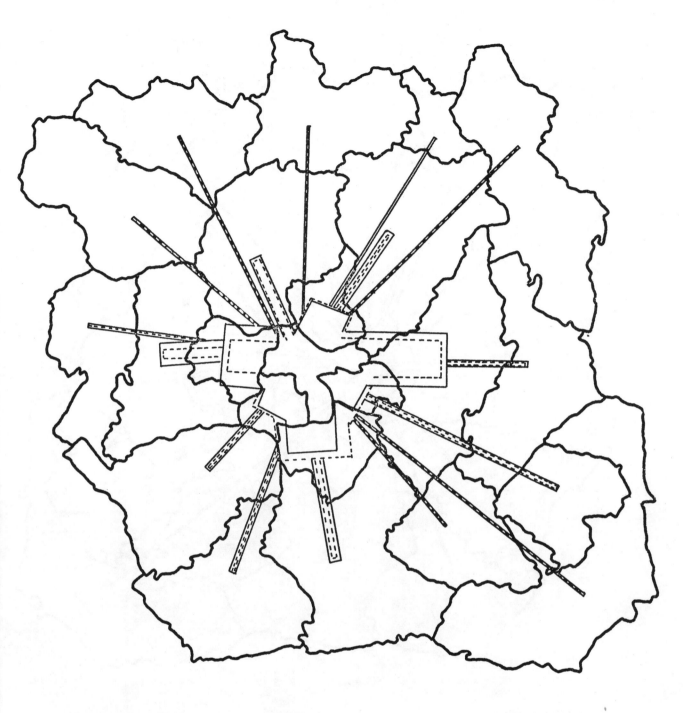

Predicted   Actual

500 trips

1000 trips

Intra-zonal flows in Abbey:

Actual   4470
Predicted 5176

Figure 9   Actual and predicted flows from Abbey zone to zones of residence –
white-collar.

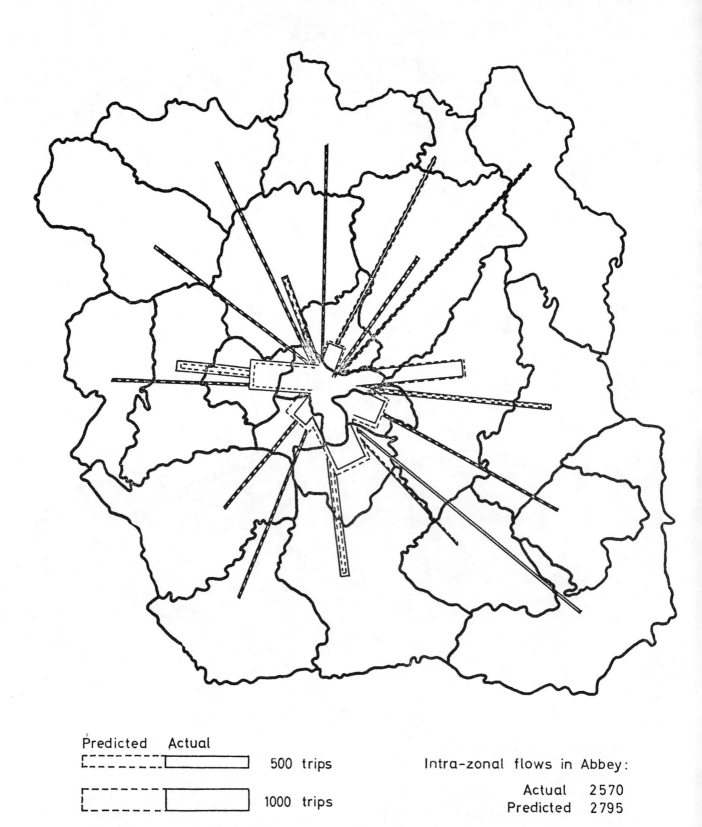

Predicted Actual

500 trips

1000 trips

Intra-zonal flows in Abbey:

Actual   2570
Predicted 2795

Figure 10 ▪ Actual and predicted flows from Abbey zone to zones of residence –
blue-collar.

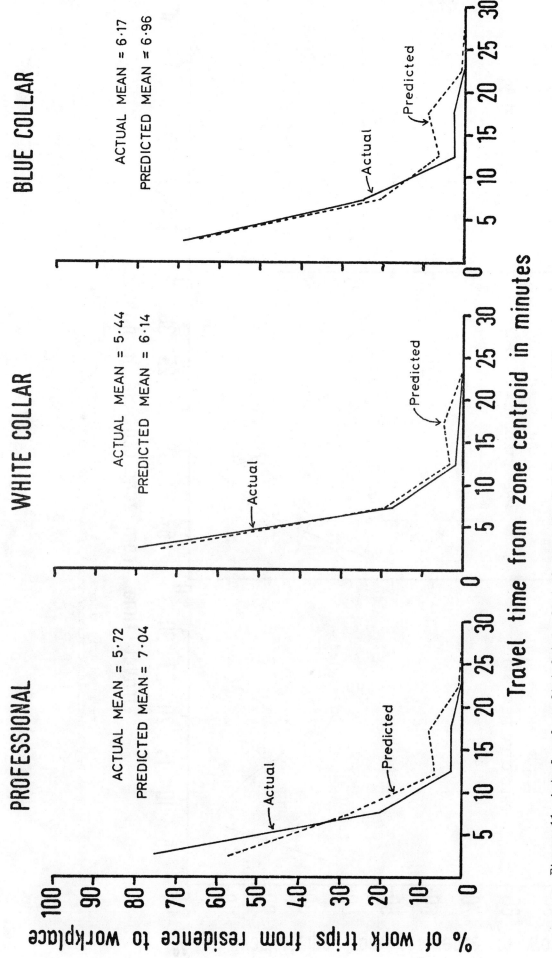

Figure 11 Actual and predicted trip distributions by S.E.G. for three different zones.
Zone 1: Abbey (urban).

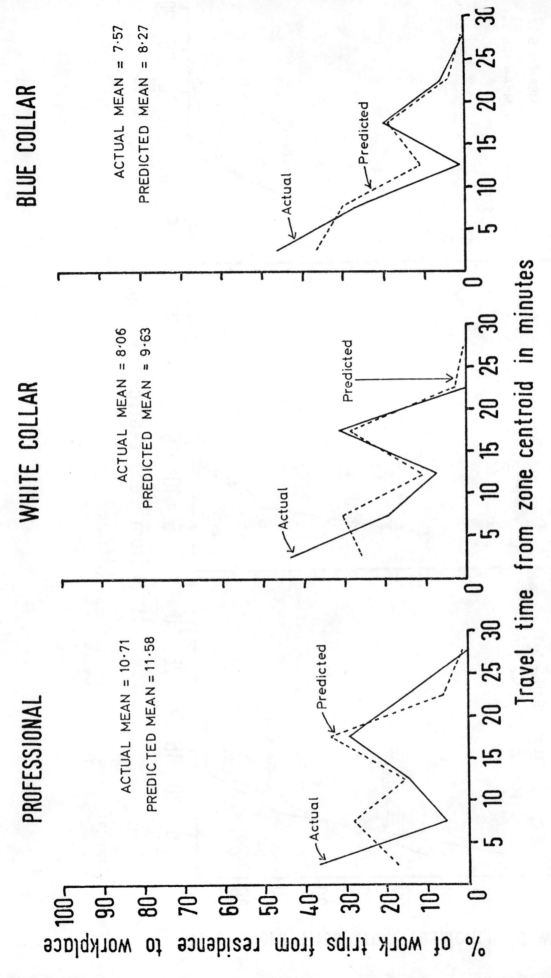

Figure 12 Actual and predicted trip distributions by S.E.G. for three different zones. Zone 9: Burghfield (suburban/rural).

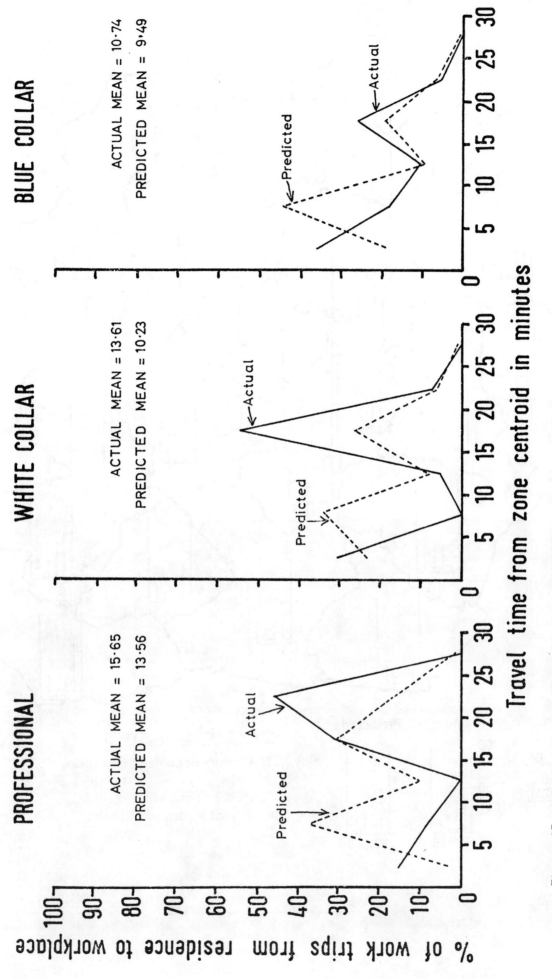

Figure 13 Actual and predicted trip distributions by S.E.G. for three different zones. Zone 17: Mortimer (rural/suburban).

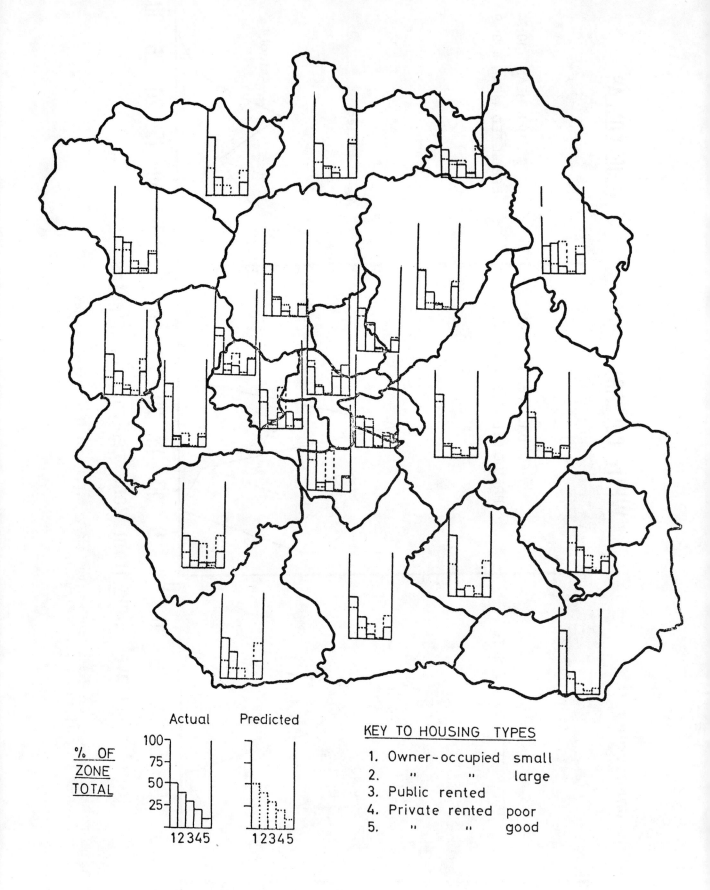

% OF ZONE TOTAL

Actual   Predicted

100
75
50
25

1 2 3 4 5   1 2 3 4 5

KEY TO HOUSING TYPES

1. Owner-occupied small
2. "   "   large
3. Public rented
4. Private rented poor
5. "   "   good

Figure 14   Zone allocation of percentages of professional workers to house type.

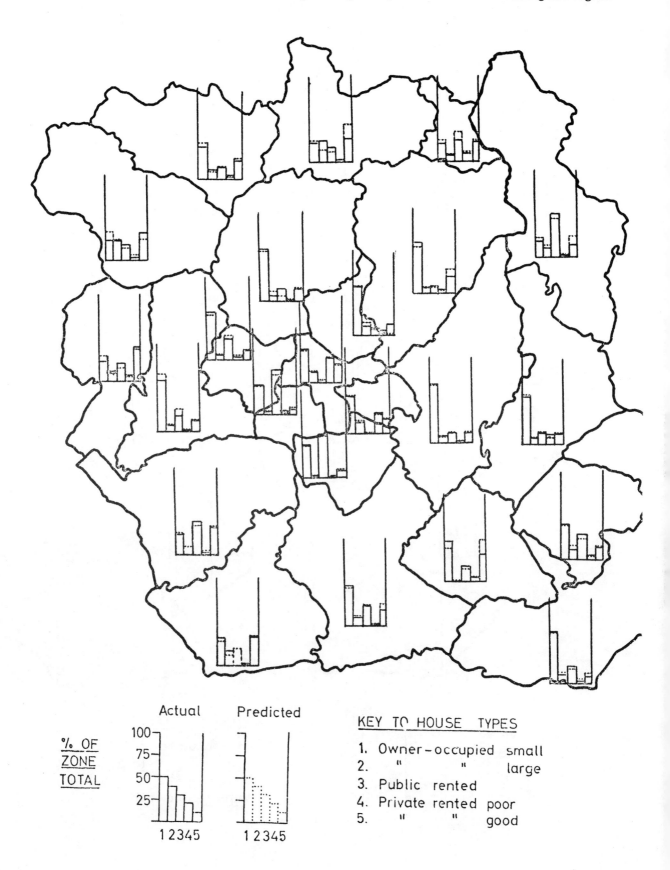

Figure 15   Zone allocation of percentages of white-collar workers to house type.

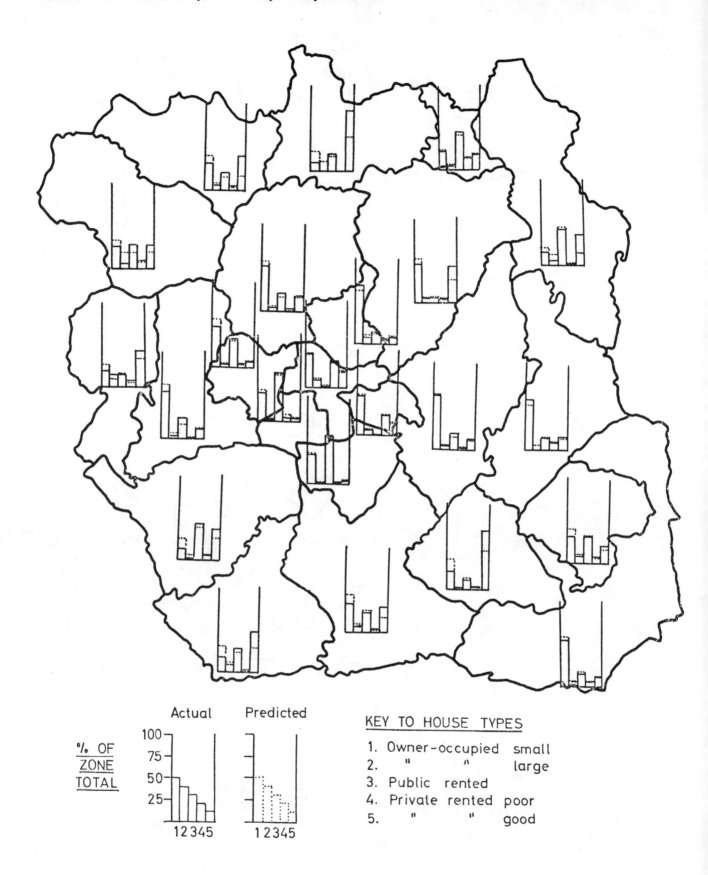

Figure 16   Zone allocation of percentages of blue-collar workers to house type.

The use of models in British planning:

applications in the Central Berkshire sub-region

Michael Batty

I am going to talk not only about the applications in Central Berkshire but also about two other model-building problems which I have been concerned with in the last couple of years. However, my main theme concerns a model of the Central Berkshire sub-region which involves an attempt to introduce the concept of time or dynamics into the basic structure of the static cross-sectional urban model.

In the quest to refine such models, my first task is to present a table (Table 1) illustrating the kind of problem areas which have already been defined by various researchers, and to hint at who is doing what in these different subject areas.

Subject area	Reference to researcher and organisation
Disaggregation of residential location model	Cripps and Cater (1972): USRU Senior and Wilson (1972): Leeds University Anthony and Baxter (1971): LUBFS
Dynamic modelling	Cordey-Hayes (1972): CES Batty (1972a): USRU Masser et al. (1971): Liverpool University
Model calibration	Batty and Mackie (1972): USRU Evans (1971): DoE Hyman (1969): CES
Zone size and shape	Barras et al. (1971): CES Broadbent (1969): CES Angel and Hyman (1971): CES Batty (1972b): USRU
Data systems and information	Baxter (1971): LUBFS Barras et al. (1971): CES
The basic-non basic split	Massey (1971): CES

USRU = Urban Systems Research Unit, Reading University
LUBFS = Land Use and Built Form Studies, Cambridge University
CES   = Centre for Environmental Studies, London

Table 1   An outline of recent research areas in urban modelling

As you probably realise by now, most of the recent modelling work has been concerned with developing the basic structure of the Lowry model. What I have to say about these subject areas refers only to this kind of model.

The first problem which has been identified earlier by Erlet Cater, by Martyn Cordey-Hayes and by Richard Barras, is the problem of disaggregating the model's variables — for example, describing the population by income group — and various researchers have been concerned with this problem. Disaggregation is a basic problem of describing the spatial system in more detail, and it is being tackled by ourselves in the Urban Systems Research Unit at Reading, by Richard Baxter and his colleagues at the Centre for Land Use and Built Form Studies and also by the Centre for Environmental Studies in their computer model package. We have already seen how this problem has been handled in previous lectures.

Another basic problem in trying to get this model to produce a better description of the real world and possibly to help in improving its predictive quality, is to introduce the concept of time. This is the problem of sorting out the dynamics of urban models and most of my talk — certainly the first half — will be concerned with one possible way of introducing some kind of dynamic element into urban models. Rather than constructing a cross sectional kind of model which simulates the structure of a spatial system at one point in time, the problem of dynamics involves trying to think about the model as it simulates the growth and change of activities over time.

Another kind of problem presented in Table 1, which is somewhat less important than these two main problems, is the zoning problem. This has been tackled most successfully, I think, by CES and by the Centre for Land Use and Built Form Studies. The zoning problem has been tackled by Andrew Broadbent and his colleagues at CES, and some of this work has been presented already by Richard Barras. He has described the hierarchical formulation of zones and the possibilities of building dummy zones into spatial models. I think that Richard Baxter will at some point introduce his cordon model which in some ways involves a very similar kind of approach to the definition of zones. I am going to say something more about zone definition towards the end of this lecture, because for the last three or four months I have concerned myself with this problem, and it is probably worthwhile introducing a few preliminary results.

There is the further problem of calibration or parameter estimation. This is what I defined in a previous lecture as the problem of trying to get the model to fit the real world. How do we actually map the theoretical structure of the model on to some kind of real world problem? How do you estimate the parameters of the model which you have already seen in the various formulations introduced earlier? Now this problem of estimation has also been tackled by various people. Richard Baxter and his colleagues have tackled it. It has been tackled theoretically by Geoff Hyman at CES, by Andrew Evans at the Department of the Environment and by various other researchers in the context of trip distribution modelling. The results of trip distribution modelling are applicable to spatial interaction models.

In the second part of my lecture, having described something of dynamics, I am going to describe certain techniques of calibration that we have been doing research in. These have already been mentioned by Erlet Cater in the context of the calibration of the disaggregated model. These research efforts have not been mutually exclusive, but I do not think there has been any very large duplication. People have tended to look at these problems in different ways over the last three or four years, and consequently they have been able to build upon each other's results.

The two other problems which have been identified in Table 1 are not really my concern or the concern of our Unit. The problem of data in general I think has been tackled most successfully by CES in the Cheshire exercise, and by the Centre for Land Use and Built Form Studies in their information data bank. The problem of the basic/non-basic split has been best investigated by Doreen Massey at CES.

So, as you can see from Table 1, this is a brief list of possible research areas into the kind of static model that we have been talking about. What I want to do first of all is to describe briefly the possibility of building dynamics into such models. I then want to say something about methods of calibration or parameter estimation, and then to finish very quickly with some comments on zoning.

The need to build dynamic models

I think the best way to present this approach to dynamics is to illustrate it diagrammatically. Let me say that I came into this work having done a couple of model applications when I was in Manchester. First of all I was concerned with an application in Central Lancashire which was primarily a research exercise designed to test the impact of Central Lancashire new town. Figure 1 illustrates the zoning system used in this model. The new town was to be located in a region of about thirty miles north-south by about forty miles east-west. The new town was located in the Preston/Chorley/Leyland area and was adjacent to an area of declining industry in North East Lancashire. Clearly there is a pertinent problem of testing the impact of this new town on such an area, which has been in economic decline since the turn of the century. There are many issues one could discuss from this.

The other application I worked on was in Nottinghamshire-Derbyshire. This was a very quick application and took about three or four months to execute. It related to the Notts.-Derbys. Sub-Regional Study, and as you can see in Figure 1 the zoning systems of both the Central Lancashire and the Notts.-Derbys. models are similar. The zone sizes are roughly the same, and there is roughly the same level of application in other respects. In the Notts.-Derbys. case I was concerned with a system of towns, rather large towns – Nottingham and its suburbs with a population of half a million, and Derby with a population of two or three hundred thousand. The objective there was to test the implications of a series of alternative plans on the sub-region.

One basic problem, a really fundamental problem, in both these pieces of work, was the treatment of time. It seemed that if we were to begin to look at time, and to try to build dynamic models, many of the problems which have been dis-cussed earlier – for example, the measurements of intrinsic zonal attraction – might be resolved. I felt that the problem of measuring intrinsic attraction could never be resolved outside a dynamic context. If you are going to allocate activity, you need to do so on the basis of some measure of attraction, and that attraction can only be measured at a point in time. Such measures obviously refer to one point in time only. As we well know, city centres are no longer attractive to residential growth, yet in many respects the residues of a growth situation remain in terms of the present data. So this is a major problem. It is a problem, I suppose, of looking at intrinsic attraction or, taking it further, of looking at the supply side of the model.

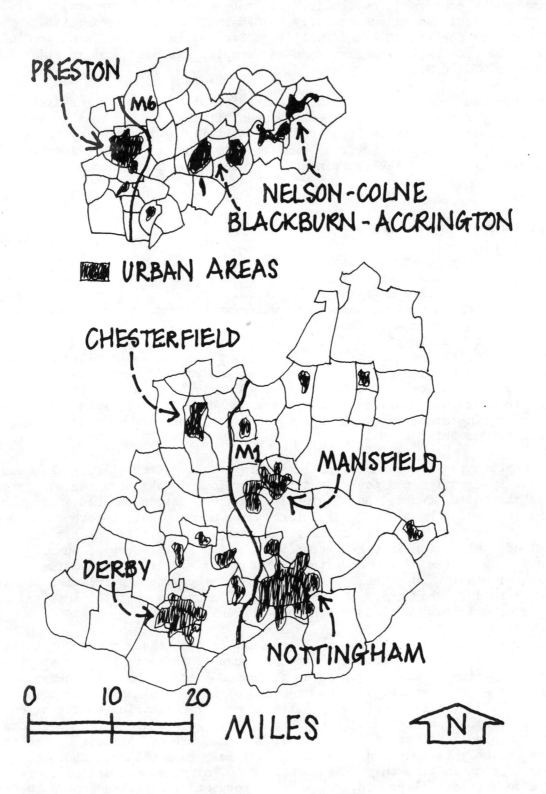

Figure 1   Zoning system for the Central Lancashire and Notts.–Derbys. models

Furthermore, there is another important problem. If we look for example at the growth of activities, such as population or employment, then we find that change in the urban system is accounted for not only by new activities or by declining activities, but also by activities which are redistributing themselves through time. Martyn Cordey-Hayes gave a very pertinent demonstration of this phenomenon earlier when he demonstrated that 30% of all change is due to people who are making changes due to their changing housing needs. Only 10% of change is concerned with changes in jobs. Clearly, any kind of dynamic model would have to take into account not only the modelling of new activities or increments and decrements, but would also have to take into account the people who are moving by redistributing themselves. For example, if you drive a new road across a city, or build a new shopping centre, it is likely people will redistribute themselves accordingly, and this was a problem we felt we could handle in the context of dynamics.

The structure of the dynamic model

The model is based on a fairly simple structure, similar in many respects to the structure of activities in the Lowry model, but it is operated in a sequence of time periods. In this case, the time period is equal to one year.

Clearly, if you are designing a dynamic model then it is important to find relationships between different points in time, and such relationships usually involve the concept of lags. There are two kinds of lag. The first involves economic repercussions. If a new industry comes into a city or if somebody changes his house, then this is likely to set off repercussions in the system. The multiplier effect in economics represents such phenomena, and generally speaking such effects work themselves out over time. The effect of fiscal policy is always measured over a period of time. We have attempted to build such multiplier effects into the model in the following way. For example, we have tried to look at problems involving the location of new basic industries in which it takes a period of time before the associated service industries get established.

The other kind of dynamic effect is a fairly obvious one. It is one which is usually referred to in the context of recursive projections. It implies that activities locate in an area not according to the attraction which is perceived at that instant, but according to attraction as perceived in a previous time period. For example, the amount of population growth or the house price in a previous time interval is likely to affect location in the next time interval. This is a kind of lag which is built into these kinds of model, providing a break-in point into the simultaneous relationships which affect urban growth.

Figure 2 illustrates the essence of the simulation process. There are a variety of sub-models at the beginning of the simulation period which in this case is 1951 and the model simulates the growth and change in Central Berkshire between 1951 and 1966 in one-year periods. Much of the data is set up using quite arbitrary models at the start of the simulation, the purpose of this exercise is as a demonstration project very largely to see how dynamics could be built into this kind of model.

At the centre of the model is a standard Lowry model in which activities are lagged through time. In the general framework, there is another series of models which examines the following problems. The first model involves determining the number of persons in the system who are likely to relocate in the

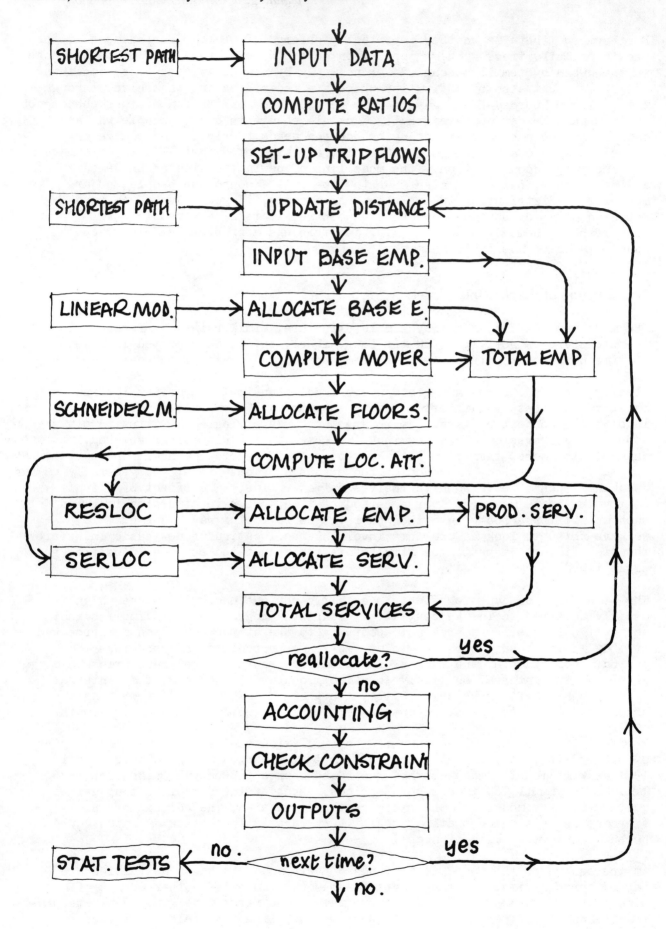

Figure 2   An outline of the operations in the dynamic model

following time interval. A rather complex mechanism is designed to calculate the appropriate numbers of locators and relocators. Before this calculation we measure the residential attraction of different zones first by using a very simple potential model to allocate floor space, and then by measuring residential attraction as some linear function of land available plus floor space. As Martyn Cordey-Hayes was demonstrating earlier, population is a very bad measure of intrinsic attraction, and in this model we have tended to use a combination of floor space and land available. The floorspace-land sub-model is based on a model by Schneider (1968) where he argues that the floorspace and land available are the two critical variables which set the urban growth process in motion. Schneider states that if you have got no land and no floorspace, then the world would never get started, but if you have got a bit of land, then it might get started. The growth process is dependent on land available which creates floorspace which in turn affects the land available. When you run out of land, then you are likely to get no more floorspace and this mechanism is a neat way of building constraints into the model.

In Figure 3, four basic sub-models are presented in abstract. First, we have a residential location model which acts in the conventional way, and second we have a service centre location model acting in a similar way. The innovations we have made are in the residential floorspace location model, which is extremely crude. In some respects the floorspace model parallels Marcial Echenique's work with residential floorspace. This model is not a great model by any means; it is just a demonstration that we feel the problem of supply is important and as a first shot, therefore, we have tried to model residential floorspace. We have another innovation here which is an attempt to model part of the basic sector. You will find that in the modelling literature some attempts to model this sector (mainly in North America) have not really been very successful. Because of such difficulties we did not take it very far. However we felt that there were certain components of basic activity which could probably be modelled, and therefore we are simply paying lip-service to the fact that this phenomenon could be modelled in the context of this model.

The structure of the comprehensive model is probably more important than the individual models themselves. As you can see from Figure 3, we are beginning to build in phenomena such as land use and floorspace which have not been incorporated in the static cross-sectional models at a sub-regional scale.

This model has been applied to an eighteen-zone description of the Central Berkshire sub-region. Figure 4 shows that the model is based on a very unsatisfactory zoning system in which 70%-80% of all activities are contained within one zone - Reading. Because the model is dynamic and works in yearly periods, I had to interpolate the data from all sorts of sources and I had to go back to the 1951 Census of Population which is not very good in terms of disaggregation into wards and parishes. In this case, the data base conditioned the geometry of the zoning system.

However, an interesting feature of this model is that we do not have quite the problem which we had in the static cross-sectional models. If we are looking at the growth or the change in activity we find that over the period 1951-56, most of the change in the activities has been due to the process of suburbanisation adding growth to the intermediate area between Reading and Maidenhead in the Thames Valley. Consequently very little change has taken place in Reading. The population of Reading was approximately 116,000 in 1951 and 119,000 in 1966, yet the total change in the sub-region is somewhere in the region of 80,000 people over that period.

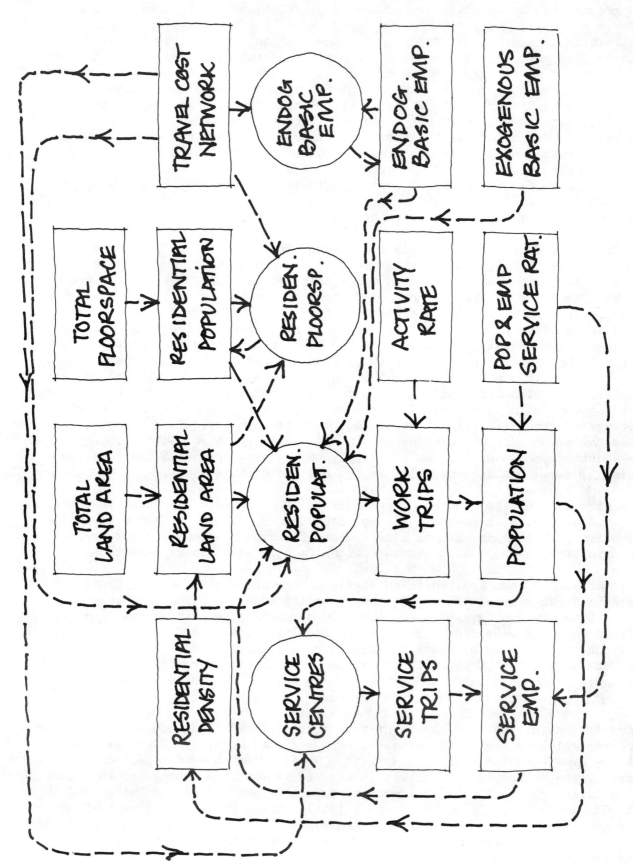

Figure 3   The sub-models of the general model

Application of the simulation model

We set the model rolling in 1951 and as you would expect from a dynamic model we can generate many different spatial distributions at each point in time. As the model is started from 1951 you can see the beginning of a build-up in activities. The time series which the model generates is rather arbitrary but Figure 4 gives you an indication of the possible outputs generated by a tool like this.

Because distributions can be generated for each of the 15 time periods, it would be rather nice to try to build a kind of cine version of the model through time, thus displaying the essential dynamic quality of the model. We could plot all sorts of variables in this way.

An interesting feature of this model is the use of a graph plotting subroutine using the lineprinter to plot the output. Because the model is dynamic the variables vary through time and we can plot both marginal and absolute changes in activity. In Figure 5, the marginal and total changes are plotted for the town of Reading and it is clear that total activities do not change very much in the simulation period. Activities drift upwards in a rather normal fashion and over the period there is little change. But, if you examine the marginal changes all sorts of peculiar characteristics are evident. People redistribute themselves in odd ways, trip lengths rise and so on. Such changes, of course, are all masked when you aggregate these into activity totals.

In Figure 6, the zone of Shiplake is examined and this shows the ability of a dynamic model to handle the problem of constraint. This question of constraint is another feature which can never be handled satisfactorily in any kind of static way because, when a constraint is met, it implies that something has changed through time. The whole idea of constraining activity is time-dependent. If we build in constraints like green belt policy into a static model, this simply means that we are building in an arbitrary computational procedure to make the model satisfy some a priori considerations. It says very little about real world behaviour. On the other hand, the dynamic model is useful because at certain points in time we might run out of land, and when no more land is available it is natural to constrain activity. In this particular zone of Shiplake, which is a suburban zone, the model ran out of land or reached its constraint in about 1962–1963. Of course, this does not happen in reality; it simply shows the dynamic mechanism at work. The model was over-allocating people into Shiplake in any case. So basically what has happened is that the model assumed that in the next time interval the attraction in Shiplake was equal to zero because there was no land left. This does not preclude any more activity ever going into Shiplake, because there may be out-migration in later time intervals.

However, we did not anticipate the problem that if we set the attraction equal to zero, those people who were moving due to changes in life cycle, etc., would also re-evaluate their locational decision to live in Shiplake. They would turn round to themselves and say well, if Shiplake is no longer attractive, let us leave. These relocators left Shiplake, its constraint was not violated, and this lead to a kind of oscillating behaviour which is very interesting from a modelling point of view. It also shows us that we can begin to design models in a kind of pseudo-scientific way; we can run them, experiment with them, and revise them, in this particular case to damp these oscillations.

Let me just finish very quickly by saying that the dynamic model to all intents and purposes is only a demonstration or pilot model. It is a demonstration of my conviction that problems can only be resolved in a dynamic context. I have not bothered to calibrate the dynamic model because of the crudity of the data,

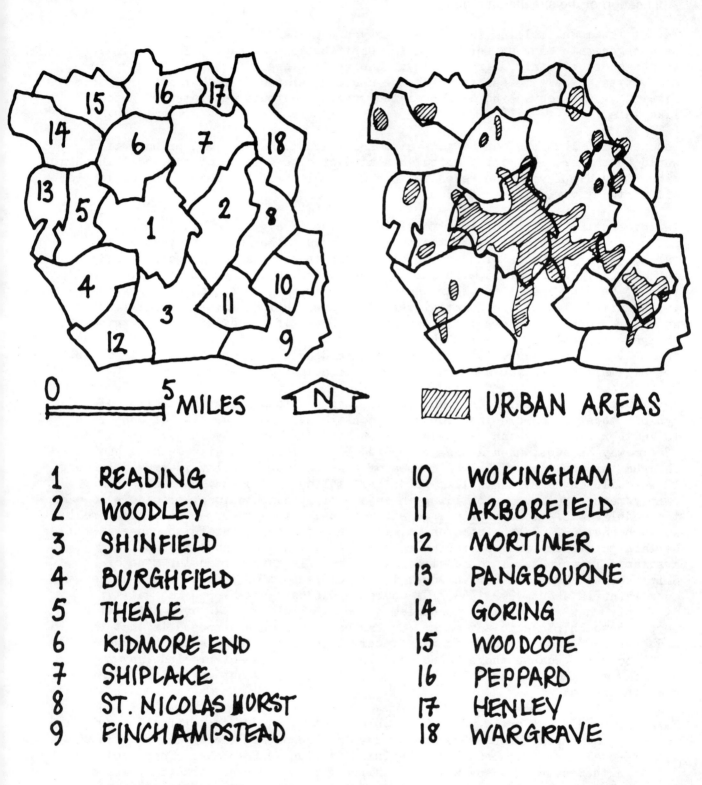

1	READING	10	WOKINGHAM
2	WOODLEY	11	ARBORFIELD
3	SHINFIELD	12	MORTIMER
4	BURGHFIELD	13	PANGBOURNE
5	THEALE	14	GORING
6	KIDMORE END	15	WOODCOTE
7	SHIPLAKE	16	PEPPARD
8	ST. NICOLAS HURST	17	HENLEY
9	FINCHAMPSTEAD	18	WARGRAVE

Figure 4   Zone geometry and size in the Central Berkshire sub-region

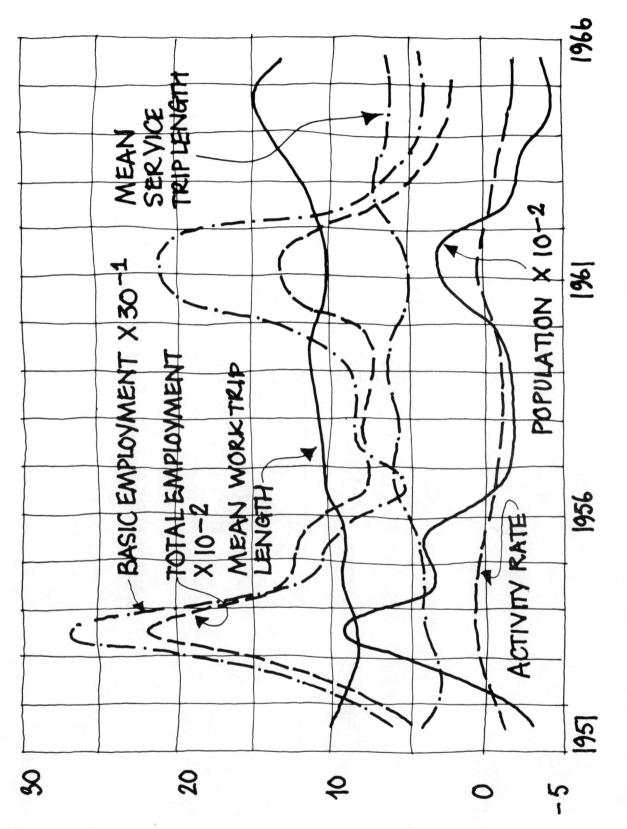

Figure 5   Changes in activities in the zone of Reading, 1951–1966

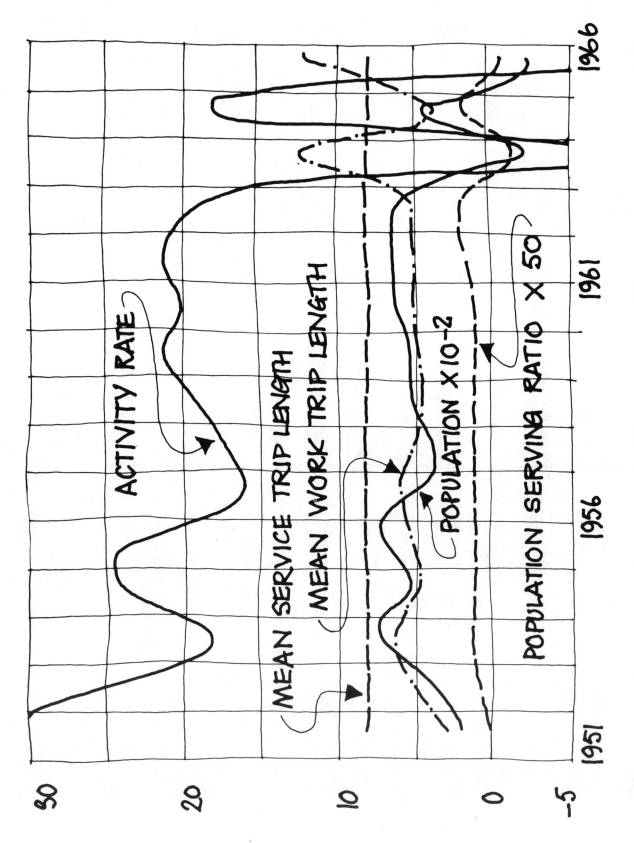

Figure 6   Changes in activities in the zone of Shiplake, 1951–1966

and the severe problems in testing such hypotheses. Some of the hypotheses are very difficult to validate. I have simply left the model in cold storage while I worked on other kinds of modelling problem, which are given in Table 1. This is not to say that I will not return to the dynamic model, because I think the dynamic modelling is important. In some respects it is a bit overwhelming because I really do not know what to do next. It would be very easy, for example, to input the M4 Motorway retrospectively, say at 1955, and see what would have happened. For the first time dynamic models can be used to generate a kind of retrospective historical analysis. Such experiments can easily be carried out, but I feel that there is a point in model building where it becomes no longer worthwhile to bash on with the same model. It may be better, on the basis of the knowledge gained, to change strategy and to build a different kind of dynamic model.

Problems of model calibration

The estimation problem is one which we have also worked on in Reading. This problem relates to parameter estimation in the context of static models. For example, there is a non-trivial problem in estimating the two parameters in the Lowry model, which control the residential and service centre location. In this model both parameters are interdependent in a functional sense and therefore have to be estimated by some technique which takes account of this.

The traditional method of calibration was simply to select values for the two parameters and to run the model over and over again in a fairly systematic way. By generating all possible combinations of parameter values at certain intervals within a given range, it is possible to pick what appear to be the best values. This is a kind of experimental technique which is often used in control systems engineering. If you look at control systems literature, you find that because scientists cannot really observe the process in hand, they have to generate the process artificially in the quest to find its optimum state.

Now the response surface of the model which is the surface formed by different parameter values can be plotted for two parameters, α and β controlling the residential sector and the service sector. The response surface based on R^2 statistic can be plotted in the search to find its best value. Furthermore, the surface could be projected on the flat plain and plotted in terms of contours, as in Figure 7. Using the hill-climbing analogy the object of calibration is simply to get to the top of the hill. First of all it is necessary to ensure that the hill which you are climbing is the correct hill, in other words, that you are using the best possible statistics. Because these model equations tend to be non-linear, calibration tends to be intractable to standard statistical methods. Two major kinds of technique have been developed in the Unit. One is a numerical technique, a standard technique used in optimisation problems based on the Newton-Raphson technique. The second is a technique which has come out of the search procedures developed in control systems engineering. This is called 'direct search technique', a procedure for starting at any point on the hill and, by systematic trial and error, reaching the top. We call this the Simplex technique which is not the same as the Simplex in linear programming although it is based on the same kind of notions. We have looked at these two techniques and are reasonably satisfied that they are the best we could use.

The calibration problem is probably the only problem we have been able to tackle in any definitive sense. The Newton-Raphson procedure is very good as long as you get a good first approximation. The problem of getting a good first approximation in a sense is anticipating the final answer; if you can, the

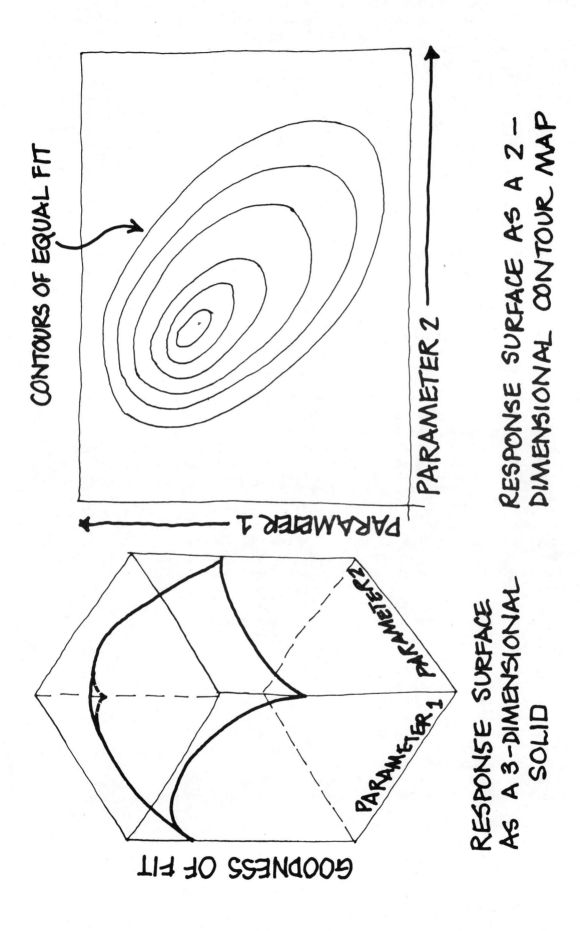

Figure 7   A typical response surface generated in model calibration

Newton-Raphson technique is extremely fast. For example, we found in the residential location model, that Erlet Cater explained earlier, that we could possibly calibrate that model in nine runs, which is really quite fast. At the moment we are working with a Lowry model of the Northampton region. We have used the Newton-Raphson technique on this model. This is in association with the East Midlands Technical Unit. In using the Newton-Raphson method we find that we can calibrate the model very quickly in a matter of nine or twelve runs. (They are in units of three because of the evaluation of the derivatives in the programme.) I am pretty satisfied with these calibration techniques for, I think, calibration is a problem which can be solved in a deterministic sense, and there are possibly ways of speeding up what we have done already, by damping the techniques and so on. In the literature of non-linear optimisation there are many speeded-up versions of the standard techniques we have used. We hope to look at some of these in the future.

Problems of zone size and shape

The final problem which I have been working with is zone size, and as you can see from Figure 4. Recently I have been working with Geoff Hyman and Andrew Broadbent at CES on this problem of zone size. We started with Andrew Broadbent's premise that if you are building a spatial interaction model, the first thing you have got to ensure is that there is some spatial interaction. If you have 80% of trip-making activity within a zone, there is not much spatial interaction with other zones. In other words, the whole model can become trivial if the zoning system is wrong. You could define a zoning system at one extreme based on a one-zone region for example, in which there was no interaction whatsoever – this would be a trivial problem.

We began to study this problem by starting off from the point of view of considering that an urban area could be modelled in a continuous sense. We could fit a continuous two-dimensional distribution to an urban area. Using such a distribution we looked at the mathematical problem of approximating an integral by a finite sum. We used a statistic of information or entropy to describe the correspondence between the continuous distribution and its discrete analog. To cut a long story short, we came out with the rather astonishing theoretical conclusion that to build any kind of model with the sort of mean trip lengths we had in central Berkshire would require between 100 and 400 zones. 100 zones is the minimum, whereas we were using 18 in the dynamic model and 23 and 64 zones in the residential model. Our data base only goes to 64 for a start, so clearly there is a basic mathematical problem, and as many people have observed here, this can be extremely important. We also resolved at the same time, or had a look at, the problem of defining the regional boundary. We have since gone on to look at zone shape, and again we have come up with some astonishing conclusions.

Much of this is due to Andrew Broadbent who first suggested that the entropy trip model is allocating the wrong thing. It should be allocating a kind of trip density, because the area of a zone is so very important. If you look at Wilson's work and recast his models to allocate density, you are allocating a function of, say, population divided by the associated area, which of course is the density. Wilson's models assume that the zones are all of equal size like those on a square grid system. Clearly, such equal sized areas do not correspond to the real world so what we did was to recast the entropy problem in two stages. First of all we took the probability of population location and maximise entropy only according to the normalising constraint on sum of the probabilities. Then you get, as you would expect, an even distribution of population in every area. If you want to describe a population in the same detail everywhere, it is best if you can build a zoning system in which you get equal population in every zone. If this result is fed into the entropy model, and then entropy is maximised, we find that the ideal zoning system varies in a negative exponential fashion around the origin zones.

I have since gone on to design some zoning systems for Reading which are based on the assumption that we are dealing with a radially symmetric city. Remarkable kinds of zoning systems can be designed in this way. Now this poses a dilemma because people have stated that the grid square system is best and grid squares have a certain appeal. However, this does not suggest that a grid square system is no good, for it does have the basic advantage of neutrality. When we are concerned with predicting the future, we may not anticipate that cities remain radially symmetric; we may be designing another kind of city. The grid system has the basic advantage of neutrality in such situations.

Clearly it would be nice to try to build a model on the kind of system in which population is equal in every zone, to see how it performs. I think that our next piece of research may be to look at some of our data in Reading and to try to do this. We have also developed a kind of a cluster analysis method based on entropy maximising, which has clustered our 64 zones down to a given number of zones using a criterion of minimising the information loss between the various sets which we are defining. All this kind of work is closely related. I think it shows that there is a lot more which could be said about Wilson's work in maximising entropy and certainly a lot more which could be said about zoning systems.

Towards the explorative use of urban models in British planning

David Crowther

My original intentions for this paper were, firstly, to describe the work of the Centre in the urban modelling field and to explain the differences between our sort of model work and the work of others; secondly, I intended to describe the directions in which we have been attempting to develop our work. Finally, I planned to move on to report progress on our pilot study in Luton, where we were hoping to apply the model (in collaboration with Luton County Borough) in order to find out how useful it is for structure planning in a practical planning context.

Unfortunately, the Luton study is not as far advanced as we had hoped when we were planning this conference and when I wrote the circulated abstract for this paper. There have been innumerable problems in preparing the data which have resulted in long delays, so that we have not yet been able to calibrate the model. Consequently there are no results, even of a preliminary kind, for me to show you and the most interesting stage of exploring the model's usefulness as an aid to practical decision-making has not yet been reached. Nonetheless, there are perhaps some morals to be drawn from our experience with the Luton study which I shall discuss at the end of the paper.

Outline of the urban model

To begin with I would like to describe briefly our work in this field. Figure 1 shows the scale at which we operate and compares the study area for the Urban Systems Research Unit in Reading with our study area for the same town. As you can see, our study area is very much smaller, demonstrating the point that we are concerned with how activities locate within towns, with intra-urban spatial interaction, while the Reading Unit is concerned with how activities locate within a region containing several urban settlements, i.e. with inter-urban spatial interaction. However, it is perhaps worth pointing out that the models are in both cases essentially the same kind. They are both based on the Lowry model. In other words, the same type of spatial interaction model can be applied at either the urban or the sub-regional scale. Although the problems at the two scales are somewhat different it is possible to combine them, with one 'nesting' inside the other, so that we can examine the spatial behaviour of an individual town and still take account of intra-regional effects, or vice versa. Within this context, our research task has been to investigate specifically the problems of applying such models at the intra-urban scale.

Figure 1 also shows that we have tended to use square grid zones. However, this is not essential. Although we have found the grid cell very useful, other types of zone of polygonal shape can equally well be used. Choice between them is in practice usually governed by the form in which the data are available. However, it is perhaps worth mentioning in passing that we have developed programs for converting from one type of unit to another.

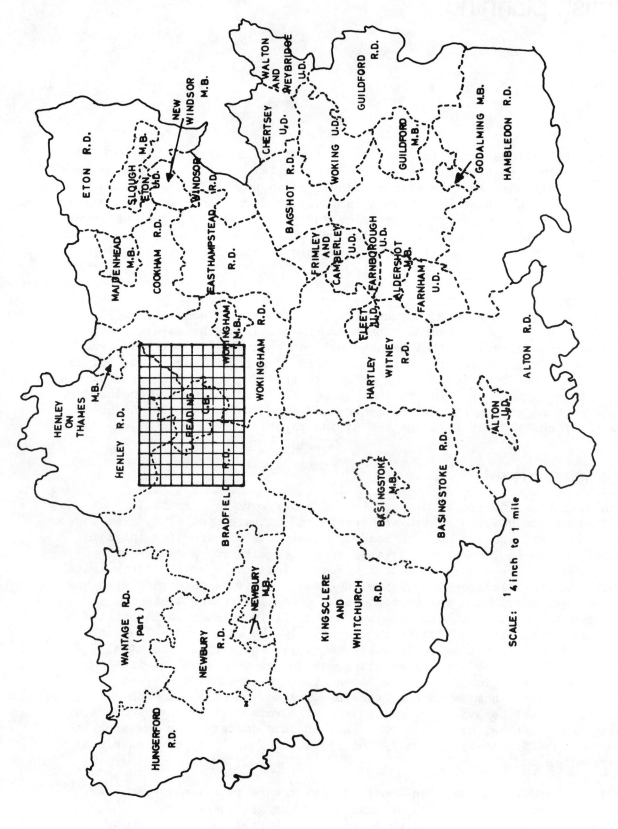

Figure 1   The study area of the Urban Systems Research Unit, Reading, with the LUBFS model grid superimposed

One of the consequences of working at the urban scale has been that we have
found it impossible to ignore the fact that activity location within a town is
heavily constrained by the stock of physical infrastructure. Figure 2 describes
the two basic components of urban spatial structure that we have identified.

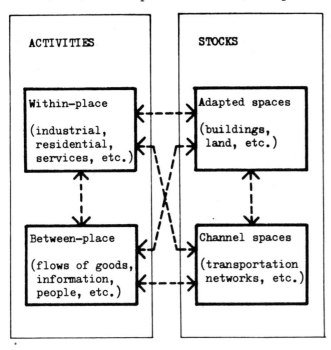

Figure 2   The components of urban spatial structure

On one side there are <u>activities</u> which can be sub-divided into 'within-place'
activities, (i.e. industrial and service establishments, households and so forth)
and 'between-place' activities (i.e. the flows of various kinds that occur
between them). On the other side, corresponding to the two types of activity,
there are two types of stock. First of all, there are the land and buildings
which accommodate within-place activities, and secondly there are channel
spaces which accommodate between-place activities. Essentially the problem
of model building at the intra-urban scale is to obtain the right relationship
between these two basic components and to simulate the way that each one
affects the other.

One of the first factors to be taken into account is that while activities may
change their location within a town quite frequently, the stock which accommodates
them changes much more slowly. This gives rise to what we call the phenomena of
stock use succession, whereby, for example, old Georgian terrace houses are
converted into shops and offices. One can therefore consider the floor space
within a town as an undifferentiated supply of accommodation which can potentially be used by any activity in the town. Some buildings may be constructed
originally as housing, but at some later date, other activities can move in
and make use of that floor space when its location is sufficiently attractive.
Thus floor space acts as the total physical envelope within which activities
jostle for position.

Figure 3 is a flow diagram of the model itself and it can be seen that the
essential difference between our type of model and similar Lowry-type models
is the inclusion of the floor space sub-model. Let me briefly explain the
diagram. The inputs are on the left, of which two are common to all models
of this type: the number of 'basic' employees in each zone and the accessibility

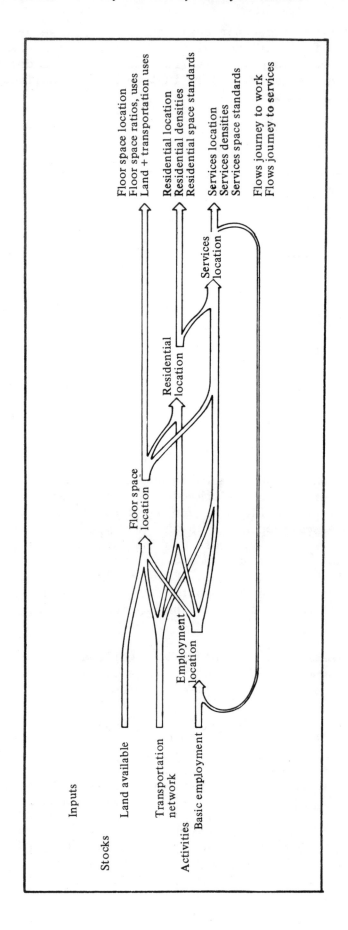

Figure 3   Flow diagram of the simple static model

of each zone to all others as measured in the transportation network. Distance, time or travel costs can be used as the measure of separation, but for simplicity, we tend to use distance. The third input is the built-up land area in each zone. This is used in the first sub-model, the floor space location sub-model, which simulates the distribution of all floorspace (undifferentiated by use) throughout the town. In the first iteration, when only the location of basic employment is known, this sub-model locates the floor space required by basic employment and by the residents and services that it generates. Having deducted the floorspace occupied by basic employees at their workplace, the residential sub-model is run and these basic employees are distributed to homes within the remaining supply of floorspace. These employees are then multiplied by an average labour participation ratio to give the residential population figures. In the third sub-model, the services generated by these residents are distributed within the same envelope of available floorspace as for residents, since both are competing for the same space. Once these services are located, they are then added to the basic employment in each zone and the whole process is repeated. This time more floorspace is distributed to zones and within this increased supply a new allocation of residential population and service employment is obtained, the latter being added to basic employment for the start of the next iteration of the complete model. In this way the totals being distributed gradually build up, more floorspace, residential population and service employment being allocated to zones in each iteration than in the previous iteration. After about six or seven iterations, however, the rate of increase has slowed so that the total amounts being distributed in the next iteration are only marginally greater than the last, and at this stage the model is considered to have reached equilibrium.

The outputs of the model are: the total amount of floorspace for all uses in each zone; the number of residents in each zone and the floorspace that they occupy; the number of service employees in each zone and the floorspace that they occupy; and the journey-to-work flows and the journey-to-service flows between each pair of zones.

The flow chart also indicates how the model is potentially useful for exploratory purposes. It can be seen from the way that the connecting arrows are interlinked that if one changes the values for any of the inputs, this will lead to new distributions of floorspace, residents and services. A single change in one of the inputs can thus lead to changes in all of the outputs. Thus, one can explore the likely effects of different policies, such as changing the transportation network, the distribution of basic (i.e. industrial) employment or releasing new land for development. There are also other inputs in the form of labour activity rates, the population serving ratios and so forth, so that the effects of changes in these too can be explored. Finally, the effects of imposing constraints, such as zoning, floorspace ratio or density constraints can also be tested in the model.

Although this model is still a static equilibrium model, and therefore subject to the criticisms put forward in Michael Batty's paper, we feel that it is nonetheless of considerable potential use for exploring alternative strategies at the town scale. By taking the location of the built-up land as a given input and by simulating the distribution of available floorspace on this land, the major constraints on activity location within towns are in this way taken into account. We feel it to be largely because the model reproduces the constraining effect of the stock of physical infrastructure that it has proved capable of simulating activity location with reasonable accuracy, despite its static equilibrium basis. A further advantage is that by taking account of the land and floorspace available in a zone, the problems of varying zone areas,

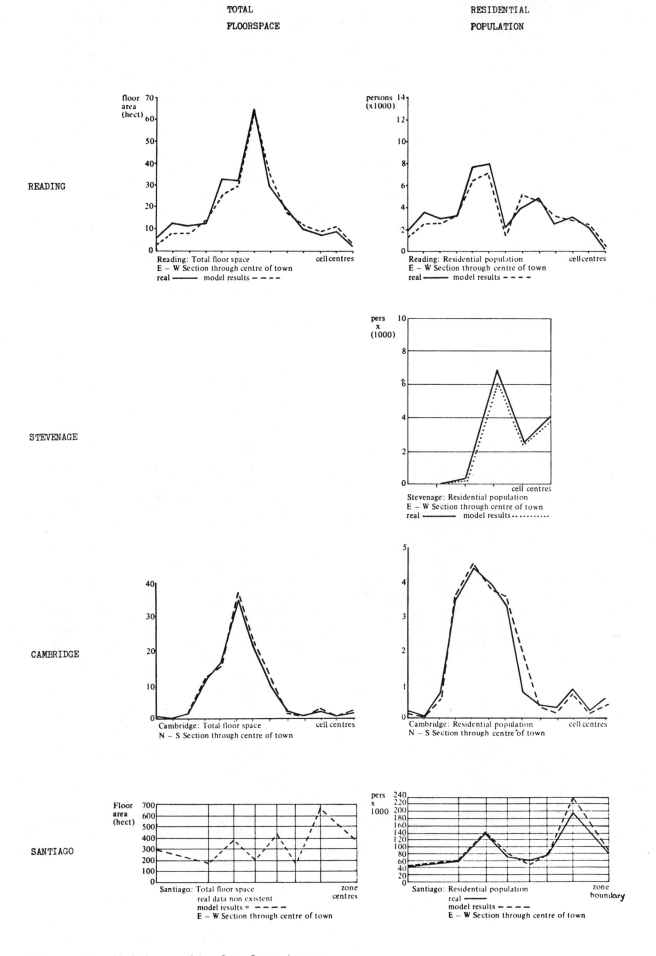

Figure 4   Model results for four towns

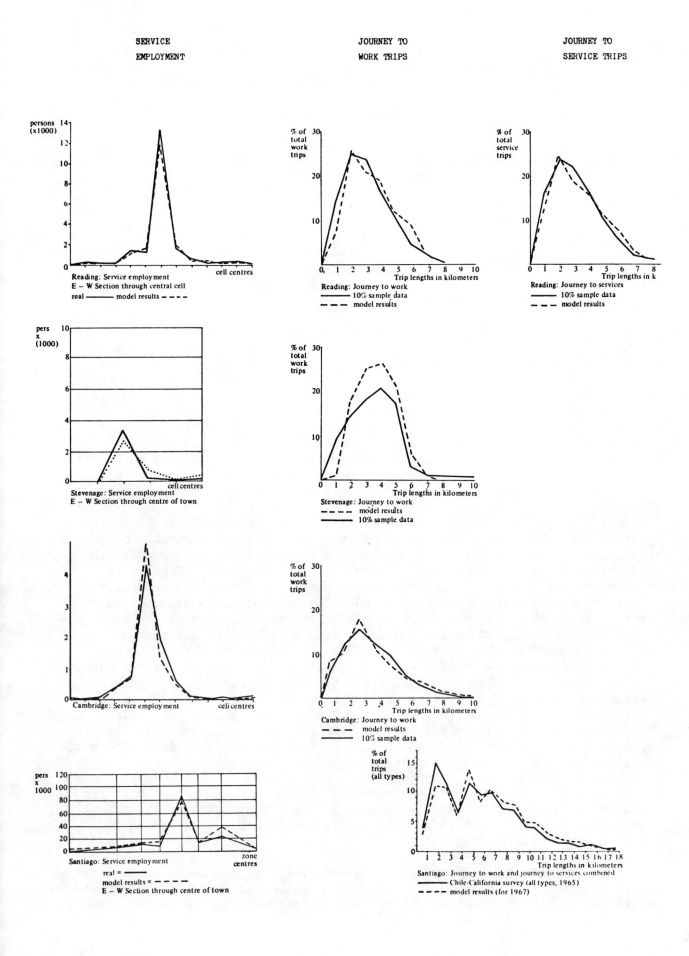

SERVICE
EMPLOYMENT

JOURNEY TO
WORK TRIPS

JOURNEY TO
SERVICE TRIPS

Reading: Service employment
E – W Section through central cell
real ——— model results – – – –

Reading: Journey to work
——— 10% sample data
– – – model results

Reading: Journey to services
——— 10% sample data
– – – model results

Stevenage: Service employment
E – W Section through centre of town

Stevenage: Journey to work
– – – – model results
——— 10% sample data

Cambridge: Service employment

Cambridge: Journey to work
– – – – model results
——— 10% sample data

Santiago: Service employment
real = ———
model results = – – – –
E – W Section through centre of town

Santiago: Journey to work and journey to services combined
——— Chile-California survey (all types, 1965)
– – – – model results (for 1967)

which Michael Batty also described in his paper, are to some extent overcome. You do not have to make the assumption that the area in every zone is constant.

Figure 4 demonstrates the extent to which the model has proved to be capable of simulating reality in a variety of different situations. Each row shows the results for one of the towns for which the model has been tested: Reading, Stevenage, Cambridge and Santiago in Chile, containing 160,000, 60,000, 140,000 and 2,700,000 population respectively. Each column shows the results for each town for one of the main outputs: total floorspace (for all uses), residential population, service employment, journey-to-work trips and journey-to-service trips. The diagrams showing the floorspace, residential population and service employment results, are sections taken through the town. Thus the base line represents a line drawn through the centre of the town (either from west to east or from north to south) and each pip represents the centroid of the zone through which this section line passes. The other axis of the graph measures the amount of floorspace, residential population and service employment respectively in each of these zones. The solid line in each case represents reality, while the dotted line represents the model results. The diagrams for the journey-to-work and journey-to-service results are shown as percentage distributions of trip lengths.

These sample results show that the model is capable of simulating reality with reasonable accuracy. There are differences in certain cases, but these are on the whole minor deviations from the general pattern which the model has reproduced successfully. One must expect differences between model results and reality, because after all a model is a simplification of reality, and there are cases where the model is too simple to take account of abnormal circumstances. In Reading, for example, there is a river cutting off the northern part of the town from the rest, and the model was unable to take account of the congestion caused by the fact that there were only two bridges across it. Since we were unable to use time as the measure of accessibility, the model tended to allocate too much activity and floorspace to the northern part.

Similarly, in Stevenage, you will notice that there is a blank space in the first column. This is because we found that the model was incapable of simulating the distribution of floorspace in a new town situation where the location of floorspace was totally dictated by the planners. This is in contrast to existing towns such as Reading where the distribution of floorspace is the result of a process of gradual accretion over time in response to market forces. It is therefore not surprising that the model was unable to reproduce the particular distribution of floorspace decided on by the planners of Stevenage. However, when we took the floorspace as given, then the model simulated the distribution of residents and services within this given supply quite successfully. There are some big differences, however, for the journey-to-work results. This is because at that stage the model did not have any dummy zone representing the effect of the environment outside the study area. Stevenage is to some extent a dormitory town for London and an unusually high proportion of trips are longer than could be fitted onto the graph. Since the model assumed that there was no commuting across the boundaries of the study area, the results for trip lengths were more inaccurate than would have been obtained by using a dummy zone to represent London. There were no data for journeys-to-services for either Stevenage or Cambridge, which explains the blanks in column 5. For Santiago, only data for journeys-to-work and to services combined were available.

In Cambridge, the problems were somewhat different in that there are a large number of students in Cambridge who do not have the same kind of journey-to-work as the rest of the population. Therefore, the students had to be taken out of the model, together with the services they generate. The model was then run without them and at the end they and the services that they generate were added to the model results. In other words we had to adapt the model to take account of this somewhat atypical situation. We also found that there were some problems in defining basic and service employment in that many of the shops in the centre of Cambridge serve visiting tourists rather than the local population. They are really exogenous to the model and should not, ideally, be counted as service employment.

I have not been able to discuss these results in very great detail (for a fuller discussion see Booth et al. 1970, Echenique 1969a and b, Echenique and Domeyko 1970. However, I hope that I have said enough to show that the model has performed with reasonable accuracy in each case and that the main errors were due to idiosyncratic factors which one would not expect the model in its most simple and unmodified form to take into account. In other words the model has proved capable of simulating the major, overall cause and effect relationships within a town, while at the same time revealing relationships special to a particular town that tend to distort this general pattern.

Figure 5 shows that the model does simulate at least one of the major cause and effect relationships within towns. This is again in the form of sections showing the results for each iteration of the model. In this case it is the residential and service location in Reading. The numbers of the various cells along a west/east axis going through the centre of Reading are shown along the bottom. In the first iteration, it can be seen that the highest number of residents has been located in the central cell (59), there being relatively few services at this stage. But as the number of services being located starts to grow with subsequent iterations there is not sufficient room for both the number of services and the number of residents who want to go in the central zone. (The model simulates correctly the way in which services are attracted to the central zone.) Already by the second iteration the number of residents in the central zone has thus gone down, being displaced by the services which are assumed to have priority over them in the competition for space. This displacement effect increases with each iteration, giving rise to the 'M-shaped' distribution of residents which is common to most towns with a dominant service centre. In this way the model simulates what happens in reality.

Directions in which the work has been developed

One of the first directions in which we have attempted to extend our work was to examine the problem of evaluation. That is to say if an urban model enables one to determine the likely consequences of alternative strategies, how does one judge whether such consequences are good or bad? This is, of course, a difficult question to answer in an entirely systematic, quantitative way. Indeed our approach has not been to attempt to develop a comprehensive system of evaluation, but rather to develop simple measures of performance which, even though they are limited in what they measure, may add to the useful information on which the evaluation of alternative consequences can be based. These measures of performance, or 'evaluation indicators', were devised in a comparative study of three British new towns (Echenique et al. 1969b).

The three new towns were Stevenage, Hook and Milton Keynes, representing three 'generations' of new town planned in Britain since the war. These were compared with the older and 'natural' town of Reading. As can be seen from Figure 6, the four towns have very different structures. Reading is a traditional, centralised town with a radial road network. Stevenage is rather smaller and

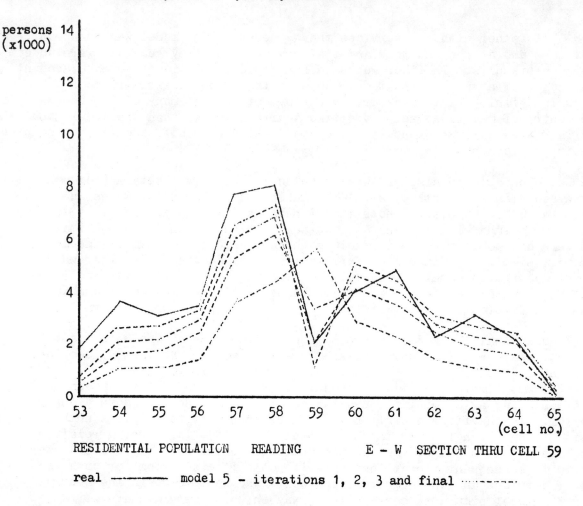

RESIDENTIAL POPULATION   READING   E - W SECTION THRU CELL 59

real ———————— model 5 - iterations 1, 2, 3 and final ············

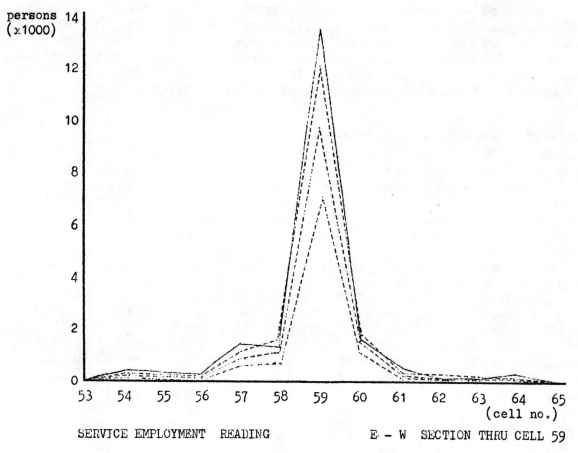

SERVICE EMPLOYMENT   READING   E - W SECTION THRU CELL 59

Figure 5   Reading: iteration of residential and service results

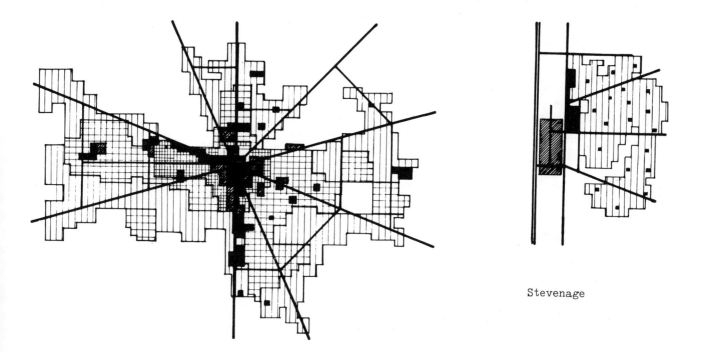

Reading

Stevenage

Milton Keynes

Hook

basic employment
service employment
residential population

Figure 6   Diagrammatic maps of the three new towns and Reading

semi-radial: all the employment is between the motorway and the railway line to one side of the town, with the service employment close by and with the population spread out in a semi-circle around it. Hook has a highly concentrated and compact structure, with a linear service centre containing almost all the service employment in the town surrounded by high density residential areas. The basic employment is contained in three industrial estates on the perimeter. In contrast, Milton Keynes is planned to be a dispersed, low-density development, with a neutral road network and scattered industrial estates, but with a highly concentrated service centre. It is also much larger than the other three towns: 250,000 population, as against 160,000 for Reading, 60,000 for Stevenage and 100,000 for Hook.

The first part of the study was to prepare the data inputs for the model from published figures for the built-up land area and the basic employment in each zone (using a 1 kilometre square grid in each case) and to measure the accessibility of each zone to all others via the proposed road network. The model was then run twice for each town: firstly with the 'distance impedance' parameters set to the same values as for Reading, and secondly with the parameters adjusted so as to obtain the closest possible correspondence between the model results for the distributions of floorspace, residential population and service employment and the distributions put forward by the planners. In this way we were able to suggest first of all how each town might be expected to develop in the absence of planning intervention, using the Reading parameter values as 'market norms'. Secondly, by determining how much it was necessary to change the parameters in order to obtain results similar to the planners' proposals in each case, we were able to arrive at a measure of the extent to which the proposals were at variance with what would in 'normal' circumstances be likely to occur. It has already been explained that for Stevenage the model was unable to reproduce the planned distribution of floorspace within the town, regardless of what values for the parameter were tried. The same problem occurred for Hook. We took this to indicate that the way in which the supply of stock had been allocated within the built-up land area in these two cases was totally at variance with what might have occurred if activities had been allowed to create their own demands for floorspace rather than to have it decided for them by the planning authority. In order to obtain 'best fit' parameters for Hook and Stevenage, the floorspace in each zone was taken as a given input. For Hook we also found that the highly concentrated pattern of services could only be reproduced by radically altering the relevant parameters, suggesting that such a pattern could only be achieved by imposing strong controls on service location. The same was true for the distribution of services in Milton Keynes, but to a lesser extent. Apart from this the model results for Milton Keynes, using the Reading parameter values, were quite close to the proposals, indicating that they could probably be implemented without strong controls.

A variety of performance indicators were then calculated for both sets of results for each town and these are shown in Table 1. The first figure at the top of the 'Reading' column is the average distance in kilometres within which any resident in Reading can reach 12,000 other residents via the transportation network. The next three figures, reading down the column, show the average distances within which a resident can reach higher target figures of other residents. Reading across the page, the corresponding values are shown for each of the three new towns, for both the results using the Reading (Model 1) and the 'best-fit' (Model 2) parameter values. Thus one can see that residents are closest to each other in Hook (as one would expect in view of its compactness). Moving down the page, the results are shown for six other accessibility measures, calculated in a similar way, such as accessibility

INDICATORS	target figure x	READING	STEVENAGE Model 1 Reading param	STEVENAGE Model 2 best fit param	HOOK Model 1 Reading param	HOOK Model 2 best fit param	MILTON KEYNES Model 1 Reading param	MILTON KEYNES Model 2 best fit param
A. SOCIAL INTERACTION	12,000	1.78	1.73	1.68	1.55	1.51	1.77	1.76
	24,000	2.34	2.15	2.67	1.99	1.82	2.48	2.42
mean distance (km) within which all residents can reach x other residents	48,000*	3.57	4.09	4.45	3.74	2.96	3.50	3.46
	96,000	5.25	–	–	7.04	6.03	4.98	5.13
B. EMPLOYMENT OPPORTUNITIES	6,000	2.30	1.60	2.44	1.64	1.75	2.71	2.03
	12,000	2.72	2.25	2.93	2.14	2.13	3.69	2.75
mean distance (km) within which all residents can reach x jobs	24,000*	3.15	2.79	3.92	3.63	3.12	5.09	3.77
	48,000	5.01	–	–	–	–	8.16	5.08
C. SERVICE AVAILABILITY TO RESIDENTS	3,000	2.48	1.92	2.66	1.86	1.91	2.07	2.07
	6,000*	2.91	2.79	3.81	2.32	2.30	2.88	2.92
mean distance (km) within which all residents can reach x service employees	12,000	3.08	–	–	4.30	2.71	3.96	3.99
	24,000	5.40	–	–	–	–	5.50	5.40
D. PROXIMITY TO OPEN SPACE	375	2.26	1.90	1.83	2.45	2.60	2.68	2.70
	750	3.26	2.94	3.16	3.81	3.77	3.57	3.57
mean distance (km) within which all residents can reach x hectares	1,500*	4.47	4.47	4.47	6.77	6.51	5.13	5.15
	3,000	6.20	–	–	–	–	7.68	7.69
E. EMPLOYMENT CLUSTERING	6,000	1.51	0.71	1.11	1.43	1.45	1.76	1.77
	12,000	1.78	1.61	1.77	2.19	2.19	2.64	2.61
mean distance (km) within which all employees can reach x other employees	24,000*	2.38	1.71	2.77	4.07	3.18	3.64	3.70
	48,000	4.29	–	–	–	–	5.31	5.22
F. SERVICE AVAILABILITY TO EMPLOYMENT	3,000	1.67	1.25	1.73	1.84	1.91	2.04	2.06
	6,000*	1.92	1.71	3.89	2.37	2.58	2.91	2.88
mean distance (km) within which all employees can reach x service employees	12,000	2.30	–	–	4.60	2.92	4.04	4.03
	24,000	4.49	–	–	–	–	5.62	5.49
G. SERVICE CLUSTERING	3,000	1.55	1.18	2.10	1.70	1.15	1.88	1.85
	6,000*	1.77	1.85	3.60	2.13	1.37	2.70	2.64
mean distance (km) within which all services can reach x other services	12,000	2.22	–	–	4.29	1.97	3.80	3.71
	24,000	4.39	–	–	–	–	5.40	5.20
H. SIZE – COMPACTNESS (km)		3.07	1.83	2.66	2.68	2.23	4.41	4.48
I. MEAN WORK TRIP LENGTH (km)		2.77	1.94	3.04	1.84	1.83	3.14	3.21
J. MEAN SERVICE TRIP LENGTH (km)		2.86	1.73	2.52	1.36	1.86	2.23	3.36
K. MEAN RESIDENTIAL DENSITY (pph)		62.43	76.82	83.87	73.89	81.37	44.84	46.41
L. MEAN EMPLOYMENT DENSITY (pph)		61.40	89.38	80.36	59.75	59.35	43.72	41.28
M. DEVELOPED LAND PER RESIDENT (m^2)		189	142		130		218	
N. TRUNK ROAD PER RESIDENT (metres)		1.04	0.98		0.59		0.88	

Table 1   Values for indicators A to N for the four towns

of residents to job opportunities (B) and to service facilities (C). The
target figure marked with an asterisk in the second column is the highest
common to all four towns. The final measures (H to N) are reasonably self-
explanatory. H is the average distance of residents to the town centre;
while K and L are weighted average densities, as an indication of the
densities at which most residents live and at which most employees work.

A close scrutiny of these figures reveals some interesting results. Indicator K
shows that the weighted average residential density in Milton Keynes is almost
half that of Hook or Stevenage. Despite this, the accessibility scores for
Milton Keynes are only slightly worse – in fact for some of the higher target
figures they are better. Although this is partly due to the great size of
Milton Keynes, it nonetheless suggests that the neutral road network and
dispersed development provides almost as good accessibility between activities
as in the more traditional form of urban structure, as well as providing the
advantages of more space per resident. Secondly, one can see in the case of
Stevenage that the Model 1 results are in almost every instance better than
for Model 2, for both the accessibility measures (e.g. I and J) and the residential density measure K. In other words better results would have been
obtained in this case (for exactly the same distribution of built-up land
and basic employment) by allowing greater freedom in allowing activities to
locate according to their preferences. For Hook, the comparisons between
Models 1 and 2 are less clear cut. Model 1 produces lower average residential
densities and a lower mean service trip length, but the other accessibility
scores vary. In general Model 1 produces better results for the lower target
figures than for the higher target figures (i.e. more activities are immediately
close by to each other than for Model 2).

The main message of these figures, however, is summarised in Figure 7. For
this diagram, all the accessibility measures A to G have been combined together
and compared with a combination of the density indicators K and L. Thus if
one judges the four towns according to their combined accessibility, or
'interaction' scores alone, Hook comes off best, as can be seen at the extreme
right-hand side of the graph. If on the other hand one judges them solely

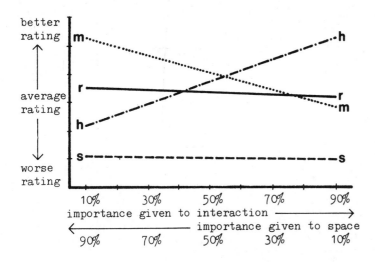

Figure 7   Comparative rating for all four towns

according to the standards of space provided (as measured by density), then Milton Keynes, on the extreme left-hand side of the graph, is the best. If one varies the weights put on the two combined scores for interaction and space, the rating of the four towns changes as shown. Thus, if one considers both good accessibilities and good space standards to be equally important, the structure of Milton Keynes is marginally preferable to Hook, since its interaction scores are less bad than Hook's space scores.

Perhaps the most interesting thing about Figure 7, however, is the uniformly consistent performance of Reading. Although it does not come out best for either space or interaction, its rating is better than the average of the four towns for both. In other words the structure of Reading is such that there is a range of choice provided for both those who prefer to be highly accessible to other activities in the town and for those who attach more importance to space. Stevenage, having high densities and poor interaction scores, performs badly, regardless of the weightings applied. This, of course, does not necessarily mean that Stevenage is a 'bad' town. These simple performance indicators only measure some of the factors which could be considered important in evaluating alternative designs: they say nothing about whether a town is a pleasant place in which to live or whether its inhabitants are happy. But, even though they are limited, they do provide additional information upon which to base assessments. Thus, one can compare alternative strategies for a town in terms of the accessibility between the inhabitants of a town and the facilities that they use, and to explore to what extent it is possible to improve accessibility without sacrificing space standards and vice versa. For more sophisticated comparisons one could adapt the programs to take account of public transportation and, if suitable rates could be established, translate some of the measures into monetary costs and benefits. Instead of treating the town as a whole, one can also examine individual zones of the town in terms of their proximity to each type of activity and the standard of space provided. Since some strategies will improve the lot of some zones but adversely affect others, by a process of experiment the strategy with the most beneficial effects on the most crucial areas can be determined. However, the purpose of these measures is simply to demonstrate the point that with the aid of a model to generate alternative structures, it is possible to use the computer to perform a variety of different types of analyses on the results, and to evaluate them.

Current developments

At present there are four directions in which we are attempting to carry forward our work in this field. The first is to use the simple model and the measures of performance that have been briefly described above to generate and compare a range of hypothetical town forms: linear, radial, semi-radial, polycentric and so forth, each at different sizes. The three inputs to the model (built-up land, basic employment and the route network) are being varied in a systematic way to generate the full range of archetypal town structures and these are then being compared by means of the evaluation indicators so that their relative merits can be assessed. Some preliminary results are described in Walton Lindsay's paper.

The second area of further work is to test the model in more cases. Apart from Reading, Cambridge, Stevenage and Santiago (Chile), the model has now been run for Oxford (by students at the Oxford Polytechnic), and it is currently being calibrated for Gotheburg in Sweden. The possibility of applying it to Mannheim in West Germany is also being discussed. With each new application of the model, we are gaining more experience of using the model in different circumstances and of the ways in which it could usefully be improved. It is becoming clear, for example, that each town has some particular feature (such as the existence of a large student population in the case of Cambridge) which the model is unable to simulate without adaptation. In most cases the adaptation of the model to suit a particular town can be achieved without difficulty (as with the students in Cambridge). Indeed one of the benefits of applying a model is it enables one to analyse the particular ways in which a town is idiosyncratic. Once such idiosyncracies have been identified they can either be allowed for in interpreting the results or, if necessary, the model can be adapted to take them into account.

The third area of work is to develop a more complex and sophisticated model in which different socio-economic groups of residents, different types of service establishment and different ages and structural types of buildings are distinguished. In other words, we are taking each of the three sub-models which comprise the complete model and attempting to develop it further by considering more variables. In order to achieve this we have been putting together from every available source a detailed and massive data bank for the town of Reading, based on the extensive surveys carried out in 1962. In this we have been considerably helped by the cooperation of Reading County Borough. We now have what must be one of the largest and most comprehensive data banks in the country. This has only been achieved at the cost of a considerable amount of time and effort on our part, however, and as a result our programme for developing disaggregated sub-models has been somewhat delayed. But it does mean that we now have an excellent data base to use for the analytical studies that we are currently carrying out and for testing a variety of alternative model formulations. Indeed there is sufficient data to support a large number of different studies, apart from our own, and we very much hope that other researchers will consider making use of it.

A team from Venezuela, attached to this centre, has been working independently to introduce economic variables into a disaggregated model for the city of Caracas. Land values, rents, income groups and costs of travel via public and private transport are all included in the model formulations. Although Caracus is obviously different from European towns and cities, we believe this work to be a major contribution to model building research.

Finally, the fourth area of work has arisen out of the work that we have put into the formation of an integrated urban data bank. What began as a relatively straightforward exercise of putting data onto magnetic tape soon became very much more difficult than we had anticipated. We found that the ease with which selected items of data could be assembled and retrieved from the data bank depended critically on the way in which the bank was structured. We also found that the problems of coding the data in an unambiguous way so that the machine (rather than a human being) could interpret instructions correctly were far harder to solve than we had at first imagined. How, for example, should one code a plot straddling the intersection of four grid squares and containing several land uses which share different types and ages of building in different proportions? Unfortunately the ambiguities often become evident only after one tries, unsuccessfully, to extract some of this information. It is certainly a mistake to think that just because the data is computerised it can be retrieved without difficulty. By a process of trial and error and by learning from our mistakes we have now acquired valuable first-hand experience of how data banks can be organised and manipulated for optimum efficiency and ease of retrieval.

In Cambridge we are very fortunate to have a wide variety of output peripherals such as plotters and visual display units, which have enabled us to develop programs for the graphical display of data in various formats. Richard Baxter discusses the lessons to be learnt from our work in this area in his paper.

Apart from these four areas of research work, however, we have always been keen to try out modelling techniques in a 'real world' planning context in order to discover their usefulness in practical planning. We have ideas about how they could become an integral part of the decision-making process, and we have always sought the opportunity to put these ideas to the test. We have carried out a study for the town of Cambridge where we used a model to test the two opposing strategies put forward by the City and the County. This study, however, was undertaken by students from the Department of Architecture purely as an academic exercise and was never part of the official planning process. Both the City and County Authorities took an interest in the study and were most helpful in providing us with data and in discussing the project. None-theless, it remained as essentially a student exercise. We would like to think that the results may have influenced thinking in official circles, but the project was done too late to be useful in this particular case. The policies had already been formulated, positions had been taken, and the issue was well past the stage of examining a wide range of alternatives as preparation for developing a few selected solutions to put through the administrative mill of official decision-making.

It is at the initial explorative stage of urban structure planning that we see urban models as being potentially most useful, for generating far more alternatives than could otherwise be tested, for catalysing discussion about the kind of consequences that might be desirable, and for re-generating further alternative strategies in the light of this discussion. In other words, we see models as being most valuable when used in a repetitive way to enable a full range of possible outcomes to be compared and analysed in a directly comparable manner. We see models as being less useful for testing a limited number of alternatives, particularly if the results of test runs are interpreted too firmly as 'hard' forecasts. Predicting the future is always a risky and hazardous business, and although models reduce the risk and enable one to determine the implications of assumptions more systematically they do not eliminate the risk altogether. Urban models are not designed to replace the human skills of experience, commonsense, local knowledge of the area and understanding of the range of issues involved, but to complement them by providing additional evidence to use in the discussions that precede decision-making. In fact unless such human skills are applied intelligently in the use of models the results may be meaningless. The results require careful scrutiny and intepretation, and when they are markedly different from intuitive expectations it is essential to understand how these results have been arrived at. If one is satisfied with the model's logic on such occasions, then counter-intuitive results can be extremely instructive, but they should not be taken simply on trust. In other words, a model should not be considered as some kind of 'black box' which magically produces the 'ideal' structure plan, or which in any way served as the final arbiter in choosing between alternatives; rather, it should be seen as an aid to understanding how one process in a town affects another, and as a means of generating and comparing possible outcomes on a common basis. Although models have been proved capable of reproducing reality with reasonable accuracy, and although they can, with care, be used for impact analysis of a particular proposal, we believe they can best be used as a piece of experimental apparatus for facilitating comparative analysis.

It follows, if these arguments are accepted, that if maximum benefit is to
be gained from the use of models they need to be integrated fully into the
decision-making process. All those responsible for the future structure of
a town (including where suitable the general public) need to take part in
discussing the results, in suggesting new alternatives to test and in debating
which outcomes it would be most desirable to achieve. If the use of models
is restricted exclusively to the research or technical teams of a local
authority their potential will not be fully realised.

The Luton project

It was with these thoughts in mind that we approached an invitation to
set up and calibrate the model for Luton County Borough. The conditions
appeared favourable. Luton had just collated a great deal of survey material
for a transportation study, and the authority possessed a suitable computer
and an active programming staff. It was agreed that a pilot project should
be mounted to see whether the model would be useful to them. Work on a new
structure plan had only just begun and there were a number of alternative
strategies which could be explored in the early stages of reviewing the
possibilities. It was also appreciated that the model would be useful for
providing inputs for the transportation study, that is to say, for generating
the alternative distributions of future land uses, from which the traffic
flows on the road network could be calculated. Unfortunately, we have run
up against a series of obstacles in this project which is worth outlining
for the general lessons that can be learnt from them.

First of all, we have had innumerable problems with preparing the data.
Although much of the available information was on computer records, it was
found to be insufficiently complete and difficult to cross-relate. The
Employment Register records, as usual, exclude all firms with less than five
employees, so that a large proportion of the service employment was missing.
The floorspace data had been collected in such a way that it was impossible
to relate different categories of employment to the floorspace they occupied.
Rather arbitrary methods had to be introduced to decide for each zone how
much floorspace was occupied by basic employment, how much by service employment and how much by the small establishments missing from the ER records.
Difficulties were also found in extracting the trip survey data from magnetic
tape.

Thus, although our model had relatively few and simple data requirements, we
have had considerable difficulty in satisfying them in a sufficiently consistent
and comprehensive manner. Indeed, one of the benefits of attempting to apply an
urban model, or any such analytical technique requiring rigorously defined
data inputs, is that it provides a valuable test of the quality of one's
information retrieval system – whether organised in a computerised or traditional form. In many ways our experience in Luton has confirmed what we have
learnt from our own experience of setting up and manipulating urban data banks.
It is surprising how difficult it is to obtain satisfactory answers to the
simplest questions, such as how many retail employees are there in each zone
of the town and how much land and floorspace do they occupy? The variety of
sources one has to collate (each with its own inconsistencies and errors), the
different areal units used, the difficulty of cross-relating one item of
information with another and the different timescales over which the data have
been collected, are all problems in producing a reliable data base for analytical
planning studies. Clearly the introduction of computers provides possibilities
for extending the use that can be made of a reliable data base within a planning

office, but the problems involved both in developing the software for storing, updating and retrieving information, and in preparing a reliable data base in the first place should not be underestimated.

The second source of difficulty arose from a lack of anticipation, on both sides, of the time and effort required to make such a study worthwhile. Thus the load on the planning staff in preparing the data inputs was seriously under-estimated. The demands made on the computing staff in Luton were also more than could be coped with, both in terms of the time and the different programming skills required. At the same time, we were not able to devote sufficient time, as part time (and unpaid) consultants at a distance, to assist in data preparation and staff-training.

In retrospect it now seems clear that if a model building exercise is to be undertaken it is only worthwhile if it is undertaken wholeheartedly, both by the local authority concerned and by the consultants providing the expertise. If the introduction of new techniques within a planning office is to be achieved successfully, sufficient priority and allocation of staff time must be devoted to their assimilation. This means that the consultants providing the expertise need to be employed as much to train staff, holding a series of seminars on the use of the new techniques and their possible role in the planning process, as to give technical advice. A consultant's aim should be to leave behind not only a report and a pile of computer output, but also a team of local authority staff that understands the new techniques and knows how to use them. It is to provide such a consultancy and educational service that Applied Research of Cambridge Limited (the sponsors of this conference) has been established.

Part 3

Evaluation

The process of evaluation

Jean Perraton

In this paper I propose to discuss the evaluation process in general terms, relating it to other aspects of the planning process, to provide a background to the more detailed and technical papers which follow. In this discussion, I propose to look first at evaluation as part of the planning process. I shall examine how evaluation fits into this process, and the implications of current views of the planning process for the sort of procedure that evaluation should be.

Secondly, I shall look briefly at some recent plan-making studies to see how evaluation is treated in them.

Thirdly, I shall look at some problems of choosing the criteria for evaluation, and at measures or indices to represent those criteria.

The context: the planning process

Evaluation as a formal procedure for examining the pros and cons of alternative plans or courses of action, and placing a value on them, is a relatively new concept in planning procedure. Of course, the activity of evaluation, in one form or another, has always been part of the planning process, though not always explicitly recognised as such. The idea of evaluation as an explicit and formal activity has emerged recently, with much discussion about the nature of the planning process. It is relevant here to sketch very briefly some recent ideas about what sort of process planning is or should be, and how evaluation fits, or should fit, into this.

It is accepted by many planners that, ideally, planning should be a goal-directed process. (Here, I am deliberately leaving aside any discussion of contrary views of planning – as adaptive, problem-solving, or the more extreme, virtually anti-planning, views of the disjointed incrementalists.) The goal-directed view implies (as Meyerson and Banfield (1955) pointed out) that planning must seek to choose those means which best promote the most valued ends. Meyerson and Banfield outlined four essential steps in the choice of a plan or programme:

i   the identification and ranking of goals

ii   the elaboration of alternative means of attaining, or moving towards those goals

iii   the prediction of likely consequences and the impact of alternatives on other goals and upon different sections of the community, and

iv   the choice of that alternative which seems most likely to promote the most valued goals.

This simple model of the goal-directed approach to planning has been accepted - but elaborated and modified - by various planning theorists and also, more recently, by planners in practice (Figure 1).

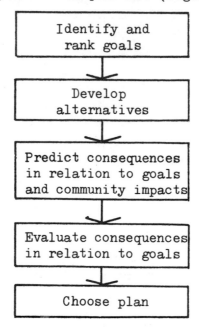

Figure 1   The goal-directed approach to plan-making

A distinction needs to be made here between abstract or general goals, and more specific ways of achieving goals - operational or instrumental objectives. These are often seen as forming part of an ends-means hierarchy (Figure 2).

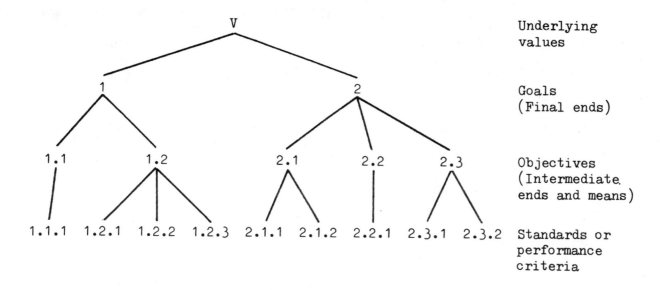

Figure 2   The ends-means hierarchy (after Boyce et al. 1971)

Whereas it may be possible to formulate general goals, at the outset, it is not always possible to define, let alone to rank or weight, more specific objectives before the implications of those objectives have been clarified during the plan-making process. Leaving aside such complications, and the need to modify in practice this ideal model, the point I want to stress here is that the goal-directed view of planning requires that the values and the reasoning upon which plans are based should be made explicit. Evaluation must relate directly to the stated goals and objectives.

The second characteristic of planning, emphasised in recent years, is that it should be a comprehensive process. This relates to the view of the city as a system in which social, economic and physical aspects are interdependent and interact. The implications of the comprehensive view are not entirely clear: some have taken it to mean that the subject matter of traditional town planning should be widened, or that it should be integrated into the wider corporate planning and management process. But, essentially comprehensiveness implies the need to take into account interactions with the rest of the system, or related systems and decision areas. It means that planning must be wide-ranging both in its efforts to consider alternative ways of achieving ends, and in tracing the impacts of plans and policies. Evaluation, likewise, must be a wide-ranging procedure.

The third characteristic of this emerging view of planning is that policies and plans should be based on the goals and objectives of the community — the users rather than producers (whether developers or planners). Theorists and practitioners alike frequently pay lip service to this view. But how this can be implemented is probably the most difficult problem presented by the goal-directed approach.

The difficulties of getting meaningful discussion of abstract goals are well known: attempts at public participation have shown that it is the local scale, concrete policy proposals that arouse public concern and debate rather than more general policies, let alone abstract goals. But even at the level of detailed, concrete proposals there are many problems in determining and interpreting public attitudes and, in particular, in assessing the relative priorities in different situations. Furthermore, even if a distribution of values could be gauged for different sections of the population these would often conflict: the decision-makers must decide whose priorities should take precedence.

This brings us to the fourth characteristic of the new view of planning, and that is the recognition that it involves inherent conflicts and the need for political choice. Conflicts arise from several sources: first, the achievement of different goals and objectives, all of which may be considered desirable, may pose direct conflicts. Second, even where there is no such incompatibility, the implementation of many objectives involves competition for scarce financial resources. Thirdly, different sections of the population have different needs, values and priorities, which lead to conflicting interests. The implementation of any policy will affect differentially particular individuals or sections of the population: some will benefit, some will lose.

No longer can the planner regard himself as a neutral arbitrator between competing uses of land, in the interest of the community as a whole. No longer can be assume that the right solution to the problem will emerge simply from the survey and analysis of the area: the right solution is a matter of judgement and choice. Evaluation is the procedure to aid in that choice.

The fifth point I want to stress about the new view of planning is that it needs to be a continuing, cyclical process. We are faced with many uncertainties: uncertainty about the present and future values of the community upon which the choice of plan or policy should be based, uncertainty about the effects of planning policies, uncertainty about the effects of future technological changes upon the environment. These uncertainties point to the need for a planning system which is capable of adapting to change: this means continuous monitoring of change, follow-up studies to assess the effects of plans, to assess user-satisfactions, to produce the feedback needed to adjust assumptions and forecasts, to redefine goals and to rethink policies.

The process of evaluation

What are the implications of this emerging view of planning for the process of evaluation?

Firstly, the goal-directed view requires that the goals and objectives, and their relative importance, be stated explicitly. This may not be possible at the outset, but it must be done before criteria are chosen for evaluation. The criteria for evaluation must relate directly to the goals and objectives of the plan.

The implications of the comprehensiveness are more complicated and problematical: it is clearly impossible (as the incrementalists point out) to trace all impacts. But the aim of evaluation must be to elucidate those impacts relevant to the chosen objectives.

The requirement that goals and objectives should be based as far as possible upon the values of the community also has implications: objectives need to be expressed in terms of sections of the community. But the values and wishes of the community are often difficult to assess, and it is often not meaningful (even to the planner, let alone councillors or members of the public) to decide upon objectives or to assign priorities to them before some of the implications and conflists have been explored. This indicates the need for the use of evaluation procedures during the plan making process – as an aid in the development of alternatives – and not simply as a final testing procedure to aid in the choice between them. It also implies finding ways of creating a dialogue between planners, politicians and the public during the plan-making process.

The conflicting nature of plan objectives requires that evaluation procedures be based upon the recognition of conflict; they must help to expose, rather than hide, the implications of different courses of action. Again, this is more likely to be possible if evaluation is used as part of the plan development process, as "a probing, exploring activity that tends to disaggregate and clarify the implications of each alternative" (Boyce and Day 1969).

Finally, the recognition that the plan-making process must be a continuing, cyclical procedure in which the goals and objectives, assumptions and forecasts, are questioned and checked against later information implies the need for post-evaluation of the consequences of planning decisions. We must remember that we are discussing here what Pearson (1970a) has termed pre-evaluation of hypothetical alternatives, based on largely hypothetical performance measures. This pre-evaluation is necessarily a much narrower procedure than post-evaluation. The latter can be based on real output measures, expressed in terms of human behaviour and satisfactions. (And, incidentally, may eventually help provide us with the information needed to make pre-evaluation a less hypothetical procedure.)

To sum up, therefore, it appears that evaluation should be:

i   goal directed – evaluation measures and their ranking must relate
                     directly to the goals and objectives,

ii comprehensive – not only must those criteria be based on the full
                     range of objectives, but the procedure must be wide
                     ranging in its exploration of impacts,

iii explicit   – in setting out clearly the essential assumptions
                     and value judgements,

iv clarifying   – to enable diverse considerations to be compared
                     and thus to facilitate rational choice between
                     them, but also

v   disaggregative and informative.

These requirements apply whether we view evaluation as an explorative, probing,
testing procedure, helping the development of alternatives, or whether it is
kept separate from the design process and used simply as a final testing
procedure, to produce a summary comparison (a goals-achievement matrix or a
planning balance sheet) setting out the pros and cons, the costs and benefits.
But, to some extent these requirements are conflicting. There is an acute
problem (particularly where evaluation takes the form of one summary account)
of balancing the need for clarity against informativeness. The cumbersomeness
of too much information is poised against the distortion of too little. This
is allied to the problem of how far it is justifiable to convert scores to
common measures to aid in comparison, and how far this gives a spurious sense
of accuracy or actually distorts the nature of important issues. The question
of converting social benefits to costs is one particular aspect of this general
problem. It may well be more meaningful to have impacts measured in different
units, even if this reduces clarity, or apparent clarity, and increases the
difficulty of making a comparison. It may be better, for example, to express
travel time as time rather than converting it to a monetary cost, particularly
if it is journey time that people are seeking to reduce.

The use of evaluation as an integral part of the development of alternative
strategies is an approach which appears to be more appropriate to the complexity of the design process in planning. It appears to give more scope for
exploring impacts and resolving conflicts. But this approach compounds the
problem of how to ensure that the assumptions involved are made explicit, and
that the implications of alternatives at each stage are presented to the
politicians and public in a clear and meaningful way, leaving room for the
important choices to be made by society.

Evaluation in recent plan-making studies

Having sketched some important points about the nature of the planning process,
and their implications for the process of evaluation, I want now to look
briefly at a number of plan-making studies, at sub-regional and urban scales,
to see how the overall task was tackled and in particular how evaluation
fitted in to this.

These studies show that there has been considerable progress in recent years
towards rational plan-making. There have been increasingly rigorous attempts
to make goals and objectives explicit, and to incorporate them into the

processes of design and evaluation. The procedures for doing this vary. In particular, the relationship of design to evaluation, and the use of objectives in these two processes, varies considerably.

Back in 1966, the South Hampshire Study (Buchanan and Partners 1966) did not define goals, although criteria for considering the suitability of the area for expansion were stated. But the concept of examining alternatives was introduced at the stage of choosing an appropriate <u>form</u> for development. Alternative idealised forms (basically road network patterns) were elaborated, and examined impressionistically in relation to five criteria.

In the same year, the Ipswich Expansion Study (Shankland, Cox and Associates 1966) was also concerned with two main problems: the feasibility of the area for expansion on the scale proposed, and the choice of a location and form for development. This study listed social and economic objectives, and discussed their implications for design. Alternative idealised forms for development were examined, as in the South Hampshire Study, but in an even more generalised way. Subsequently, in the Basic Draft Plan (Shankland, Cox and Associates 1968), the chosen linear form was elaborated to produce a theoretical town diagram, which was adapted (or bent-on) to fit the particular opportunities and constraints of the site.

In the Telford Plan (The John Madin Design Group 1969) the goals of the plan were clearly stated, and their implications for the structure plan discussed (Figure 3). The plan generation process in this study was an attempt to derive a plan directly from the goals: it was a synthetic procedure in which an ideal structure was designed by considering the needs and standards at the smallest scale, and building up the components hierarchically to form one ideal structure. This ideal structure, as in the Ipswich study, was then bent-on to the site.

In the Northampton Master Plan (Wilson, Womersley et al. 1969a) the objectives of the plan were also clearly set out (Figure 4). These were a rather disparate mixture of general aims, and more detailed design criteria, most of which were presumably incorporated directly into the design of the alternatives. This plan included a formal, quantitative evaluation of alternative land use/transportation patterns, based on a narrow range of criteria relating to the costs of the network and average journey times for private car users.

These first four plans were all prepared to cope with large-scale planned immigration of population: the next four sub-regional studies were prepared as advisory documents for the coordinated development of areas under more than one local planning authority. These sub-regional studies have made some interesting developments in approach to plan generation and evaluation.

The Teeside Survey and Plan (Wilson and Womersley et al. 1969b and 1971) began with two broad substantive aims, but the more detailed objectives emerged after a study of the alternative possibilities for development (Figure 5). This study also included a formal, quantitative evaluation of alternative land-use strategies, using a somewhat broader range of criteria than in the Northampton Plan. A traffic model was used to predict future traffic patterns and to evaluate the transportation aspects of alternative urban structures.

In the Leicester and Leicestershire Sub-Regional Study (1969) there was no formal statement of goals, and the stated objectives were essentially the policy variables to be considered (Figure 6). Again, alternative patterns for development were generated, and evaluated in terms of explicit criteria.

MAIN STAGES IN PLAN-MAKING

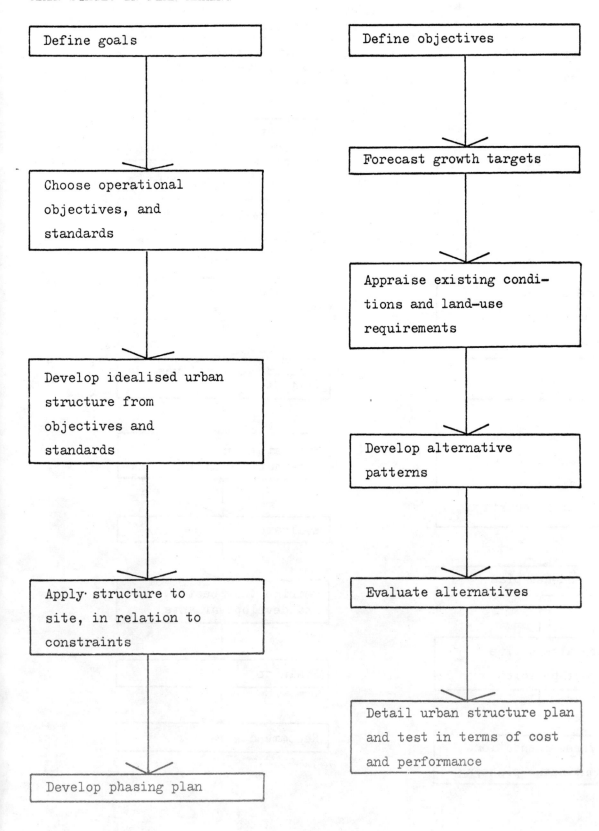

Figure 3
Telford Development Proposals (1969)

Figure 4
Northampton Master Plan (1969)

MAIN STAGES IN PLAN-MAKING

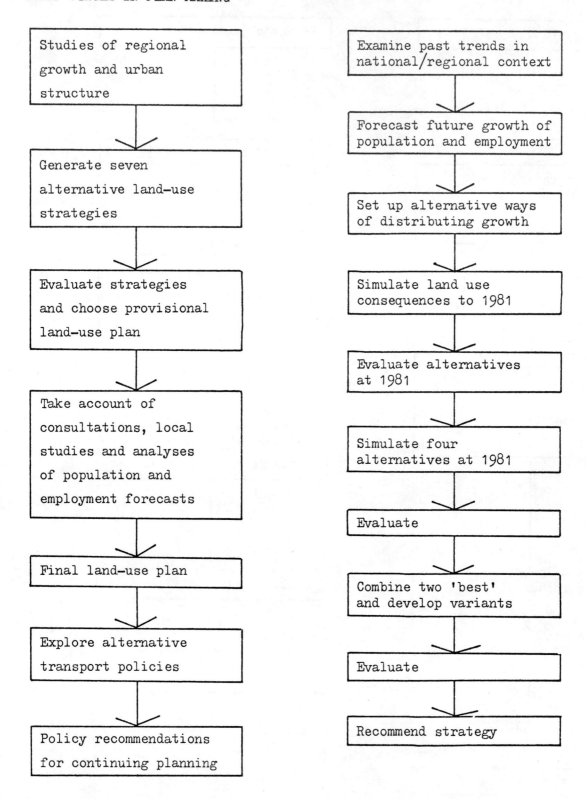

Figure 5
Teeside Survey and Plan (1969)

Figure 6
Leicester-Leicestershire Sub-
Regional Planning Study (1969)

The alternatives were evaluated at two dates, in relation to a wider range of criteria than in the previous studies, using a variety of techniques. The two 'best' strategies from the second evaluation were then synthesized to combine their advantages, and the chosen strategy emerged from a further evaluation of variants of this synthesis. Evaluation, here, was used to help develop alternatives as well as choose between them.

In the Nottinghamshire-Derbyshire Sub-Regional Study (1969) the general aims were stated and a large number of objectives put forward (Figure 7). The alternatives were developed initially without references to the objectives. They were then evaluated in relation to criteria (reflecting the objectives) using a variety of techniques. The evaluation was repeated four times, each evaluation stage being used to help develop better strategies. Here, evaluation was an integral part of the plan development process - an explorative learning process rather than a final testing procedure. But, possibly partly as a result, the whole plan-making process is much less clear-cut and explicit than in our next study.

The Coventry-Solihull-Warwickshire Sub-Regional Study (1971). Here we see the most clearly defined attempt to follow a strictly goal-directed procedure (Figure 8). Broad goals were stated, operational objectives defined, and for each objective a performance criterion and performance assumptions were set out. The alternatives were derived directly from some, but not all, the objectives. These alternatives, differing within narrow limits, were then evaluated in relation to the full range of objectives using a comprehensive goals-achievement matrix. Both the development of the alternatives and the evaluation of them rested upon the weighting of objectives to reflect their relative importance. And, because of the uncertainties in weighting objectives, the evaluation procedures included sensitivity analyses to check the effects of changing the weighting of objectives upon the performance of the strategies.

In the last study considered here, the Brighton Urban Structure Plan (1971), the plan-making procedure was split into two main stages: the choice of a strategy based on alternative function and growth patterns, and the choice of a transportation pattern to serve the preferred function-growth pattern (Figure 9). In the first stage (to which the 1971 report relates) the objectives were formulated and broad alternatives differing in terms of growth and function were put forward. These alternatives were evaluated in two stages. First, a coarse evaluation produced a short list of four broad alternatives. These were detailed in terms of land-use, and subjected to more detailed evaluation using a goals-achievement technique. The scores from this account were aggregated and weighted in accordance with the relative importance of the objectives as assessed by the public.

The relationship of evaluation to plan design

It is clear from these brief summaries that the evaluation procedure cannot be considered in isolation from the design. Clearly, where the plan development procedure is a linear process giving rise to one plan, there is no room for evaluation. And, where the design procedures give a poor range of alternatives, evaluation cannot produce a good plan however comprehensive, careful and complicated that procedure may be.

MAIN STAGES IN PLAN-MAKING

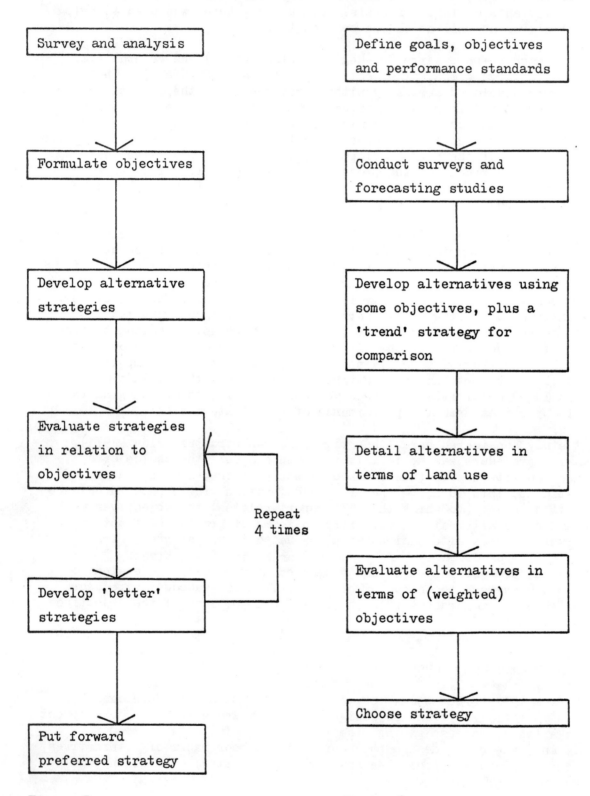

Figure 7
Nottinghamshire and Derbyshire
Sub-Regional Study (1969)

Figure 8
Coventry-Solihull-Warwickshire
Sub-Regional Study (1971)

In this handful of plans we see basically three contrasting approaches:

i   The development of a plan directly from objectives, leaving no
         room for the evaluation of alternatives,

ii   the development of alternatives, either intuitively or using
         some of the objectives, which were then evaluated either once,
         or at increasing levels of detail,

iii   the use of evaluation in an iterative way to help in the
         development of better strategies.

The first approach, the development of <u>one</u> plan, has serious weaknesses.
Where, as in Telford, this builds up to one ideal structure, one may assume
that the components reflect objectives satisfactorily at the detailed scale,
but one does not know how the structure functions, whether better or worse
than any other, at the urban scale. Furthermore, when such a structure is
'bent-on' to the site with many constraints, as it was in Telford, there is
no guarantee that the modified structure retains the merits of the ideal form.
(Optimising procedures, using mathematical programming, are even less likely
to be appropriate to the complexities and uncertainties of urban structure
planning.)

The development of alternatives was, in some of our earlier examples, also
based on contrasting urban forms. Again, where (as in Ipswich) these were
considered in isolation from the site the comments about 'bending-on' are
equally applicable. Clearly, such alternatives must be evaluated after they
are applied to the site.

The planning team for Coventry-Solihull-Warwickshire, however, decided against
using contrasting urban forms, and sought to develop realistic alternatives
more directly from objectives as a quicker way to arrive at a range of
strategies worthy of evaluation. Their technique for doing this, development
potential surfaces, is an advance on the sieve technique, but involves using
the same partial range of objectives to develop all alternatives. The danger
here is that if development potential surfaces are used as the sole method of
developing alternatives, the range of alternatives put forward for evaluation
may be limited and biased towards those objectives which have been included
in the development process, and may exclude other possibilities which might
do well on evaluation in relation to all objectives.

In the Brighton Study evaluation was also used simply as a procedure for
choosing between alternatives, but at two different levels of detail – a
progressive refinement approach which was carried much further, for example,
in the West Midland Study (Stevenson 1971) (Figure 10).

Thirdly, there is more untidy, less explicit approach of the Nottinghamshire-
Derbyshire Study, in which evaluation was used as an aid to design as well as a
final testing procedure. Here, development potential surfaces and mathematical
models were used to explore the potential for development and the interaction
between patterns of development. But it is by no means clear from the published
documents precisely what was done and with what results at each stage. This is
partly, no doubt, because the procedures were more exploratory and complicated,
but, one suspects, it also results from the paternalistic attitudes of the
planning team towards the public for whom they were planning (see Thorburn 1970
and Steeley 1970). This last approach appears to lend itself to the complexities
of the design procedure in urban structure planning. But a way must be found

MAIN STAGES IN PLAN-MAKING

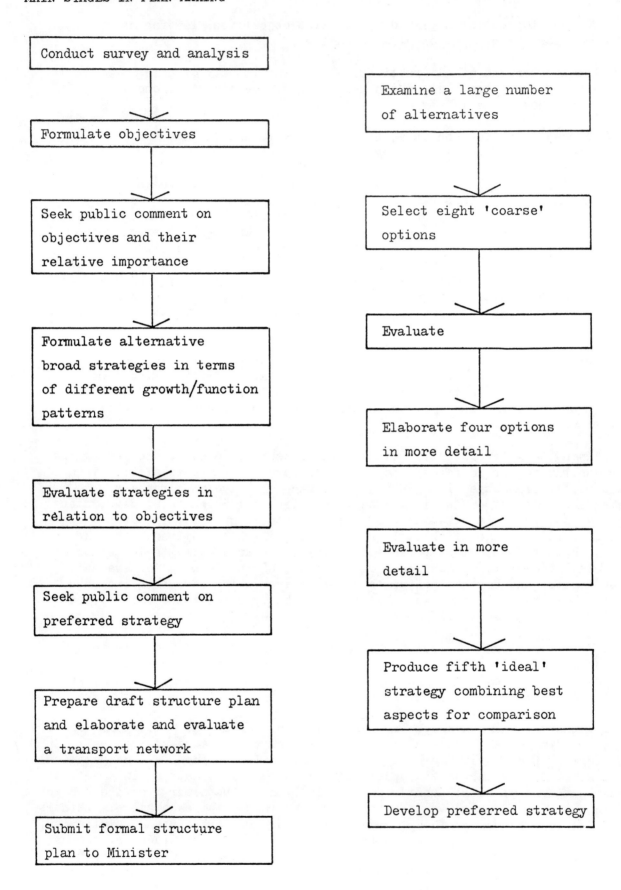

Figure 9
Brighton Urban Structure Plan
(1971)

Figure 10
West Midlands Regional Study
(from Stevenson 1971)

for the procedures, assumptions and results at each stage to be made explicit, so that the decision-makers can appreciate the full implications of different policy choices.

These differences in planning and evaluation procedure rest upon some basic similarities in the philosophy and approach to plan-making. Two similarities stand out. First, where alternatives were put forward for formal evaluation, they were all framed in terms of overall strategies. There appears to be room for considering approaches based on evaluating alternative means of meeting objectives at sub-system level, or in terms of basic design standards. There is also a need to consider non-spatial ways of meeting objectives, particularly in structure planning for an existing urban area.

Second, the generation and evaluation of these plans all reflect a unitary conception of the public interest. There were no attempts to express objectives in terms of different sections of the population and virtually no atttempts to evaluate the impact of strategies on different sections. Yet plans or policies designed to benefit the community as a whole usually benefit some people at the expense of others. The Teeside Study, for example, put forward a strategy based on maximum car use, to meet the objective of freedom of choice. Yet clearly measures facilitating the maximum use of cars in cities tend to conflict with maximum public transport provision, and benefit the car-owning sections at the expense of non-car owners. This failure to recognise, or to make explicit, the conflicting nature of objectives as they affect people, and to evaluate their implications in these terms, is the most serious weakness of these plans.

Evaluation criteria

In the final section of this paper, I want to take a quick look at some of the evaluation criteria. The choice of appropriate evaluation criteria, and appropriate performance measures or indices to represent those criteria, is crucial to the validity of the evaluation process. However sophisticated the methodology, the exercise will be useless, or even a hindrance to rational decision-making, if the criteria upon which it is based are irrelevant or unrepresentative of the full range of objectives – or if the indices chosen to represent those criteria are irrelevant or of dubious predictive value.

Where alternatives are put forward for evaluation the criteria should relate directly back to the objectives. They should reflect as fully and closely as possible all the objectives of the plan, or rather, all those objectives which are relevant to the choice between alternatives. (Some objectives may be incorporated as essential constraints into all the alternatives, and other objectives may relate to the continuing planning process.)

One must remember, of course, that there can be no one-to-one relationship between objectives and evaluation criteria, or between evaluation criteria and performance measures. The criteria chosen represent an interpretation and a choice among various possible criteria and various possible ways of measuring them, and this interpretation is likely to be narrower than the original objective. In this sense, there cannot be any really objective evaluation measures.

I want to stress this point, for there seems to be a tendency to assume that if a measure is expressed quantitatively and especially if it rests upon some observed regularity in existing behaviour, it thereby becomes an <u>objective</u>

measure. Yet, as we all know, the criterion of minimising journeys to work could be measured in various ways: in terms of linear distance, in time or in costs (based on various different assumptions). Which measure is most suitable rests upon a judgement, a judgement that should be an attempt to interpret public preferences. The tendency to regard measures based on observed behaviour as 'objective' often appears to rest on two other mistakes. One is to assume that observed behaviour necessarily reflects preferences. (Here, I use 'preference' as a psychologist would, rather than an economist.) The second is the failure to distinguish between what 'is' and what 'ought' to be. Evaluation is about what ought to be.

Thus the measures we choose for evaluation are necessarily subjective, but we must try to make them reflect as fully and closely as possible the chosen objectives of the plan. Let us look briefly, now, at how this was done in the plans examined earlier.

Criteria used in recent plans

There was a tendency in the earlier plans for evaluation to be based on a narrow range of quantitative measures, relating mainly to transportation aspects and selective costs. These measures represented typically only a few of the objectives, and not necessarily the most important. Indeed, an analysis of these plans revealed that questions of costs were almost totally absent from the stated objectives, but entered frequently into the evaluations. In the Northampton Master Plan, for example, a fairly wide range of objectives was put forward, but the alternatives appear to have been evaluated solely in terms of average work journey times for private car users and the costs per head of the road network.

In the Coventry-Solihull-Warwickshire and the Brighton plans, great strides were made towards explicit, comprehensive evaluation, by setting out the objectives, matching them with appropriate performance measures and explaining the performance assumptions upon which their use was based. In both studies, too, the results of the performance of alternatives in relation to each measure were also given. In the Coventry-Solihull-Warwickshire study, so neatly are all the objectives matched by all the performance criteria, all of which are expressed in quantified terms, that one is forced to wonder whether the choice of objectives may have been influenced by the desire for a neat and tidy evaluation. If so, this is putting the technical cart before the planning horse; it is a dangerous fallacy that evaluation can be an entirely neat and quantified procedure.

This suspicion does not arise in the Brighton Plan. For although all the objectives are clearly set out, with the corresponding evaluation criteria and performance assumptions, there are gaps where appropriate criteria could not be found, or where only qualitative criteria appeared to be relevant. In many cases, too, there were several criteria put forward for one objective: the result is less neat and tidy, but possibly more realistic.

Let us look more closely at some of the evaluation measures used in the Coventry-Solihull-Warwickshire study and the Brighton Plan, for they illustrate some of the problems of choosing appropriate indices. Both these plans, unlike the other plans we have looked at here, included measures for the goal of flexibility. Flexibility, as a characteristic of the plan as a programme of action and not simply a characteristic of the physical form or road network of the area, has been an increasingly important goal in planning, but only recently have indices been developed to measure it. There are several different meanings of plan flexibility: the most flexible plan has been interpreted as the one that leaves most options open, or the plan which will function most satisfactorily if the forecasts upon which it is based vary from the most likely.

It is clear that the goal of flexibility, interpreted in these ways, is different in kind from other goals. This point was recognised and emphasized in the Coventry-Solihull-Warwickshire study: "The other objectives and the tests applied to them dealt with a set of circumstances which we considered 'most likely' to arise in 1991 ... Flexibility was concerned with the variations in these circumstances which, if they arose, might make the strategy in force less satisfactory than an alternative". Therefore, the Coventry-Solihull-Warwickshire team summed the results of their four flexibility tests separately from the results based on other objectives.

They applied four criteria:

i   The ability of the plan to adapt to changes within a range of departures from the most likely forecast. This was tested by a robustness test to examine the effects of changes in the rates of growth from the most likely forecast upon the effectiveness scores.

ii   The ability of the plan to respond to changing social values. Again, a robustness test was used to examine the effects of changes in the weighting of objectives.

iii The ability of the plan to cope with sudden and unexpected events. This was tested in terms of accessibility to jobs and the choice of transport mode.

iv   The possibility of switching from one strategy to another. This was tested in terms of an index of interchangeability, calculated from the number of kilometres of new development common to one or more strategies. This last test is the "keeping options open" idea, and was measured in a similar way in the Brighton plan.

Fortunately for the Coventry-Solihull-Warwickshire team the plan which did best on the flexibility tests was also the plan which did best in relation to the other criteria. They were not forced to choose. Clearly there is a potential conflict between the requirements of flexibility (upon which the planner lays great stress) and those based on other goals (which may mean more to the community). The way in which flexibility is interpreted and measured may have policy implications: if it is interpreted solely in terms of keeping options open this is likely to inhibit radical changes in direction in planning. Thus, it cannot be regarded simply as a non-controversial technical criterion.

There are other plan requirements which are apparently technical considerations, such as feasibility and consistency, which also might conflict with the achievement of other objectives. Again, much depends on precisely how they are defined and measured. At first glance feasibility would appear to be a necessary precondition of any plan. Lichfield, for example, listed feasibility as one of several constraints to be taken into account before evaluation (Lichfield 1970). But to what extent is it satisfactory to regard feasibility, like internal consistency, as a technical requirement to be satisfied before plans are evaluated in relation to other criteria? Much depends on how they are measured, which was seldom made clear in the plans we have examined here. If, however, one measures feasibility — as was done by several planning agencies in the

States studied by Boyce and Day (1969) - as the degree of consistency with current trends, one is making a choice in favour of maintaining existing trends rather than changing them. Again if one tests internal consistency in relation to, say, existing patterns of travel behaviour, which appears to have been the case in the Nottinghamshire-Derbyshire study, one is choosing to reinforce such patterns rather than to change them. Thus, how these apparently technical criteria should be defined and measured, and how much importance should be given to them, is a problem which needs to be brought into the open and discussed with the other substantive aims and criteria.

The indices used in the Brighton Plan were in many ways similar to the Coventry-Solihull-Warwickshire study, but there are some interesting differences. The Brighton Plan included a greater range of evaluative indices: some are straightforward and clearly relevant to the objectives, but others are more hypothetical and their relevance or predictive value is more questionable. An unusual feature of the indices used in this plan is the extent to which population growth was taken as a proxy for various undesirable consequences. "Total population" or "population increase" was used as an indication of the extent to which several objectives might not be achieved, by contributing towards:

i   the disruption of the physical and social character of residential districts,

ii   the incidence of trespass,

iii   the incidence of demolition of houses,

iv   the disturbance of areas of natural history interest, and

v   the possibility of intrusive developments.

This recognition of the undesirable effects of population increase is not found in the other plans, and is in marked contrast with the development potential or trend strategy philosophy of the Coventry-Solihull-Warwickshire and Nottinghamshire-Derbyshire studies.

Clearly, in many cases, the use of indices based on population growth are relevant, particularly in relation to conservation objectives. But population growth or size is not a satisfactory proxy for other undesirable effects. It is not adequate, for example, to use the total number of trips (which appears to depend primarily on total population) as an indication of the accidents and stress in different strategies. Surely one should be seeking here an index which will reveal, independently of population size, which strategy is most likely to meet these objectives. There is clearly something wrong, too, in using the last index, the total number of trips, as an indication of impedence to traffic flow, to measure the suitability of the strategies both to public and to private transport. Clearly, such an index is of marginal relevance and little predictive value.

It is probably quite unfair to single out these questionable examples from the Brighton study, when so many more are no doubt hidden from view in previous, less explicit, studies. Indeed, the authors of the Brighton Plan are aware of the hypothetical nature of some of the indices put forward. But these examples serve to illustrate that the indices chosen for evaluation, at this "pre-evaluation" stage, are often essentially hypothetical. They are usually physical input measures for outcomes which we would like to be able to express

in terms of human behaviour and satisfactions. This point needs to be
remembered when interpreting the results of evaluation.

Conclusion

I am aware that I have presented here an oversimplified view of a complex
issue, and left out of consideration many complications. But I hope that one
underlying message has come across, and that is that evaluation is a difficult,
complicated and ultimately subjective process. Our choice of evaluation
technique must not oversimplify it. Our choice of evaluation criteria must
be related to what matters rather than what can be measured easily. And we
must leave room in the process for the assumptions, doubts and value judgements
to be made clear to the decision makers.

Some theoretical aspects of evaluation and their application to plan-making

Tony Houghton

The previous paper dealt with the process of evaluation in general. There are many ways of applying these techniques, but I am not going to deal with any particular application of evaluation techniques in a plan-making study. Instead, I am simply going to pick out a few of the techniques which are used in evaluation and describe them in a little more technical detail.

The first point I want to make about evaluation is that an evaluation technique is not, strictly speaking, a model. If you define a model as a representation of reality in mathematical terms, evaluation is not a model. Therefore the criterion of the usefulness of an evaluation technique is not the goodness of fit, as it is in the case of a model. In an evaluation technique one has not got the same sort of calibration problem, and the criterion of evaluation is not how well it fits the situation, but whether it is useful in the decision making process. This is not to say that a given evaluation technique may not incorporate behavioural models where the calibration criteria still apply; but the overall criterion for a successful evaluation technique must be its usefulness rather than its goodness of fit.

Before I go on to describe some of the techniques in more detail, I would like to set the scene by putting forward a view of the planning process in its technical aspects. I am going to look at a plan as a set of values assigned to a set of decision variables. In a purely physical plan, for example, the decision variables might be how much land to allocate for housing in a particular zone, and a given plan will have a value assigned to that variable – say, ten acres.

The process of evaluation is basically trying to establish whether that plan is a good plan. An important point I want to make before describing the techniques is that if it is possible to say what makes a plan good – that is, if it is possible to evaluate the plan in a global sense – it should be possible to say how to make the plan better. In other words, one should be able, by looking at the decision variables, to map out the effect of changing the decision variables in terms of the evaluation criteria that you are using for your plan. This process of marginal evaluation is particularly important in the plan formulation process.

Let me expand this a little further. We have up to now talked about evaluation as a means of choosing between alternative plans. We generate alternative plans – say, six plans; we evaluate each of them; and we then choose one of them on the basis of this evaluation. This very simple way of looking at the evaluation process is open to much criticism. In particular, if there is not really very much to choose between the six plans, and there is a seventh plan somewhere which you have not formulated which is far better than any of the six, then it is a waste of time. The way to get over this, as other contributors have mentioned earlier, is to introduce a cyclical procedure. The key to this cyclical procedure is the process of marginal evaluation. This means looking at a plan and saying not how good it is in relation to other plans, but how it can be improved on the basis of the evaluation criteria.

Now, I have been accused of a lot of things, one of which is misusing linear programming and optimisation techniques. I ought to say a word on optimisation techniques at this stage. Clearly, if the evaluation process is a well defined one it should lead to a process of plan formulation which can be automated. In other words, if one has a set of objectives one wants to maximise and if one can combine these objectives, there should be a solution in terms of the values assigned to the decision variables which maximises the objectives. It should therefore not be necessary to generate alternatives in a simple sense.

Is there, then, any need for alternatives? Well, having done quite a bit of work on the techniques of optimisation in plan making, I have come to the conclusion that there probably is the need for alternatives for two quite separate reasons. The first reason is a purely technical one. If the evaluation process were simply a case of finding a set of linear indicators, then there would be a unique solution, that is, a global optimum that would be fairly easy to find. But the real world is not like this; urban systems are not linear. A process of optimisation from a given point would inevitably lead to a local optimum. For example, if we have a single decision variable and a criterion, then we must find the value assigned to this decision variable, and measure the goodness of the plan by our criterion. If we look at the whole solution space presented by this decision variable and map the relationship between this variable and the criterion continuously in a complex situation you would get something like the graph in Figure 1. Then in mathematical terms we have three optima and the only way of finding out which is the global optimum is by examining each of them.

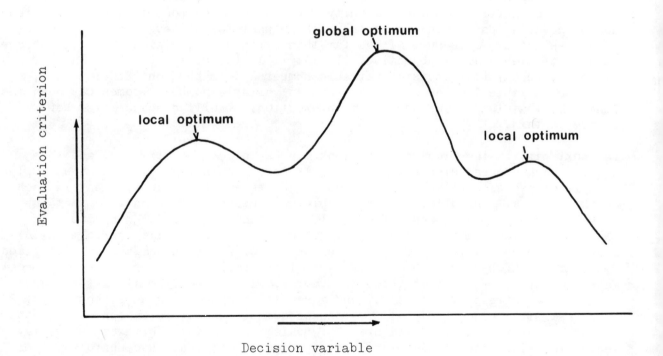

Figure 1   Relationship between an evaluation criterion and one decision variable

Obviously planning is far more complicated than this. There are many
decision variables. So, the process is obviously quite a complicated one,
and one suspects that local optima abound. I will give an example of this
in planning terms. There may be two decision alternatives for growth policy:
one of peripheral growth of existing settlements and one of growth based on
a new town policy. Clearly, within each of these strategies, one can envisage
a local optimum appearing: the best new town solution and the best peripheral
growth solution. The problem is generating these and choosing between them.
But, to look at this problem purely in terms of figures, is rather a simplistic,
mechanistic view of the planning process. There is also a need for alternatives
which arise from political objectives, the political intervention in the planning
process. Basically, this arises from the different ways of interpreting
criteria. Different weighting sets could be put on the criteria which must be
used to produce a global criterion of goodness. But it is more complicated
than this for there will be a lot of criteria involved in a particular plan
that cannot be quantified. This leads to more uncertainty as to which is the
best plan, and one needs to generate alternatives to explore these non-
quantifiable criteria.

The goals-achievement matrix technique

I would now like to look in a little more detail at some of the techniques of
evaluation. I am going to start by looking at what is probably the simplest
technique: the one that was used in the Coventry-Solihull-Warwickshire Sub-
Regional Study (1971). This is loosely referred to as a goals-achievement
matrix. Let us see how this technique is applied and what criticisms we can
level at it.

Table 1 shows a very simple example. Basically, one starts with a set of
objectives or goals. Here, I have suggested three objectives: to minimise
journey to work costs, to maximise residential amenity, and to maximise the
provision of services to the community. Let us also suppose that we have three
decision variables: three zones in which we want to put development. One then
puts a weighting, a measure of how far this particular decision variable achieves
this particular goal or objective. In matrix A, for example, in the case of goal
number 1, we say that decision variable number 2 does best onthis criterion,
decision variable 1 comes next and decision variable number 3 comes way down the
line. So that is part of the input information. I will discuss later how we
arrive at this.

The next part of the process is to look at the policies (matrix B), and here
again I have chosen three alternative policies. Again we will look at a simple
example of decision variables 1, 2 and 3, as the amount of development in each
of three zones. In policy 1, for example, we put most of the development in
zone 1. By a simple process of multiplication and addition we can combine
these two tables (matrices A and B) to find out how each policy performs with
respect to each goal. For example, ten units for decision variable 1 multiplied
by 12 gives the performance of that part of the policy with respect to that goal.
Matrix C gives a summary of these two tables, we can see from it that policy 1
does best with respect to goal 1, and also with respect to goal 2, but policy 2
does best with respect to goal 3. Then we compact this information even further
by looking at the relative weighting of goals (matrix D). For example, we may
decide to value amenity twice as much as accessibility, and access to services
three times as much as amenity. Thus, by the same process that we got matrix C
from A and B, we now get matrix E from C and D. This gives us an overall
summary of the particular policy in terms of the goals we have set ourselves.

Matrix A

		Goal		
		1	2	3
	1	12	12	6
Decision	2	15	10	12
Variable	3	5	8	8

Matrix B

		Policy		
		1	2	3
	1	10	7	5
Decision	2	4	5	1
Variable	3	3	5	11

Matrix C (AxB)

		Policy		
		1	2	3
	1	195	184	130
Goal	2	184	174	158
	3	132	142	130

Matrix D

		Weighting Set		
		1	2	3
	1	1	1	1
Goal	2	2	1	2
	3	3	2	1

Matrix E (CxD)

		Weighting Set		
		1	2	3
	1	959	643	695
Policy	2	958	642	674
	3	936	548	576

Table 1   A goals achievement matrix

We can introduce alternative weighting sets. There may be other weighting sets we wish to consider, and there are two ways at arriving at these. First of all, the Coventry-Solihull-Warwickshire Study's method was to generate a plan that places more emphasis on one objective, say amenity, than any other. Alternatively, this could be a way of introducing the way the plan affects different sections of the community. We could say that one weighting set represents the interests of a particular section of the population, and another represents the way another section would weight them. So, what we have done is to look at each of the three policies, apply the weighting sets, and get a summary measure for each policy against each weighting set. We find that policy number one, for example, does marginally better than two, and much better than all of them under every weighting set. So, conveniently, we come to the stage of saying that policy number one comes out best in all weighting sets and therefore must be the best policy. We have found it; let us publish it, and away we go.

This is precisely what happened in the Coventry-Solihull-Warwickshire case. I do not think it was quite as blatant as that, but certainly one of the policies did better under every set of conditions than practically every other policy. This makes one a little suspicious of this as a technique. It is a fairly easy technique to understand and it is a fairly easy technique to use. You could even do it without the use of a computer.

This goals-achievement technique is the one that has been most widely used by practising planners. We have heard several people lamenting that there are all these techniques being developed in all these research establishments and nobody is using them, and if we look out into the field we find practising planners using their own techniques. It is not that the techniques are not being used, it is just that there is a gap between the techniques that are being developed in research establishments and the techniques being actually used by practising planners.

The criticisms of this sort of technique are fairly obvious. It is far too simplistic an approach; it assumes certain linear relationships; it assumes that no matter how much development one puts in a particular area, the return will still be the same per unit of development. It does not really help us with the important non-linear relationships that occur in real life. In particular, it cannot cope very well with the whole problem of transportation, which is essentially a non-linear problem. It is entirely subjective. You can apply a gloss of public participation to it, but I suspect not very successfully. At the end of the day, it involves six planners sitting round a table and arguing over what number they are putting against which objective. I suspect – although I have not really worked it through – that the assumptions one makes at this stage are absolutely critical to the end result and it is not sufficient to say intuitively that zone 2 is better than zone 1 on this particular objective or goal, and therefore put a number 15. It may be absolutely critical whether the number is 15, 16 or 17, albeit all of these numbers are higher than the other two we have selected.

There is also the problem with the weighting set. A feature of the Coventry-Solihull-Warwickshire study was that the weighting sets, although different, were not very different. Again, this leads to the inevitable result that one plan comes out better than all the rest.

The other interesting sidelight on this sort of technique is that if this is the only technique used for evaluating a plan, then the best plan could be found analytically from these criteria. In fact it is a traditional linear programming problem. One has an objective which one wants to maximise; one has the objective function stated explicitly; one has a set of constraints; and for each of these alternative weighting sets, one can generate a best alternative plan. Why was this not done? I suspect the reason it was not done, apart from the fact that possibly they did not know much linear programming, was the danger, despite all the work that was put into these objectives, one could come up with a plan that seemed to maximise the achievement of the objectives and still be a not very satisfactory plan. This leads me to suspect that an awful lot of the evaluation in a plan-making process is done subjectively at the plan formulation stage. One is careful not to formulate unsatisfactory plans, although one does not say explicitly at that stage what makes a plan satisfactory.

So this really, I think, leads me to an important criterion for evaluation techniques. One should look at an evaluation technique to say "What will happen if we use this evaluation criterion and we test it to destruction? If more of this means a better plan, what sort of plan is the 'best' possible plan based on this criterion or set of criteria?" In other words, we should judge evaluation techniques by their ability, when taken to their logical conclusion, to produce good plans. The goals-achievement technique is a useful technique in its place. It is very useful at sub-regional study level for sorting out coarse objectives at a fairly high level. It is probably a useful technique for clarifying ideas, but – as I have indicated – it is a technique with a lot of limitations.

I want now to go on to discuss some other evaluation techniques, and in particular some of the work that we have been doing on the development of evaluation techniques on this sort of basis.

I think inevitably the criticism that one can level at this sort of technique is that it does not really make explicit the measurement, if you like, of achievement or objectives. You know, it is all very well to sit around and say "You know looking at this plan, it looks as though it is a better plan", or "Looking at this particular variable, it looks as if it will do better under this criterion, namely accessibility". But, if this is entirely subjective, it may in fact be wrong however one defines this. It would be nice I think to be able to come up with some more objective measurement of goal achievement. I should hasten to add that I am not suggesting that if one measures it it is necessarily right, but at least it is slightly more objective, if not entirely so.

Cost modelling

I want to talk about two sorts of technique. First I want to talk about cost modelling, because this really is the simplest to understand. Now clearly whatever one's views are on the planning process and evaluation generally, it would seem a good idea to work out the capital cost implications of a plan. Even if one is not using this as a criterion for selection, at least it is useful simply to say whether or not the plan is going to be feasible. It is useless to produce a policy that involves vast expenditure when the money is just not going to become available. So, from that very mundane consideration, cost modelling is probably a useful tool, but obviously one can develop this further and weave it into the evaluation process.

The sort of cost model I want to discuss, very briefly, is one that a number of people have developed. We have developed one at the Unit, and I think Vorhees have developed one. Basically it is concerned with the analysis of sewerage costs. This is a very mundane sort of subject, but it is worth explaining. One of the major public expenditure components in some plans is likely to be the development of the main drainage required for the plan and different plans can lead to different costs under this head. It must be an important part of evaluation to make this more explicit. The sort of model that we have developed is fairly simple in concept. One sets out with an existing area which typically has an existing drainage network. If further development is going to take place on the periphery of this area, this network has to be extended, so we introduce possible extensions. We should, in theory at least, be able to find out what are the sizes and gradients of the pipes, and we should be able to work out from this their capacity in terms of flow. The second stage is to look at the proposed land use distribution, and to translate this into discharge into the sewerage system. We relate this to the sewerage system, and where there is an excess of flow against capacity it makes a case for either a new link or the duplication of the existing link. We can cost these alternatives.

This is a very simple concept but there are a number of problems. First, there is the simple problem of engineering design. The criteria that are used for designing new sewerage systems are not necessarily those that one would use for working out the capacity of existing systems, simply because engineers have the habit of putting in safety factors. You quite often find that existing systems which theoretically should be flooding are not, simply because of the safety factor element. But there is a rather deeper problem than this, which I had not realised until I actually tried to do this. I imagined that every Borough Engineer knew where his sewers were, and in fact this is just not the case. They know that they disappear at various points and they know that certain other sewers appear at various other points, but short of sending a man down, they really do not know how the two link up. Data is lacking on this and it presents an awful lot of problems.

The other problem is that actual sewerage systems are far more complex than a simple diagram would suggest. So here is probably a substantial cost, but a lot of work may have to be done before one can make it explicit. It is very useful if you can make it explicit. The costing can be extended to incorporate marginal evaluation: that is, one can trace back to where one is duplicating links, and find the area of development that requires this duplication and, therefore, the implications of adding still further development to these areas. In other words, one can make explicit the marginal costs for development, and again this might be a useful tool in plan formulation. This is an example of the sort of thing which we can do in evaluation cost modelling.

Behavioural models in evaluation

I would like to bring this chapter to a close by discussing an important approach to evaluation which ties up with a lot of the discussion we had earlier. This is the place of behavioural models in evaluation. I am going to try and describe this in terms of a very simple numerical model. I would stress that this is a simple numerical model for explanation purposes; it is not a working model and I do not intend to go out into the field and apply this model. It is simply to give you the feel of how the behavioural models tie up with evaluation, and how there is a very strong link between them. Just in passing, I would say that in Marcial's talk earlier, he drew the distinction which I do not think exists, between the economic approach and the social physics approach. In fact there is a very close tie-up between behaviour in the market, the values that people put on alternatives, and the Lowry-type model which really can be shown to be a model of this behaviour in aggregate.

What I have suggested here is that we have three sites for housing and we have twenty households looking at these three sites. If it were possible to ask people how they would value, how much they would be prepared to pay to live in each of three types of houses on three sites, one might very well get the result shown in Table 2. Person number 1 would say he would be prepared to pay 76 units, whatever these are, to live in a house on Site A, 92 units for a house on Site B and 105 units for a house on Site C. The important thing about the housing market is that different people value the same house in different ways. A young couple with three children at primary school are obviously going to put a fairly high value on living in a house relatively close to a primary school, whereas an old-age pensioner is going to put a very low value on this particular aspect and therefore this particular site. What happens in fact is that a preference emerges. We have assumed, very simply, that the houses are freely available and that there will be enough houses to satisfy whatever preference emerges, and a certain preference does emerge.

Person	Site A	Site B	Site C
1	76	92	105*
2	85	111*	90
3	92	88	101*
4	72	81	91*
5	77	86	104*
6	97*	82	82
7	73	90	101*
8	87	91	96*
9	60	76	114*
10	92	109*	100
11	80	84	97*
12	80	81	111*
13	90	67	106*
14	89	99*	93
15	65	95	98*
16	77	85	111*
17	65	98	98*
18	84	96	103*
19	67	99	100*
20	97	97*	95
Total values	1604	1806	1996
Mean values	80	90	100
Total persons preferring to live on each site	1	4	15
Mean benefit derived from preferred distribution	97	104	102.4

Table 2   Assumed value placed on each site by each person (* denotes the site on which a person places the highest value)

We can deduce two things from this very simple example. First of all we can find out what the average value that people put on the site is, and we see that Site A has the lowest average value, Site C has the highest - 80, 90 and 100. The other thing is we can look at the preferences. I have put a little asterisk beside those people who prefer to live in a particular site, and we find that the preference follows a pattern. One person prefers to live in Site A, four people in Site B and fifteen people in Site C. In other words, very simply, most people prefer to live in the site with the highest mean value, and if we take this a little further and define this mean value as a measure of the attractiveness of the site - the average value that the whole community are prepared to put on a particular site - we can say that more people prefer to live in the most attractive site, but not everybody. This is important.

We can make a further deduction from this example. If we take the average value after people have located themselves, we can consider this as a benefit. If we add all the figures with an asterisk, and divide by 15, 4, 1 in these columns, we can get a measure of the average benefit that people who choose to live in these houses would derive. We can see that there is a difference between the attractiveness, the mean perceived values, and the derived benefit, and in fact the economist will recognise this as related to, although not directly a measure of, consumer surplus.

I have said that when people go into the houses in accordance with their preference, the value of the house becomes a benefit. I have added the figures with the asterisk and divided by the number of people to get an average. Now, if we say in the simple example that all the people work in the same place, we can add to this another factor - the journey to work cost (Table 3).

Site	Cost of journey to work
A	10
B	5
C	25

Table 3   Journey to work cost from each site

If we subtract the journey to work costs from the initial net value, we get Table 4. Here, the mean net value is slightly different because although Site C is the most attractive, it is also the least accessible, so that the net value falls below that of Site B, and Site A still remains the least valued site. Again, we can work out the preference on this basis. We can derive an average benefit in exactly the same way. This simple numerical example indicates the way people locate themselves in proportion to a measure of attractiveness and, inversely, to the cost of travel to work. Exactly the same sort of hypothesis was built into the Lowry model, but here we have looked at it in an economic way. But what we are really interested in is not the attractiveness necessarily or even the attractiveness less the cost of travel to work as our measure of return, but the measure at the bottom in which there is a discrepancy. In other words, these values will change as people exercise their right to choose where they are going to live and as they move to the sort of areas which they personally value most of all.

Finally in Table 5 we look at what happens when we restrict supply. We have said that the distribution that occurs in the absence of any restriction is 1, 15, 4 to Sites A, B and C. If we now introduce a pricing mechanism - if we

Person	Site		
	A	B	C
1	66	87*	80
2	75	106*	65
3	82	83*	76
4	62	76*	66
5	67	81*	79
6	87*	77	57
7	63	85*	76
8	77	86*	71
9	50	71	89*
10	82	104*	75
11	70	79*	72
12	70	76	86*
13	80	62	81*
14	79	94*	68
15	55	90*	73
16	67	80	86*
17	55	93*	73
18	74	91*	78
19	57	94*	75
20	87	92*	70
Total net value	1404	1706	1497
Mean net value	70	85	75
Total persons preferring to live on each site	1	15	4
Mean benefit derived from preferred distribution	87	89.4	85.5

Table 4　Net value placed on each site by each person (* denotes the site on which a person places the highest net value)

Differential price between Site B and other sites	Persons changing preference	New preference	Total preference for houses in sites			Total benefit
			A	B	C	
0	–	–	1	15	4	1770
1	3	A	2	14	4	1769
2	5	C	2	13	5	1767
5	20	A	3	12	5	1762
7	1	C	3	11	6	1755
7	11	C	3	10	7	1748
9	7	C	3	9	8	1739
9	8	A	4	8	8	1730
10	4	C	4	7	9	1720
13	18	C	4	6	10	1707
15	14	A	5	5	10	1692
17	15	C	5	4	11	1675
19	19	C	5	3	12	1656
20	17	C	5	2	13	1636
22	10	A	6	1	13	1614
31	2	A	7	0	13	1583

Table 5　The effect of increasing the price of a house in Site B

make the houses in Site B more expensive than the other two sites — preference will shift. If the differential in price between Site B and the other two sites increases by more than one unit, then person number 3, who was more or less indifferent as to whether he went to A or B will now go from B to A because A becomes that much more attractive. Preferences will change. The important thing is that now the total benefit — the values that people put on it when they actually move into a house — will in fact go down. As we increase the pricing level of site B with respect to the other two, the benefit will go down and the demand will go down until eventually nobody would wish to live in Site B because the price is so high.

I have been looking here at the behavioural aspects of the housing market, especially those modelled by a Lowry-type model and its close relative the simple transportation model. We begin to see that we can interpret this model to yield a measure of benefit. This is really measuring the way that people respond to the housing stock that is available in the market, the sort of values that they put on it and the benefit they derive from it. I would have liked to have said a bit more than that, but perhaps we can bring further points in in the discussion.

In conclusion, I would like to suggest that evaluation really boils down to looking at the sort of constraints that the planning process applies on the market. In other words, one can hypothesise that the housing market, imperfect though it may be in some senses, represents an optimum in the sense that people are moving into the sort of houses they would like to move in and houses are being provided. The planning process basically is concerned with applying constraints on this process in such a way as to reduce the benefit that people derive. It may conceivably be doing this for other reasons, for example, to minimise public expenditure. That is a point we could discuss later.

The place for evaluation
in the planning design process

Robert Cheesman

What is the context for new town design and what place has evaluation within the ensuing design process?

A study of the British new town design process[*] reveals that many evaluation processes have been developed and applied 'after the fact', i.e. their main – and often only – application is in selecting the 'best' plan from a number of intuitively derived alternatives. Such evaluation employs blanket and subjective value judgements without considering the important issues in detail. If a rational and systematic process of generating designs is used, evaluation can be applied as an integral part of the process, providing a detailed check against desirable performance standards.

It is also apparent that the subject matter of the evaluation often fails to reflect the original stated objectives of the planners. While this could be due in part to the fact that plans may be evaluated by a different set of people with different frames of reference to the original set of planners, more often, the fault arises from the general absence of a clear and comprehensive specification – a pre-requisite in any rational process of design synthesis.

In presenting alternative plans, there are few clear references to the methods used in combining the physical and spatial components of the urban system. As well as making explicit the method used in each case, evaluation should reflect the decision priorities that are established during the design process.

The design problem

If we make a broad survey of the evaluation process, as Jean Perraton has done in the preceding paper, we cannot help but obtain an insight into the design processes that have been applied, because evaluation is almost always an integral part of those processes. Alexander (1964) has simply defined the design problem as a complex, two directional interaction between the context and the form. Alexander's illustration (Figure 1) represents a static and finite problem. "It is based on the idea that every design problem begins with an effort to achieve fitness between two entities; the form in question and its context. The form is the solution to the problem; the context defines the problem. In other words, when we speak of design, the real object of discussion is not the form alone, but the ensemble comprising the form and its context." (Alexander 1964).

---

* During 1971, the New Towns' Study was established at the Centre for Land Use and Built Form Studies with the aim of comparing initially the physical and spatial characteristics of all the British new towns as designed. This is described so far in three publications (Lindsay et al. 1971, Cheesman et al. 1971, and Porzecanski et al. 1971).

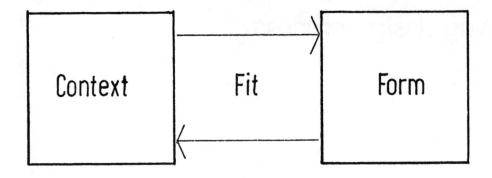

Figure 1   The design problem

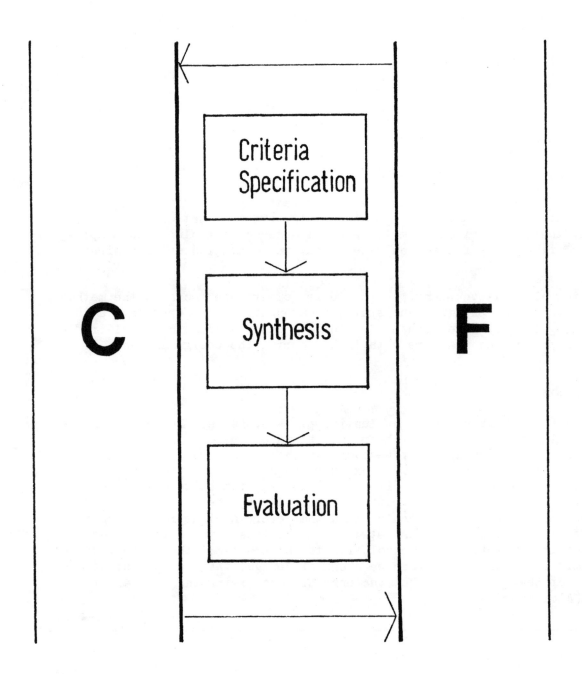

Figure 2   The design process

Design methodology and development

Essentially design methodology, or the fitting process, comprises three continuous phases which are in no way discrete (Figure 2).

1   Criteria specification
2   Synthesis
3   Evaluation

Certainly these phases are applied consciously or unconsciously to a greater or lesser degree in every design problem.

Within the New Town Study, it was possible to follow the development of the design process relevant to the new towns over the past twenty five odd years. In this time the process has become more sophisticated possibly as a result of the increasing amount of experience and information available, as well as the increased research and interest in the new towns.

Let us briefly study the design development periods.

For the first new towns possibly up to Cwmbran the criteria specification involved establishing basic social and physical needs in terms of stock. These depended heavily on suggestions outlined by Lord Reith (Ministry of Town and Country Planning 1946) such as the number of schools, pubs and churches required, and in addition conformed to broadly defined space and location standards, especially those relating to open space. The synthesis involved the intuitive juxtapositioning of these quantities, while evaluation was the subjective assessment of the resultant land use plan with little or no reassessment of the criteria after evaluation and only a partial redesign cycle (Figure 3).

In the second period the criteria specification benefited from earlier attempts. There developed a greater awareness of the need to define systematically planning goals and objectives, not only for land use but for population structure. The plan for Hook (London County Council 1961) is a good example in its use of many empirically derived standards. While the synthesis was still intuitive the evaluation phase experienced a radical departure from subjective assessment with the advent of evaluation techniques in the '60s.

Traffic assignment and gravity models became commonplace, as did cost benefit analysis, while simple simulation models of urban structure and activity were attempted with limited success in evaluating some plans. Irvine Development Corporation in their Master Plan of 1971 state that "for a number of reasons the model is not a satisfactory method in the context of the corporation's requirements for refining particular aspects of the selected plan." (Irvine Development Corporation 1971)

This development in evaluative techniques has increased the apparent cyclic nature of the design process (Figure 4). However, the intuitive nature of the synthesis phase, together with its time consuming graphic representations, still causes reluctance to reassess the basic criteria or goals. Hence there is still a tendency to prepare a limited number of alternative plans and systematically select the 'best' one, or that which nearest fits the criteria statement.

What have we gained from this apparent increase in sophistication in the design process? Do we honestly believe that there will be any real improvement in the end result of Skelmersdale over Basildon or Washington over East Kilbride other than possibly a few additional material benefits such as one or two extra trees

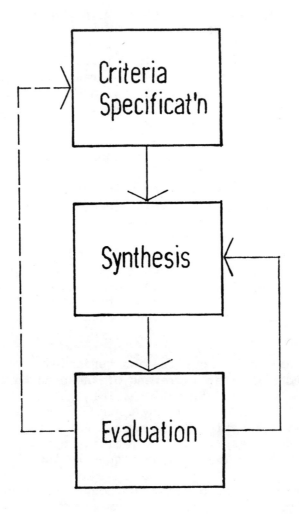

Figure 3   Process development − 1

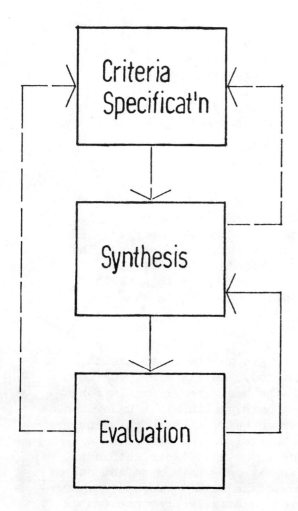

Figure 4   Process development - 2

or shops. Is it possible or even desirable to adopt a fundamental and systematic rationale in the design process, such that we follow through an iterative and complete process cycle to arrive at the best plan? (Figure 5)

I believe that new towns will continue to look and function like new towns unless we re-examine our principles.

Planning problems

I would like to elaborate here and discuss two problems which beset planners but which are certainly not unknown to most people here:

1   that most of us continue to think and design linearly, and

2   that we are unable to come to grips with the time element in design as it applies to all three phases – criteria specification, synthesis and evaluation.

Linear design

In dealing with linear design I am not so much referring to the non-cyclic nature of the design process as it is practised as to the tendency to think in hierarchical trees and nesting sets in all three phases of design. The diagram in Figure 6 must be familiar to many – a tree at the top, its equivalent Venn diagram of nested sets below. The axiom for this is that for any two sets in the group either one is wholly contained in the other or else they are wholly disjointed (Alexander 1965).

If we examine the criteria for at least the first 14 new towns there is a remarkable similarity which seems to have its origin wholly in the Reith Report (Ministry of Town and Country Planning 1946). In the mid 1940s Lord Reith's committee examined in reasonable depth the basic requirements for the new towns and established standards dealing mainly with stock under basic headings such as town size, designated area, green belt, main shopping centre, industrial zones, residential zones, etc. At this stage the committee did consider, to a small degree, the extent of overlap between these sets but this referred to their desirable spatial juxtaposition. This made the job of new town planners very simple. Reith had removed the need to reconsider overlap and had handed to the planners cut and dried, spatially preconceived nesting sets. In fact the committee's definitions of the three basic road types – radial, ring and residential – help to define these nesting sets even more clearly; they are containers around discrete zones. Such a situation could not encourage fundamental and rational judgement by the planners. This was dogma – the individual town criteria were established by it and the end results evaluated against it.

The organisation and administration of many planning departments has the same sort of influence – their tree structure is often a necessary and efficient means of getting the job done, but the lack of interaction between departments means that more often than not the integral parts are considered and prepared in relative isolation. In this situation, basic organisational premises and priorities prevent fundamental reconsideration and it follows that evaluation establishes its premises too high up the scale of clustered criteria.

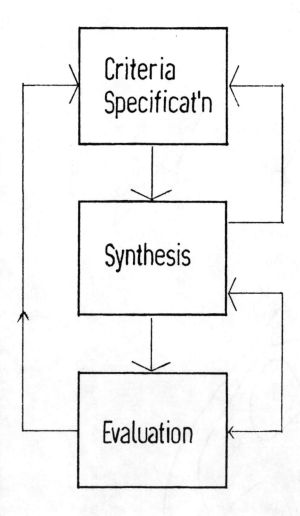

Figure 5   The complete design cycle

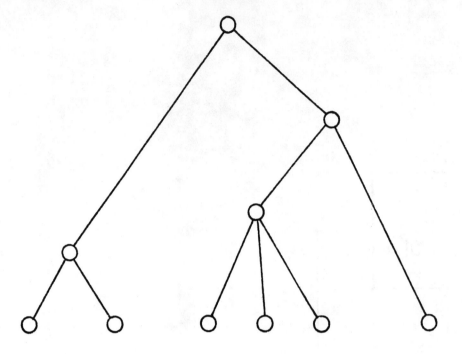

Tree

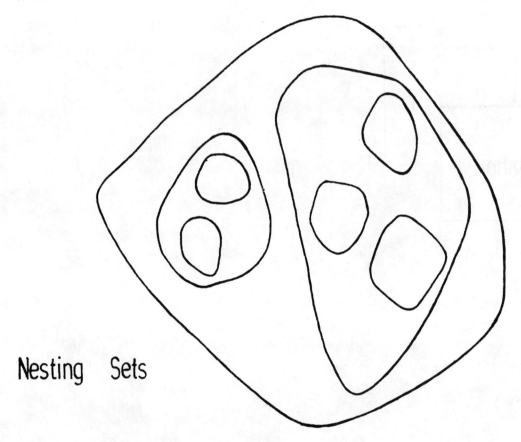

Nesting Sets

Figure 6   Tree and nesting sets

What of governmental spending and taxation policies? These are certainly organised in nesting sets and apply incredible constraints in defining spatial zones. It is hard to understand, for example, how a special development area boundary can be allowed to cut across a designated area boundary causing an inevitable concentration of industrial floor space in one location, as in Washington New Town. David Donnison (1967) has disoussed the government of housing, and it is not hard to see how the total preoccupation with the problems of financing, programming and erecting housing keeps it as a well defined and discrete set.

In cost benefit analysis, often used to select the 'best' plan from a number of alternatives (see, for example, Lichfield 1969), there are clear examples of the reduction of consumer benefit preference to principal residential areas, principal industrial areas, principal open space and recreational areas, central area and secondary centres. The nested evaluation sets reflect the nested criteria sets.

The recent Coventry–Solihull–Warwickshire Sub–regional Planning Study (1971) is a commendable and comprehensive attempt at defining systematically a regional development strategy. However in section 5 of the supplementary evaluation report No. 4 we see that it was necessary to rank strategy objectives. A questionnaire was prepared and "confined to town planners because at this stage we were concerned with the experience of professionals within the planning field ... The Study Team's mean rank scores were weighed by length of experience ... Having done this, the mean rank scores were examined relative to four natural groupings of the remaining preliminary objectives."

1   Land resource objectives
2   Residential location objectives
3   Economic activity objectives
4   Transportation objectives

Certainly it is necessary to weight objectives but why the need to form such discrete groups at an early stage?

Finally an example from the Department of the Environment's 'Information needs of the New Planning System' (S.D.D. and M.H.L.G. 1971). In section 5, which deals with planning decisions, we see that "In identifying the decision fields, we found that care was needed to remember that each was intended to illustrate a group of planning decisions. For example, housing or shopping are without doubt planning decision fields since the location, amount of land and so forth devoted to these purposes are matters on which the planner must formulate policies and make decisions." Such deterministic intuitive taxonomy pervades our most systematic attempts at evaluation.

I am quite sure that the artificiality of new town development is partly the product of this sort of approach and while it is often unavoidable, we should at least develop an honest sensitivity when confronted by an apparent need to consider nesting sets.

Static planning

In dealing with the time element in planning, we seem to continue to maintain a static approach probably because it is difficult to represent constantly evolving systems in terms of graphic morphological structures.

The British new towns are still too young to display any signs of decay and resulting deterioration of the local urban environment. In fact most are still moving towards maturity whilst shedding such causes of 'New Town blues' as unbalanced population structure, inadequate provision of social and recreational facilities, and uncoordinated activity relationships during the period of planned growth.

One might suppose that on reaching the planned target population, if no extension order is applied before the town has achieved maturity, its success as a town at this time is measured in financial terms, i.e. whether it is maintaining a favourable export/import ratio having paid back the original government advances. At this time, the corporation hands over all its responsibilities to the Commission for the New Towns. The New Towns Act (1965) states that "the Commission is incorporated for the purpose of taking over, holding, managing and turning to account the property previously vested in the development corporation" and in addition "it shall be the general duty of the Commission to maintain and enhance the value of the land held by them and the return obtained by them from it ..."

There is a strong indication that at this stage the desirable social and physical relationships within the town have low priority as it is assumed that by reaching the target population according to the master plan, the town should be in perfect harmony and running order. There is no indication of any further need for planners and in addition, to ensure continuing economic success and prosperity, the administration continues to attract manufacturing and service industries. East Kilbride is a town at present at this stage of growth.

The first new town master plans described in broad simplistic terms a desirable physical state of the town at the end of a period of natural growth, following the period of planned intake. I think most of us are aware that unless the town ceases to prosper as a result of say economic recession, there can be no end to the period of growth as it will continue to attract immigrants. Certainly it is folly to believe that at any stage in time a prosperous town will remain physically static after reaching a planned target, whether surrounded by a green belt or not and any design should attempt to reflect two important characteristics:

1   that by nature a town is an open ended situation and therefore should not be described by any ultimate finite form,

2   at any time during this continuous growth, the cybernetic processes within the town are attempting to reach an equilibrium.

Milton Keynes appears to be the only master plan to consider seriously these two characteristics (Llewelyn-Davies et al., 1970a). Here a series of balanced stages is considered a priority in maintaining social harmony within the town during its early period of accelerated growth. The Milton Keynes Development Corporation has developed a realistic plan to monitor and evaluate the growth of the town with the aim of facilitating continuous reassessment of the design criteria at any time, thereby maintaining an ongoing planning policy (Pearson 1970b). But in Cumbernauld there is evidence of the dangers which develop from abiding rigidly to a morphological concept, designed as an entity to function in its 'finite' form. The proposals for extension to the designated area appear incompatible and create previously unconsidered problems of balance and accessibility in relation to existing activities. In fact it could be shown that such an entity will invariably inhibit any attempts at extension in much the same way as Frank Lloyd Wright's Guggenheim museum defies extension. Finally to this point, it is interesting that one of the stated main aims of the Hook report was that "the town should have a coherent structure, easy to understand ... The main elements of the plan should be arranged to assist the design of the town as an entity" (L.C.C. 1961).

I think that at the structure plan design stage we should pay less attention to the formal graphic patterns of the plan, and a lot more attention to the interacting elements of the system, and that includes the people.

The problems presented by static planning and tree thinking may be summarised: if the criteria specification is deterministic then both the synthesis and evaluation stages, however sophisticated, will reflect that determinism and no amount of cyclic iteration towards optimization can markedly improve the situation, unless of course the evaluations are based on a different set of criteria.

Even if the criteria are fundamental non-deterministic objectives, and even if we evaluate our plans against these for one point in time (the entity state), the result of the evaluations will give little indication of the actual performance of the town through time.

A complex dynamic system

What then is the context for the design process and the place of evaluation within the process? Certainly it involves lattice thinking and dynamic planning and possibly more informal growth patterns and possibly even a permissive planning team.

I should like to diverge briefly and discuss a tribe of natives in the New Guinea central highlands (reported by Rapaport 1971). The Tsembaga are an agrarian society, planting vegetable gardens in small clearings in the tropical rain forest to provide 99% of their everyday diet.

To prepare a garden, the underbush is roughly cut, smaller trees felled and thick trees are stripped of limbs and left standing. The resulting debris is burned which, of course, liberates mineral nutrients in the cut vegetation. Logs are used to build fences and retain soil on sloping ground. As planting stock the Tsembaga primarily use cuttings and amazingly they name at least 264 varieties of edible plants, representing some 36 species.

Now unlike modern specialised agricultural processes, the species are not segregated by rows or sections (discrete sets) but are intricately inter-mingled, so that as they mature, the garden becomes stratified and the plants make maximum use of surface area and of variations in vertical dimensions. For example, taro and sweet potato tubers mature just below the surface; the casavata root lies deeper and yams are deepest of all. A mat of sweet potato leaves covers the soil at ground level. The taro leaves project above this mat; the hibiscus and sugar cane stand higher still, and the fronds of the banana spread out above the rest.

In this complex ecosystem, the successful species are not those that merely capture energy more efficiently than their competitors but those that sustain the species supporting them. Needless to say, harvesting is a gradual and partial process which allows the plants to recover in the interval between successive harvestings.

Apart from achieving high photosynthetic efficiency, the system has many scientific and ecological advantages which are extremely interesting but not relevant here. The significant point, for this discussion, is that the Tsembaga have demonstrated an intuitive understanding of the surrounding rain forest by imitating its organic, dynamic and diverse structure in the design of their gardens. They have not tried to control growth with blanket constraints to some predetermined pattern but understood the system and given it positive and permissive direction. The economics of this planning system lie in the fact (as proven by Rappaport) that the gross expenditure in energy units is more than balanced by the return in nutrient energy. The success of the system is reflected in the survival of the tribe as a healthy and happy ethnic group.

Of course, this is a simplistic analogy and if we try to draw too much from it we are sure to find conflict but it does have its relevance.

The dynamic design context

I should now like to outline a dynamic context for design, and within this to discuss not only the evaluation phase, but also criteria specification and synthesis.

We have already suggested that the design problem is a fitting process, and that fitting process or methodology is made up of three phases: criteria specification, synthesis and evaluation. The dynamic context can be described by an infinite series of static problems or finite states (see Cheesman 1971); a parallel to this is the process of integration in calculus. Thus in Figure 7 we have a series of problem fits through time

$$P_0, P_1, P_2, \ldots P_n$$

The increments of time are given by d_t. The form F_0 is the fitted problem solution for Context C_0 over a period increment say $2d_t$. At the end of time period t_1, the original problem statement C_0 is reassessed in the light of the developed form F'_0 and a modified statement C_1 is the context for problem fit P_1 resulting in a projected problem solution F_1.

It can be seen then that the series

$C_0, C_1, C_2, \ldots C_n$	represents the change in problem statement resulting from a change in demand.
$F_0, F_1, F_2, \ldots F_n$	represents the change in projected distribution of stock and activities
$F'_0, F'_1, F'_2, \ldots F'_n$	represents the observed change in activity and stock distribution

Thus we have an open ended dynamic design process. It is significant to note that we probably never realise the idealised or projected series F_0, F_1, etc. This is because while our administrative organisation and programming

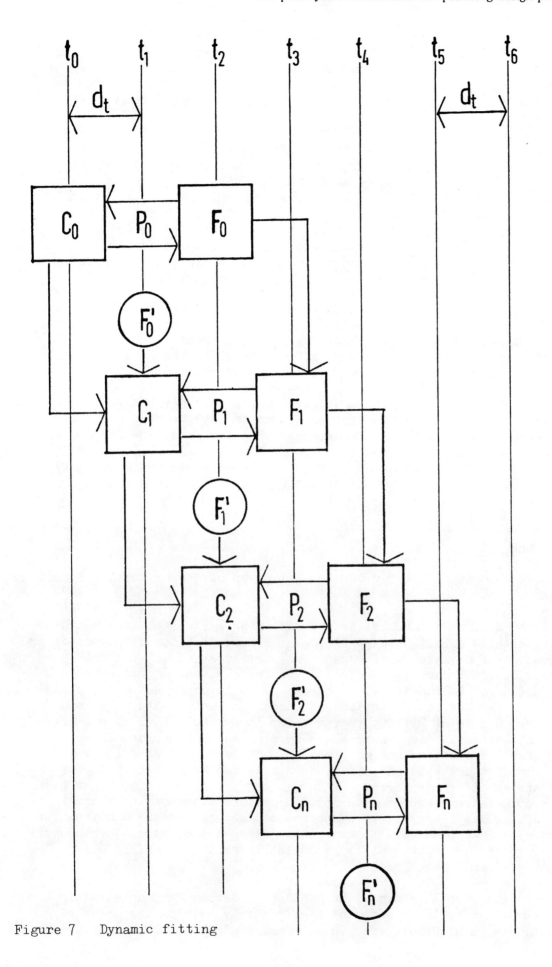

Figure 7   Dynamic fitting

is based on this series, every new individual proposal for development is assessed against the criteria specification prior to location. The benefits of the location both to the development and to the rest of the system are carefully assessed and if desirable, the location is changed and thus the series of actual development F'_0, F'_1, etc. differ from the projected series F_0, F_1, etc.

The time increment d_t depends solely on the efficiency of the administrative and organisation processes but ideally it should be the smallest increment of time which allows planning to keep ahead of the evolution of the urban system or as often as necessary to keep the planning criteria up to date. The increment need not be constant and it is quite feasible that it could increase with deceleration of the town's growth rate. Within the process, the resulting form F'_n could be a totally free solution, or conform to a predetermined structure plan, depending on the number of inflexible criteria carried over in the context series; but too much inflexibility would defeat the purpose of the exercise.

Obviously such an idealised process raises implementation problems. For example, we can hardly be expected to pull up and relay roads in different locations just because desirable patterns of accessibility change with time. There is, however, a compromise between the theory and reality.

Certainly this process in operation should give us, as planners, more confidence and understanding based on rational judgement. We need not necessarily resort to blanket controls and deterministic sets. We can establish our criteria within a specification of fundamental elements and we can more realistically discuss and design for the overlaps which actually occur in the urban system, i.e. we can consider intersecting sets and semi lattices (Figure 8).

Criteria specification

I would now like to comment briefly on the setting up of the criteria specification.

When an architect designs a hospital as a functioning system, he is concerned about many criteria to do with that building. He needs to consider types of materials, quantities of materials, capacities, services and in fact with unlimited scale he would have to consider an infinite number of elements. But the building would not be functional or habitable if it could not accommodate the occupants and the desired activities of those occupants. Its measure of success is in the degree of utility provided for those occupants. There are patients and patient activities, nurses and nursing activities, chemists, researchers, janitors, porters and many more. Each one receives utility in the degree of comfort and even satisfaction experienced as a result of clever synthesis of the specified criteria. If the system were perfect it might be possible to provide each occupant with optimum satisfaction but the reality of the situation presents many types of dependent and independent constraints: spatial constraints, environmental constraints, financial constraints, and very often the pure geometrical constraints presented by criteria conflict – incompatible performance requirements.

Now if the architect were a pessimist he could consider as many constraints as possible and design by the constraints, effectively eliminating the need for a decision between alternatives. These constraints would also provide

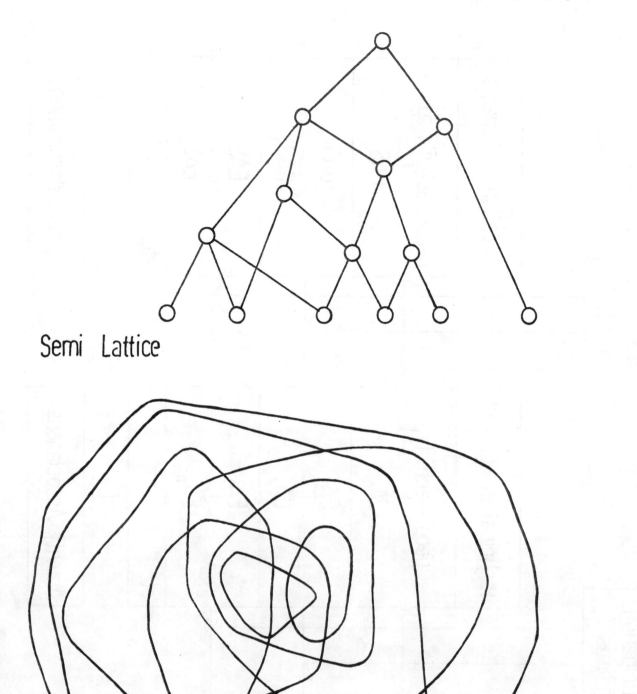

Semi Lattice

Intersecting Sets

Figure 8   Semi lattice and intersecting sets

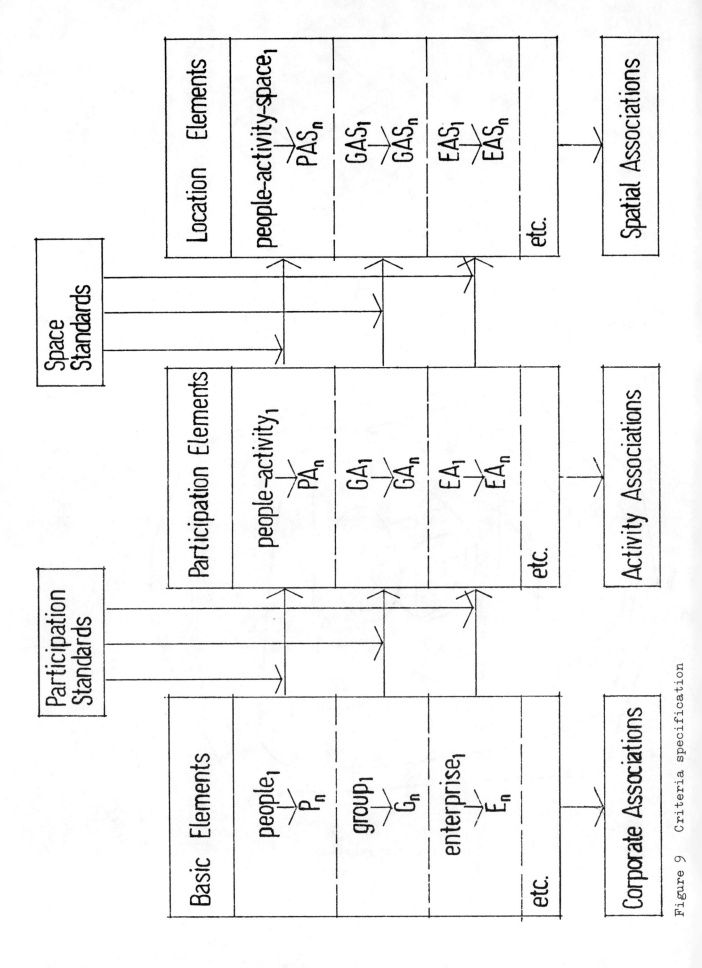

Figure 9   Criteria specification

him with a useful armoury of excuses in the event that occupants aired their dissatisfaction with particular situations. I should prefer to think that the architect could think positively, possibly a little idealistically, so that his first move would be to investigate the desirable requirements of all the individuals involved and consider the constraints when they become a reality. Of course, to simplify his task we would have to allow him to consider types of individuals and even types of groups of individuals, but I would hope he maintained a certain sensitivity and awareness of the dangers of preconceived nesting sets.

The point of this analogy is that in setting up the criteria specification for a town, or any urban development for that matter, our first fundamental concern should be the individuals or if we must, types of individuals and types of groups, that may occupy the town.

We are all familiar with demographic studies, but these are so often a means for estimating more accurately the possible stock requirements (meaning spatial quantities) for the development and we know that it is easier to cost stock than people and certainly the geometry of stock is easier to handle in graphic representations. This is the stuff of master plan maps.

Milton Keynes Development Corporation spent some time researching the demographic base of their proposed urban occupants (Llewelyn-Davies et al., 1970b).   But it appears that the real application of this detailed study is in housing development and it has only superficial use in estimating the desirable requirements for other urban activities. While it is necessary to consider the urban individuals, and their requirements, in terms of socio-economic groups, (SEG), such groups do not necessarily reflect the individual needs of the town. The age/sex distribution table of Milton Keynes population suggests that in 1989 approximately 30% of the population of 235,000 will be in the 0-14 age group;   but in the plan, the spatial amenities for these individuals tend to be distributed by rule of thumb.

Dr Mark Abrams (1964) has examined the way in which the population as a whole spend their time and money, and has concluded that stage in family cycle is a more significant variable than SEG. How best we represent the needs of the individual in a criteria specification is open to debate, and Ray Pahl has dealt with this matter is detail. Certainly it is central to the theme of planning for people.

The idea that a criteria specification can be a long list of confused goals and objectives worries me because this is hardly conducive to systematic rationale at the synthesis stage. I see the specification as being a statement of the fundamental elements of the urban system, together with their desirable quantities and desirable interactions and associations. Figure 9 shows the subdivision of the criteria into

1   Basic elements
2   Participation elements
3   Location elements

This subdivision can occur for both consumers and producers in the system. Within each subdivision there is a lattice of desirable interactions which can be recorded in quantifiable terms in a matrix form. Also, within each sub-division we can identify desirable constraints and realistic constraints. For example, constraints to location elements may be spatial restrictions and cost restrictions while cost restrictions and sociological restrictions may be relevant to participation elements. It can be seen that many elements are dependent and tend to occur in successions of dependencies. If the information resources available do not suggest a desirable standard for a particular requirement, then we can derive one, objectively or subjectively, and design for this; or we can record the fact that we did not adopt a standard or design for this particular elemental requirement.

One point of this record is that if we are to adopt a policy of criteria reassessment as suggested in the dynamic planning context then we must have a clear and comprehensive base for reference. Also, such a base, which defines between types of criteria, is a more meaningful aid for rational methodology in synthesis.

Synthesis

The process of syntehsis or combination of the elements in accordance with desirable criteria using mathematical processes can never be achieved success-fully in a one-shot operation nor would it be desirable to attempt such an operation. Allen Scott (1971) states that "clearly it is beyond any known mathematic or computational process to define an optimum over all the systems which exist in a single town". We have only to look to unsuccessful attempts to see the difficulties involved.[*] However, Scott optimistically discusses the effective analysis and planning of realistic combinatorial systems in geographic space, using combinatorial programming methods. Now it is true that such methods can be extremely powerful in solving small well-behaved problems; so essentially the procedure is to define small problems such that synthesis is achieved using a set of optimizing models with heuristic interface. We are bound, therefore, to organise clusters of elements for progressive suboptimization according to priorities established from the criteria specification. The taxonomy involved has been studied by both Philip Tabor and Michael Batty (see Tabor 1970 and Batty 1971).

It is most important though, within the dynamic planning process, to maintain a record of the procedure adopted in the synthesis so that successive syntheses can imitate or reassess and improve the previous procedure.

Evaluation

Now within the design process so far I have suggested the need to establish a criteria specification which details the desirable performance requirements for individual elements, and it has been shown that in synthesis we need to adopt a taxonomic methodology for establishing sets of elements for successive suboptimization. The success of the synthesis therefore lies in correlating the measured performance of the individual elements of the form with the recorded desirable performance requirements in the specification. This is evaluation in the planning design process. By changing the synthesis methodology we achieve a different form but the performance of this also can be checked against the original specification. It would be dangerous to adopt a different form of evaluative procedure as it could negate the criteria adopted. The procedure suggested in theory measures the success of one plan, and in the same way this evaluation would facilitate selection of the best policy direction from two or more planning proposals.

---

[*]   The Local Government Operational Research Unit (Reading) attempted to establis an objective function for a 'one-shot' operation development plan for Macclesfield and district, in Cheshire, which proved unsuccessful (Farnsworth 1969).

Conclusions

During the course of this paper, I have given what may appear to be an improperly small amount of time to the actual process of evaluation within the planning design process. But too often we have seen evaluation processes applied which are rather pointless and have little effect on an already determined plan and planning policy. Therefore, the emphasis here has been in showing how true evaluation must be considered as an integral part and set in context within the total scope of the planning design process, and certainly at no time acting as a detached function of that process.

For any specific planning problem, we must first design a relevant planning process. But the main point is that whatever methods we adopt, we should take care to see that they are relevant, rational, recorded, and reflect the fundamental requirements of the people.

Evaluating urban form

Walton Lindsay

The purpose of this chapter is to demonstrate how the urban system model can be used in some form of experimental way to help with the design and evaluation of urban forms. There are four sections :

i)   a brief description of the model and the policies which were explored, and a comparison of the resulting distributions;

ii)   a discussion of the types of evaluation;

iii) an analysis of the effects of each policy on a set of evaluation indicators; and

iv)   a general comparison of all these policies.

The structure of the model has been discussed by David Crowther, and the diagram he presented (page 98) shows the interdependence between the input data and the output. Once the model has been fully tested it can be used as an experimental tool by systematically changing the inputs to correspond to some changes in planning policy. The effects of the different results can then be observed and compared. The set of inputs in the flow diagram are basic employment distribution, available land and roads. The outputs are floor space, residential and service populations and flows. The model is also calibrated with a set of parameters which control the overall labour and service rates, the demands for floor space and the mean journey to work and service trip lengths.

The experiments and results

This paper presents an analysis of two of the inputs shown in the model and examines their effects upon the distributions of population and floorspace. The inputs examined were the shape of the town, expressed in terms of development land, and the policy of basic employment location. The road network was varied slightly to suit the land patterns. The parameters and ratios were also set constant; these were derived from new towns data for towns of the same size. Figure 1 shows the 16 layouts which were used in the experiment. They are all highly theoretical. Each has a similar area of nine square kilometre cells and a population of 100,000. The plans can be divided into four land types (A, B, C, D) and each of these has four different policies for employment (1-4). The land pattern can be categorised as follows: type A is a radial town with centralised roads; type B is a semi-linear grouping of the cells with a double strand road system; type C is a linear system; type D is a ring structure with the road network connecting - the lines showing the connections between the road networks.

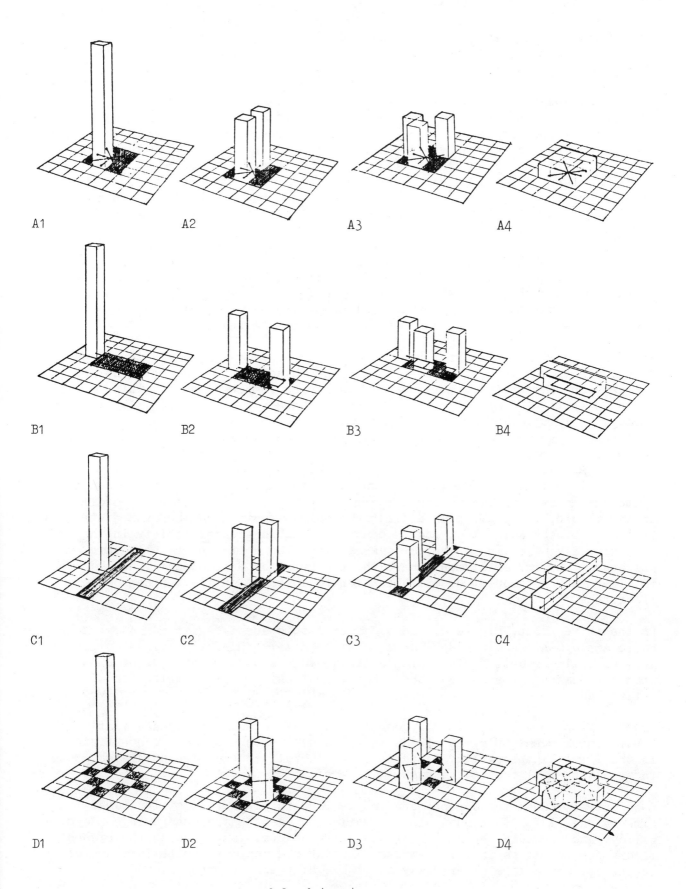

Figure 1   Basic employment and land inputs

Figure 1 also shows the location of basic employment, the second of the input variables. Here it was decided to explore a variation in the distribution of employment rather than adopt a single policy of location. The distributions varied from a policy of concentration (1), two-site location (2), three-site location (3) and dispersal.

It was not intended to maintain identical employment distributions with each town since the constraints imposed by shape affected the location of basic employment. The single site where a variety of positions was possible was located on the edge of the development as in early new towns. As the number of sites increased (2, 3 and 4) the relative location was controlled by the available land. This is clear in the most dispersed category 4 where the relation of the nine sites is entirely determined by the shape of each town. It is one of the aims of this exercise to examine these differences in employment location.

The model was then run for these 16 layouts and the results can be seen in Figures 2, 3, 4 and 5. Each figure distinguishes the four categories of town shape (A-D) and the results of the employment types are separated on four lines (1-4). The outputs are the residential population, the floor area, the services and the flows. Let us look at these results more closely.

Group A (Figure 2), the first group of results shows very clearly the effects of a concentrated land pattern. Despite the changes in employment distribution the pattern of residents, services or floorspace remains stable. This is due to the constraints imposed by the land on all the variables especially the basic employment input. Even when the latter is dispersed the distances between employees does not vary significantly. The concentration of services and flows reflects this pattern of centralisation.

The semi-linear group of towns in Figure 3 responds differently. The concentrated employment policy causes a sharp decay in all activities, especially in the floorspace. This peaked distribution contrasts with the even distribution in the previous radial town and is caused by a much greater variety in the accessibility of cells to the employment site. Some of the cells in this example are over 3 km from employment where the pressure for development is weak. This is clear from subsequent decentralisation policies which flatten demand for floorspace.

In the third group, Figure 4, the decay of floorspace is again marked, but when basic employment is dispersed there is still a large difference in the relative accessibility of cells. This simple linear town shows the effects of distance upon the demand for space and the greater contrast in the distribution of activities.

Example D (Figure 5) is linear, connected at both ends, and gives a flat distribution when employment is decentralised. It is also very concentrated in the first example. It is apparent that the distances between related areas in this town will tend to be high.

Two general tendencies can be seen in the results of these distributions: firstly the radial town shows little variation despite the change in employment policy, and secondly the policy of concentrated employment causes the highest floorspace densities in all examples. Let us now compare the performance of these types in a more ordered way to highlight these tendencies.

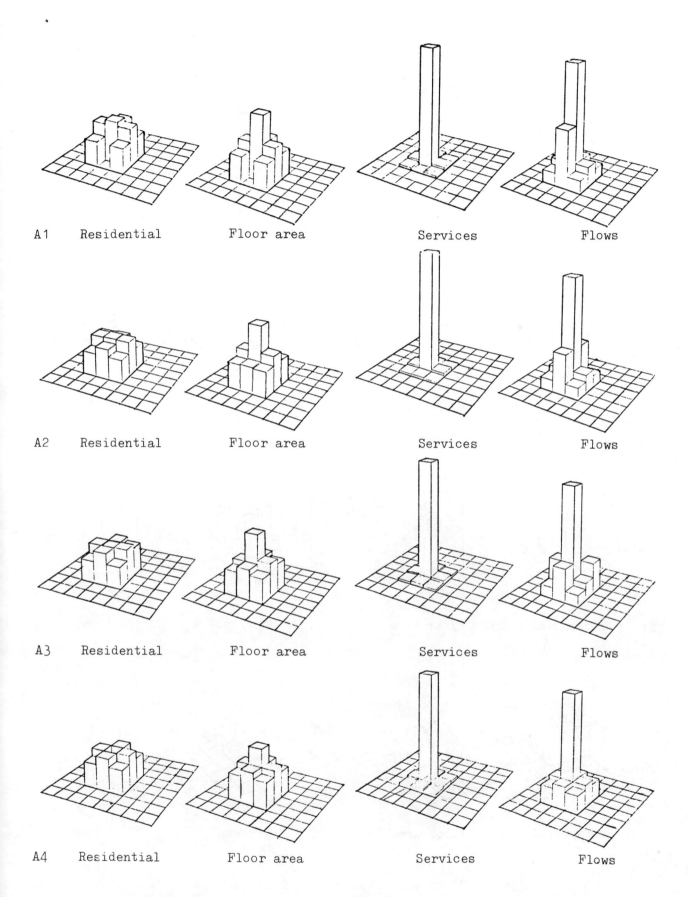

A1 Residential Floor area Services Flows

A2 Residential Floor area Services Flows

A3 Residential Floor area Services Flows

A4 Residential Floor area Services Flows

Figure 2 A: Radial output distributions

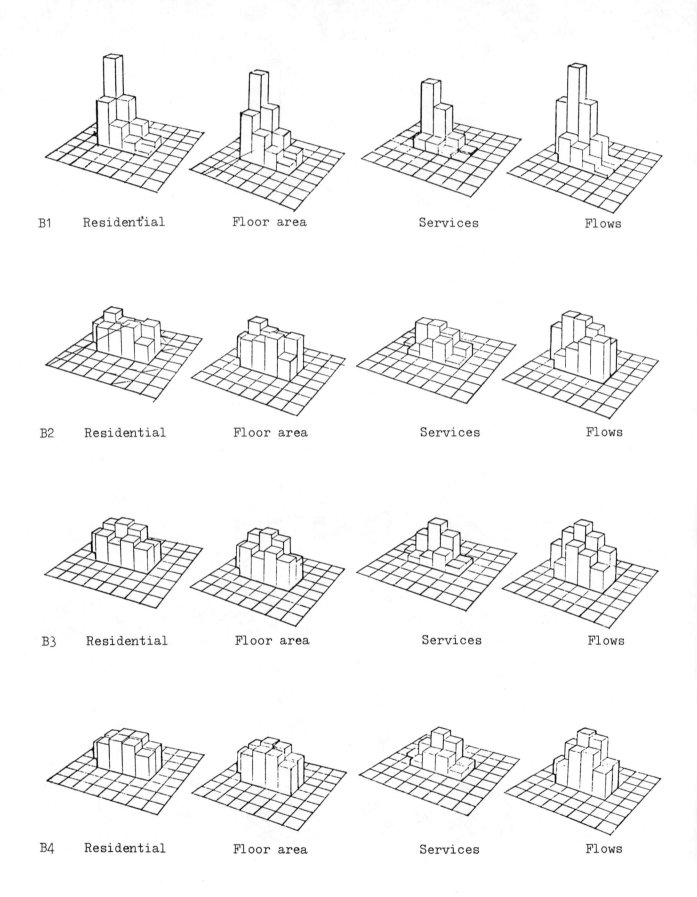

Figure 3. B: Semilinear output distributions

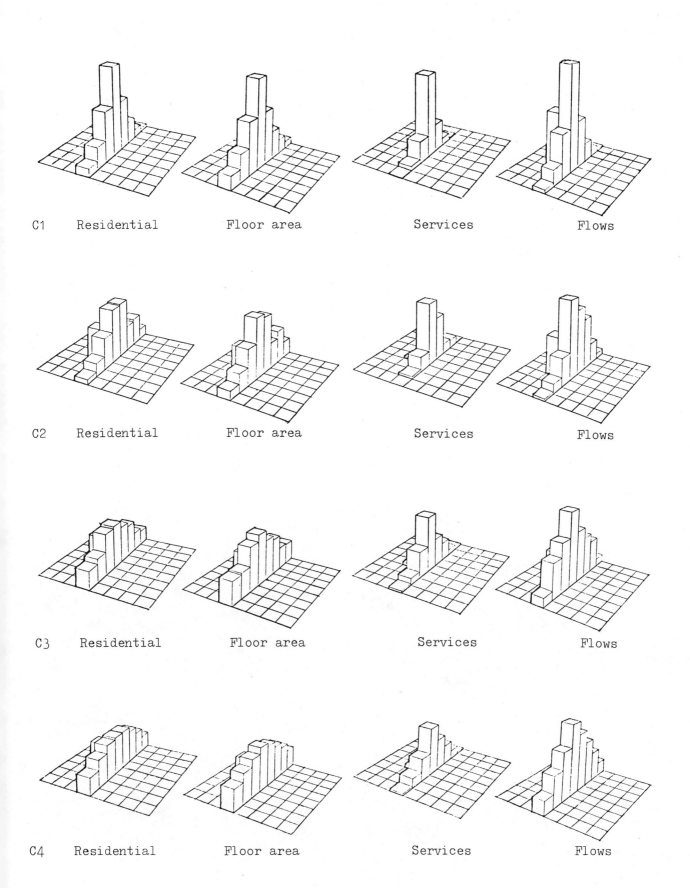

C1   Residential   Floor area   Services   Flows

C2   Residential   Floor area   Services   Flows

C3   Residential   Floor area   Services   Flows

C4   Residential   Floor area   Services   Flows

Figure 4. C: Linear output distributions

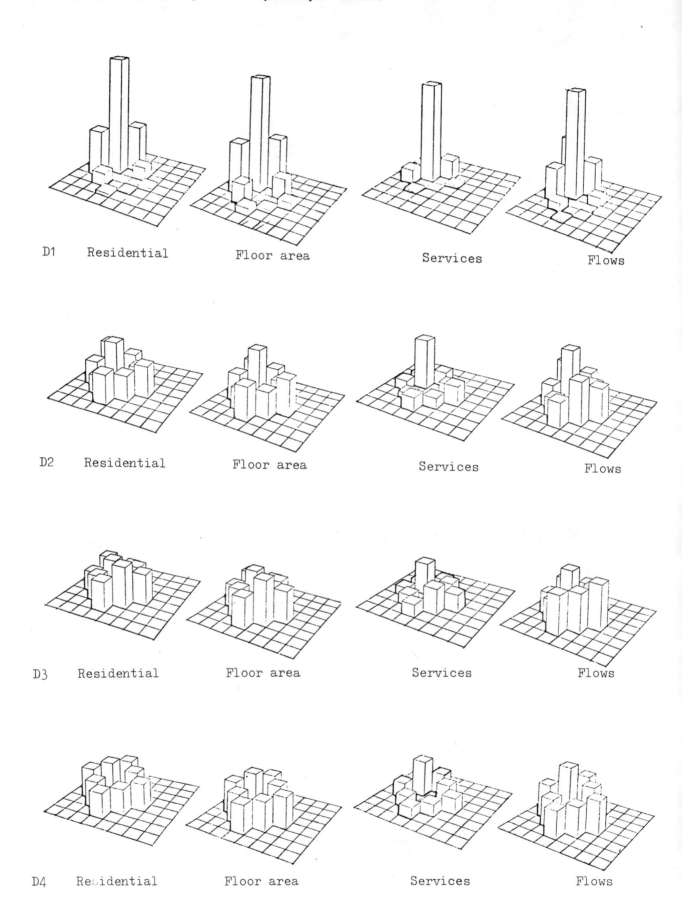

D1   Residential   Floor area   Services   Flows

D2   Residential   Floor area   Services   Flows

D3   Residential   Floor area   Services   Flows

D4   Residential   Floor area   Services   Flows

Figure 5. D: Ring output distributions

Evaluation of each policy against five indicators

In general it may be possible to evaluate the urban structure in terms of specific planning objectives such as the need to provide adequate space standards for housing, education or industry - or to improve the level of communications between interrelated activities. In our experiments, however, the evaluation is limited and we can only examine certain aspects of the urban system connected with the distribution of, and the relationship between, our original variables - corresponding in planning to an analysis of density and accessibility. The 16 distributions are subjected to five tests: three are concerned with interaction between activities and two with density.

The interaction indicator measures the distance which one type of population, say residents, needs to travel to reach a given number of opportunities, say jobs. This opportunity for interaction varies according to the distribution of this population in the town, and an average measure is derived which is the mean distance that the population must travel to meet a specific target over the whole of the town. The three interactions shown in the study are the opportunities for residents to reach jobs, residents and other services. The size of targets can also be varied to include either a few neighbouring cells or larger opportunities, in this case 20% and 50% of the total opportunities in the town.

The indicators which form the other type of test are derived from an analysis of the distributions of the different populations. In this case the distributions of the residential and employment densities were plotted as histograms, and the means of these distributions provided a measure of the average weighted population density in each sample. Both the density and the interaction indicators have been used in other new town studies and have been explained in greater detail elsewhere (Echenique et al. 1969b).

The effects of each policy upon the evaluation indicators

How do the 16 layouts respond to the five tests? Since none of the plans can be represented by strict numerical quantities (town shape is difficult to measure) the values of each test are compared as a set of ordered results. The results of the experiments have been grouped in two sets of figures on separate pages and classified first by land and second by employment policy. Figure 6 shows the samples across the page A, B, C, D corresponding to the different shapes - radial, semilinear, linear and ring. Each employment policy is marked on the horizontal axis of the graphs. Figure 7 shows the groups in relation to different employment policies with the results of each shape shown along the horizontal axis (A-D).

The results of the five tests are shown on separate lines of each page: three types of interaction (two target figures are given) and two types of density (both shown on the same graph). The scaling is given in terms of kilometre distances (interaction) and persons per hectare (density).

What do these results show? Let us first examine the effects of our two main policies upon the five indicators and see if we can distinguish the causes of variation. If we examine the variation in the graphs we see that in general the small target indicators (20%) do not show much movement and never more than 1 km compared with the $2\frac{1}{2}$-3 km variations in the larger (50%) targets. That is to say the opportunities to reach local services are not greatly affected by either changing land or employment policies, and we will therefore concentrate more closely on the larger indicator which represents (50%) of the opportunities in the town.

The top indicator in Figure 6 for residents to jobs shows little variation for each policy of employment within the separate town groups but a tendency to rise from 3-4.5 kilometres across the groups from the radial to the ring structure. The trend is clearly seen in the corresponding graph in Figure 7 which shows this large variation caused by the land patterns within the different policies of employment. The two and three site examples show maximum variation of 2.5 kilometres with the largest value caused by the ring structure (D).

The third interaction, residents to services, demonstrates these features in a more exaggerated form. The maximum variation between ring and radial is over 3 kilometres. Thus the increases in distances between home and work and services are caused more by land than by employment, especially in example D where the constraints imposed by the town shapes upon the location of basic and service employment outweighs effects of the employment policies themselves.

The second indicator, residents to residents, shows the opportunity for inter-action within the population and reflects the distribution of residential density. The value of the indicator in Figure 6 is generally lower than the residential/work indicator as the distribution of residents is more continuous. Here, the variation caused by the different employment patterns is more striking and the policy of concentration both in Figure 6 and Figure 7 forces the residents to occupy a small area of town at high density, with a consequent increase in opportunities for interaction.

The fourth set of graphs along the bottom of the page shows the average density in each of the 16 tests. We see from Figure 6 that the effects of different employment policies upon the pattern of land is large. Similar variations occur in each structure due to the decentralisation of employment. This appears in Figure 7 where density decays with each employment set and little variation is caused by the different shapes of the town.

It is apparent from these results that some of the indicators show a degree of correlation. All the interaction indices have similar upward trends caused by the spread of the town shape or the dispersal of employment. The density indicators show the reverse – a decrease of density in each graph. In order to bring out the overall effect of the variations an average value of the three interaction indices was calculated and the results plotted as a three-dimensional histogram in Figure 8, when the town shape (A-D) and employment policies (1-4) were measured against a common scale of kilometre distances. An analysis of variance was performed on the samples and greatest variation was shown by the different land policies, due largely to the eccentricity of type D. A similar analysis was performed in the lower graph and showed greatest variance in the concentrated employment policy (1). It is thus interesting to observe from these histograms that although the land pattern more greatly affects the relationship <u>between</u> the variables, it is the policy for employment location that dominates the distribution and thus the <u>density</u> of each separate variable.

A general comparison of each policy

As well as distinguishing the effects of our input policies upon the performance of individual indicators, we can also compare their effects on the towns as a whole, that is on all the indicators at once. This should bring out overall trends and common groups, and helps to identify those combinations of policy which vary and those which remain stable under different conditions.

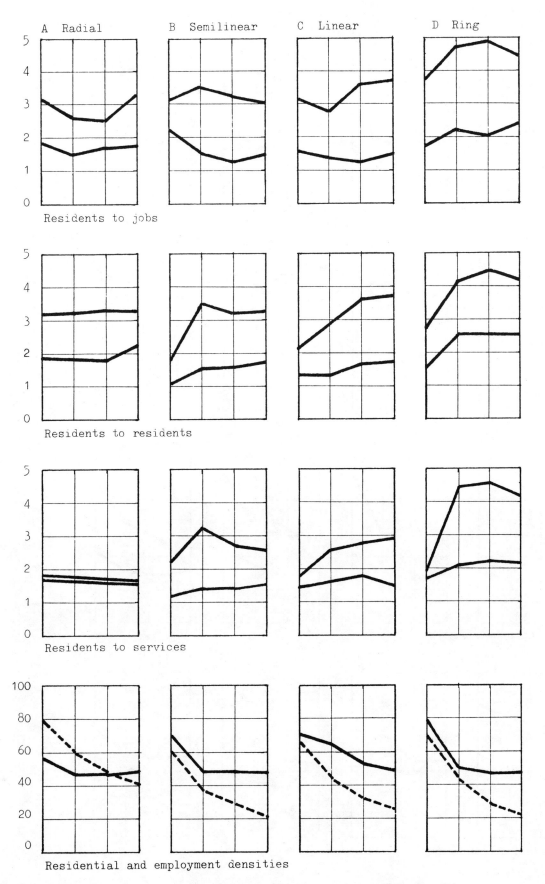

Figure 6   Evaluation indicators grouped by type of land policy

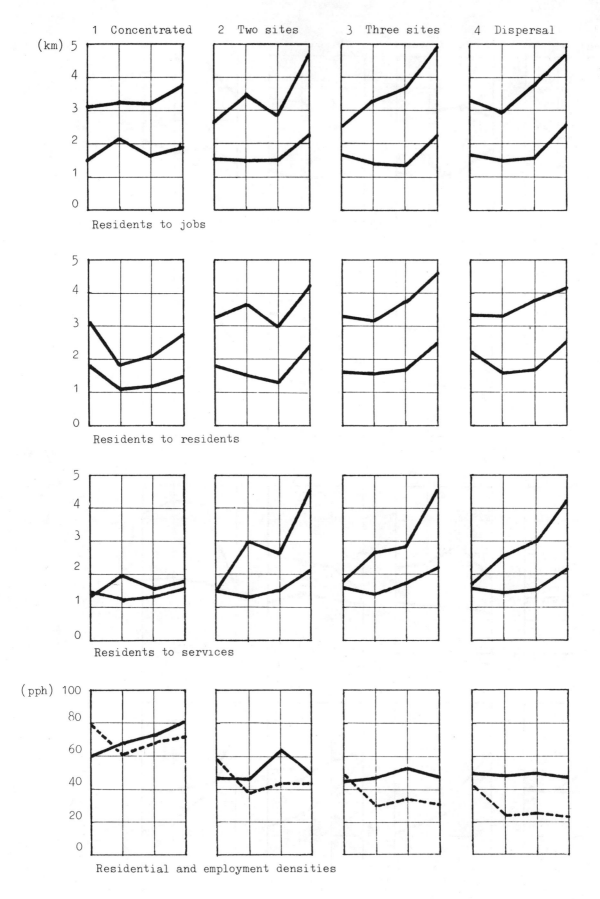

Figure 7 Evaluation indicators grouped by employment policy

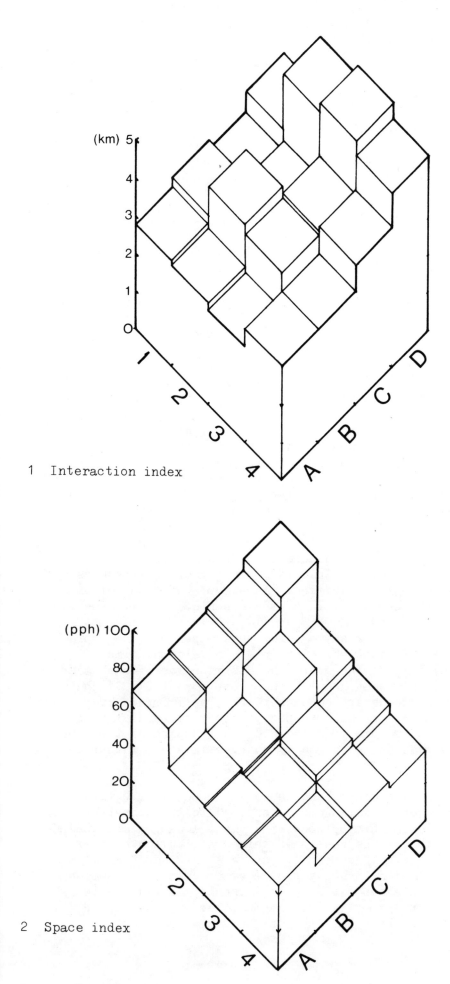

1 Interaction index

2 Space index

Figure 8   General indices for interaction and space

The first step, however, must be to reduce the number of tests to a reasonable number of significant indices. In the previous section an attempt was made to summarise the effects of our two policies by reducing the five indicators to two sets of averages. Two related problems arise from such a method: the degree to which the indicators correlated with each other, and the relative importance of the indicator itself. These problems could be partially overcome by using more systematic analytical methods to correlate the results of each indicator and vary the relative importance of one measure against the other, but lack of time prevented such methods in this study. Cross comparison of our results had shown an obvious similarity in the performance of each of the interaction and density indicators, which divided clearly into two separate groups.

It was also undesirable at this stage to give prominence to any single indicator in either group since each test was considered equally important. The five indicators were therefore collapsed into two general indices: one related to interaction and the other to density. These were then plotted for each layout in Figure 9. The upper graph is scaled in terms of hectares and kilometres; the lower graph is transformed into standard units with a zero mean.

Looking at the general distribution within the upper graph we see that 14 of our 16 points fall within the area of the graph bounded by the 2-5 kilometre mark and the 40-80 p.p.h. on the Y-axis, while ten of the points occupy a much smaller area. The size of each town and the total employment and residential population impose these overall constraints. Within this space the samples fall into three groups. The central cluster, grouped around the common mean (3.43 km and 50.8 p.p.h.) consists of all those towns which have both average density and average interaction, that is land types A, B and C and employment types 2, 3 and 4. The upper cluster consists of concentrated employment samples: A1, B1, C1, and D1. The right hand cluster is reserved for the spread land types: D2, D3, and D4. It is interesting to note in passing that none of the samples occupies the top right hand quadrant where densities are high and interrelated activities are greatly separated, since the model ensures a reasonable relationship between all activities. An example of towns of this type can be seen in some of the new town plans (see Echenique et al. 1969b).

The graph on Figure 9 provides a clear summary for this paper and demonstrates what happens when we combine different policies into single town forms. Along the horizontal (interaction) axis of the graph the distribution of each sample is evenly spread and there is a tendency (with the exception of D1, C1 and C2) for its value to increase with the shape of each town. The principal variation in the lower part of the graph occurs with respect to this horizontal axis. It is, therefore, reasonable to assume from the ordered grouping of the towns along this axis, that the variation is caused by changes in shape rather than in employment policy.

The vertical axis (density) on the other hand shows a skewed distribution with a clear progression from the concentrated employment (1) to the dispersed (4) indicating once again the relationship between employment location and the distribution of density. Although the centre of this distribution clusters around the interaction axis its tail is clearly separated and contains all the samples with concentrated employment. The presence of D1 on the extreme edge of this graph clearly shows how a concentrated employment policy can outweigh the effects of a dispersed town shape for even in this most extreme example it is density rather than distance which has increased.

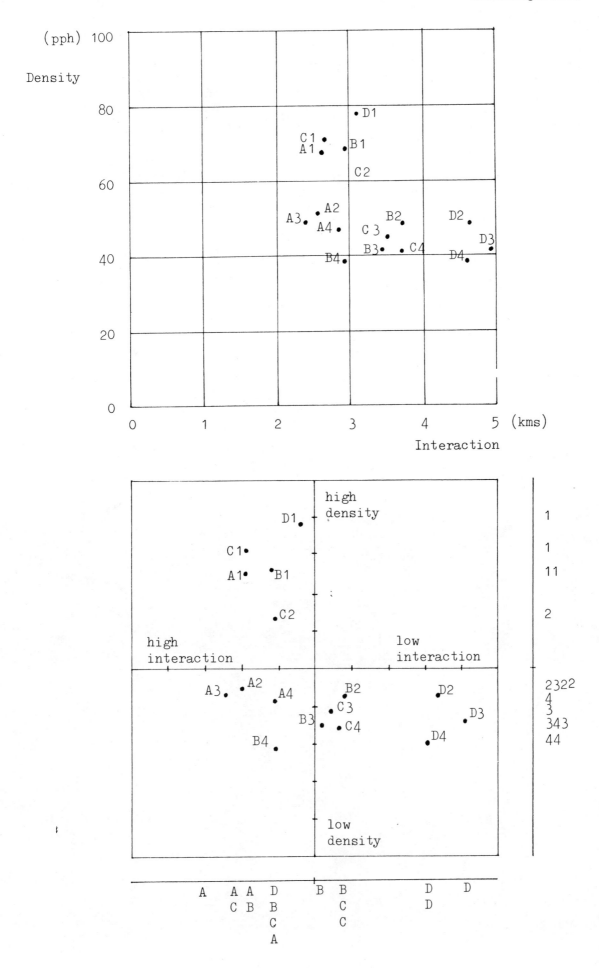

Figure 9 Plot of interaction and density by sample type

This brief analysis has attempted to show the effects of two different types
of urban policy upon the distribution of 16 sample layouts, and to show how
these policies interact upon such features as density and interaction of
populations. It has not been our aim to make any assessment of the results
at this stage nor to judge the merits of one type over another since this
depends ultimately upon the importance of each type of test. Some policies,
for example the dispersal of land in a town, may provide the population with a
close connection to the countryside and the choice of a wide variety of housing
but may do this at the expense of long commuting times. Other policies, for
example the concentration of employment at a single centre of industry, may
reduce industrial disturbance and centralise services but at the expense of
congestion and high density. Policies of this sort are evidently extreme cases
which perform well for a very limited number of criteria while failing most
other tests. Perhaps the results which we should be looking for fall into the
intermediate category and can only be found by adopting a more balanced set
of strategies which present no real extremes, but may satisfy a greater number
of people and increase the variety and choice of opportunities open to them in
the urban environment.

Part 4

Information systems

Computerised information systems for planners

Erlet Cater

The statutory requirements of the 1968 Town and Country Planning Act mean that
in order to prepare structure plans, local planning authorities need the backing
of a much more comprehensive information system than previously envisaged. This
is a fundamental requirement because the Act embodies the essential principle of
viewing cities and regions as complex systems in their own right. Not only must
the local planning authority examine all the components of the urban system as
laid down in the Act, but it must maintain continuous review and monitor changes
as well. In fact, this latter requirement for review and the monitoring of
change implies the need for a continual updating and amendment of the data base.
The many references in the Act to the need to consider adjacent areas, wherever
relevant, also indicates the reliance of a local authority on data bases in
adjacent areas as comprehensive as their own. Clearly, then, there is an
argument here, if not for a centralised data collection system, at least for a
unified approach to the problem of data collection amongst local authorities.
The formulation of policy, as outlined by the Act, must have regard to the
information collected and also bear in mind regional policy. So we can see
then that greater rationalisation and coordination of data bases is required.

How far do our national information sources meet the planner's requirements
for continuously updated data describing all the complexities of the urban
system? In a survey of information needs of planners I conducted in 1969,
I found that their prime source of information was the Census of Population.
Obviously this falls far short of many of the requirements, particularly
because a full census is conducted on a decennial basis, and therefore does
not provide for a continually updated data base.

There are similar problems involved with most central government sources.
Sweden is rather more fortunate. There, the central population register,
for example, dispenses with the need for a periodic head count, since
up-to-date information is available on the number and location of people
and certain of their socio-economic characteristics. A real estate register
and a national computer based land data bank are also being developed. The
nearest thing we have to a national register is the Central Register of
Businesses developed by the Business Statistics Office, which provides an
up-to-date list of names and addresses of businesses and various statistics
(although the National Health Service Register, the Register of Births and
Deaths and the H.M. Land Registry might, if reformed, provide bases).
Obviously, the scale of resources needed to set up a system of this kind
in Britain, is far greater than in Sweden. It would also be beyond the
capacity of computers at a national level, so some sort of regional registers
would have to be evolved. There is also the problem of invasion of privacy
brought about by the interlinking of the records in these central registers,
as they do in Sweden, which may not prove acceptable in this country.

Classification of planning data

Having seen, therefore, that the national information systems fall short of the planner's requirements for data, let us examine more precisely the nature of the planner's needs for information so that we can make more concrete suggestions as to the type of information necessary.

Information that a planner collects and uses must have regard to the nature of the city or region as a system and the information must therefore be organised in a systematic way in order to match the system he is trying to control. As McLoughlin points out, the system is dynamic so that the planner needs to know how its parts and interconnections change and how the whole system changes. He also has to be able to identify what has caused these changes and why. The continuous nature of the planning process means that there must be a continual feed-back of information on change and on the result of planning policies. The nature of the planner's information needs suggests the necessity of a systems approach to the structuring of the information system, in which major components are inter-related.

The problem then is to identify and classify the major components of an urban system and to identify the most important or fundamental variables which should be indexed to describe these components. If we know this, we can ascertain the content of the planning data bank, where the fundamental variables used in system description can be stored and amended.

We also want to achieve economy of description. There is the danger, on the one hand, of adopting a magpie approach to the problem of data collection, and collecting too much data, or, on the other hand, of collecting too little data for an adequate description and understanding of the complex nature of urban systems. It is essential therefore to establish an overall strategy for the design and development of the information system and to identify the major components of the urban system that we are concerned with.

Chapin (1965) has provided a useful classification of the components of the urban system. (It is quite comprehensive and we have used it in our work at Reading.) Chapin distinguishes between the activities and the adapted spaces which are the physical expression of these activities, and he considers the within-place and between-place aspects of both (Figure 1). An example of

		Sub system examples	Variables that could be used to index the sub-systems examples
Within-place	Activities	Residential	Family composition
	Adapted spaces	Houses	Type and size
Between-place	Activities (flows)	Journey to work	Numbers of persons making trip
	Adapted spaces (Communication channels)	Roads	Road capacity

Figure 1   A classification of the components of the urban system

a within-place activity is the residential sub-system, and the corresponding adapted spaces are the houses. An example of a between-place activity, or flow, is the journey to work, and the adapted space which accommodates this activity could be a road or railway.

There are a very large number of variables which can be used to index these various components. If we look at houses, for example, we can see that two possible variables that can be used to describe them are type and size; there are many others. So this gives us some sort of framework for analysis.

It is insufficient, however, to categorise data into isolated compartments like this without recognising the ties between the components. The components are all inter-related; for example, it is obvious that people live in houses and they make journeys to work using the physical networks. How can we tie them all together and recognise the interactions that occur within the system?

The components of the urban system all have one quality in common; they all have some locational tie. This is generally speaking a property unit, so it remains for all the data to be referenced in terms of this basic unit. Coordinate referencing is a unique and infinitely flexible mode of referencing. The spatial context of data is clearly the most important element for planning information and the need for a unique geographical tag to data is indisputable, although the level at which this must be done to satisfy most planning needs can be open to question.

The role of information in decision-making

Having justified the need for an information system then, let us examine the role of information in decision making in urban planning. At each stage in the planning process, the planner needs information to help him formulate his decisions. I will go through the planning stages, as outlined by McLoughlin (1969), and point to the information needs at each stage.

Firstly, McLoughlin begins with the actual decision to adopt planning. That is to recognise that planning is needed. This initial decision implies that the planner must have an understanding of his power to promote a better environment, and implies also that he has some understanding of desirable quality and standards.

To go on to the next stage, which is the formulation of goals and objectives, the information required by the planner in this stage of planning helps him to understand the urban system. This initial taking stock may be viewed as an inventory. As well as taking physical stock of the situation, such as existing population densities or number of fit houses, the planner must also have information on the relevant standards and constraints, and on the echomics and financing of development of land and transport. He must also have knowledge of the various powers and responsibilities of central and local government and other public bodies concerned with urban and regional planning.

The planner then goes on to outline alternative courses of action. These must be backed by projections, such as of future population and housing totals, and by more comprehensive models of the urban system, derived from the data set. Even the simplest models are quite demanding in terms of data, especially small area data, so the information system must have regard to the demands of such techniques. Studies of possible courses of action show how the system might change through time as a result of public and private actions.

The next stage in the planning process is the comparison and evaluation of alternative courses of action. This is achieved by a process of increasing refinement of detail and therefore needs a considerably refined information system capable of furnishing the necessary disaggregated data. In order to evaluate the alternatives, information must be held on social values and on the relative costs or benefits arising from the alternative courses.

The taking of action or implementation stage of planning requires information and research to keep the plan continually under review and to check the assumptions and goals on which the plan was based. The results of the initial projections and recommendations should be checked to see if they remain consistent with the present conditions, and the implications of any new events that may have changed the situation should be examined. Detailed examination of the updated data base is necessary, to consider such factors as changing population structure.

The final review and assessment is the examination of the completed development including the critical appreciation of standards and the actual use of facilities planned. The process of planning is a cyclical one and the planner must learn the results of his previous actions so that his decision-making becomes better informed in the future. Continuous amendments to planning techniques, programmes and proposals in the light of current knowledge and the changing patterns of demands and tastes, give rise to revised objectives. There is need for continuous review and monitoring and this implies the need for a continuously updated comprehensive information system.

Organisation of the data base

Having justified the need for an information system and illustrated its role in the planning process, I will now go on to examine various aspects of the organisation of the data base necessary to fulfil the demands made upon it.

In the light of the various needs of planners, certain general and necessary principles to be embodied in the information system can be outlined. Firstly we need to structure an overall systematic framework for analysis. The information system should itself reflect completely the urban system it seeks to describe and have regard to change. There needs to be a complete description of the study area in terms of the activity systems and interactions, adapted spaces and communication channels that I outlined earlier. Models can provide rigorous frameworks for the analysis of the complex web of relationships that exist in the urban system.

Secondly, the organisation of the data system and its automation should be able to accommodate the changes in the urban system, over time. It therefore needs to be continually updated by feedback of data through amendment and updating procedures.

Thirdly, since most of the data is collected and supplied by different agencies, standard procedures need to be devised for the collection, coding and storage. Inconsistencies of data over space, time and definitions need to be ironed out. The present sets of data from different sources used by the planner are often incompatible as far as areal definitions are concerned. The spatial units used differ between data collecting authorities, both at central and local government levels, but they also differ within local authorities. For example, the traffic zones used by the highways department may differ from the planning areas used by the planners. They may also differ even within departments, such as comprehensive development areas and street units used within the planning department. Now, obviously, this difference in definition is necessary from the point of view of analysis. There will in fact be as many areal divisions as there are problems to analyse.

However, the point to be made is that unfortunately the data are collected for these widely differing areas. The answer is that it should be collected for the smallest basic unit and then it can be aggregated to any required zone size for different purposes. This would save great duplication of effort, as quite often at present separate surveys are mounted to collect the same sort of information by different agencies. The ideal solution is to retain reference data at the most basic level to enable aggregation to any level. Coordinate referencing of the basic data units would provide the most flexible means of achieving this.

A standard referencing system would also cope with the problem of changing areal definitions over time, such as the change in enumeration district boundaries between the 1961 and 1966 census. Data should also be consistent as far as the temporal or time dimension is concerned. It is useless if the planner has to relate two data sets which have been collected at different dates. The boundaries of the areas he wants to consider over a time period may also have changed. Topical inconsistencies or differences in definitions are a further problem facing the planner in using different data sources. For example, an industry may be assigned to the wrong Standard Industrial Classification (S.I.C.) or to different S.I.C.s over time, or the S.I.C.s themselves may change.

The fourth principle in the organisation of information systems is the computerisation of the data base. It is only by computer storage that the vast complexity of data I have outlined can be made operational. The computer allows for flexibility of organisation and permits multiple access by different departments for different purposes. It also facilitates statistical analyses.

Allied to this, the fifth consideration is file organisation. It is probable that the local authority will find it necessary to organise the computer data files at two levels. There will be the basic files which contain the basic information and means of access to the more detailed, or topic, files which can be linked by a common referencing system. Topic files would include the employment file, population file and the land use file. An integrated file could be one which gives both employment and land use for any location.

Models and other analytical tools

Finally, a mention must be made of the role of models and other statistical tools of analysis in the information system. The relationships between variables are of considerable importance to the planner in understanding and planning urban systems. He must also know how such variables change over time and the way they respond to intervention. Models of urban development and other statistical techniques structure these relationships between the major variables and help us to analyse the system. They look at activity and interaction in a spatially disaggregated way, but at the same time they abstract the principal planning variables used for the purpose from the mass of information that would be contained in a comprehensive information system.

The abstraction of such variables is represented in the models in a symbolic way, such that the activity systems involved can be presented at an abstracted

enough level for the planner to comprehend the whole and the interactions involved between the parts, and he can begin to understand some of
the likely results of his intervention in the system. The model is therefore
a very useful tool in understanding the complexity of the urban system, and
the data bank and the model are therefore very much inter-connected within
the information system.

A strategy for developing computerised information systems for local government: the end of the mega-system

Jeffrey Willis

Before the conference organised by PTRC and the TPI in 1968 (TPI/PTRC 1968), very few people in local government had heard of data banks or information systems. By 1972 almost every major local authority in the country was discussing how an information system could be devised to meet their needs and many were already committing themselves to investments in systems of one form or another. However there is no profession that can naturally take responsibility for information system design. Indeed there is no recognised conventional wisdom, no textbooks, and very little expertise or experience available. As efforts continue, and experience is reported and evaluated, various approaches are beginning to emerge. Conclusions are being drawn, lessons are being learned and the beginnings of a methodology is emerging. But, at best, the ideas are still controversial and, at worst, naively dangerous.

This paper aims to dispel the myth of the oversimplified, ideal, comprehensive system that can solve everybody's problems. It aims to describe some of the decisions to be made in choosing a strategy for system development, to list some technical problems to be solved, and finally to move towards some recommendations for action that has a good chance of leading to success.

A working definition of an information system distinguished it from a data bank, which is simply a set of files of disaggregated data that can be processed to provide a variety of summary tabulations. An information system is an image of the management process it serves. It is a data bank linked to a set of procedures for collecting data, and coupled to a set of techniques that can transform data into information for decision making and transmit them to decision points where they can be used (see Willis 1972). It is intimately connected with the suppliers and users of data (Figure 1) and is centralised in a model of the management process, which could take many forms (Figure 2).

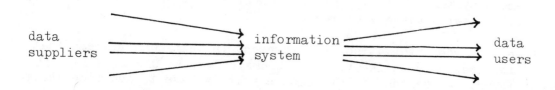

Figure 1

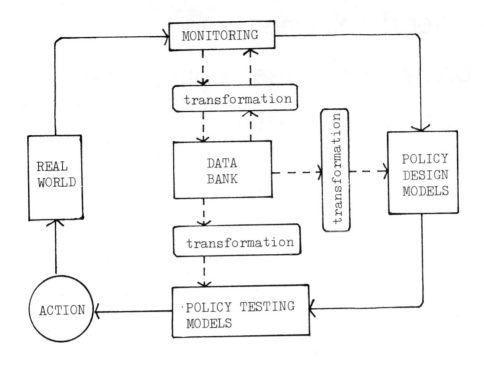

Figure 2   The management process

The mega-system ideal

Information systems caught the imagination when the work of the Swedes was introduced to Britain in 1969 (Salomonsson 1969). The well-known conceptual model of the Swedish system (Figure 3) is perhaps the ideal of planners toiling daily under the burdens of decision making with current British data sources. The Swedish 'mega-system' is based on three linked registers of entities: population, land parcels and businesses. Each entity is labelled with a unique identifier which is cross-referenced to one or both of the other registers as well as its own register. Topic files are similarly integrated: for instance educational records and occupational details can be integrated via the population register and in turn linked to the property register, so that the location of every university drop-out can be determined. Links to the business register mean that the ones who made it can also be discovered! An added attraction is the possibility of automatic spatial processing via a special topic file containing the coordinate references of each land parcel. Theoretically, aggregates of data for any combination of land parcels over any combination of topics can be assembled. Conceptually, the system is completely integrated and completely flexible.

Systems as sophisticated as this are unlikely to be established here for a long time, even if they are desirable at all. The preparation of the first wave of structure plans, the corporate planning systems that are now emerging, and the management systems that implement them, will rely on systems that are much less ambitious for a variety of reasons.

First, attitudes towards information in government in this country mean that investment on this scale is unlikely. But such systems are unproven in cost-effectiveness terms. Advocates of information systems have to overcome their general lack of credibility amongst traditional managers by adopting a soft-sell incremental approach. Intermediate pay-offs must be demonstrated at each point in the system's development before further funds are allocated.

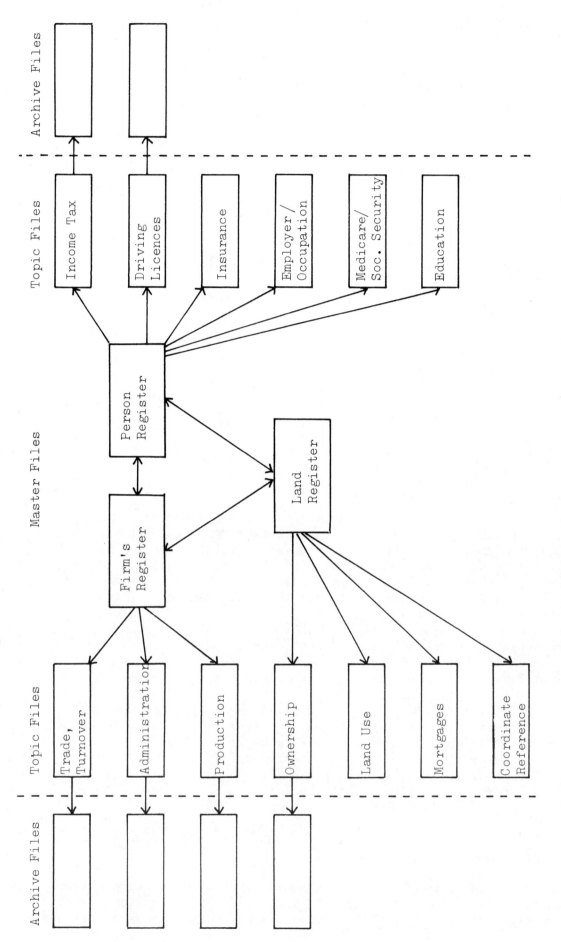

Figure 3   Conceptual model of fully integrated information system (after Salomonsson 1969)

Information systems will enter the town halls usually by the back door in all but the most enlightened and courageous authorities.

Second, there are problems in designing one centralised system that will satisfy the full range of potential users. The requirements of the planner manning the development control desk, are quite different from the urban economist working on a housing policy, or the designer of a school building programme. For some users routine summaries and reports batch-processed on a regular basis would be adequate. Some would require the association of data from separate files over constantly changing spatial areas. For others instantaneous access to individual records would be essential. It is doubtful whether operating procedures could be designed to allow one mega-system to satisfy all these users efficiently and economically.

Third, there may be a danger in making commitments on the basis of existing technologies. Developments in hardware and software might open up new design options. As in all planning, a strategy robust enough to handle technological uncertainty is to be favoured and premature commitments are to be avoided.

Fourth, mega-systems must be imposed on organisations from above or outside. Present local authority departmental structures mean that there is no unit that has the power or resources to provide a totally centralised system for all the departments. At the same time there is no evidence to suppose that large users of data, such as the town planning department, or the programme budgeting section, are in the best position to run the information services of the whole local authority. Local government departments jealously guard their own supplies of information and strive for information autonomy. All this argues against massive centralisation.

Fifth, although it is theoretically and technically possible to have fully integrated comprehensive systems there are enormous operational difficulties. The practicalities and cost of assembling and outputting the data required by a wide range of users, of responding to users in time to meet their needs, and of managing the data base should not be underestimated. The original estimates for the Swedish system have risen from £900,000 in 1966 to at least £9 million in 1971 (Black 1972a) and it is still not fully operational. And there is little evidence to suppose that even those parts which are working contribute significantly to decision making.

Sixth, the mega-system approach is analogous to the grand-design, city-beautiful style of the old fashioned town planners. Their plans were rarely realised. Just like towns, information systems should be adaptable and flexible. System development is more likely to succeed if it is seen as a learning, adaptive, iterative process. From small beginnings development must be slow with tests at each stage, searching constantly for the direction of improvement with the biggest pay-offs, taking decisions that close off the fewest options, and striving to develop the design that is as robust as possible in the face of all kinds of uncertainty. Progress is more likely to be untidy and improvised, as one crisis is followed by another, rather than a smooth path to a perfect ideal.

Choosing a design strategy

Information system technology is already sufficiently developed for a number of key issues to emerge. The optimum strategy for information system development will vary with the structure of the organisation and the local conditions prevailing, but it will involve negotiating a path through these key issues and

choices of approach. It is unlikely that any two agencies could go through
this check list and emerge with the same set of decisions.

The first approach could be dubbed the O & M (Organisation and Methods)
approach. The system designers interview and observe the officials and
prepare job descriptions of everything they do. The work of the local
authority is broken down into tasks and sub-tasks and the information
requirements at each stage are listed. They look for overlaps of requirements, duplication of data collection, inconsistencies between data sources
and begin to define common information requirements. They see where the
information required by one task could be supplied by another, where two
tasks have a common requirement and where data supplies could be improved.
Files are set up around the tasks and sub-tasks (usually called 'computer
applications'). Data supplies are amalgamated and unnecessary duplication
is eliminated. This approach is commonly pursued in private industry and
rarely leads to disaster but it compares unfavourably with the second alternative. It can be summarised as building up files around well defined existing
tasks.

The Operations Research (OR) approach rejects the first as being totally
inadequate. Computerised information systems represent a new technology
which releases us from the procedures imposed by manual methods. By automating existing ways of working, by making the existing processes more
efficient, there is a danger of simply entrenching the overall management
deficiencies. A new technology provides a fresh opportunity for examining
how tasks are structured and how they relate to each other; for devising
a new management model. There is a chance to re-examine the basic objectives
and sub-objectives of the organisation, begin to specify how best these can
be achieved, sort out the information required to achieve them and exploit
the technology to the full to provide that information. In other words the
aim should be to build up operational files around well defined objectives.

The third approach builds up files around well defined activity systems
(see Chapin 1965). The idea of an activity system is based on a systems
theory approach to representing towns. Within the total urban system,
where everything relates in some degree to everything else, there are well
defined sub-systems, within which interactions are strong, and between which
interactions are weaker. This is the basis of the theory building which
underpins most of the models discussed in this conference. The residential
location model and the shopping activity model are examples of systems theories
formulated and operationalised around well defined activity systems. The
residential location model uses residences and work places as its entities,
and seeks to infer one by considering its relationship with the other,
expressed as the journey to work. In the shopping activity model, the shop
replaces the work place and the journey to shop is the relevant relationship.

Of course there are problems with this approach. The main drawback is that,
within the urban system, the sub-systems that are defined are by no means
permanent or inviolate. They are merely transitory tools that are exploited
for a while and then rejected as our concepts change. Systems are defined
for a particular purpose and there is no one set of sub-systems that can
meet all requirements. Just as shopping activity models, residential models
and transport models, developed separately during the fifties, gave way to
the 'comprehensive' framework of the Lowry model, this in turn is being
rejected in favour of disaggregated housing market models based on a completely new systems definition. As the acceptability of various theories
is constantly changing, the data files which represent them must change.

It may be reckless to structure information systems around them. Some, however, will be durable enough to merit this treatment and these can be exploited.

The fourth approach is that which produces the mega-system and all its problems. This approach is based on the belief that technology can solve all the problems. Data is collected at the finest level of disaggregation possible and placed in pigeon holes with linked identifiers so the whole data base can be restructured to meet any unforeseen requirement. There is no need to decide whether to concentrate on present work methods, devise new ones or go for files representing activity systems: the system is so flexible and closes off so few options that it can meet any requirements.

The main shortcomings of this approach are that it fails to take account of the phasing of system development from small beginnings and it fails to recognise the price, in terms of operating efficiency, of high flexibility and centralisation.

The fifth approach is based on exploiting the relationship between planning data and administrative data. Administrative data are the data generated by the local authority in carrying out its day to day functions. Planning data are what policies are based upon. They are usually combinations of data from many separate files arranged to coincide with the functional structure of the urban system. They can be performance indicators or activity systems or similar combinations. The exponents of this approach say that most of the planning data required is floating around somewhere in the local authority in the form of administrative data. If only it were captured and organised in the right way and made accessible it would need little supplementing to meet all the planning requirements.

There is no doubt that a great deal of data are not presently exploited to the full, but unless data from the full spectrum of public agencies are integrated, there is little chance of realising this dream. If the employment data from Employment Exchanges, the physical survey data from local Ordnance Survey offices, the personal data from water, gas and electricity accounts, the floorspace data of the Inland Revenue, the social data from Social Security Offices and so on, could be integrated with the administrative data within the local authority on planning permissions, rent and rate rebates, car parking, social services, education records, electoral roll, etc., then most of the policy enquiries could be answered.

Control of the information system

An important issue is the question of where the responsibility for the information system should lie. The initiative for system development usually comes from a heavy user of data, such as the planning department, but heavy users are not necessarily best placed to run successful systems. In fact, a heavy user offering to provide a centralised information service for the whole authority is motivated, not by altruistic feelings, but by a desire to get access to other departments' data. The service provided by any one department will be biased by that department's particular requirements. In Coventry the Point-Data-System, with a strong emphasis on spatial retrieval facilities, which was eventually abandoned in favour of an authority-wide management information system, with an emphasis on file integration, reflected the initiating planning department's preoccupation with physical infrastructure.

The alternative is to have a central intelligence unit, charged with the responsibility of supplying the authority's information needs. The main problems in system development are not technical at all, they are social, political, human or institutional. These might best be solved by a central intelligence unit which would be responsible for devising the strategy for system development. It would have its own budget, and it would have the power to impose the necessary disciplines of standardisation and procedures on other departments. It could arrive at useful definitions for collecting units, sort out problems of paying for data, provide information about the availability and quality of data, and what techniques were available for processing them. It could make sure users understood the limitations and the potential of the data. It could discipline its clients by making them clarify their objectives and tell them how other users were solving similar problems. It could ensure that consistency was achieved between users. It could provide a statistical service. In general it would ensure that the users understand what the data can and cannot do.

Technical decisions

A system designer must consider the sort of data base management system to be adopted. Jones (1972) distinguishes various software approaches and begins to specify the conditions where one might be preferable to another. The choice lies between a general purpose software system available from the computer manufacturer or a system specially tailored to the particular requirements of the local authority.

In general, specially designed systems are more efficient in machine terms but it is unlikely that a local authority starting from small beginnings could justify a specially commissioned system. And the generalised system does have advantages. It can be implemented quickly and, although often inefficient in machine time, it can save user time. It may also be better at meeting unanticipated needs, where a system tailored to a particular set of requirements might break down.

Most information systems with a town planning bias emphasise the desirability of very flexible spatial processing facilities. This question is quite trivial, compared with other problems of system development, although it is eye-catching and has received a lot of attention. Perhaps greater pay-offs would follow from concentrating on facilities for integrating separate files; as long as the data are uniquely identified it is often sufficient to locate them to some spatial aggregate.

The currently favoured spatial referencing system is borrowed from Swedish experience (Joint Local Authority Study Team 1972). Each land parcel has a unique reference to its centroid. This is stored as a piece of data in that parcel's record. Spatial retrieval options include point-in-polygon searches, grid square summaries, radial and pathsearches and special calculations such as accessibility searches, and shortest routes through geometric space.

However, it does suffer from some shortcomings. Files ordered on the basis of coordinate values bear little relationship to the functional areas on which most enquiries are based. Retrieval will be slow and expensive if whole files have to be searched to assemble the information for the parts of a polygon spread over the length of the file. The geometric searches, based on the coordinate geometry of the referencing system, rarely match the functional areas of a town. These tend to be aggregated in terms of block faces or streets, and distances tend to be required along networks rather than 'as the crow flies'. Point referencing does not lend itself to storing data on networks or boundaries. Finally there is an increasing suspicion (borne out by the requests for 1971 Census data available on this basis) that for the great majority of enquiries the cost of point referenced data is out of proportion to the cost involved in establishing and updating them.

An alternative approach would be to use area codes such as enumeration districts or planning zones. Another alternative system is segment referencing (U.S. Bureau of Census 1970). This system, known as DIME, was developed to handle the spatial small area side of the 1970 U.S. Census, and has been modified elsewhere (Black 1972b). Basically, the spatial unit is a link drawn between two nodes. Nodes are usually road junctions, and links (which have a left or right subscript) are block faces joining nodes. Data is spatially referenced only to the precision of the block face or segment. Areas can be built up by aggregating block faces and networks and other linear features such as shore lines and railways can be readily incorporated.

The advantages are that the files are ordered with some correspondence to the intrinsic topology of the area, as expressed in the network. Contiguity relationships incorporated in the file sequence can be exploited for more economical spatial searching. Shortest route and accessibility measures are more meaningful. Above all, the system is said to be up to twenty times cheaper than point referencing for only a marginal decrease in spatial accuracy and flexibility.

Towards some recommendations

It is unlikely that any one strategy could be devised which would be suitable for all authorities but there are certain factors they have in common. There is a built-in resistance to heavy investments without obvious pay-offs. There is a shortage of experienced computer people. As legislation, problems and values change and as new priorities are established, any information system must operate in a dynamic environment. After local government reorganisation there may be a multiplicity of computers in any one authority, and this will be certain in the Metropolitan countries. Reorganisation and the new division of functions will mean that the links between policy makers and policy implementers will be stretched. The chances of meeting policy requirements from aggregates of administrative data will diminish.

Factors that vary between local authorities are their attitudes towards reform of management structures, the distribution of power between departments, the level of cooperation and integration between departments and the local perception of priorities concerning the different potential users of information.

In spite of the widely varying contexts within which information systems are to be developed it is possible to move tentatively towards some firm recommendations. Because the success of a system depends to a large extent on the status and power of the department that promotes it, it would seem advantageous to establish a new department with information responsibilities, staffed by the right mix of experts and supported by resources and power necessary to do the job. A unit such as this would have more chance than any single user of data (such as the planning, or treasurer's department) of imposing the necessary reforms on the suppliers and users of information, as well as achieving the benefits already mentioned above.

Another firm recommendation would be to opt for a phased programme of development with intermediate pay-offs rather than to go for a one-shot mega-system. Development should be seen as an iterative learning process, pursuing strategies that are robust enough, and flexible enough, to handle the uncertainty of future requirements and future technology.

Designers must distinguish between a conceptual model, as in Figure 3, and an actual operational system. There is much to be gained by having an overall conceptual framework in mind but in practice it is unlikely to provide a blueprint for what can actually be achieved.

Figure 4 shows how an information system might look after about five years of effort. It represents a combination of some of the choices discussed above. It consists of a number of files linked together in terms of 'applications'. Some of these, such as the public housing application, have been designed around well defined tasks (the O and M approach). Some, such as the development control system, may be designed around an operations research approach to the redefinition of objectives and how they can be met. Some, such as the 'Lowry model data base' have been designed around well defined activity systems.

It is obvious that many of these disintegrated sub-systems overlap with each other. The rent rebates and arrears file is part of the 'personal services' sub-system, and is linked with the personal services master file. It is also part of the public housing sub-system, and is linked with the public housing master file. Similarly the area of land built-up is part of a combination of files designed to provide the model with attraction factors, and it is updated with information accumulated in the development control system.

As each separate file is established every opportunity is taken to label records with identifiers that enable files from one application to be cross-referenced with files from another. Master files at key points in the system contain directories which enable identifiers devised for one application (e.g. a rating number) to be linked with a different identifier, referring to the same entity, but more appropriate for another application (e.g. a public housing reference number). This is the basis for the partial integration of the separate sub-systems, and an example of how this might look is shown in Figure 5.

With patience the partially integrated system could be reformulated into a neat diagram similar to Sweden's conceptual model (Figure 3). Master files corresponding to the land register, the business register and the population register are recognisable. The difference is that in this case the registers are sometimes only partial, the system's relationships are represented in terms of how it might actually work and in practice every piece of data is not given an equal chance of being linked with every other piece of data. The sub-systems are defined in operational terms, are only notionally linked, and would probably be intimately connected with (even located within) the departments that use them most frequently. Possibilities for storing data in more than one file are allowed. Data storage may be duplicated but the task of the C.I.U. is to ensure that the collection of data and their use for the creation of new files or the updating of old files, is not duplicated.

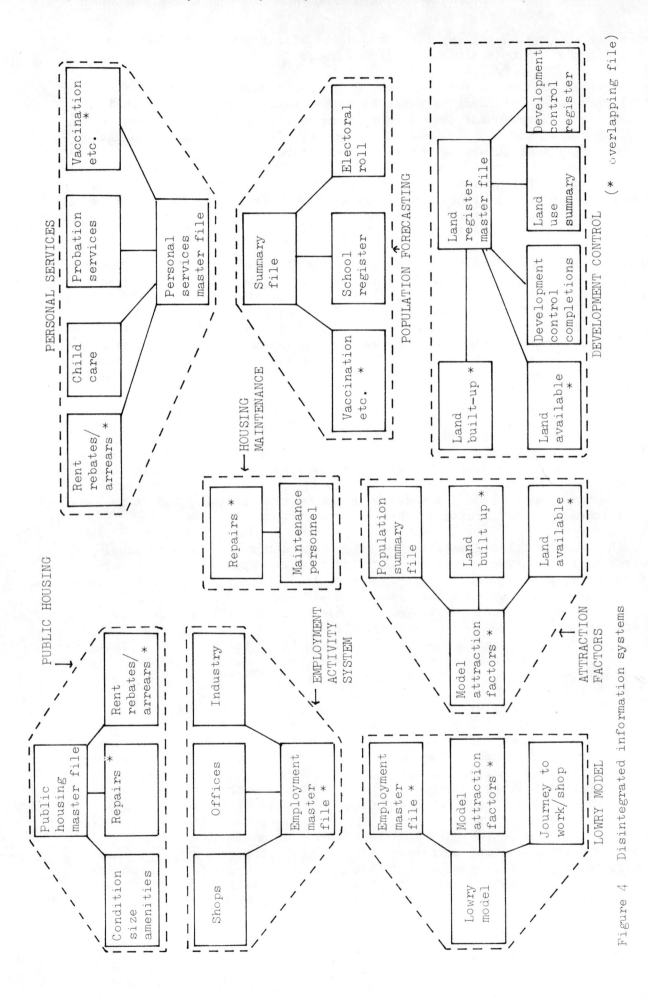

Figure 4 Disintegrated information systems

(* overlapping file)

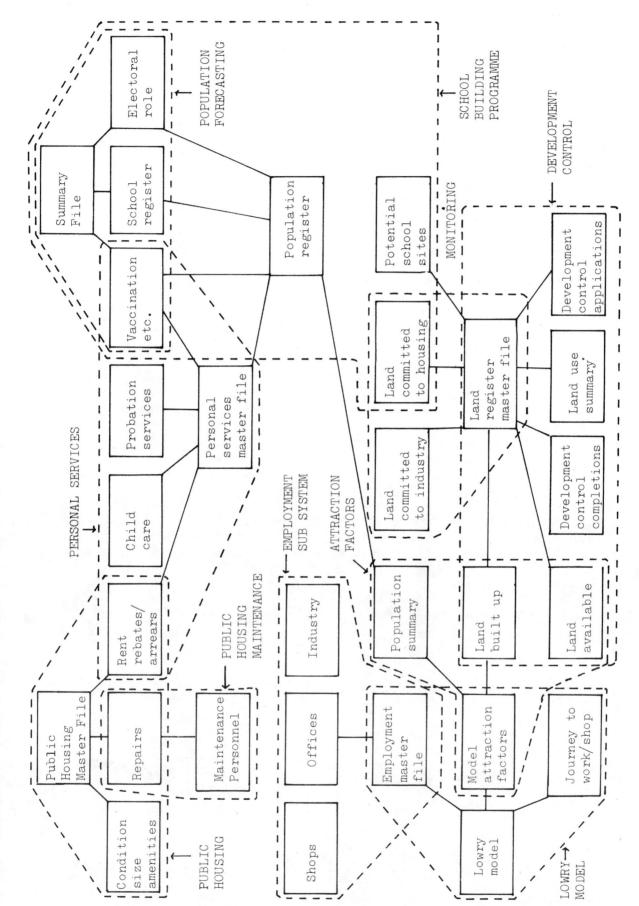

Figure 5   A partially integrated operational model

Provided the identifiers and integration keys are imposed at every opportunity the system can be adapted and reformulated by shuffling the files around. New operational sub-systems can be defined. New sources of data from outside the local authority can be keyed in to supplement the 'administrative' data and provide new 'planning' data as new tasks emerge, or as new theories are tested.

The strategy of developing separate systems on a piecemeal basis like this, but in the context of an overall conceptual framework, overcomes to some extent the problem of split functions under local government reorganisation. It allows priorities to be redefined, it allows the management model to develop and is robust enough to meet unanticipated events. The operating efficiency of the local government service is preserved and opportunities for getting new combinations of data are provided.

As 'applications' become operational intermediate pay-offs are achieved which improve the credibility of the total information system concept. The system can be seen to 'pay its way' and no one department is bidding for a huge sum of money to finance a mega-system which may or may not work at some unspecified future data. Computer personnel and system managers have a chance to cut their teeth on smaller applications before making the massive commitments to full integration. The piecemeal, iterative approach allows improvements in computers to be exploited and the lessons learnt from one stage can be used to improve the design of the next.

The group served least well by this approach would be the researchers who, by definition, constantly break out of the traditional activity systems and task-oriented compartments. Their work is innovatory and their enquiries ad hoc. It is perhaps no coincidence that pressure for the flexibility of the fully integrated comprehensive mega-system has been coming from that direction. However researchers are trained to deal with problems of imperfect or partial data. They are deluding themselves if they think that mega-systems will ever be able to meet their data needs at the press of a button. Information systems should be designed to meet the operational needs of the people who run local government. If the options for reformulating the system and integrating files in new ways are provided then research requirements will be met without threatening the operational effiency of the local government machine.

Information systems for planning:
some emerging principles

Stewart Cowie

This paper discusses some of the theoretical and technical considerations influencing the development of computerised information systems for planning in UK local authorities. Its purpose is not to debate fundamental issues 'ab initio' but rather to state some guiding principles which are emerging from recent work in this country and abroad.

Much of the state of the art thinking in this country is contained in the GISP Report (Joint Local Authority Study Team 1972) which has recently been published (see also Gaits 1971). Since the GISP Report was prepared considerable experience has been gained by local authorities pioneering the development of information systems. Central government departments, particularly the Department of the Environment, have continued to investigate information handling problems (see, for example, DOE, forthcoming, and Cowie 1972), and much literature has been published reporting research findings and describing system developments in the USA, the Scandinavian countries, and elsewhere (see PTRC 1972 and UNESCO/IGU 1972). This paper restates much that is contained in the GISP Report but also discusses principles emerging from the more recent work.

It should be emphasised that the paper concerns only the scope and structure of systems. It is not concerned with questions of data nor with questions related to the choice of data items to be included or excluded. The GISP Report has indicated that most data needed by an authority for planning purposes already exists somewhere within the local authority or elsewhere in the public sector, although not necessarily in the most suitable or accessible form. Local authority information problems are seen to be largely concerned with the organisation of data collection and storage, and with facilitating the dissemination of information (Note 1) to authorised persons throughout the authority (Notes 2 and 3).

The place of a planning system within an overall system

When local authorities begin to develop systems they are working towards the longer term goal of creating authority-wide management information systems. These will take time to develop not only because authorities have limited resources compared to the size of the task but also because an organisation needs time to accept technological innovations. The size of the task rules out the possibility of a single system being able to cope with all data processing within an authority. In the longer term it can be envisaged that local authority information systems will consist of several linked sub-systems. In the shorter term it is likely that authorities will come to different conclusions about which sub-system to implement first and the scope of the various sub-systems to be developed.

---

* This paper is published with the knowledge of the Department of the Environment, UK, but does not necessarily represent the policies or view of the Department.

Many different kinds of sub-systems may be implemented as the initial phase of system development in authorities, since authorities will have different priorities and since there are potentially several ways of approaching the common goal. Some authorities for example might wish initially to implement the skeleton of a system to serve the needs of management. Here the priority would be centred around corporate planning in general or on a particular form of innovatory management technique such as a Planning, Programming and Budgeting System (PPBS). Alternatively some authorities may wish to begin by developing a system to cater for forward planning and research activities such as might be required, for example, for the preparation of a Structure Plan. Other authorities might feel that their greatest priorities lie in the automation of routine services and administration. (Routine services and administration include such things as answering enquiries from the public, processes and procedures which involve a sequence of steps leading to an action, for example a land charges search, or processes which have a number of decision points occurring in a known sequence, for example, progressing of a planning application. In routine administration each transaction entering the process follows the same procedure.) For these authorities the desire would be to improve efficiency and the quality of the services they provide.

In considering the first stages of system development an authority will have to choose between the alternatives because it lacks resources for simultaneous development of sub-systems. It may also feel that it must decide either to concentrate on developing a sub-system to satisfy a short term objective or to approach development by making general preparation for the variety of sub-systems required in the longer term. Often the choice has been posed as "should an authority develop a GISP or should it prepare for an authority-wide system". The choice has been posed in these terms since, as implied by the title of the GISP Report, the initiative for system development in this country has tended to come from the planning department in an authority.

The initial concern should not be seen in terms of choice between the two as conflicting alternatives. It should be to ensure that if the authority's priority area centres on the needs of planning, a planning sub-system can be defined which can be integrated with or linked to other sub-systems developed later. In other words an information system for planning should not be designed as a separate system but should be thought of as an integral part of an authority's overall system. (Recommendation 6 of the GISP Report states that, "Because of the indivisible nature of most local authority operations, GISP, although primarily conceived for the planning department of the local authority, can ultimately only operate successfully as part of an overall information system for all departments of the local authority.")

In general terms the initial choice is for the authority to decide where its information handling priorities lie. When this has been decided the next decision concerns the scope of the initial sub-system. The sub-system chosen initially should fit logically with other sub-systems planned for the future. It should not range widely but selectively into data areas which are to be the bases of future sub-systems. The implication is that a strategy for development leading to the longer term overall system is desirable before initial phases are implemented. Conversely the concern is to ensure that the system required in the longer term can be conceptually sub-divided in such a way that its constituent sub-systems can be gradually implemented in an orderly fashion. As far as a planning sub-system is concerned, the timing of its implementation will depend on an authority's priorities but its scope should have been largely determined by the time work begins on the first sub-system to be developed. Approaches to determining the scope of sub-systems within an overall system are discussed in the next section (Note 4).

Approaches to defining the scope of a planning system

One approach would be for the system designers to stand back from the real
and apparent constraints existing within an authority and to consider what
kind of total system would constitute an idealised solution to its information
handling problems. The solution evolved from this kind of approach may be
very good in the abstract, but the gulf between the ideal and what is likely to
be possible is so great that the approach is unlikely to be practical. This
would be especially true if such a 'grand design' approach questioned the
existing organisation of the authority and produced a new management structure,
as it would be tempted to do. Such an approach would also be unrealistic in
that it would have to make assumptions about the future (for example in the
provision of computing facilities). These would tend either not to take account
of what might be possible in the future or to place too much reliance on
anticipated changes actually coming about.

Alternatively approaches can be followed which have regard to the practical
difficulties of altering information processing procedures in authorities and
take a realistic view of what kind of improvements may be possible. Two such
types of approach are possible. For convenience the two are termed adoptive
and adaptive approaches. An adoptive approach, while bearing in mind the
various constraints to producing a radical solution, would hold them in the
background. It would allow the inherent logic of the data and its linkages
to the functions it performs, to suggest the structure of the total system
and the scope of constituent sub-systems. The approach would be optimistic
in its view of how much change in data handling procedures might be possible.

An adaptive approach would be more pessimistic. It would hold the functional
rigidity of departments, and various other limitations and constraints (in such
things as staff resources and computing capability), very much in the foreground.
An adaptive approach would seek to effect improvements in such a way as to
minimise alterations to the structure of the authority and political balance
between departments. It would also seek to avoid radical changes in procedures.

An adoptive approach to system design and definition of sub-systems would
first involve an authority-wide analysis of data holdings and flows. The
analyses would provide an objective assessment of the size and nature of the
authority's information processing problems. They could also be expected to
identify the data areas where improvements are urgently required and thus
point to a broad strategy for system development. Following the analyses, an
adoptive approach would proceed to classify data items into related sets on
the basis of the functions and activities requiring the items. Each related
data set would form the base of a separate sub-system. The extent of the
relationships within the data would define the scope of sub-systems.

The approach is implicit in the USAC six cities project which initially
anticipated that data items in US local authorities could be classified into
four related sets, each set being the base of a major sub-system (see US
Department of Housing and Urban Development 1969). The four sub-systems
anticipated were: Finance and Administration, Public Safety, Economic and
Physical Resource Development and Human Resources Development. Now that
analyses of data holdings and flows have been undertaken in the project
cities it is apparent that a fourfold classification does not correspond
with the logic of the data. It appears that possibly 10 or 11 related data
sets, and hence sub-systems can be defined. The number is not as important
in the present context as the approach which allows the data base to define
the number of sub-systems and the scope of each sub-system.

The research in the six cities has suggested a variation to the adoptive approach outlined above. It has suggested that it might be possible to define sub-systems without reference to the function of data items per se. Rather the suggestion is that classification of items into related sets may be undertaken with reference to the commonality of and frequency of need for data. Commonality is a measure of the degree of duplication or redundancy in the data base. Alternatively it is a term describing the amount of data which is collected more than once or used by more than one department. For example, in Wichita Falls, a city of about 100,000 population, an authority-wide analysis of data holdings and flows revealed that 25,000 data items were in use (Dunn and Hearle 1972). Not all the 25,000 were different data items however. In fact further analysis showed that there were only 6,000 different data items, that 25,000 items were counted in use yet only 6,000 items were collected or used more than once, and indeed that many items were duplicated several times. The figures indicate a commonality rate for Wichita Falls of approximately 80%. Following this approach, sub-systems would be defined around data sets which exhibited high degrees of commonality. A major benefit of the approach could be expected to be in a reduction in the number of data items collected more than once.

The definition of sub-systems following an adaptive approach would be likely to have more regard to the departmental organisation of an authority. The temptation would be to consider that since the functions of departments are different, so too are their data requirements, and hence to conclude that the separate departments require their own sub-systems. The tendency would thus be to define a sub-system for each department or group of departments having closely similar data requirements.

Planning sub-systems defined following the various approaches can be expected to differ in scope. Following an adaptive approach it is likely that the existence of a planning sub-system would be accepted a priori. Its scope would be defined so that it would meet the needs of the planning department in an authority. Following an adoptive approach the existence of a planning sub-system would not be assumed a priori. The data base would define sub-systems. It is likely that the sub-system most central to the needs of planning would emerge as a land and property sub-system. The needs of planning could be expected to extend to many of the other sub-systems such as person related, finance, and highway network sub-systems which would be defined by the logic of the data base.

Data bank and data base philosophies

The scope of an information system for planning does not solely depend upon the approach to sub-system definition. It also partly depends upon the approach adopted to the acquisition and storage of data. Here again approaches can be polarised for emphasis to contrast data bank and data base philosophies. The first approach would suggest the creation of a general purpose data bank catering for as many present and potential uses of data as possible. Creation of a data bank would involve the gathering together of whatever data was thought to be relevant from whatever source and in whatever form it could be obtained. This would include data files in different departments, data collected for particular purposes in special surveys, and data obtained from secondary sources such as for example the Census of Population. Such a collection of data would tend to be unsystematic in its coverage and ad hoc in nature. There would be no certainty that the data stored would be required in the future. It would tend to be static in that once collected and stored, a data file would be regarded as a self-contained entity with no arrangements made to keep it regularly up-to-date.

Data files are likely to be incompatible one with another in that data on common topics could be stored on the basis of different units of records, have varying identifier numbers for records, and varying definitions of data items.

The contrasting philosophy holds that data forming the data base in an information system should be derived from automating processes and procedures of management and routine administration. The data base would be acquired as a by-product of normal functions and at the same time be available to support these functions. Collection of data in this way would be systematic in coverage. It would be certain that what was collected was required for at least one purpose. The data base would be dynamic in that as changes occur they would come to the attention of the authority through the administration of services and the act of administration would cause the relevant data records to be amended. If data is stored at the unit of collection level (the level of routine transaction) there will be few problems of incompatibility of data files.

One place for argument concerning these approaches relates to whether data which is to be held for future use need be stored at such a fine level of detail as it is needed to support administration. More generally the argument concerns whether data needed for management, research and forward planning is in some qualitative or quantitative sense different to that required for (and generated by) administration. The American research and development projects are beginning to show that in the US situation, at least in the context of town and country planning, there is little difference between the data required by and available to the two sets of activities. In one city analysis of data holdings and flows revealed that over 100 items of data were used for the rating assessment function, while in the same city the Planning Department used an exact subset of these items. Further research is required to show whether this result is generally applicable in other data areas in US local authorities and whether similar conclusions would be arrived at in UK authorities. If it were generally found that there is little difference between planning and administrative data, the result would argue in favour of a data base approach since what would be required for planning would be available as a by-product of routine administration.

In the UK situation it may be that a significant proportion of the data required for planning would not be available for automating routine processes within an authority. The choice between approaches would then depend on the extent to which this kind of data normally comes from sources outside the authority as opposed to its being collected unsystematically by the planning department. If non-correspondence between administrative and planning data is due to the role of data collecting agencies outside the authority then the the needs of planning would have to be met in part by a data bank. If it is for this reason then a data bank approach would only be preferred if new arrangements to collect the required data systematically could not be made. (For the foreseeable future there will be a need for a data bank containing data for planning purposes which is not nor cannot be collected and regularly updated by a local authority, e.g. data files from national censuses. The longer term need for a data bank will depend upon whether agencies collecting official statistics themselves adopt the principles and practices of information systems.)

A data base approach is accepted as the preferred approach by both the GISP Report and the US six cities project. In the latter case acceptance is taken to the extent that once an authority process has been automated the computer process is expected to replace its clerical forerunner. Adoption of a data base approach implies the acceptance of computer systems to the limits of their capabilities and cost effectiveness as integral parts of an organisation. A data bank philosophy would view a computer system as a useful adjunct to be used in moderation within existing organisational frameworks. It should be apparent from the above discussion that a data bank of the kind described cannot be used to support routine administration. Conversely a data base approach cannot be adopted if an authority's information processing priorities do not involve the automation of routine processes.

View of the planning process

The argument concerning data bank and data base approaches has centred on the role of computer systems with respect to an authority's routine administration. A further consideration concerns an authority's view of the process of plan-making. The view of the US six cities project is that once systems are developed in local authorities the process of planning will involve a five step paradigm of data use. The intended sequence of steps is for data in the dynamic data base derived from routine administration in turn to:

    i   indicate and define a problem,
    ii be used to analyse the problem,
   iii be used to generate alternative courses of action,
    iv be used to implement a programme to alleviate the problem as
            suggested by item iii,
    v   provide feed back for monitoring.

The hope in the long term is to have so much data coming from routine administration that there will be little or no need to undertake ad hoc data collection. The paradigm contrasts with traditional practice in forward planning in this country which has tended to have problem definition separated from formal channels of data collection, i e. in other ways than through close inspection of an existing data base. Traditional practice has in addition usually involved a stage of survey and data collection after problem definition but before the problem can be analysed.

It will be apparent from the discussion that a change from traditional practice to the kind of planning process envisaged by the paradigm described above necessarily implies the adoption of a data base approach. A data bank of the kind described could not support the paradigm although it might allow greater flexibility in the use of data collected for the purpose of plan making. Much of the initiative towards information system development in this country has come from planning departments who have felt that the ideas of continuously reviewed Development Plans imply a dynamic data base as a substitute for large scale but periodic data collection exercises such as often preceded the creation, or the quinquennial review of, a pre-1968 Development Plan.

If it accepts the link between continuous review and a dynamic data base, an authority may be able to argue for system developments on the grounds of require-ment to fulfil statutory responsibilities. In this sense an authority is unusual. Many other organisations would introduce innovations such as computer systems only if there was good reason to believe that they could be justified in terms of costs and benefits.

Not all authorities may be able to adopt a data base approach to support their plan-making functions. In particular authorities who have a responsibility for strategic planning in a subject area but do not have executive responsibilities in the same area, will find that data which would normally be required for planning is not under their control but is the responsibility of another authority. Some implications of this situation are explored in the next section.

Updating

An information system includes a range of administrative and organisational procedures for the collection of data and dissemination of information in addition to computer systems which perform manipulation and retrieval functions. In developing an information system these non-computer aspects must be considered in parallel to hardware and software systems.

Updating is one such aspect of crucial importance to the success of an information system. It would seem pointless to mount major file building exercises to support a computer system if the files are built to refer to one point in time and are then allowed to go out of date. In a system constructed following a data base approach the updating function is performed by the routine transactions and processes which the system is designed to support. Updating files in a data bank of the kind described would be much more difficult to organise. The degree of difficulty would depend on the extent to which the data bank files represent once-off surveys or files derived from sources outside the authority which do not regularly bring the files up to date at a frequency desired by the authority.

Organisation of appropriate updating arrangements is required at all stages of system development, but a plan for updating is needed before the first phases of implementation. This is because the degree of difficulty in making proper arrangements can influence the choice of what part of the desired overall system is developed first. It can also influence the scope of sub-systems.

The effect of updating is particularly acute on a planning system as can be seen from the contrasting approaches of county councils and non-county authorities who have already started to develop sub-systems based on land and property data. The effect is related to the need for an authority to agree on what is to be its basic spatial unit for recording land and property data. The basic spatial unit (BSU) is the lowest level of unit for which data can be cross referenced in the system. Ideally the unit adopted as the BSU should be capable of being aggregated to form the spatial dimensions of other units of records of interest, for example, properties, land parcels, areas of homogeneous land use, planning applications and hereditament ratings (among others). The problem is that it may be impractical to adopt as the BSU the most suitable unit of record because of difficulties of updating.

The GISP Report recommends the hereditament rating as the BSU in urban areas. Adoption of the hereditament rating implies a central updating role for the department responsible for rating. This is a source of difficulty however since not all authorities are rating authorities. Authorities who are rating authorities have been able to consider a land and property system based on hereditaments partly because of the ease of updating of basic spatial units via routine operations of the rating department. County councils who are not rating authorities have anticipated greater difficulties in arranging for a continuing flow of information about properties. In large part because of difficulties in updating, county authorities have preferred to begin system developments in other ways. The tendency has been for counties to begin by automating planning applications for development control purposes and to provide data on land availability. Development of a land availability system is seen to be feasible partly because it can be updated by the routine process of updating planning applications.

If updating is administratively possible and if different units of records can be related to a common basic spatial unit then there would appear to be no technical reason why a system (or sub-system) could not extend throughout an authority to wherever relevant data exists. If arrangements for updating appear to be a serious difficulty the scope of a planning system will have to be more limited.

The value of a data file rapidly decreases if the file is allowed to go out of date. To obtain maximum benefit from information system developments it is thus essential that updating procedures be put into effect as soon as data files are computerised. Since an information system will only be as good as its updating, the emerging view is that the source of updating should be the routine processes of the authority.

The utility of data files may also be affected by other considerations. Some of these are described in the next sections. These sections form a second part to the paper concerned with matters of a more technical nature.

Avoiding longer term problems: by cross-referencing and planned flexibility

Whatever the scope of a sub-system for planning there are several steps which can be taken to ensure that the system has a high degree of utility and to ensure that the system can be integrated with other sub-systems.

One of the keys to a successful information system is the ability to cross-reference between data files. Several cross-referencing facilities should be built into a system. At one level facilities are required to cross-reference files within a sub-system; for example, between property records, land use records and planning applications within a planning or land and property sub-system. At another level facilities are required to cross-reference data files in different sub-systems; for example, between property records and person records or between property records and highway network records.

One problem that will face many authorities is that different departments sometimes use different numbering systems to identify units of record which are also the units of record in data files in other departments. The solution recommended in the GISP Report is that two kinds of files be constructed. These are data files, both at unit of collection level (basic files) and at aggregate level (zone or subject files), and a series of index files whose function is to form links between data files. For land and property data three indexes are suggested. One is a General Hereditament Index which has the function of providing a definitive record of all properties in built-up areas and is a guide to where data about properties is stored. It contains all file codes used by departments in transacting business with occupants of property or in collecting data about property. A second is an Address Index which provides a comprehensive gazetteer of properties and is to enable correlation between rating number references, full postal addresses, post codes and locational references. The third is a Planning Master Index the functions of which are to locate all basic spatial units to correlate them with hereditaments in built-up areas and to indicate where in the system all BSU data are stored.

Within a planning sub-system the General Hereditament Index would ensure cross referencing between land and property data files. For purposes of integration with other sub-systems further indexes might be required, for example, to facilitate cross referencing between property files and highway network files. More generally cross-referencing will be facilitated if key reference numbers identifying records of each of the various units of record can be commonly agreed throughout an authority. In this respect the adoption of the rating assessment number to identify all property records in built-up areas is one possibility recommended in the GISP report.

Identifier reference numbers written on to data records should be in a form suitable for computer processing. Postal addresses would thus not be suitable identifiers in data files. Because a large proportion of enquiries to the computerised data base will initially identify records by means of the postal address it is essential that the system incorporates the interface between records and their postal address. Within the GISP framework the place for this is the Master Index.

An earlier paper in these proceedings has discussed difficulties of processing and analysing data in current local authority data bases. These arise because much data is held at aggregate level rather than at the unit of collection level; because data sets often refer to different points of time, especially if they are obtained from sources outside the authority, and because data sets are often incompatible one with another because of differences in definitions, classification and coding schemes, and the spatial units of records. These difficulties could be largely avoided if the recommendations of the GISP Report are accepted by data collecting agencies. It is suggested in the report that data should be stored in units of record as close as possible to those used for data collection and that data be stored as actual values rather than coded values (e.g. actual age rather than age group). It is further suggested that records should be referenced to the time of data collection or to the time they were last updated and that records should be referenced to their spatial location in such a way as to permit flexible aggregation into larger units of varying size and shape.

Geographic referencing

Records can be referenced to their spatial location in a number of ways. There has been recent debate about the relative merits of the various kinds of referencing systems as they have been adopted in difficult countries and authorities. The argument has tended to claim that one is in some sense better than another. The view of the GISP Report is that at least three kinds of locational referencing systems will be needed in advanced information systems. These are Point, Area and Network systems (corresponding to what are referred to in GISP as Geosystems). Point referencing assumes that data is located at a point somewhere inside the boundary of the area to which the data refers. This kind of system is most suitable when the area of the data units is small compared to the scale of data analysis. Area referencing, by which is meant the definition of an area by a series of coordinates describing its boundary, might be required if a description of the boundary is essential information about the area. This kind of referencing would be suited to systems which are concerned with large land units or with qualitative characteristics of land units or where interest is in relative proportions of a measurable attribute (e.g. amount of different land uses within an ownership unit, proportions of an area having different ranges of relative relief). In a network system (often referred to as a segment or line segment system) the unit of record is a link in the network referenced by coordinates to its end points. This kind of system is clearly most appropriate to data systems concerned with such networks as roads, gas, electricity, water supply or sewerage systems.

If the different kinds of referencing system will be required in an advanced overall system the question arises whether one should be adopted before the others. In theory the first referencing system implemented should be the one most suited to locating the units of record of the sub-system to be implemented first. In practice there may be an element of opportunity influencing the adoption of a referencing system. In one authority, for example, the exercise of putting rating records into a computer file provided the opportunity for restructuring the file and for adding point references at a marginal additional cost. In another authority the obligation to undertake a land use survey provided the opportunity to define basic spatial units for the information base. Again it was felt that referencing of the units could be undertaken at a marginal additional cost compared to the cost of the survey. These examples illustrate the further information system principle that developments are easier to justify if they can be undertaken in association with work that is to be done in another context which itself can be justified in terms of costs and benefits. Referencing is unlikely to be justifiable as an isolated exercise out of context of data file building or restructuring.

In general authorities are developing referencing systems suited to the data forming the basis of their priority sub-system. The priority in authorities tends to centre on land and property data. In urban areas where it is possible to establish a master index of properties in association with rating records at hereditament level, authorities have been led towards coordinate points as their first referencing system. County authorities beginning systems development with the automation of planning applications have also opted for point referencing as a cheaper alternative than area referencing while being suitable for the kinds of applications they have in mind.

Current orientation of objectives

Authorities who adopt a data base approach to data collection and storage are necessarily concerned with the automation of routine processes. It was explained earlier that they may also adopt the approach in order to support their plan-making functions. Conversely it has been implied that a data bank could not be used to support routine processes but might assist research and plan making activities. As a result of preparation of the Manual on Point Referencing Properties and Parcels of Land it is possible to assess the current orientation of local authority objectives.

One exercise undertaken for the Manual was an investigation of the processing requirements of authorities related to spatially located data. It was discovered that most processing requirements were concerned with the retrieval of records from data files in various ways, the extraction of records lying within areas of various shapes and sizes, and the extraction of groups of records which have common characteristics or attributes. It was apparent that there was little felt need for sophisticated research techniques.

The study group outlined a Spatial Retrieval and Analysis System (SPARS) to meet the identified processing requirements. The SPARS outline is reproduced in Figure 1 (see Cowie 1972). The views of many of the authorities most active in systems development work and the descriptions of their current applications as included in the Manual indicate that the major uses of SPARS will be in extraction and simple manipulation of data (Modules 1 and 2), at least in the short term. The analysis module (Module 3) included in SPARS recognises however that an extensive capability for research may be required in the longer term. Current work and views thus indicate that authorities are most concerned with supporting their routine operations.

In the longer term authorities may find their priorities changing to give a greater emphasis to model building and research generally as data bases are extended and as more sophisticated techniques for analysing locationally referenced data become available. Authorities who currently feel that a data

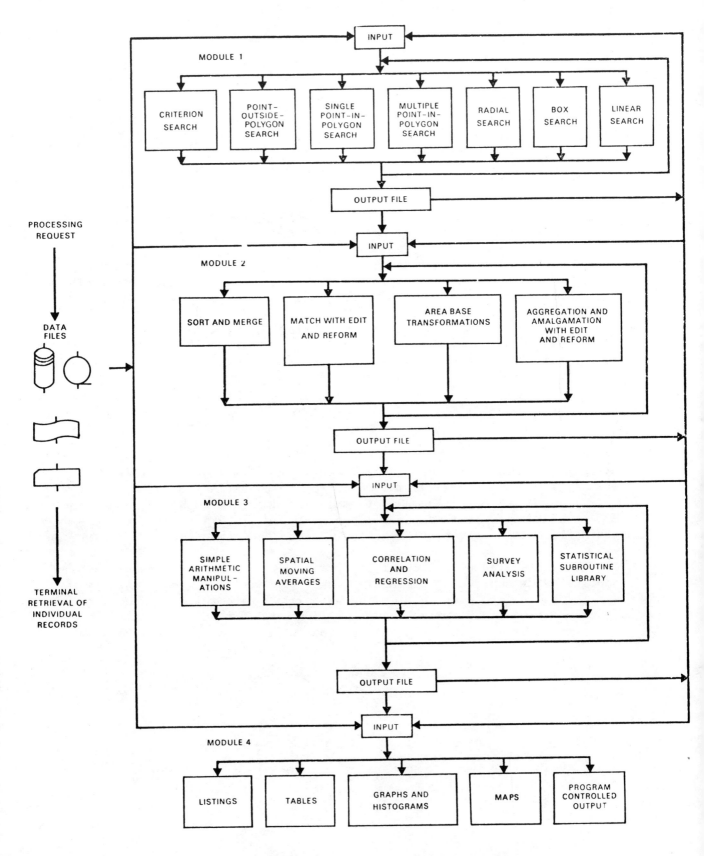

Figure 1   Spatial retrieval and analysis system (SPARS)

bank approach is sufficient for their anticipated purposes may find a data base approach more appropriate for model building since large quantities of good quality data is required to make realistic planning models operational.

NOTES

1   In this paper data is distinguished from information in the following way. Data or items of data are observed or measured facts or values. Data becomes information when meaning is attributed which is not explicitly contained in the data. Thus for example, that a property has two bedrooms, three of the five basic amenities, and that it houses five people, are items of data. The meaning derived from the data (information) would be different to an officer considering the property for an improvement grant than to an officer in a Social Services Department. The purpose of an information system is to process facts or data items in order to derive information. A number of departments would consider the same data items but would derive different information. It appears to be doubtful whether an information system can in fact process information.

2   Privacy and confidentiality are sensitive issues especially with respect to data relating to individuals. The topic is not discussed in the paper other than to note that the emerging view is that the problems are administrative and political rather than problems of systems per se. The technology is neutral. It can be protective or revealing according to how it is used. Privacy and confidentiality are issues of the use of information, not of the collection and storage of data.

3   The emergence of the views expressed in Notes 1 and 2 can be largely attributed to Dr W.H. Mitchel, former chairman of the United States Urban Systems Interagency Committee (USAC) responsible for the Six Cities Project organised under the US Department of Housing and Urban Development (HUD). Statements in this paper concerning the six cities projects are derived from talks given by Dr Mitchel unless otherwise noted.

4   That there are a number of possible approaches is partly the result of a planning department being primarily a user of data collected by other departments and agencies outside the authority, rather than a generator of data. It is also partly because a planning department has data requirements which extend or could extend to data collected and held by most local authority departments. The GISP Report discusses both points.

The management of data and the presentation of results from a computerised information system

Richard Baxter

If anybody were interested in reviewing the existing literature on the subject of information systems for planners, he would find a rather unbalanced picture. The debate has centred around the system design of a computerised information or management system and the experiences of specific applications. Yet in this debate the question of the computer environment is rarely discussed. This paper attempts to rectify this omission to a small degree.

Perhaps it is useful to state at the outset what I am not going to include I do not intend to argue the pros and cons of an information system for planning. Nor do I want to direct my remarks to any specific design of a spatial information system. Whilst accepting that file contents and the structure of any system of cross-referenced files are important considerations, I do not intend to discuss the options, but to use the concepts only in a general sense. Further, I am not interested in the details of manipulating, searching, sorting and updating files as constituent tasks within an information system but I intend to criticise the thinking that has categorised tasks in this way. Finally, I am not going to assume that you have any intimate knowledge of computing systems, but will try to introduce the topic from basic principles.

Computer hardware

At this juncture it would be useful to define some terms, especially as these will recur in the ensuing discussion. Because the world of computing has built its own jargon at an alarming rate it is difficult to discuss this subject without unintentionally leaving doubts and questions in the minds of the uninitiated. For a start there are the physical units or hardware which make up a computer system. (The programs or software which control the running of the machine will be introduced later.) At any computer installation there are a number of hardware units which together constitute the computer configuration. In all such configurations there are some essential components which are readily identifiable. These are shown in Figure 1.

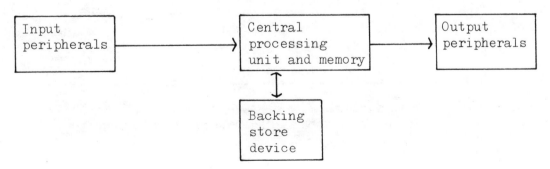

Figure 1   Essential components of a computer configuration

There is a common need for programs and data to be entered into the computer. This is undertaken through various input devices which perform translations into the internal code of the machine at the same time. Most configurations have input devices capable of reading either punched cards or paper tape. Porta-punch cards permit the direct transcription of field observations on to punched cards without any intermediate manually written document. Mark sense cards have similar advantages but the reading mechanism is not electro-mechanical but of the optical category. Devices to recognise characters are a relatively new development. They fall into two classes: those relying upon magnetic ink character recognition and others recognising handwritten characters. Having used the IBM 1287 reader. which falls into the latter category, it is easy to see its potentialities — for example, the reading of Census tables — but at the moment it fails to reach a sufficient level of accuracy. Encoders are able to transfer information directly from a key-board on to magnetic tape whilst on-line systems can enter data directly into core or on to disc from a teletype terminal. Visual display units offer scope as input devices but they tend to be expensive. Since the input of data is still a comparatively slow procedure within the computer system it is not surprising that the industry continues to develop faster and improved peripherals.

The central processing unit is the nerve centre of any digital computer system since it coordinates and controls the activities of all the other units and performs all the arithmetic and logical processes to be applied to the data. Much of the money spent on computer installations ends up in this unit and, as with most things in this life, you get what you pay for. There are many considerations in the purchase of a central processor but two parameters assume significant importance. These are the store size of the memory and the speed of operation. The memory (for programs and data) of the computer is generally in the central processor (although extensions are made on to backing store devices). It consists of a series of magnetic storage devices organised to hold data or program instructions in a series of addressable locations. The number of such locations limits the informa-tion content of the memory at any one moment in time and is a measure of the machine's core capacity. This measure (in multiples of 1024 addressable locations) is one of the. vital parameters in all computing systems. It is also necessary to know a little more about the nature of the addressable locations (their bit lengths) before being able to judge the true capacity of the machine.* For all intents and purposes it is as fast to get informa-tion into and out of any of these store locations and for this reason the store is called random access. The actual speed of extracting information (access store) reflects the state of the technology. The first, second and third generation machines have seen the transition from electro-mechanical, through valves into transistors and other small semi-conductor circuits. This drastic shrinking in size increases the capacity and speed, with no loss of accuracy or reliability. Access times which were once measured in milliseconds (thousandths of a second) are now measured in nanoseconds (billionths of a second).

Random access storage is limited and expensive, and so there is a need to provide additional space for storing information before, during and after program runs. For these purposes backing store is provided which has a

---

* All storage media are binary consisting of two-state devices which hold a binary digit or bit. It follows that N distinct objects require at least $\log_2 N$ bits to describe them.

larger capacity but slower access time than the main core memory. In the
case of magnetic disc or drum the access method is cyclic but still relatively fast. Magnetic tape is the most common alternative, but information
is stored sequentially and access times are correspondingly slower. The
characteristics of main and backing store are demonstrated in Figure 2.

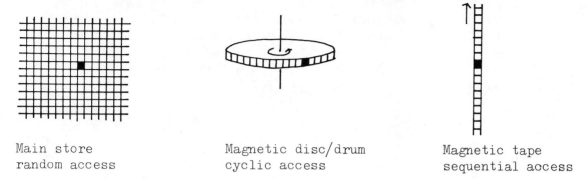

Main store
random access

Magnetic disc/drum
cyclic access

Magnetic tape
sequential access

Device	Typical storage capacity	Approximate access time
Main core store	512k	0.001 milliseconds
Magnetic disc	500 million bits	50 milliseconds
Magnetic drum	8 million bits	10 milliseconds
Magnetic tape	200 million bits	several minutes

Figure 2   Characteristics of main and backing store

Magnetic tape is the commonest form of backing store for the storage of the
large data bases, typical of any information system, because of its cheapness
per unit of stored data. Disc or drum tend to serve as storage media for
short programs or data in constant use. At the time of running programs the
computer controls the disposition of data sets and they might be moved
between any of these various forms of storage devices.

Lastly there are the output devices. Their purpose is to translate the
information held in the machine's internal code into a format acceptable
to human interpretation. There are various types of unit designed to present
information in a particular manner or deliver it at appropriate speeds. The
commonest type of output unit is the lineprinter. There are also page printers
which operate xerographic printing techniques as the result of electron beam
recording. Punched cards and paper tape can be produced as output as well
as serving as input. Once output, however, they still have to be interpreted
and these media are best reserved for situations where the data has to be
processed further by other equipment. In some cases output can be directed
to a typewriter or microfilm base. Information which is diagrammatic or

graphic can be presented on a plotter or visual display unit. The former can be of the digital incremental or vector type and draw on a drum with a pen or on a flat bed using a light spot or electron beam. The visual display units are either of the transient or refresh cathode ray tube type in which the picture has to be regenerated approximately 60 times a second or they take the form of storage tubes (like the Tektronix) in which the image is retained on the screen without computer intervention. Recent advances in Cambridge have produced a display device using laser beams which draw with a high resolution at much faster speeds. Three dimensional output has been converted directly into a solid model cut by a laser beam operating on a polystyrene block. These are early days, however, for the general distribution of laser scan output devices.

Catering for the planner's needs

Following on this brief introduction to the basic elements of any computer configuration I would like to review the planner's needs in this area. In terms of inputting data to the computer, the planner is likely to have three contrasting requirements. Firstly there is the data which already exists but which has to be transferred to a computer acceptable form. For source data, which requires sorting and ordering, it is usual to rewrite the information on forms and then have it punched on to cards and verified. These two stages could be reduced to one by using optical reader forms. When the source material is already ordered (such as Census returns) the punching can be undertaken directly from the source document but in the future an automatic scanning device might avoid the need for any manual intervention. The second situation arises when new information is collected from surveys. The use of specially designed optical reader forms could produce significant savings in resources and even mark-sence or portapunch cards are an improvement over the two stage document and punching process. The third type of information is that necessitating spatial identification. Such a need arises in the compilation of any master gazetteer for a spatial information system. Although crude manual methods of spatial coding are feasible the best results are obtained using digitisers. The main distributors in this country – D-Mac, Ferranti and Graphic-Display – provide a variety of models. In some cases the coding is punched on to paper tape for subsequent input to the computer. On more recent models the output is buffered and then sent to computer compatible magnetic tape, whilst the Ferranti Freedcraft is a freescan digitiser on-line to a small dedicated computer with a storage tube for the display and editing of data. The extraction of information from Ordnance Survey maps offers interesting potentialities. Automatic and multiple manual digitisers exist at a cost; there are computer controlled interactive line followers in the development stage; and the British Admiralty is assisting in the development of an instrument capable of optical character recognition from a map. There are flyspot and vidicon scanners which can digitise automatically linear information on a transparency. At a different level of sophistication there is a whole new world in the application of remote sensing to the collection of spatially located information. In Britain this development area is unlikely to affect planners within this decade.

For computer output the present situation is clearly established. Most planners rely upon lineprinters and plotters for the display of results. The plotters are well suited to planning data which has a spatial attribute and for the future the potentials of visual display units cannot be overlooked. It is worth drawing attention to the present disposition of these input/output peripherals amongst local authorities with a view to comparing them with similar statistics at some future date. Figure 3 gives a fair indication of the situation at

December 1971 and apart from indicating the sparsity of spatial data output peripherals (plotters and video terminals) it presents a more comforting picture of backing store facilities in the form of magnetic tape and disc.

Peripheral	Percentage of all Local Authorities possessing a computer installation
Magnetic tape	49.9
Paper tape	43.9
Punched cards	43.2
Magnetic disc	36.8
Graph plotter	2.9
Terminal and keyboard	2.9
Video terminal	1.8
Direct input	1.4

Figure 3   Configuration of Local Authority computing systems.
(after Baxter, 1972)

Although somewhat separate from the main discussion it is worth mentioning the work of the Ordnance Survey in the digitisation of large scale maps and the storage of the digital information on magnetic tape. The theoretical advantages of holding maps in this form are considerable, but the practical advantages might be delayed because of the lack of suitable hardware and software in local authorities. One interesting possibility is to establish such digital data bases from which the spatially located planning data can be extracted. A project to compile a planning gazetteer from a digitised Ordnance Survey map using a video display attached to a computer is in the research stage at the Computer Aided Design Centre in Cambridge. Progress in digitising specified information directly from maps using optical scan devices is slow but one interesting development is the measurement of coloured or shaded areas directly from a map. The Quantimet computer, which can measure percentage cover by different land uses, could be of widespread interest in planning. Certainly the results are encouraging at this stage (Baxter and Lloyd 1971).

When looking at the entire computer installation, the main constraint would appear to be financial. Few local authorities will ever aspire to the type of configuration existing within a University environment or that at the Computer Aided Design Centre in Cambridge (Figure 4). Whilst core storage is becoming cheaper and disc access speeds and storage capacities are increasing, they are likely to remain critical constraints when purchasing machines and deciding how to store information economically. In this context it is interesting to look at the current use of computers by departments within local authorities (see Figure 5). The present existence and shape of computer configurations within local authorities is undoubtedly due to the overwhelming importance of financial work as the main application area. It is interesting to conjecture on the future pattern of computers with the increasing demands made by other departments and the impending reorganisation of local government.

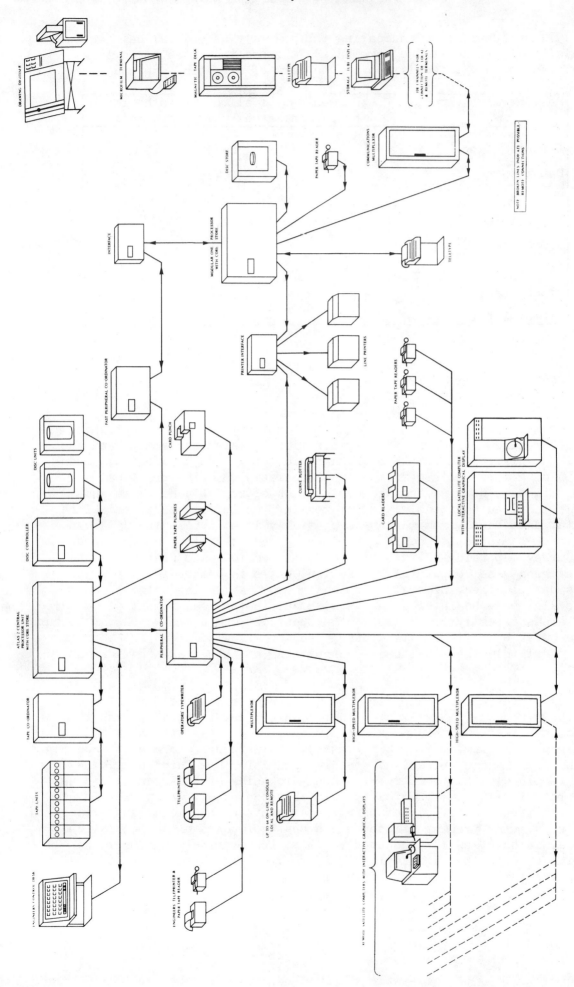

Figure 4   The C.A.D. Centre system at Cambridge

Uses	Percentage of all local authorities possessing a computer installation
Financial	97.9
Engineering	30.2
Statistics	18.6
Management	13.0
Health	12.3
Planning	8.4
Education	7.4
Architecture	3.5

Figure 5   The uses of computers in local authorities
(after Baxter 1972)

The future pattern of computers in local government

As of April 1974 the number of local government authorities in England and Wales will be reduced from 1425 to 433. The best provision of computing facilities to cater for the needs of these new authorities is a matter of concern. Whatever the final pattern, it is likely that a willingness to see through a redeployment of resources will be necessary and the outcome may be a hierarchy of computing facilities. This will inevitably pose problems with those departments already developing information systems, but it makes the question of data compatibility and transferability important when planning data interchange between the two tiers of local government under its new structure.

The compatibility between machines exists at a number of levels. The users' main concern is the ability to transfer software and data from one installation to another. As far as the data transfer is concerned there is an obvious need to use industry compatible magnetic tapes and standard recording formats. More ambitious schemes of long distance relay of data use shortwave radio transmission or the telecommunications network. The Post Office Datel service is an interesting development in the latter field and already international standards of signalling have been agreed and an inter-regional network of circuits within Britain worked out. These developments favour the multiple access computer environment in which remote terminals are used for data entry. The time when computers can be linked to other computers is not too distant. When the machines are of the same make and model the engineering problems are not too formidable but linking different manufacturers' machines poses considerably more difficulties. The Computer Aided Design Centre in Cambridge has a plan to link Atlas to the ICL 1900 range of computers and hopes to extend the range to include Univac, CDC and IBM. Once this is achieved we will be a step nearer unlimited access to information for planning. We will have to consider all the issues that that raises.

Software considerations

I would now like to turn my attention away from the hardware components of the computer and talk about the software which is a necessary prerequisite for running jobs. Information systems by their very size pose special problems and planning information systems, because of the spatial element, pose even more taxing problems. Successful software can help solve some of these problems, and it remains to identify the need for and existence of such software systems. At this stage it is vital to differentiate between the various types of software. Strictly the term is applied to those programs which assist all users to make the best use of a machine, which are supplied with the machine (but not necessarily free), as distinct from the user's own problem solving programs. Manufacturers generally supply file processing programs, debugging routines, utility programs to perform data handling operations, executive programs and operating systems, assemblers and compilers, and subroutines. The existence of much of this software is assumed by the user but under the heading of subroutines there is much scope for what actually is provided. These subroutines are usually provided by a manufacturer to perform large numbers of routine calculations. Together they form a software library package from which the user can incorporate members in his own program.

Only two of these various types of software need concern us here: the file processing programe already mentioned and the application package designed to perform the routines associated with a general problem area. The latter group can be seen as a more sophisticated type of subroutine in which the user employs the package and defines his own requirements by means of parameters.

File processing involves all operations connected with the creation and use of files. In the case of a planning information system there are usually a number of integrated files and the user is interested in creating, comparing, collating, sorting and merging these files. This is normally achieved by calling into operation a Data Base Management System (DBMS). Before examining such systems it is worth looking at the problems they are designed to solve.

A data file consists of entities (observations) which are described by characteristics (properties, variables) that take on attributes (values). Each characteristic has a domain of values and any particular value in the domain of its definition is an attribute. Attributes are finite on a nominal, ordinal, interval or ratio scale. A file can be represented as a data matrix $A = (a_{ij})$ where a_{ij} is the attribute possessed by the entity e_i for the characteristic c_j. For computer manipulation it is unlikely that the whole matrix is required in store at the same time. It is most likely that data relating to one characteristic, or possibly two characteristics to perform overlays, or one entity, are required in store at any moment in time. In this case the data matrix is best thought of as a sequence of records or inverted files (see Figure 6).

The complete data matrix is inefficient in terms of storage, the more so when the attributes are sparse, and is inflexible to change. The records and inverted files are more flexible but more complicated in their arrangement. In the case when new entities are to be added it is better to have a structure of records, but if new characteristics are added the inverted file structure is better. In this case it emphasises that the choice of file structure and data representation should be affected by the possible types of processing and analyses that will be performed.

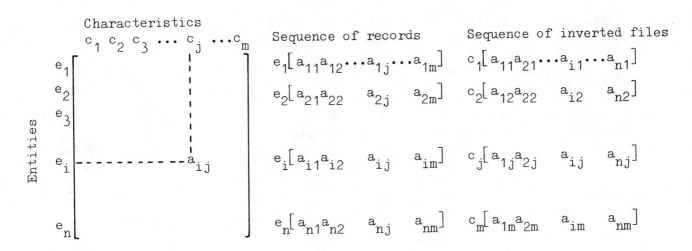

Figure 6   Data matrix with records and inverted files

All these structures can be ordered and the benefits are best illustrated with reference to a file consisting of a number of entities (dwellings for example) one of whose characteristics is the house number. The attributes of this characteristic constitute a list and the file can be ordered or unordered with reference to this characteristic (Figure 7).

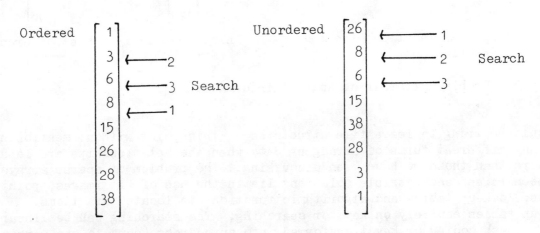

Figure 7   Ordered and unordered lists

When faced with the task of searching for a particular attribute the two lists exhibit different properties. Unordered lists must be searched sequentially and N/2 tests are needed on average to locate a specific entry. For an ordered list a search by successive halving requires only $\log_2 N$ tests. Hence searching is faster for an ordered list. For updating purposes additions to the list are easier when unordered as the new entity is merely added to the bottom of the list. If the list is ordered the addition of new entities necessarily involves a search and merge if the resulting list is to remain ordered. Deletions or manipulations of a specified entity in an unordered list involves a lengthy search. These are more efficient in an ordered list because of the faster search techniques.

It is feasible to ascertain the benefits of either an ordered or unordered list based upon an assessment of future applications of the file. If it is ordered it is likely to be so for only one of the characteristics. In the case of spatially located data in which the geocode is the key characteristic there is a problem in deciding the criterion for ordering as Figure 8 indicates. Considering a twelve digit geocode in which the first six digits represent the easting and the second six digits the northing, if the ordering is undertaken from west to east the list will be very different from one ordered from north to south. The implications are considerable because many applications of the data base will involve aggregation of information into areal parcels. For these reasons it is foolhardy to discuss a spatial data system as merely the extension of the rating file. If the spatial component is to be useful, and real time systems become the norm, there is a need to rethink some of the methods of file structuring and handling.

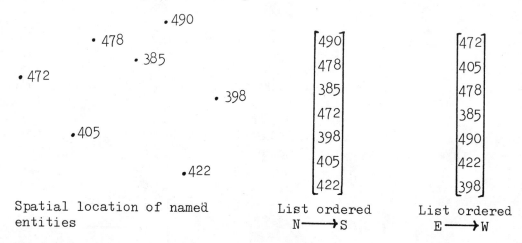

Figure 8   Problem of ordering spatial information

It would be wrong to leave file structures at this point without mentioning the many different forms of arranging data when the relationships are less standard than those we have been discussing. The problem of sparse arrays has been raised and possible solutions lie in the use of bit images, pointer chains, look-up tables and algorithmic functions to locate data items. Look-up tables can rely on keys or searching. The searching can be linear, binary, hash coding or key transformed into an address (many-to-one mapping). Records or inverted files of variable length can be structured in chains with relations stored as pointers. Other data structures might be better represented as trees, lists (as used in LISP), graphs, sets or ring structures. All these pose considerably more problems and require more fluent expertise than demonstrated by our initial array of data. The language becomes technical with addressing, tables, mapping functions, parallel files and directories, pointers, double chained trees, scanning, impasse detection, loops, isolated vertices, invalence, outvalence, orientated tree, arborescence, sieving, etc. Some structure to the whole area of interest is provided in the following schema:

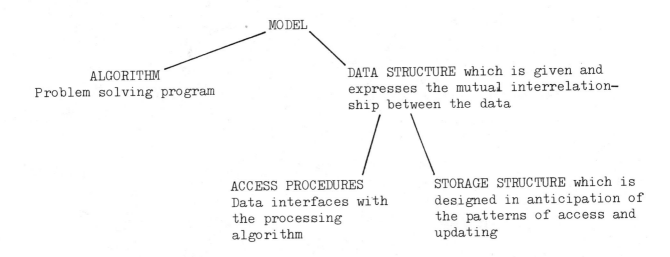

The data structure results from the contents and integration of the planning
information system. To a certain degree this dictates the form of the storage
structure in the computer, although the previous discussion has suggested that
much flexibility exists in this process. This flexibility allows for the form
of the local computer environment and envisaged pattern of use. Nothing, as
yet, has been said about the access procedures.

Data base management systems

The essential characteristics of a planning information system is that it
comprises a system of interlinked files. The data must, therefore, be organised
in files so that it is amenable to linkage, stratification and aggregation.
This is no easy task but generally implies some recognition of application files
which contain all the information needed for specific applications and linked
files in which information is not duplicated. Access procedures are likely to
be complex, the more so when the data storage design is complex but efficient.
It is in this context that the DBMS is necessary.

Such systems are needed to integrate application orientated files into a
working whole, to retrieve information from such data bases rapidly, to develop
a set of basic data processing functions which might be used as a systems level
language, and to manipulate the contents of a data base in accordance with
changing requirements. The data base task group of the CODASL Programming
Language Committee defined extensions to COBOL to handle data bases. Their
definition of an outline specification pinpoints the elements and relationships
common to most information systems:

Data structure	Item
	Group
	Entry
	File
Functions	Data definition, interrogation and update
Storage structure	Organisation of data within a stored entity
	Entries within a file
	Files within a multiple system
Operational environment	Hardware and software

ADAM	Advanced Data Management System	IBM 7030 (stretch)
GIS	Generalised Information System	IBM 360
IDS	Integrated Data Store	GE 625/635
ISL–1	Information System Learning Corporation –1	IBM 360; RCA Spectra 70/45; Univac 1108
MARK III	File Management System	IBM 1401
MARK IV		IBM 360
NIPS/FFS	NMC Information Processing System/ Formatted File System	IBM 360
SC 1	System Control 1	IBM 360/40
TDMS	Time Shared Data Management System	IBM 360/50H
SPAN		IBM 7090/7094
UL/1	User Language 1	RCA Spectra 70
COLINGO		IBM 1401, 1410, 7030
DMS 1100		Univac
CIBAS		
DATSY		
FASTOR		
PROFIL		
IMS		IBM
ICI		Burroughs
MIISFIT		IBM 360
FORTE		Burroughs
QUEST		
SAS–FIND		IBM
DBMS	Announced June 1972. Software Science funded by DTI's Advanced Computer Technology Project and Scheme	
LAMIS	1972. Local Authority Management Information System developed by ICL with DTI funding and applied in Leeds.	
L*	1971. Research development at University of Cambridge Computer Laboratory and Applied Research of Cambridge Limited.	

Figure 9   Data base management systems

There are a number of DBMSs in existence (Figure 9) but it is probably true to say that the perfect system does not exist. None of them makes special provision for the spatial component of planning information systems although the recent additions are geared specifically towards the problems of information systems in local authorities. There is a twofold division of DBMSs into host language and self-contained systems. Host languages allow the same degree of procedural control over the machine as, for example, COBOL. They enhance the facilities of COBOL and PL/I by offering a more extensive hierarchical structure or by providing for the expression of network relationships among records and providing facilities to initiate data transfers between disc and core. Self-contained languages have no language connection with any procedural language; they are suitable for the non-programmer, provide interrogation, selection, sorting and updating and give rapid satisfaction. The success of a comprehensive information system will depend upon a good Data Base Management System, probably of the host language variety.

Application packages

Having made a broad case for the file processing programs it is now time to look at the application packages designed to perform the routines associated with a general problem area. Their application to planning information systems can be viewed within the framework of SPARS put forward by Stewart Cowie. In the case of modules 1 and 2 we are concerned with spatial searches, transformations, sorting and editing. In module 3 there are the statistical routines. Algorithms for spatial searches and transformations exist in diverse places and the main omission is some form of centralisation and distribution. Sorting and editing packages are available from the manufacturers. On the statistical side there is a surfeit of packages: IBM's Scientific Subroutine Package with its unbundled version SL-MATH, the Harwell subroutine library, the Nottingham Algorithms Group Library, Dixon's Biomedical computer programs, Kansas State Geological Survey programs, Michigan State Geography Program Exchange, Computer Applications in the Social Sciences and Collected Algorithms from Communications of the Association for Computing Machines. With the exception of the last, which are written in Algol, the packages are written in Fortran. For the individual user it is always a question of knowing what software packages exist and how easy it is to acquire them. Even then the costs of obtaining, transferring and modifying them may be greater than writing one-off programs internally. This is especially true when local authorities are likely to use only a small selection of the library routines.

The question of programming languages is relevant at this juncture. It is not surprising that most local authority computing departments rely mainly on COBOL as a high level programming language. The specification of this language makes it most suited to business applications. As a language it is not suitable for arithmetic operations for which FORTRAN and ARGOL are ideal. In the developments of planning information systems we are manipulating large data bases for which COBOL is most suited and at the same time requiring the arithmetic capabilities of scientific languages such as FORTRAN and ALGOL to perform the spatial searches and statistical analyses. In this respect the recent report by LAMSAC is interesting (Computer Panel of Lamsac 1972). They consider COBOL, PL/I and ALGOL 68 within local authorities (why not FORTRAN?) and suggest adopting the following:

Single standard	PL/I
Dual standard	PL/I for the data processing and FORTRAN for the scientific work (on the face of it this would appear to be an absurd combination).
Mixed standard	Mixed modules of COBOL and FORTRAN

They state that ALGOL 68 should not be entertained and point out that ICL will not implement PL/I. (This is a significant statement bearing in mind that 50% of local authority computers are ICL.) They favour PL/I even though only 15% of USA users have adopted the language even accepting IBM's provision of packages to translate existing FORTRAN and ALGOL modules into PL/I. This whole question of programming languages is a vital issue if we aim for transferability in the future and yet we have an advisory document which only dabbles with the critical issues.

Whilst discussing software packages, it is nice to complete the story by turning attention away from the manipulation of the data in the machine to that of getting the answers out. Computers have an insatiable appetite for numbers at both the input and output stages. Generally it is expensive in human resources to put redundant data into the machine and by the same token it is wasteful to output unnecessary information. One of the simplest procedures is to change the voluminous lineprinter lists and tables into lineprinter graphs and histograms which convey a simpler message. The programming for this task is straightforward and simple. For spatial data sets the natural output is the map. Sophisticated packages such as SYMAP, LINMAP and COLMAP theoretically fulfil this role. The first is available from Harvard University for use on an IBM 360 computer but suffers from being heavily CPU bounded. The last two are the outcome of work at the then Ministry of Housing, and their general availability is subject to negotiation. The COLMAP version requires specialised peripheral equipment. Further applications are indicated in Taylor (1972).

Digital plotters are becoming more common and here the opportunities to display spatial data sets are increased. The problem of peripheral compatability is a recurring one but routines are generally called from high level languages to draw diagrams. Sophisticated extensions of these manufacturer supplied inter-faces can be found. In this country there is GINO in Cambridge, GIMMS in Edinburgh, KOMPLOT in Swansea, DISSPLA from Computer Cooperatives and the work at the Experimental Cartography Unit of the Royal College of Art. Probably the most exciting developments are in visual display units in which a keyboard is linked to some form of storage tube. As the price of these terminals fall they become more attractive propositions for the display of all forms of spatial data.

This paper has considered the computer environment as it relates to information systems for planners. The problems involved in designing a computerised data bank are many and lie far beyond those identified in the recently published GISP document. The expensive parts of the system lie in the computer environment and its ability to replace human resources. As yet we know too little about the cost effectiveness of different approaches to computing systems applicable to information systems.

Part 5

Appendix

Demonstrations & Seminars

URBAN SYSTEMS STUDY DEMONSTRATIONS AND SEMINARS

The last two days of the conference were given over to demonstrations and seminars illustrating the application of some of the ideas expressed earlier in the week. To provide an informal atmosphere, participants were divided into groups and attended three sessions:

Session I
INFORMATION AND DATA PROCESSING SYSTEMS
a)   Searching and retrieving planning data from computerised files and subsequent display on a Textronix tube and digital plotter.
b)   Changes in road networks and the effect on accessibilities. Interactive handling on a cathode ray tube display.
c)   Population predicting using cohort analysis.

Session II
THEORETICAL AND FUNCTIONAL ASPECTS OF URBAN MODELS
a)   Entropy: a theoretical approach to urban model building.
b)   Exposition of a simple residential location model.
c)   Computer demonstration of a simple residential location model.

Session III
AN URBAN MODEL AS AN EXPLORATIVE AND EDUCATIONAL TOOL
Demonstration of the experimental use of a computerised urban model for the generation and evaluation of alternative urban strategies.

What follows is a brief description of the theme presented in each of these sessions. All the demonstrations described are part of an on-going program of work at Land Use and Built Form Studies in Cambridge.

The three sessions attempt to give planners an awareness of computer
potentialities. The advent of the computer has an impact in two dimensions.
Firstly, it changes expensive manual techniques in planning into trivial
exercises which can be performed at will. Secondly, it enables the implementation of conceptual models which hitherto were beyond the calculating
capabilities of any planning officer. The limiting factors when using a
computer are no longer the actual calculations involved in any quantitative
work but rather the collection and input of sufficient accurate data, the
specification and writing of a program to perform the technique, and the
analysis of the results.

The demonstrations which follow are necessarily self-contained and might,
therefore, appear fragmentary. In an attempt to overcome this limitation
let us consider a hypothetical town and use this as a basis for discussion.
This town is subdivided into nine square cells as illustrated. The main
road network is superimposed together with a possible new road link across
the river. The accessibility matrices for the initial road network and the
network with the link added are listed. The fabric of the town's structure
is only drawn for one of the cells. With this common basis it is possible
to describe the objectives of the demonstrations.

One cell of the town (cell 2) is chosen as a digitised data base from which
to search and retrieve land use information. The town's road network provides the basis upon which to implement network changes and calculate accessibility surfaces. The forward prediction of the town's population by cohort
survival techniques is the third demonstration. The accessibility matrices
for the two networks are used in the examples of the residential location
model. In this demonstration spatial interaction models are applied to the
same nine cell town. The remaining demonstration is applicable to a real
town situation but in theory could also be applied to our hypothetical town.

The computer applications that are described in the following sections
have been developed on the Titan computer at the Computer Laboratory of
the University of Cambridge and the Atlas 2 computer at the Ministry of
Technology*CAD Centre, Madingley Road, Cambridge. These are almost
identical large multi-access computers to which are attached a selection
of on-line teletype terminals and graphical devices (see diagram). The
graphical devices take the form of small satellite computers with cathode
ray tube displays such as the PDP 7/9 computer with DEC 340 display or
the Elliot 905 computer with 928 display, other devices such as the CALCOMP
digital plotter, the COMPLOT on-line plotter and the Tektronix storage tube,
are directly connected to the main computer. The Atlas 2 and Titan also
support all the normal facilities such as card, paper tape and line printer
peripherals, with backing store provided by magnetic tape and disc units.

The computer programs which have been developed for the demonstrations are
written entirely in the high level language FORTRAN. Certain parts of the
demonstrations illustrate the use of graphics and these are also written
in FORTRAN. This has been possible by using a general purpose graphics
software package, GINO (Graphical Input and Output), which has been designed
and implemented by the University of Cambridge Computer-aided Design Group
[The Design and Implementation of the GINO 3D Graphics Software Package,
P.A. Woodsford, Software-Practice and Experience, Vol. 1, No. 4, 1971].
GINO takes the form of a library of subroutines, accessible from FORTRAN
(and some other languages), enabling the user to generate displays. The
programs using GINO are independent of the particular graphical device to
which the display is destined, an initialisation routine is provided for

*Department of Trade and Industry

Hypothetical Town

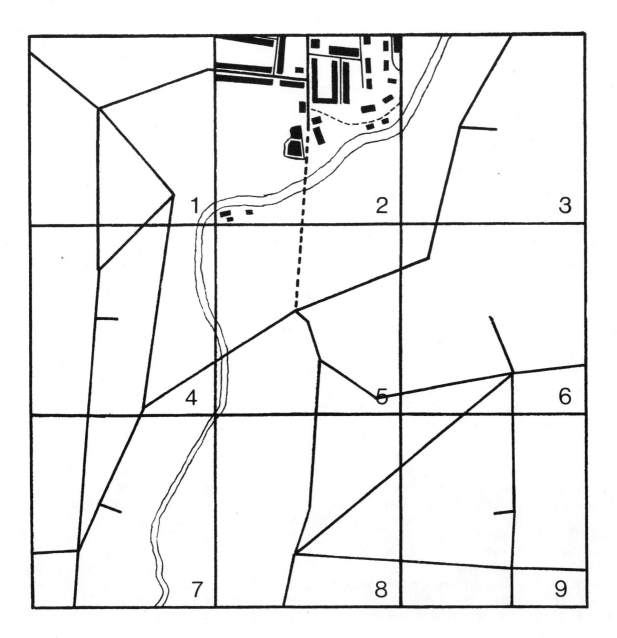

Accessibility matrix for road network with link added

	15	79	299	78	130	211	113	180	240
15		20	138	134	51	132	138	101	161
79	20		20	237	87	168	166	137	197
211	299	20		18	158	239	90	208	268
79	134	237	18		15	81	87	50	110
132	211	87	158	15		15	168	103	57
213	292	168	239	81	15		15	137	197
113	192	166	96	87	168	15		10	92
182	261	137	208	50	103	137	10		15
242	321	297	268	110	57	197	92	15	

Accessibility matrix for initial road network

each device and this alone requires modification to redirect the display to an alternative device. The present system incorporates facilities for all the graphical devices mentioned above, and is written in such a manner that new devices can be readily accommodated.

In the GINO system, the unit in terms of which pictures are generated is the picture segment — the smallest unit that can be independently displayed or plotted. Picture segments are generated sequentially by the user, who controls the size and content of the segment. Any number of segments can be viewed together. A picture segment consists of a sequence of picture parts, each added by a call to a GINO routine. Routines are available for a group of built-in picture parts which include points, lines, characters and circular arcs. This is supplemented by a facility to create user-defined picture parts, constructed from built-in picture parts and other user-defined picture parts; the user-defined object thus created can then be called as many times as required. Picture segments can be generated in two dimensions or in three dimensions displayed as two-dimensional projections. Windowing or clipping routines exist for both 2D and 3D, enabling the suppression of picture parts falling outside a specified region and thus allowing selective viewing of parts of a large picture. Transformations can be applied to all or any subset of picture parts making up a segment. These take the form of translation, rotation, scaling, shearing, reflection, parallel projection or point projection. This means that the user is able to define his picture parts to any scale or orientation that is convenient, and then use transformations to position the resulting display as required.

The preceding properties of GINO are relevant to all the graphics devices mentioned, but certain extra facilities exist to enable the user to interact with the display tubes. The basis of light pen interaction is the facility to name picture parts. Any picture part, built in or user-defined, may be given a unique numerical name so that it can be identified by the light pen. Only named picture parts are sensitive to the light pen, and when a pen hit occurs on a named picture part, the name is available in the satellite computer. A special satellite program, the interactive handler, is provided to control the feedback from the satellite to the user's program in the main computer. Occurrences of pen hits on named picture parts can be registered and stored by the handler in a list. The list may then be passed to the user's FORTRAN program when required, where it is decoded and suitable user defined action taken. New or replacement picture segments may then be sent to the display to await further interaction. Other facilities are available to handle interaction via a button keyboard and a joystick.

Using the GINO package enables sophisticated graphics applications to be developed on a wide variety of devices without recourse by the programmer to consideration of all the technicalities of picture manipulation.

SEARCHING AND RETRIEVING PLANNING DATA FROM COMPUTERISED FILES AND SUBSEQUENT DISPLAY ON A TEKTRONIX TUBE AND DIGITAL PLOTTER

Richard Baxter

INTRODUCTION

Successful planning and urban analysis is heavily dependent upon information about the study area. The sorting and retrieval of this information is greatly enhanced if the data is manipulated within a computer. For this reason computerised information systems for planning data have been developed in a number of authorities over the last decade. It is likely that these developments will increase during the next decade.

Rather than discuss the feasibility of conceiving the ideal information system it is worth making two basic points. In the first place the amount of data involved in a planning information system is very large. At the present time there is no sound software system existing which manages data and allows processing by multiple applications and can be interfaced by multiple languages. The need for a sophisticated data base management system (DBMS) will be more evident as information systems are extensively used. The second point concerns the nature of planning data. Land use data are spatially located and retrieval exercises tend to be across an areal domain. This has two implications. Firstly, the data in files must be structured systematically and secondly, the retrieval mechanisms must be efficient in terms of system overheads.

What follows is a brief exposition of a structure for a planning information system, the mechanics of collecting and storing the data, and the demonstration of selected retrieval exercices.

DATA ORGANISATION

The starting point is the Ordnance Survey map. For land uses two basic units are recognisable [Point referencing properties and parcels of land, Techniques for planning, DOE, 1971]. In the first case there is the hereditament which can be located to the nearest metre on the National Grid. Facing the problem of differentiating between multiple hereditaments at the same location it is necessary to append a suffix. This geocode plus suffix is the unique identifier for each hereditament. On the map it is necessary to add a visual identifier and the rate code satisfies this requirement. The other basic unit is the areal parcel. This involves the definition of the boundary of all parcels needing separate identification together with tne geocoded centroid.

A digitiser provides the most accurate way of obtaining this data. In this case the hereditament locations and parcel boundary coordinates are entered directly from the positioning of the cursor. Digitisers are designed so that miscellaneous information (such as rate codes) can be entered through a hand key. In this case a layout was constructed whereby all information could be entered by the cursor. Labelled boxes with fixed digitiser table coordinates were established and points within the appropriate boxes are digitised as required. The setup is illustrated. This simplifies the whole process, reduces errors and achieves a high throughput from the operator. For each map the result is a length of paper tape containing the digital information.

TRANSFER TO A COMPUTER

The paper tape containing the digital information is read into the computer
and filed on magnetic disc. A program (in Fortran) uses this data file to
construct two basic data files. The first of these is the property file
containing the individual geocode plus suffix, rate code and other information. The second file is the parcel file containing the geocoded centroid
and the string of parcel boundary coordinates. These two files can be
seen as part of a whole integrated information system, an example of which
is illustrated. The purpose of the program is to interpret the meaning of
the miscellaneous information entered through the fixed boxes, separate
the property and parcel files data, and perform the translation and rotation
from map coordinates to National Grid coordinates. Parts of the end products are listed. These files form the basis for the subsequent exercises
involving retrieval and file interlinkages.

APPLICATIONS

Four demonstrations are presented which use these two data files for a
number of search and retrieval exercises. Firstly, the parcels file is
used to redraw the maps of the land area. The remaining demonstrations
use the property file and perform a number of spatial searches.

(1) Display of maps from parcel data file

In this demonstration the areal parcels are drawn on the Tektronix tube
for any user defined space within the town. The user merely states the
coordinates of the south-west corner of the required space and gives the
east/north extent in hectares. This last figure determines the scale of
the map. A square with its hectare subdivisions is drawn and the grid
limits are added. The land parcels falling totally and partly within the
boundary are drawn together with their associated centroids and numeric
identifiers. Unlike the standard Ordnance Survey map a system of this
form has no limitations on scale and the map borders are under the control
of the user.

Package:

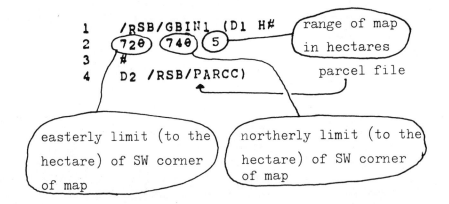

This simple package runs in 4k of 48bit words. It could be enhanced in
a number of ways. The parcels to be drawn could be subjected to filtering
on a number of criteria. For example, only the public open space might be
drawn as a result of checking the land use entry. It would be a simple
operation to compute areas for each parcel and print them on the map, on
the lineprinter, or in a data file for subsequent analysis. A further

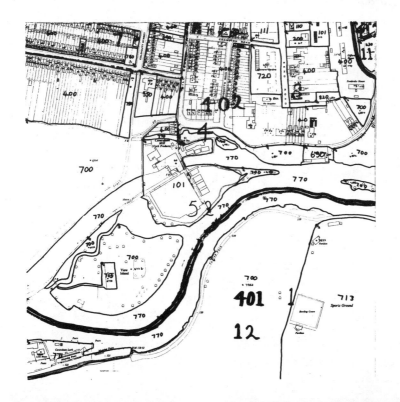

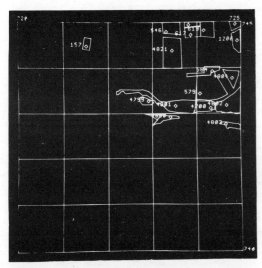

(1) Display of parcels

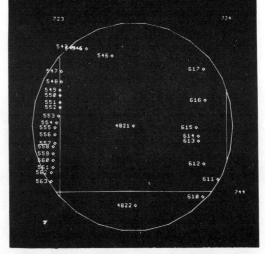

(2) Radial search of properties

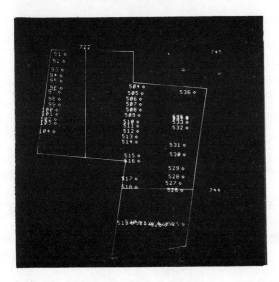

(3) Polygonal search of properties

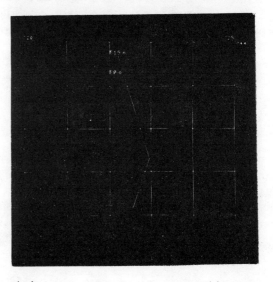

(4) Path search of properties

development could allow interactive editing of the data base. This would allow the user to subdivide parcels or join others together. Developments in this direction tend to be expensive in overheads as the package requires more store and locks out other users.

Significant advances have been made by the Ordnance Survey in the use of digital data held on magnetic tapes as an alternative to the standard map sheet [Developments in Automated Cartography at the Ordnance Survey, Capt. M. St. G. Irwin, Cartographic Journal, Vol. 8, No. 2, 1971, pp. 133-8].
Conceivably these data bases could be manipulated in a similar way to the example described.

(2) Radial search of property data file

In this demonstration the properties within a specified distance of a user supplied central point are searched and displayed on the Tektronix tube.
The user merely states the precise coordinates of the central point (possibly after referencing a gazetteer) and a distance in metres over which the search is performed. The circle is drawn and the hectare grid inserted together with the grid references. The properties falling within this circle are selected and located. The associated numeric identifiers are added to the display file.

Package:

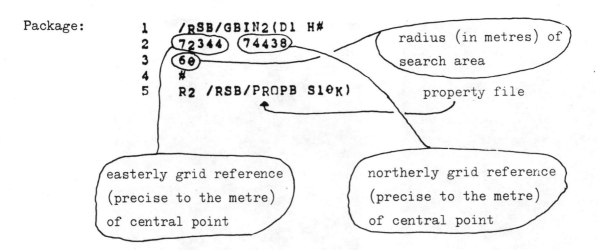

To illustrate the use of such a system consider a situation where a planning application has been received for the development of the allotment area illustrated. Before making a decision it might help to review the other planning applications within a certain distance of the current application.
Using the property file as a gazetteer it is possible to give the grid reference of this central point. It is a simple matter to decide over what distance the search is to operate. The present output merely retrieves all properties within this distance of the central point.

(3) Polygonal search of property data file

In this demonstration the properties within a user defined polygon are searched and displayed on the Tektronix tube. The user merely provides the precise coordinates of the vertices of a closed polygonal shape. The polygon is drawn and the hectare grid inserted together with the grid references. The properties falling within this boundary are selected and located. The associated numeric identifiers are added to the display file.

Package:

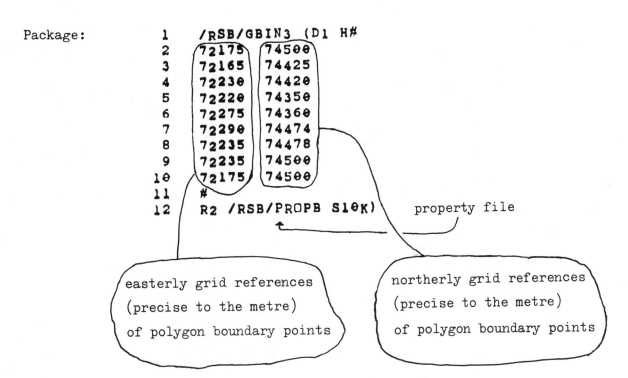

```
 1    /RSB/GBIN3  (D1 H#
 2    72175   74500
 3    72165   74425
 4    72230   74420
 5    72220   74350
 6    72275   74360
 7    72290   74474
 8    72235   74478
 9    72235   74500
10    72175   74500
11    #
12    R2 /RSB/PROPB S10K)
```

property file

easterly grid references (precise to the metre) of polygon boundary points

northerly grid references (precise to the metre) of polygon boundary points

Uses of such a system are diverse. The boundary coordinates might represent an enumeration district and the task be to update population figures for such a unit. The properties selected in this demonstration could be passed to another file containing household populations and these properties (matched by the geocode) retrieved and totalled. In this example all the properties falling within the polygon are displayed.

(4) Path search of property data file

In this demonstration the properties within a specified distance of a user defined path alignment are searched and displayed on the Tektronix tube. The user merely provides the precise coordinates of a notional central line of the path and the width of the path on either side of this line. A hectare grid for the appropriate area and at a suitable scale is constructed. The grid limits are added and the central line of the path is displayed. All properties falling within the specified distance of the central align-ment are selected and located. The associated numeric identifiers are added to the display file.

Package:

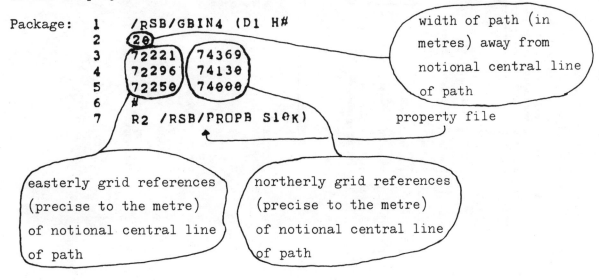

```
 1    /RSB/GBIN4  (D1 H#
 2    20
 3    72221   74369
 4    72296   74130
 5    72250   74000
 6    #
 7    R2 /RSB/PROPB S10K)
```

width of path (in metres) away from notional central line of path

property file

easterly grid references (precise to the metre) of notional central line of path

northerly grid references (precise to the metre) of notional central line of path

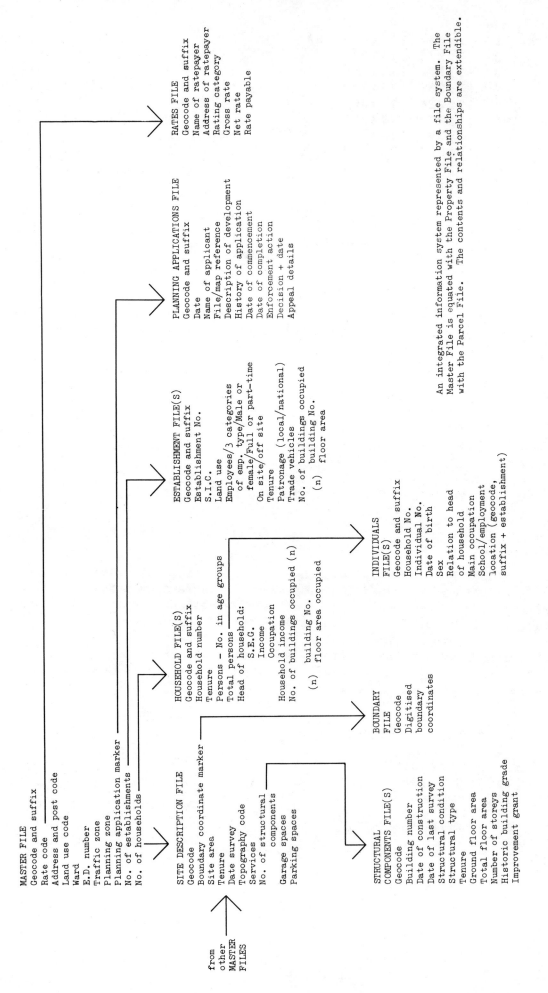

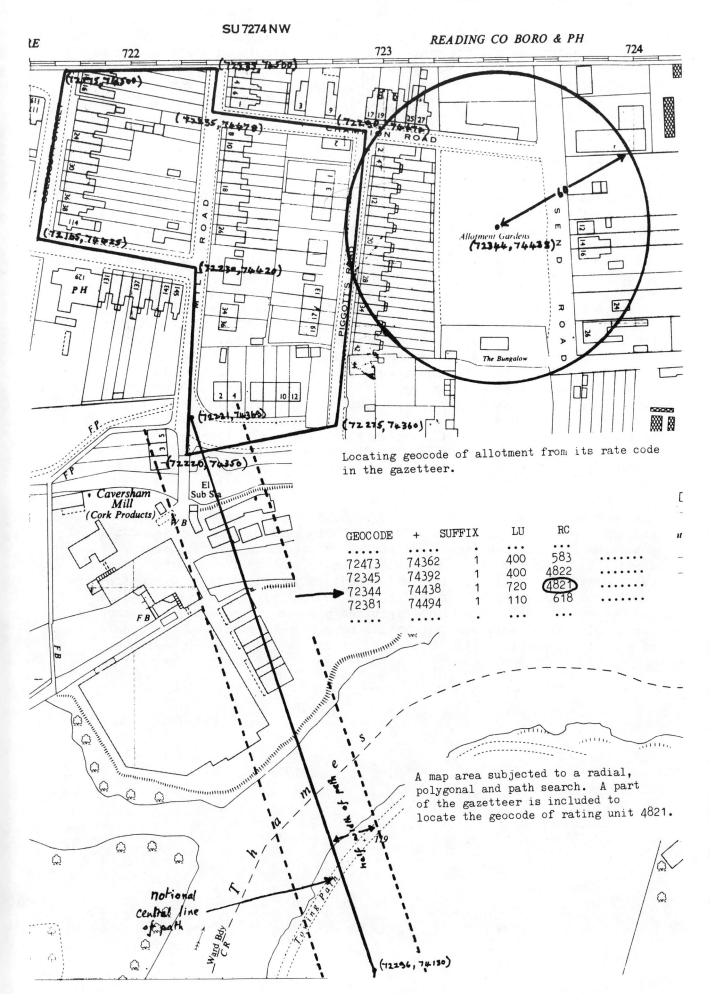

Locating geocode of allotment from its rate code in the gazetteer.

GEOCODE	+ SUFFIX		LU	RC	
72473	74362	1	400	583	......
72345	74392	1	400	4822	......
72344	74438	1	720	4821	......
72381	74494	1	110	618	......

A map area subjected to a radial, polygonal and path search. A part of the gazetteer is included to locate the geocode of rating unit 4821.

The most obvious use of such a system is in road alignment planning. For any given alignment all the properties within a specified distance can be retrieved and subsequently analysed. Reference to the rating file (matched by the geocode) would permit rapid tabulations of the total rateable value of all properties along any specified alignment. This example sorts and displays all the properties along the path.

FUTURE DEVELOPMENTS

Graphics are an expensive tool on two accounts. Firstly, the hardware is expensive to buy and can only be justified if the benefits themselves can be costed. For this reason graphics for planning are only likely to be introduced where this hardware already exists by virtue of usage in other local authority departments (transportation and highways especially) or by access to a computer bureau. Secondly, the software is also very expensive. Manufacturers of graphic plotters provide software packages to support their machines. Unfortunately these tend to be machine dependent and compatibility and transferability are difficult to attain. GINO, however, is a general purpose graphics software package which is independent of the particular graphic device to which the display file is destined. Once the display is generated a post-processor interfaces it with the characteristics of specific peripheral devices. These post-processors can be extended with the addition of alternative graphical devices. GINO, therefore, is independent of these peripherals and it only remains to make the basic software package computer independent. When one realises that the cost of software involved in these demonstrations approaches £250,000 the benefits of making such systems generally available are obvious.

The four demonstrations described could be extended in countless ways. Any development the user sees as useful could be implemented with additional penalties in running costs. Any incursions into this field, however, must await a suitable climate of opinion and until this is forthcoming it is worth drawing attention to the less visual component of these demonstrations, namely the ability to scan geocoded data and satisfy radial, polygonal and path searches and to regenerate digitised parcels. These will be common application areas wherever authorities have been convinced of the benefits of computerised information systems as an aid to successful planning.

CHANGES IN ROAD NETWORKS AND THE EFFECT ON ACCESSIBILITIES –
INTERACTIVE HANDLING ON A CATHODE RAY TUBE DISPLAY

Catherine Stoneman

INTRODUCTION

This computer demonstration is designed to show the great potential for the
use of interactive graphics techniques in the planning field. For this
particular example we have confined ourselves to considering a simple road
network, but there is great scope for further applications.

The aim of the present system is to enable the user to speedily analyse
and compare various modifications made to an existing road network. The
two processes, modification and analysis, split the system into two logical
phases. Phase 1, modification, presents the user with a displayed picture
of his network on the cathode ray tube, which he may then alter in any way
he wishes using the light pen. The second phase performs various analyses
on the network taken from the first phase. The user may then return if he
wishes to the first phase and instigate more modifications, the cycle continuing for as long as required (see systems flow diagram).

DATA ORGANISATION

The system requires two types of data inputs, the network data and some
parameters. It is assumed that the network can be obtained in such a way
that each of its junctions or nodes is uniquely positioned with reference
to a two-dimensional coordinate system. Each junction is then given a
unique numerical name, followed by its grid coordinate and a list of the
names of other junctions to which it is directly connected (see example).
The data may be coded by hand directly from maps and transferred to paper
tape or cards or a digitiser can be used to produce a paper tape containing
the required information. The parameters that are required are to assist in
the scaling of the network to fit it on to the available display screen, and
also to specify the positioning and mesh size of a square grid which may
overlay the network on the display screen. The significance of the square
grid is that it can be used to define the level of aggregation at which the
analysis is made on the network.

TRANSFER TO COMPUTER

The cards or paper tapes containing the digital information are fed into
the computer and stored on magnetic disc ready for use. Once the initial
network has been transferred to the computer in this way there is no need
to repeat the process if the network is subsequently altered. This is due
to the fact that on termination, the modification phase of the system
automatically outputs new files containing the modified network and can
thus be used without phase 2 as a file updating process.

SYSTEM FLOW DIAGRAM

Program in main computer   Satellite and Display

Enter phase 1 program
  ↓
Read network data from
disc file and store in program
  ↓
Construct ancillary ————————————→ Ancillary segments displayed
picture segments   on screen
  ↓
Construct network ————————————→ Network displayed
picture segment   on screen
  ↓   ↓
  Wait   User indicates with light
  ⋮   pen changes to network
  ⋮   or completion required
  ⋮   ↓
Message received- ←———————————— Message sent to main
decode   computer
  ↓
Is completion indicated? ——————→
  ↓
Incorporate changes indicated
into network data in store

Output current network data
to a file on disc
  ↓
Terminate phase 1 program
Enter phase 2 program
  ↓
Read current network data
from disc file
  ↓
Compute minimum path for network
  ↓
Compute accessibility measures and ——→ Accessibility measures displayed
construct picture segment   on screen
  ↓   ↓
  Wait   ↓
  ⋮   ↓
Message received ←———————————— Indicate with light
  ↓   pen return required
Terminate phase 2 program
  ↓
Re-enter phase 1 program
with current network file

NETWORK DATA FILE

NODE NAME	X-COORD	Y-COORD	N1	N2	N3	N4	N5
1	55	145	11	12	0	0	0
2	105	145	14	0	0	0	0
3	155	145	16	0	0	0	0
4	55	95	18	0	0	0	0
5	105	95	20	21	0	0	0
6	155	95	24	0	0	0	0
7	55	45	28	0	0	0	0
8	105	45	21	30	0	0	0
9	155	45	33	0	0	0	0
10	30	166	11	0	0	0	0
11	49	151	1	10	36	17	0
12	69	128	1	17	19	0	0
13	105	169	14	0	0	0	0
14	105	158	36	13	2	0	0
15	160	170	16	0	0	0	0
16	146	146	3	15	23	0	0
17	49	108	11	12	18	0	0
18	48	95	4	17	27	0	0
19	61	72	12	28	20	0	0
20	102	98	5	19	23	0	0
21	108	85	5	8	22	0	0
22	123	75	21	24	0	0	0
23	138	112	16	20	0	0	0
24	161	82	6	22	25	30	33
25	180	84	24	0	0	0	0
26	30	33	27	0	0	0	0
27	43	34	18	26	28	35	0
28	49	48	7	19	27	0	0
29	98	20	30	0	0	0	0
30	101	34	8	24	29	32	0
31	160	20	32	0	0	0	0
32	160	30	30	31	33	34	0
33	161	45	9	24	32	0	0
34	180	30	32	0	0	0	0
35	42	20	27	0	0	0	0
36	78	161	11	14	0	0	0

APPLICATIONS

This demonstration is best seen as two phases.

Phase 1 – network display and modification

Phase 1 initially reads into store a specified file of network data, and its parameters. The network file may be for the initial network input to the computer, or a file containing a modified network produced during a previous session. The algorithm used to convert this data into a picture

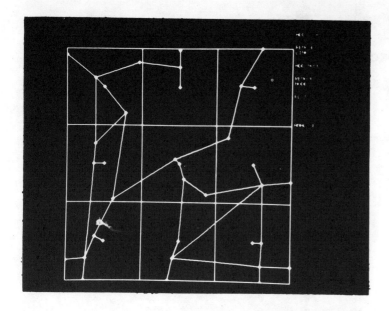

Basic road network display, overlaid with square grid. The light buttons for the various operations are also visible.

A new link has been added.

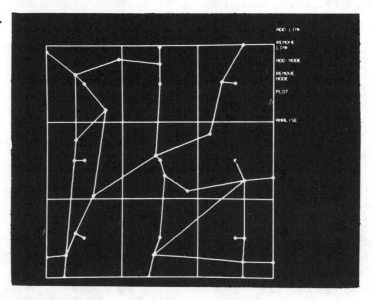

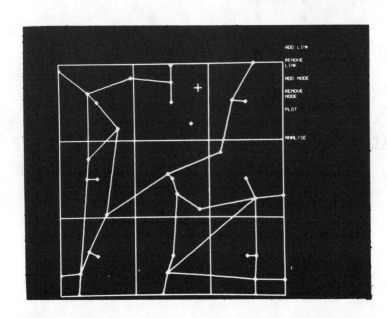

A new node has been added. New links can now be connected to this. The tracking cross is also visible here.

segment to be displayed is then basically very simple. Straight line links are created between the junctions or nodes specified as connected. Where this produces great inaccuracies when compared with the real road map, dummy 2-link junctions can be created to improve the fit. If the analysis of the network is to be based on square grid cells then it is also desirable to include some dummy nodes. These will be placed at the centroid position of each of the grid cells, and linked to the nearest point on the actual road network.

When the network picture segment is displayed on the screen, the required modifications can be made using the light pen. The junctions of the network are defined by the system as named picture parts, allowing them to be uniquely identified by the light pen. A set of function names (or light buttons) is similarly represented and identifiable.

To add a new road link, for example, the user just registers light pen hits on the two junctions to be joined, registers the function name 'ADD LINK', and a signal is sent to the phase 1 program which modifies its network data and returns a replacement picture segment to the screen. Other functions are available to enable the user to add junctions (using a special displayed item called a tracking cross which can be positioned anywhere on the screen using the light pen) and also to remove links and junctions. Combinations of these four functions enable the user to perform any desired modification to his network.

The user can continue modifying his network until he reaches a point where he wants to analyse the changes he has made. The function button 'ANALYSE' can then be indicated by the light pen, and when the message is received, the phase 1 program outputs the network data in its current state and terminates.

Phase 2 - analysis and evaluation

Phase 2 of the system performs an analysis of the road network as it stands at the completion of the first phase. In the present system, this analysis consists of computing accessibility measures for each of the grid cells. These allow comparisons to be made between the areas covered by the network, and indicate the relative effects of various modifications.

To compute the accessibility values, the program must first determine the distances via the shortest route between each pair of junctions. There are a number of standard algorithms to solve this problem; the one used here is a fixed matrix method described in a paper by J.D. Murchland [A Fixed Matrix Method for all shortest distances in a Directed Graph, J.D. Murchland, LBS-TNT-91 (1969)]. This has the advantages of being efficient and simple to program and is especially suitable for small networks. However, disadvantages grow with the size of the network and, therefore, the author is developing a new program based on an algorithm more suitable for the larger networks. Once the distances have been computed, the program calculates the accessibility measure for the central node of each grid square as a function of the distances to each other central node. The actual function used is explained in detail at the end of this section.

When the program has completed its computations, the accessibility measures obtained are displayed on the screen overlaying the network which is still present (see photographs). There is also a facility for the user, by picking out pairs of junctions using the light pen, to obtain an intensified display of the shortest path route between two junctions. When the user has considered the results of the analysis, he can then indicate the function button 'RETURN'. This causes the phase 2 program to terminate and phase 1 to be re-entered, reloading the network file it created on its previous run. The process can continue cycling in this way indefinitely.

The accessibility measure

Accessibility measures are only calculated for the centroid nodes of each grid cell, using the distances to all other centroid nodes. The relative accessibility of cell j to cell i, a_{ij}, is given by

$$a_{ij} = \exp(-\beta\, d_{ij})$$

where exp is the standard exponential function, d_{ij} is the distance from cell i to cell j, and β is a parameter which determines the rate at which the exponential function decays. The general accessibility, A_i, of cell i is then computed as the sum of its relative accessibilities:

$$A_i = \sum_j \exp(-\beta\, d_{ij}) \cdot 1000/N$$

where N is the total number of cells, and 1,000 is a scaling factor. The overall accessibility, Δ, of the whole network is computed as

$$\Delta = (\sum_i A_i)/N$$

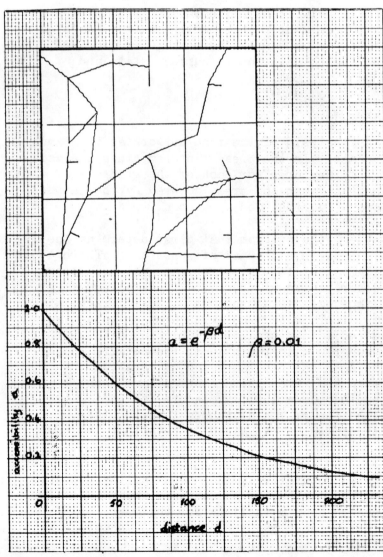

Relative accessibility function shown with network to scale

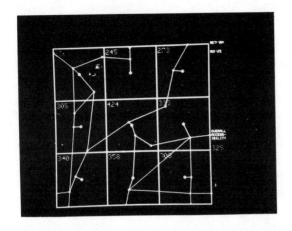 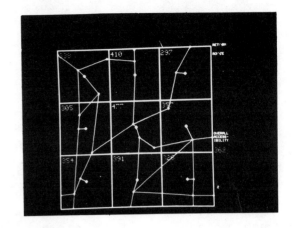

Accessibility measures for the basic road   Accessibility measures obtained after adding
network shown overlaying the network itself   a new link

FUTURE DEVELOPMENTS

There are several possible future developments which can be envisaged for
this system, either by the extension of existing facilities or the
addition of new ones.

The display and modification program could be extended to cope with a
more sophisticated network representation, possibly distinguishing between
road types such as two-lane, dual carriageway, etc., and junction types
such as roundabouts, traffic lights, etc., and also including details of
traffic flow restrictions such as one way streets, no right turns, etc.
If larger networks are to be used with the system, there is also a need
for the provision of 'close-ups' on small subsets of the network.

It would be possible to extend the analysis program (phase 2) to include
information about actual traffic flows in the network, and other measures
of network performance. Or a suite of phase 2 modules could be built up,
each performing different analyses for various applications. The user
would then need only to select the module he required and 'plug' it in
to the system.

One can also envisage the addition of a third phase to the system, on
the scale of a transportation model, or even an urban model. It would
not be viable to run this phase while the user sat at the display tube
because of the long computation time involved. However if the phase 2
program contained some basic analyses which gave an idea of how the
network was performing, then the user could obtain satisfactory results
using only phases 1 and 2, and then initiate phase 3 to run at its
leisure.

POPULATION PREDICTING USING COHORT ANALYSIS

Nigel Lloyd

INTRODUCTION

The computer is excellent at performing operations requiring the repeated
application of a known series of logical steps to a set of inputs. It is
for this reason that their principal use in local authorities so far has
been in the Treasurer's Department [Computers in Local Authorities,
R.S. Baxter, RTPIJ, Vol. 58, No. 6, 1972], where the arithmetical steps
are simple, and the repetitive nature of the work is easily performed by
a computer with an increase in accuracy and a decrease in time over
manual methods. Planning Departments also have many processes which are
repetitive and obey a well defined logical sequence. By computerising
such operations it is possible to repeat the calculations with greater
frequency leading to more up-to-date forecasts and to test the validity
of the outputs by changing the assumed values of the inputs (i.e. testing
the sensitivity of the results to the inputs).

When using computers error is possible at 3 stages: in providing
inaccurate data as inputs, in using a program that has not been fully
debugged, and in misinterpreting the output. Since the inputs are all
supplied at one time as a computer file, it is simple to check that they
contain no errors. A mistake in the computer program is no more likely
than a similar miscalculation of the same process by hand. Errors in
the interpretation of output exist whether using manual or computerised
techniques, but typically there is more output from the computer than
from humans. Hopefully, however, the computer output is presented in a
more digestible form.

EXAMPLE

In order to demonstrate the advantages of using computers, a program has
been written to perform population projections using the cohort survival
method. It is assumed that most of the audience will have carried out an
exercise of this kind, conceivably of greater sophistication. The particular cohort survival method adopted is not of vital importance. The
objective is to demonstrate the advantages of computerising any such
model and to familiarise the audience with the characteristics of the
computer operation.

The example chosen has been taken from the Leicester-Leicestershire
Sub-Regional Study [Leicester and Leicestershire Sub-Regional Study,
Vol. 2, 1969]. The population is considered in 5 year male/female
age-groups (cohorts) from 0-4 to 85+, giving 2 x 18 cohorts. For
simplicity no account has been taken of marital status, and fertility
rates are applied to female cohorts within the child-bearing range. Time
is also considered in five year periods (quinquennia).

Initially, estimated values for survival factors, fertility rates and
migration rates are input for each quinquennium, together with the ratio
of male to female live births (which remains remarkably constant over time).
The survival factors are derived from life tables in the 'Annual Abstract

of Statistics' and are estimated for future quinquennia using figures produced by the Government Actuary. National fertility rates by age of mother are also provided by the Government Actuary, and are estimated for the region by comparing the overall birth-rate trend for the nation and the region. The male to female live birth ratio is also culled from the Annual Abstract of Statistics. Migration figures by aggregated cohorts are available for Leicestershire, but do not take account of emigration to outside the UK. They can also be estimated by calculating the 'natural' changes in each cohort from 1951 to 1961 and comparing them with the actual changes observed by the census. From these two sources a table is made up showing the percentage composition by cohort of net immigrants. Where a cohort is found to emigrate, there will be a negative value.

The operation of the cohort survival model is illustrated in the accompanying flow diagram. The total number of net migrants in any quinquennium is divided amongst the cohorts using the table just described, and these immigrant cohorts are added to the resident cohorts at the beginning of each quinquennium. Fertility rates are applied to the female cohorts to give total live births and these are divided by the male-female ratio. All cohorts are now survived and aged to give the cohorts at the end of the quinquennium. These cohorts are used as the starting values for the next quinquennium.

COMPUTER APPLICATION

The required figures and tables are extracted from the official statistics and punched on to cards or on to paper tape for input to the computer. The data file will usually remain unchanged from one requirement for a projection to the next so it is stored either on magnetic disc or on magnetic tape ready for immediate use by the program. When more recent information becomes available revisions or editing of the data - locating the number to be changed and substituting a new value for it - can easily be performed.

The cohort survival package itself has been written in standard ASA Fortran to run on the Titan and Atlas computers at Cambridge. The program enables projections to be made over any numbers of periods, with or without migration.

Package:

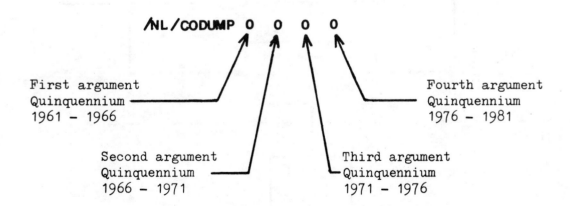

Input

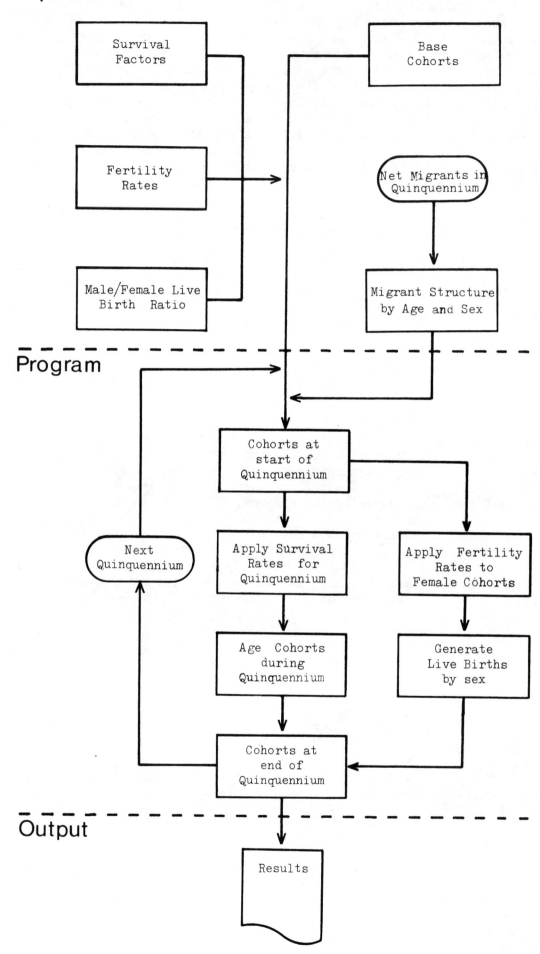

Program

Output

SURVIVAL RATES

```
1.0000 1.0000 1.0000 1.0000 1.0000 1.0000 1.0000 1.0000
0.9962 0.9966 0.9970 0.9974 0.9976 0.9974 0.9977 0.9979

0.9980 0.9982 0.9983 0.9986 0.9984 0.9987 0.9989 0.9990
0.9967 0.9971 0.9976 0.9978 0.9987 0.9988 0.9989 0.9990

0.9950 0.9954 0.9960 0.9963 0.9978 0.9981 0.9984 0.9985
0.9950 0.9954 0.9960 0.9963 0.9972 0.9976 0.9980 0.9981
0.9950 0.9953 0.9960 0.9963 0.9968 0.9970 0.9972 0.9975
0.9929 0.9934 0.9939 0.9946 0.9944 0.9953 0.9959 0.9962
0.9886 0.9894 0.9901 0.9910 0.9917 0.9925 0.9932 0.9939
0.9805 0.9817 0.9828 0.9841 0.9865 0.9876 0.9887 0.9897
0.9670 0.9681 0.9692 0.9713 0.9796 0.9807 0.9819 0.9833
0.9396 0.9420 0.9462 0.9477 0.9670 0.9701 0.9726 0.9740

0.8960 0.9004 0.9045 0.9105 0.9500 0.9519 0.9544 0.9578
0.8370 0.8425 0.8480 0.8533 0.9190 0.9203 0.9238 0.9272
0.7622 0.7674 0.7728 0.7790 0.8630 0.8676 0.8723 0.8768
0.6510 0.6602 0.6693 0.6745 0.7700 0.7759 0.7817 0.7875
0.5220 0.5291 0.5349 0.5438 0.6455 0.6515 0.6576 0.6637
0.3730 0.3779 0.3830 0.3876 0.4827 0.4846 0.4881 0.4931
0.2025 0.2039 0.2853 0.2861 0.3760 0.3793 0.3871 0.3889
```

FERTILITY RATES

```
0.000 0.000 0.000 0.000
0.200 0.250 0.260 0.275
0.890 0.935 0.990 1.000
0.905 0.900 0.900 0.900
0.525 0.465 0.440 0.415
0.240 0.210 0.195 0.185
0.065 0.065 0.060 0.055
0.004 0.004 0.004 0.004
0.000 0.000 0.000 0.000
```

LIVE BIRTH RATIO

0.51 0.47

BASE COHORT

```
27046 26585
25284 24148
29359 27596
24509 23348
20927 20687
21783 20991
23157 22446
24759 24149
21950 21762
23004 23651
22074 23674
20950 22257
16491 20041
11918 16670
 8519 13191
 5623  9612
 2966  5662
 1361  2808
```

MIGRANT STRUCTURE

```
0.000 0.000
0.070 0.066
0.078 0.058
0.024 0.014
0.029 0.043
0.201 0.053
0.149 0.038
0.075 0.025
0.034 0.035
0.008 0.009
0.000 0.000
0.000 0.000
0.000 0.000
0.000 0.000
0.000 0.000
0.000 0.000
0.000 0.000
0.000 0.000
```

Computer Input

PROJECTIONS FOR 1981

AGE	MALE COHORTS	FEMALE COHORTS	COHORT TOTALS
85-89	1688	5545	7224
80-84	3855	8281	12136
75-79	8243	13367	21611
70-74	12840	17651	30490
65-69	16173	19889	36062
60-64	17950	19613	37563
55-59	22294	22620	44914
50-54	21716	21537	43253
45-49	20979	20383	41362
40-44	20413	20358	40771
35-39	24047	23088	47134
30-34	28904	27384	56288
25-29	24967	23996	48963
20-24	27620	26402	54022
15-19	30927	28575	59502
10-14	32119	29632	61751
5- 9	35061	32328	67389
0- 4	36031	33205	69235

AGE-SEX PYRAMID FOR 1981

PERCENTAGE OF TOTAL POPULATION

Computer Output

The program is initiated by typing /NL/CODUMP followed by a number of arguments. Each argument is separated by two spaces and the number of arguments determines the number of quinquennia through which the projection will be made. For this demonstration no more than four arguments (i.e. four quinquennia from 1961) may be used.

A table of possible migration assumptions for the Leicestershire region is given. These can be used for the present demonstration. Quite evidently, the existence of a computerised model obviates the need to try merely four different rates of migration.

Migration Assumptions

Period:	1961/66	1966/71	1971/76	1976/81	1981/86	1986/91	1991/96
Migration Pattern	+	+	+	+	+	+	+
Fast	11,300	15,000	15,000	30,000	30,000	30,000	30,000
Fast-trend	11,300	15,000	15,000	15,000	15,000	15,000	15,000
Slow-trend	11,300	10,000	10,000	10,000	10,000	10,000	10,000
Slow	11,300	5,000	5,000	5,000	5,000	5,000	5,000

A brief summary of the output is returned to the console but the full output is sent to the lineprinter. The console prints the number of males and females in 4 aggregated age-groups for the base and final years.

```
      AGE GROUPS
                0-14          15-44         45-RETIRE          RETIRED
1961
MALE            82589         115135         105369             30287
FEMALE          78329         111531          91344             67984
TOTAL          160918         226666         196713             98271
POPULATION          682568

      AGE GROUPS
                0-14          15-44         45-RETIRE          RETIRED
1981
MALE           103211         136464         103352             42791
FEMALE          95165         129445          84897             84346
TOTAL          198376         265910         188249            127137
POPULATION          779671
```

There are 3 possible outputs from the line-printer any of which can be chosen. The standard output is a complete list of male and female cohort sizes at each quinquennium. As well as this, an age-sex pyramid for each quinquennium can be produced in order to highlight changing population structure. And lastly, as a precautionary measure, the input data can be listed in full so that its validity can be checked.

ENTROPY: A THEORETICAL APPROACH TO URBAN MODEL BUILDING

David Crowther

These diagrams demonstrate how certain problems can be analysed using
the principle of maximum likelihood. Although the concepts of entropy
and likelihood are not precisely the same, the following examples
illustrate certain statistical phenomena which help to explain the
relevance of both.

1   The most likely result of throwing two dice

The first diagram illustrates all possible ways of combining the scores
of two dice. It can be seen that the result "7" for the total score can
be arrived at in the highest number of ways, i.e. 6 out of a possible 6^2
or 36 ways. Based on the a priori assumption that all 36 permutations
of the dice are equally likely, it is possible to conclude that the
result "7" is therefore the most likely.

Each result from "2" to "12" can be assigned a probability of occurrence
according to the number of ways in which it can be obtained. Thus the
results "2" and "12" have a probability of 1/36th (or 0.0278) each, since
both can only be arrived at in only one way. The last row of figures in
the diagram therefore shows both the number of ways in which each result
can be obtained and its probability (expressed as a fraction of 36).
These figures demonstrate that the result "7" is six times as likely as
either "2" or "12", but only 1/36th more likely than either "6" or "8".

This analysis does not indicate that if two dice are thrown, the result
will be "7". Rather it shows that if prior to the throw one was forced
to make a guess as to the result, "7" would be the most sensible guess
to make, that is to say the guess with minimum uncertainty.

2   The most likely result of throwing three dice

The second diagram shows the same problem, but this time for three dice,
each box representing one of the 216 possible permutations of the dice.
Making the same a priori assumption that each of these permutations is
equally likely, it is possible to conclude that the results "10" and "11"
are the most likely, since they both can be arrived at in the highest
number of ways. The number of ways by which each result can be obtained
is again shown at the bottom of the diagram, representing the probability
of occurrence for each result expressed as a fraction of 216.

In the case of two dice, the difference between the most likely and the
least likely results was not great — only 6 times. This time, with three
dice, the difference is much more marked, the results "10" or "11" being
27 times as likely as "3" or "18".

3   The results of throwing two, three and four dice compared

These graphs show how the difference between the most likely and the
least likely results become more marked as more dice are considered.
In the case of four dice, the difference is now 148 times.

The rapidity with which the graphs become more and more peaked as further dice are considered is difficult to represent graphically. If the graph for five dice were to be drawn at the same scale, it would be only slightly wider at its base (five points wider), but the peak value for the number of ways of obtaining the most likely results (17 and 18) would be way off the page at 798. For six dice the peak value is 4376, and for ten dice it if 4, 401, 937. Drawn to the same scale, the graph for ten dice would be only twice the width of the diagram at its base (representing the 51 possible results from 10 to 60), while its peak would be nearly 400 miles away from the base line. The graph for 100 dice is impossible to conceive of in these terms.

4 A simple trip distribution problem

In this example the same principles are applied to an extremely simple problem involving movement between zones. In order to keep the numbers small and manageable, a system of two zones and six objects is considered.

At the start it is known that the left hand zone contains four objects and the right hand zone two. It is also known that during a fixed period each object will move in such a way as either to stay within the same zone or to pass from one zone to the other. The problem is to predict, in the absence of any other knowledge, the number of objects in each zone at the end of the process. For the moment, the question as to what these objects are can be left unanswered: they could be molecules of gas, mice or people, but before tackling this question, the properties of the system can be examined in abstract by making the same assumption as for dice that all permutations are a priori equally likely.

The diagram sets out all 64 possible ways of permutating the system. The permutations are arranged into columns, each column representing one of the seven possible results. From this it is clear that the result "3" in each zone is the most likely since it can be obtained in the highest number of ways.

In the case of throwing dice, it was shown that the difference between the most likely and the least likely results became rapidly more distinct as more dice were considered, so that even with as few as ten dice a small group of results stood out as overwhelmingly more likely than any others. The same rapid peaking effect can be observed for this problem: as more zones and objects are considered, a small group of similar results will assume rapidly increasing dominance over other possible results.

This peaking phenomenon is in fact common to many different types of system consisting of a number of elements which can be combined together in a variety of ways. In each case two phenomena can be observed as more elements are considered: first of all the total number of possible permutations rises very steeply (i.e. very much more rapidly than the total number of possible end results), and secondly a large proportion of these permutations all give rise to the same end result (i.e. the increases in the permutational flexibility of the system are unevenly distributed, tending to favour relatively few of the most likely end results at the expense of the rest).

It is these statistical phenomena which form the basis of the maximum likelihood approach to predicting the outcome of situations which can be analysed in terms of the number of ways by which end results can be

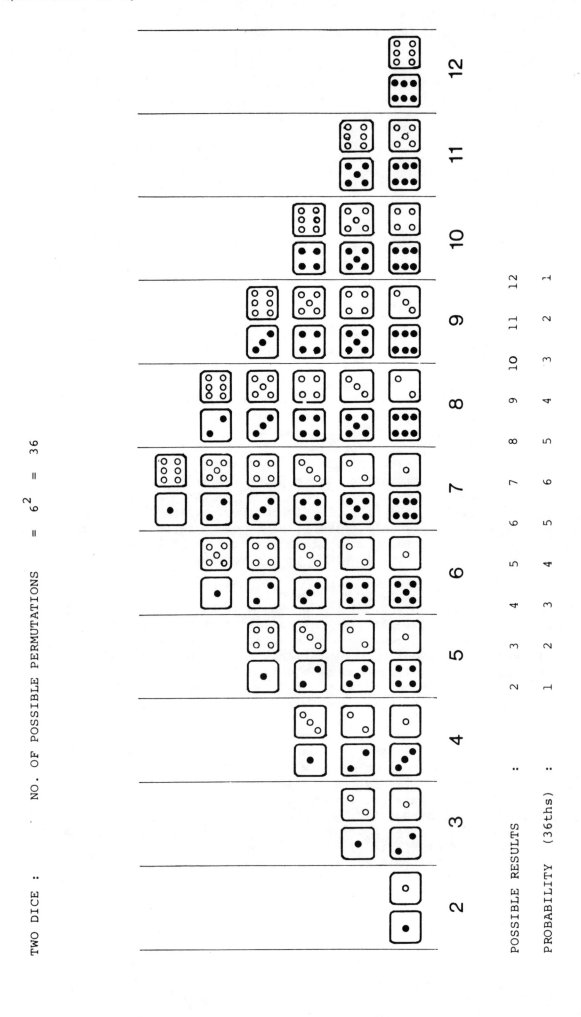

TWO DICE :   NO. OF POSSIBLE PERMUTATIONS   = 6^2 =   36

2	3	4	5	6	7	8	9	10	11	12

POSSIBLE RESULTS :
2	3	4	5	6	7	8	9	10	11	12

PROBABILITY (36ths) :
1	2	3	4	5	6	5	4	3	2	1

THREE DICE : NO. OF POSSIBLE PERMUTATIONS = 6³ = 216

$$\text{THREE DICE : NO. OF POSSIBLE PERMUTATIONS} = 6^3 = 216$$

POSSIBLE RESULTS	3	4	5	6	7	8	9	10	11	12	13	14	15	16	17	18
	1 1 1	1 1 2	1 1 3	1 1 4	1 1 5	1 1 6	1 2 6	1 3 6	1 4 6	1 5 6	1 6 6	2 6 6	3 6 6	4 6 6	5 6 6	6 6 6
		1 2 1	1 2 2	1 2 3	1 2 4	1 2 5	1 3 5	1 4 5	1 5 5	1 6 5	2 5 6	3 5 6	4 5 6	5 5 6	6 5 6	
		2 1 1	1 3 1	1 3 2	1 3 3	1 3 4	1 4 4	1 5 4	1 6 4	2 4 6	2 6 5	3 6 5	4 6 5	5 6 5	6 6 5	
			2 1 2	1 4 1	1 4 2	1 4 3	1 5 3	1 6 3	2 3 6	2 5 5	3 4 6	4 4 6	5 4 6	6 4 6		
			2 2 1	2 1 3	1 5 1	1 5 2	1 6 2	2 2 6	2 4 5	2 6 4	3 5 5	4 5 5	5 5 5	6 5 5		
			3 1 1	2 2 2	2 1 4	1 6 1	2 1 6	2 3 5	2 5 4	3 3 6	3 6 4	4 6 4	5 6 4	6 6 4		
				2 3 1	2 2 3	2 1 5	2 2 5	2 4 4	2 6 3	3 4 5	4 3 6	5 3 6	6 3 6			
				3 1 2	2 3 2	2 2 4	2 3 4	2 5 3	3 2 6	3 5 4	4 4 5	5 4 5	6 4 5			
				3 2 1	2 4 1	2 3 3	2 4 3	2 6 2	3 3 5	3 6 3	4 5 4	5 5 4	6 5 4			
				4 1 1	3 1 3	2 4 2	2 5 2	3 1 6	3 4 4	4 2 6	4 6 3	5 6 3	6 6 3			
					3 2 2	2 5 1	2 6 1	3 2 5	3 5 3	4 3 5	5 2 6	6 2 6				
					3 3 1	3 1 4	3 1 5	3 3 4	3 6 2	4 4 4	5 3 5	6 3 5				
					4 1 2	3 2 3	3 2 4	3 4 3	4 1 6	4 5 3	5 4 4	6 4 4				
					4 2 1	3 3 2	3 3 3	3 5 2	4 2 5	4 6 2	5 5 3	6 5 3				
					5 1 1	3 4 1	3 4 2	3 6 1	4 3 4	5 1 6	5 6 2	6 6 2				
						4 1 3	3 5 1	4 1 5	4 4 3	5 2 5	6 1 6					
						4 2 2	4 1 4	4 2 4	4 5 2	5 3 4	6 2 5					
						4 3 1	4 2 3	4 3 3	4 6 1	5 4 3	6 3 4					
						5 1 2	4 3 2	4 4 2	5 1 5	5 5 2	6 4 3					
						5 2 1	4 4 1	4 5 1	5 2 4	5 6 1	6 5 2					
						6 1 1	5 1 3	5 1 4	5 3 3	6 1 5	6 6 1					
							5 2 2	5 2 3	5 4 2	6 2 4						
							5 3 1	5 3 2	5 5 1	6 3 3						
							6 1 2	5 4 1	6 1 4	6 4 2						
							6 2 1	6 1 3	6 2 3	6 5 1						
								6 2 2	6 3 2							
								6 3 1	6 4 1							
PROBABILITY (216ths)	1	3	6	10	15	21	25	27	27	25	21	15	10	6	3	1

MOST LIKELY RESULTS : 2, 3 & 4 DICE

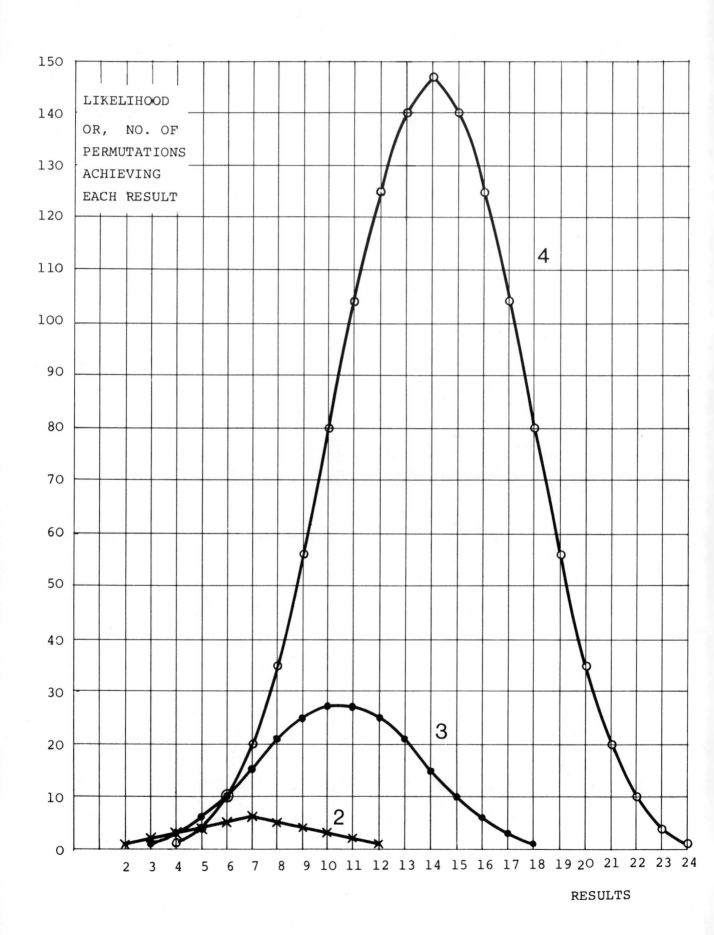

LIKELIHOOD
OR, NO. OF
PERMUTATIONS
ACHIEVING
EACH RESULT

RESULTS

obtained. In the examples shown here the problems have deliberately been made extremely simple, so that all possible permutations can be presented graphically and the most likely result determined by inspection. For normal problems, of course, this is not possible because of the sheer number of permutations, and mathematical techniques have to be used to determine the most likely results. Frequently, in fact, one does not need to determine the most likely result expressed in terms of a single numerical value. For example, in the case of the dice, we might want to derive a general equation expressing the most likely result in terms of the number of dice thrown. Typically, therefore, the maximum likelihood method is used to derive a mathematical expression describing the most likely end result as a function of the variables defining the system.

The major disadvantage of illustrating the maximum likelihood approach by means of such simple examples is that one is, in fact, presenting the cases where the method is least useful, that is to say where the peaking effect for the most likely result is least evident. Despite the difficulty of representing this peaking effect graphically for anything but the smallest number of permutations, it is important to appreciate its significance. For the case of ten dice there were over four million ways of obtaining the most likely result, and for any system involving a large number of elements and ways of combining them the difference between the most likely results and any other possible results will in some cases be almost infinitely great. This means that in such circumstances the solution derived by applying the maximum likelihood approach will have considerable relevance for the purpose of prediction.

The usefulness of this approach will be further enhanced if one does not need to predict the most likely result with absolute accuracy. Considering the case of four dice again (the third diagram), the prediction "14$\bar{+}$2" is clearly very much more safe than "14" exactly. When dealing with larger numbers, the group of very similar results covered by the tolerance limits around the most likely result is precisely that group which stands out so dramatically above all others.

Indeed there is something of a paradox involved here, in that intuitively one might have thought that the behaviour of a system consisting of a large number of elements and ways of combining them was inherently less easy to predict than a simpler system with fewer elements. However, the above analysis shows that because so many of the permutations of the larger system give rise to the same end result, it is on the contrary possible to predict the end result of such a system with greater confidence.

Constraint building

This is an important part of the maximum likelihood approach, since it is the means by which one's prior knowledge about the behaviour of a system can be taken into account when deriving a value or a mathematical expression for the most likely outcome or end result. In the case of the two zones and six objects, for example (the fourth diagram), one of the pieces of given information was that four objects started in one zone and two in the other. Each of the permutations shown in the diagram takes this into account. However if one were to derive the answer mathematically (as opposed to by inspection), this piece of information would have to be fed into the process of derivation as a specific constraint to limit the number

SIMPLE MOVEMENT PROBLEM :   6 OBJECTS & 2 ZONES :   POSSIBLE PERMUTATIONS = 2^6 = 64

START   FINISH

GIVEN :   (4) (2)   PROBLEM ::   (?) (?)

POSSIBLE RESULTS	⑥⓪	⑤①	④②	③③	②④	①⑤	⓪⑥

PROBABILITY (64ths)	1	6	15	20	15	6	1

of permutations considered to only those involving four objects starting
from one zone and two from the other. Moreover one would need to ensure
that for each permutation the <u>same</u> four started in the left hand zone
and the same two from the right hand zone (i.e. an object which started
in one zone in one permutation should not be considered to start from
the other in another permutation). Clearly the total number of ways
of permutating six objects and two zones would be much greater if this
constraint were removed.

Similarly other constraints representing initial knowledge of the system
can be "built in". For a larger system of many zones and objects, for
example, the numbers of objects finishing up in some of the zones may be
known and the problem is to determine the most likely distribution of
objects in the rest. Alternatively the number of objects passing between
certain specific zones may be known beforehand, or else the total distance
travelled by all objects added together might be given. These and many
other similar types of constraint can be taken into account in deriving
the most likely outcome, so that only those permutations which obey them
are considered.

A priori possibilities

The constraints described above are of the kind whereby initial information
concerning the system being analysed is used so as to reduce the number of
permutations considered. (In most practical instances, although the number
of permutations is reduced, there is still a sufficiently large number of
them obeying all the constraints for the method still to be as viable as
before – although the danger of imposing such severe constraint that there
is no permutational flexibility left in the system needs to be guarded
against.) Further types of initial information can be taken into account
by altering the assumption that a priori all permutations of the system
are equally likely. That is to say that if one has reason to believe
that some permutations are more likely than others, these permutations
can be weighted so that the most likely outcome is the one with the
highest total for the number of permutations by which it can be obtained
multiplied by their respective weights. In the case of the zones and
objects, for example, it may be known that some zones are larger and
can accommodate more objects than others, or there may be some other
reason to believe that objects will tend to be attracted to some zones
more than others, all other factors (such as permutational flexibility)
being constant.

By combining changes to the a priori probabilities with the imposition
of constraints, the maximum likelihood approach can be adapted for a
wide variety of different types of problem according to one's initial
knowledge of the system being analysed. In other words, faced with a
problem involving the prediction of the outcome of a process, one can
separate out all the information about that process that is known at
the start and apply the maximum likelihood approach to determine the
most likely outcome in the light of this information. By employing a
variety of a priori assumptions one can also examine the degree to
which the outcome is likely to be changed according to which assumption
is proved correct.

Suitability for social science studies

At this point it is useful to return once more to the example of the zones and objects, and to consider the question of what the objects are. While there is usually general agreement that the approach described here can suitably be applied to the study of the movement of such inanimate objects as gas molecules, a common response from those new to the subject is that it is invalid to consider human beings in this way. To a large extent this response is based on a fundamental misunderstanding or misinterpretation of the problem. For a start, it is a mistake to assume that the behaviour of individual gas molecules in space is totally predictable; it is not. Indeed, it is precisely because it is difficult to predict the state of a gas from a consideration of the behaviour of individual molecules that the maximum likelihood method is applied. Similarly, when studying travel behaviour in an urban situation, or the distribution of residents around their work places, one is faced with exactly the same problem as the atomic physicist. One has certain information about the behaviour of individuals but this is not of the kind from which it is easy or even possible to build up a representation of the overall workings of the whole system, which consists of a large number of individuals all affecting each other's behaviour. In other words it is as valid to apply the maximum likelihood approach to people as it is to gas molecules. In both cases one is overcoming a lack of detailed knowledge of the precise mechanisms by which each individual person or molecule affects the others by analysing the inherent characteristics of the system as a whole which tend to make some outcomes very much more likely than others. Thus, to say that if the maximum likelihood approach is applied to urban studies it is in effect treating people as though they were gas molecules is exactly as meaningful as to say that if the approach is applied to the study of gases it is in effect treating gas molecules as though they were people.

In considering these arguments it is important to remember what it is that one is trying to achieve: in a situation of uncertainty to make as reasonable a guess as possible as to the outcome of a process in the light of whatever knowledge may be available. In both the case of gas molecules and the case of human trip behaviour, one only makes the assumption that a priori all permutations of the system are equally probable, because in the absence of any knowledge that suggests the contrary, this is the least biased assumption one can make. If one does have reason to believe that the a priori probabilities are not equal then this knowledge can be taken into account by altering the probabilities as described above.

In principle therefore the maximum likelihood approach is both useful and suitable for the study of urban phenomena. In this context it is interesting to observe that the approach can be used to derive from first principles many of the formulations that have proved successful in practical urban model building (see Wilson 1970 and Wilson 1972). The approach can also be used to derive entirely new model formulations and for this reason is an important theoretical technique.

Entropy

The difference between the entropy and the maximum likelihood approach
is partly conceptual and partly mathematical. Conceptually entropy is a
measure of uncertainty used in information theory, which is concerned
with the problems of deriving maximum useful information from a given
signal. If the "given signal" is considered to be data which partially
describes the urban system, then information theory provides a framework
for analysing the data in such a way as to extract from them the least
biased description of the state of the urban system as a whole (i.e. to
fill in the missing data not contained in the original "signal", making
as few assumptions as possible). In the context of the arguments contained in the previous paragraphs concerning the validity of applying
the maximum likelihood method to the study of aggregate human behaviour
in a defined situation, information theory provides additional support
for the principle that all a priori probabilities for the permutations
of a system should be assumed to be the same, unless there is specific
prior information that suggests otherwise, since any other assumption
would introduce a greater degree of bias.

Methematically entropy, being a measure of uncertainty, is similar to
the concept of likelihood as discussed in this paper. However, the
mathematical means of deriving the entropy of a system are somewhat
different from the derivation of the likelihood of any one outcome
occurring by examining the various permutations possible. By using
the concept of entropy one arrives at the same value or expression
for the most likely outcome but by more direct means. Within the
context of information theory, the concept of entropy can also be
used to analyse problems where the maximum likelihood approach is
difficult to apply. It is thus a more general and more flexible
analytical concept. For the purposes of this paper, however, the two
concepts can be considered as essentially the same in that they can
both be used to predict the outcome of a process and to measure the
extent to which some outcomes are very much more likely or less
uncertain than other outcomes.

REFERENCES:

A.G. Wilson   Entropy in Urban and Regional Modelling. Pion.
               London: 1970.

A.G. Wilson   Papers in Urban and Regional Analysis. Pion.
               London: 1972.

EXPOSITION OF A SIMPLE RESIDENTIAL LOCATION MODEL

Chris Doubleday

A model is an attempt to simplify reality, to make it easier to comprehend and to facilitate predictive calculations. A balance always has to be found between too large a degree of simplification – in which the essential workings of the process being modelled are not adequately represented, and too little simplification – in which case the model is very difficult to understand and use.

The aim of this lecture is to develop from a series of observations a model to describe the spatial distribution of the places where people live in a town.

<u>1st observation:</u> In most towns, the substantial majority of journeys starting from people's homes are for the purpose of going to work.

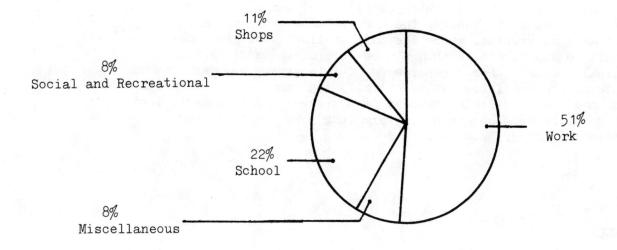

This suggests that the location of residents is primarily related to location of employment rather than to location of any other activity with which the residence is linked.

Equation of the model:

$$R = f(E)$$

    R is employed residents
    E is employees
    f represents a function, i.e. a dependence of one
       measurement upon another

<u>2nd observation</u>: Increasing distance from a place of employment reduces the probability that a particular location is chosen as a residence.

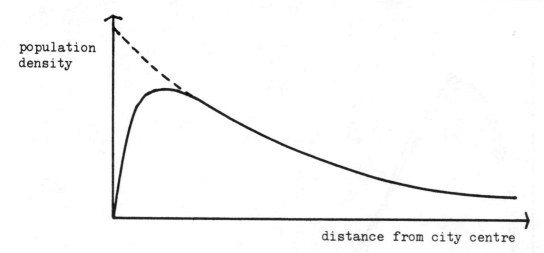

Note the declines of density in the central area of a town. Commercial land uses outbid residential ones for central sites and residents are displaced.

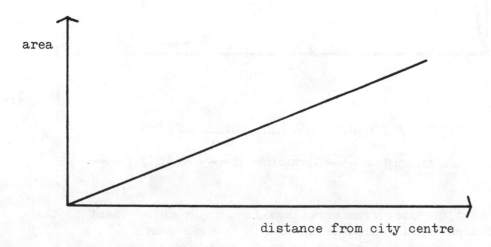

The area at any particular distance from the centre of the town increases in proportion to that distance. Hence, the distribution of population is obtained.

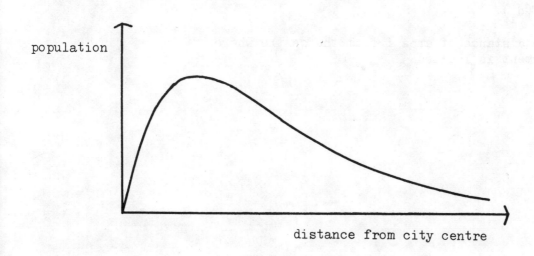

This relationship is reflected in the distribution of the lengths of journeys to work

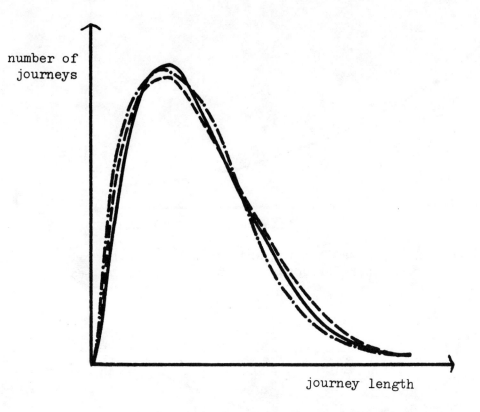

JOURNEY TO WORK BY ALL MODES OF TRAVEL

Northampton—·—Gloucester———Reading——

This suggests that distance from workplace is a major determinant of the probability of a particular area being chosen for residence. It may also be noted that the effect of distance is most marked over the shorter distances.

Equation of the model:

$$R_i = E\, f(d_i)$$

d_i is the distance of area i from the centre where employment is located

3rd observation: Different parts of the town at the same distances from the centre have different probabilities of being chosen as residential locations.

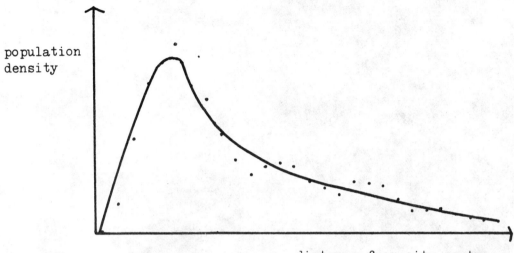

This effect is included in the model by defining different attractiveness factors. These might be related to the constraints imposed by planning policies or geographical disadvantages (e.g. river floor plains or unacceptably steep ground).

Equation of the model:

$$R_i = W_i \; E \; f(d_i)$$

W_i is attractiveness of area i for residence

4th observation: Employment opportunities occur in many areas, not just in the centre.

This suggests that the model must be able to aggregate distributions from many centres and hence requires employment totals to be specified by area. We therefore define zones or cells.

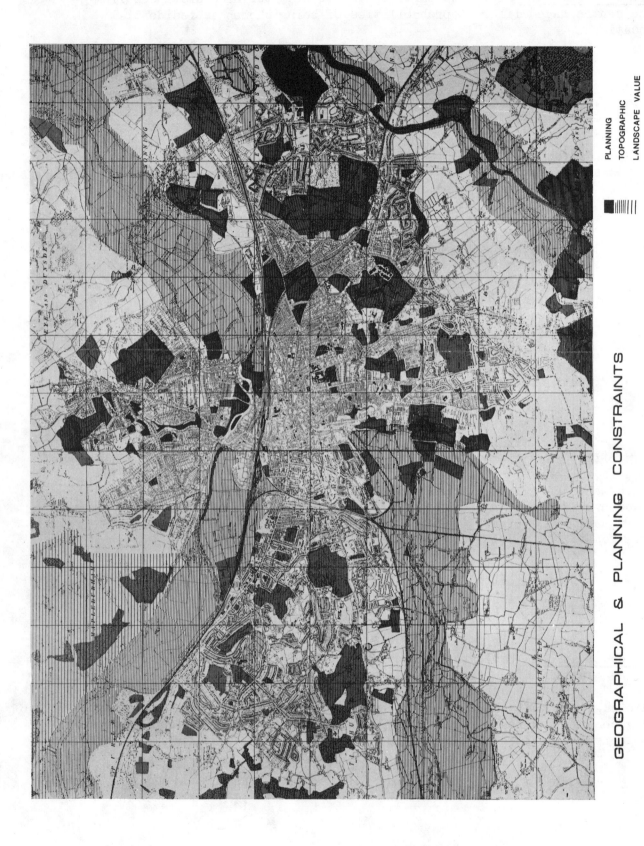

GEOGRAPHICAL & PLANNING CONSTRAINTS

PLANNING
TOPOGRAPHIC
LANDSCAPE VALUE

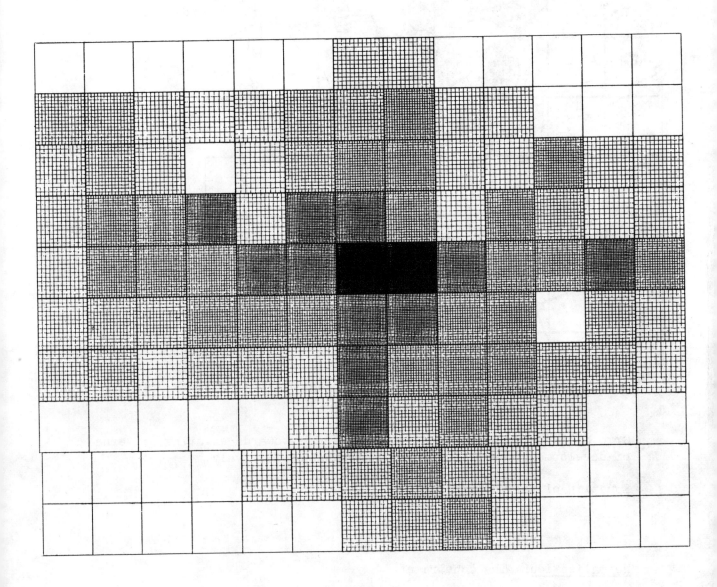

DISTRIBUTION OF EMPLOYMENT (READING,1962)

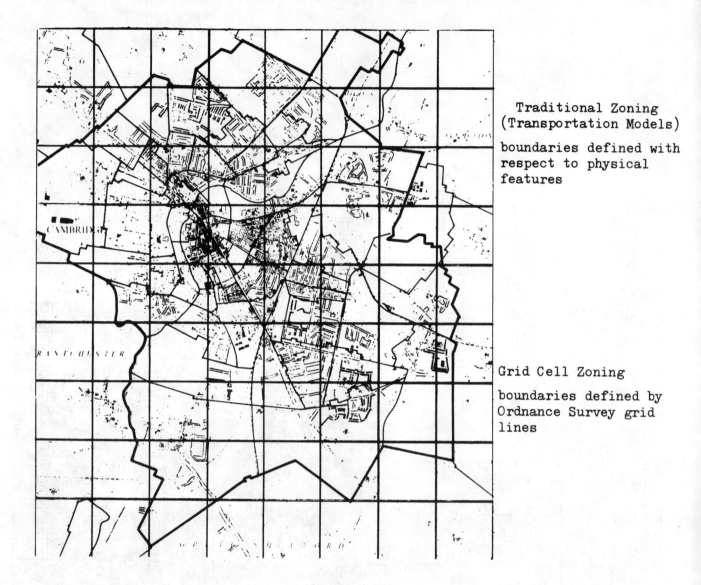

Traditional Zoning
(Transportation Models)

boundaries defined with
respect to physical
features

Grid Cell Zoning

boundaries defined by
Ordnance Survey grid
lines

Grid cell zoning eliminates systematic bias towards existing patterns
of development when a model is being used predictively.

Equation of the model:

$$R_i = \sum_j W_i E_j f(d_{ij})$$

<u>Normalisation</u>: The constraint

$$\sum_i R_{ij} = E_j$$

ensures that the sum, given by the model, of the number of workers in j
living in each residential zone i is the same as the number of employment
opportunities in zone j.

The normalisation term, B_j is calculated as:

$$B_j = \frac{1}{\sum\limits_{i} W_i \, f(d_{ij})}$$

and when included in the model expresses the competition between residential zones for employees since

$$\frac{W_i \, f(d_{ij})}{\sum\limits_{i} W_i \, f(d_{ij})} = B_j \, W_i \, f(d_{ij})$$

expresses the relative attractiveness of zone i for residence.

Equation of the model:

$$R_i = \sum\limits_{j} W_i \, B_j \, E_j \, f(d_{ij})$$

Labour Participation Rate: A model of the distribution of residents rather than just the distribution of employed residents is required. Therefore the number of employed residents, R_i, must be multiplied by an average city-wide labour participation rate, a, to obtain P_i, the residential population in zone i.

Equation of the model:

$$P_i = a \sum\limits_{j} W_i \, B_j \, E_j \, f(d_{ij})$$

airline distance, d_{ij} *

not appropriate in an
urban model

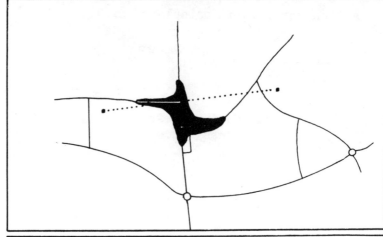

shortest road distance,
d_{ij}

but congestion at the
district centre makes it
slower than the by—pass
route

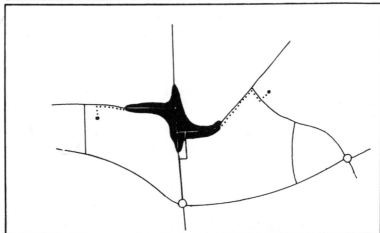

shortest time, t_{ij}

but this is characteristic
of the existing
residential distribution
and could not be used in
a predictive situation

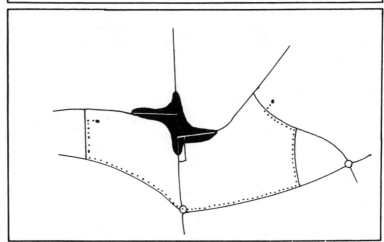

minimum cost, c_{ij}

avoids congestion and
although not so fast as
shortest time route is
shorter in distance

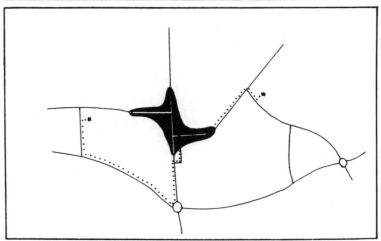

Functional Dependence on Distance:

Alternative functions

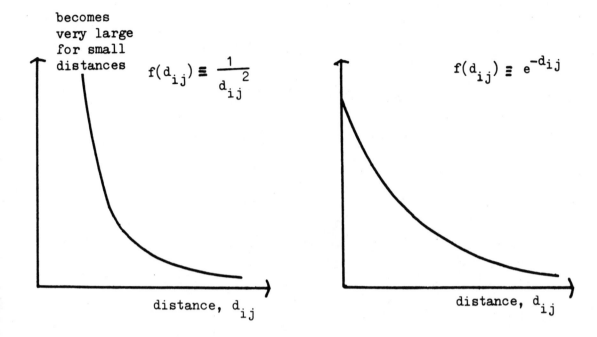

becomes
very large
for small
distances

$$f(d_{ij}) \equiv \frac{1}{d_{ij}^2}$$

$$f(d_{ij}) \equiv e^{-d_{ij}}$$

distance, d_{ij}

distance, d_{ij}

Effect of β on Population Distribution

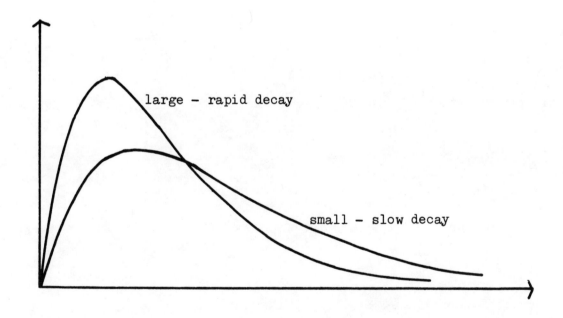

large – rapid decay

small – slow decay

β reflects the propensity of people to travel to satisfy their aims.

HAND WORKED RESIDENTIAL LOCATION MODEL

Ian Williams

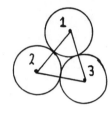

3 Zone Town

Inputs:

Accessibilities: $f(d_{ij})$

Zone	j=1	j=2	j=3
i=1	$f(d_{11})$	$f(d_{12})$	$f(d_{13})$
i=2	$f(d_{21})$	$f(d_{22})$	$f(d_{23})$
i=3	$f(d_{31})$	$f(d_{32})$	$f(d_{33})$

Zone	j=1	j=2	j=3
i=1	3	2	1
i=2	2	3	1
i=3	1	1	2

Employment: E_j

$E_1 = 90,$ $E_2 = 50,$ $E_3 = 70,$

Attractiveness: W_i

$W_1 = 1,$ $W_2 = 2,$ $W_3 = 2,$

Labour participation ratio: $a = 2$

Equation:

$$R_i = a \sum_j E_j \, W_i \, B_j \, f(d_{ij})$$

where $B_j = 1 \Big/ \sum_i W_i \, f(d_{ij})$

i.e. $R_i = a \sum_j \left[E_j \dfrac{W_i \, f(d_{ij})}{\sum_i W_i \, f(d_{ij})} \right]$

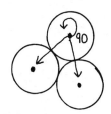

Zone 1

Number of employees to be distributed is $E_1 = 90$

Attractiveness x accessibility of;

Cell 1 to cell 1 $= W_1 \, f(d_{11}) = 1 \times 3 = 3$

Cell 2 to cell 1 $= W_2 \, f(d_{21}) = 2 \times 2 = 4$

Cell 3 to cell 1 $= W_3 \, f(d_{31}) = 2 \times 1 = \underline{2}$

Thus B_1^{-1} $= \sum_i W_i \, f(d_{i1}) = \qquad 9$

Relative attractiveness x accessibility of;

Cell 1 to cell 1 $= W_1 \, f(d_{11}) / \sum_i W_i \, f(d_{i1}) = 3 / 9$

Cell 2 to cell 1 $= W_2 \, f(d_{21}) / \sum_i W_i \, f(d_{i1}) = 4 / 9$

Cell 3 to cell 1 $= W_3 \, f(d_{31}) / \sum_i W_i \, f(d_{i1}) = 2 / 9$

Number of employees working in cell 1 and:

Living in cell 1 $= E_1 \left(W_1 \, f(d_{11}) / \sum_i W_i \, f(d_{i1}) \right) = 90 \times 3/9 = 30$

Living in cell 2 $= E_1 \left(W_2 \, f(d_{21}) / \sum_i W_i \, f(d_{i1}) \right) = 90 \times 4/9 = 40$

Living in cell 3 $= E_1 \left(W_3 \, f(d_{31}) / \sum_i W_i \, f(d_{i1}) \right) = 90 \times 2/9 = 20$

Zone 2

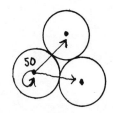

Number of employees to be distributed is $E_2 = 50$

Attractiveness x accessibility of:

Cell 1 to cell 2 $= W_1 \, f(d_{12}) = 1 \times 2 = 2$

Cell 2 to cell 2 $= W_2 \, f(d_{22}) = 2 \times 3 = 6$

Cell 3 to cell 2 $= W_3 \, f(d_{32}) = 2 \times 1 = \underline{2}$

Thus $1/B_2$ $= \sum_i W_i \, f(d_{i2}) = \qquad 10$

Relative attractiveness x accessibility of;

Cell 1 to cell 2 $= W_1 \, f(d_{12}) / \sum_i W_i \, f(d_{i2}) = 2 / 10$

Cell 2 to cell 2 $= W_2 \, f(d_{22}) / \sum_i W_i \, f(d_{i2}) = 6 / 10$

Cell 3 to cell 2 $= W_3 \, f(d_{32}) / \sum_i W_i \, f(d_{i2}) = 2 / 10$

Number of employees working in cell 2 and;

Living in cell 1 $= E_2 \left(W_1 \, f(d_{12}) / \sum_i W_i \, f(d_{i2}) \right) = 50 \times 2/10 = 10$

Living in cell 2 $= E_2 \left(W_2 \, f(d_{22}) / \sum_i W_i \, f(d_{i2}) \right) = 50 \times 6/10 = 30$

Living in cell 3 $= E_2 \left(W_3 \, f(d_{32}) / \sum_i W_i \, f(d_{i2}) \right) = 50 \times 2/10 = 10$

Zone 3

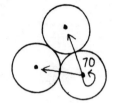

Number of employees to be distributed is $E_3 = 70$

Attractiveness x accessibility of;

Cell 1 to cell 3 $= \quad W_1\ f(d_{13}) =$

Cell 2 to cell 3 $= \quad W_2\ f(d_{23}) =$

Cell 3 to cell 3 $= \quad W_3\ f(d_{33}) =$

Thus $1/B_3$ $= \sum\limits_i W_i\ f(d_{i3}) =$

Relative attractiveness x accessibility of;

Cell 1 to cell 3 $= \quad W_1\ f(d_{13}) / \sum\limits_i W_i\ f(d_{i3}) \quad =$

Cell 2 to cell 3 $= \quad W_2\ f(d_{23}) / \sum\limits_i W_i\ f(d_{i3}) \quad =$

Cell 3 to cell 3 $= \quad W_3\ f(d_{33}) / \sum\limits_i W_i\ f(d_{i3}) \quad =$

Number of employees working in cell 3 and;

Living in cell 1 $= \quad E_3\ (\ W_1\ f(d_{13}) / \sum\limits_i W_i\ f(d_{i3})\ )\quad = 70\ x$

Living in cell 2 $= \quad E_3\ (\ W_2\ f(d_{23}) / \sum\limits_i W_i\ f(d_{i3})\ )\quad = 70\ x$

Living in cell 3 $= \quad E_3\ (\ W_3\ f(d_{33}) / \sum\limits_i W_i\ f(d_{i3})\ )\quad = 70\ x$

Final set of equations

$$\qquad\qquad j = 1 \qquad\qquad\qquad j = 2 \qquad\qquad\qquad j = 3$$

$$R_i\ = a\ \bigg[\ \Big(\ E_j\ \frac{W_i\ f(d_{ij})}{\sum\limits_i W_i\ f(d_{ij})}\ \Big) + \Big(\ E_j\ \frac{W_i\ f(d_{ij})}{\sum\limits_i W_i\ f(d_{ij})}\ \Big) + \Big(\ E_j\ \frac{W_i\ f(d_{ij})}{\sum\limits_i W_i\ f(d_{ij})}\ \Big)\ \bigg]$$

$i = 1 \quad R_1\ = 2\ \big[\ (\ 90\ x\ 3\ /\ 9 \quad) + (\ 50\ x\ 2\ /\ 10 \quad) + (\ 70\ x \qquad)\ \big]\ =$

$i = 2 \quad R_2\ = 2\ \big[\ (\ 90\ x\ 4\ /\ 9 \quad) + (\ 50\ x\ 6\ /\ 10 \quad) + (\ 70\ x \qquad)\ \big]\ =$

$i = 3 \quad R_3\ = 2\ \big[\ (\ 90\ x\ 2\ /\ 9 \quad) + (\ 50\ x\ 2\ /\ 10 \quad) + (\ 70\ x \qquad)\ \big]\ =$

COMPUTER DEMONSTRATION OF A SIMPLE RESIDENTIAL LOCATION MODEL

Ian Williams

Explanation of the significance of changes in the model output as a result of different inputs.

Run 1: Here the program is run using the data as listed in the data file /INW/ACC1. This corresponds to the present state of the hypothetical town. It is with the output of this run that the other runs are compared in order to show the effects of various changes in the town.

NO. OF RESIDENTS				CHANGE IN RESIDENTS		
1309.	387.	522.		-0.	0.	-0.
1180.	1493.	2104.		0.	-0.	0.
903.	799.	280.		-0.	-0.	0.

	WORKPLACE								
	CELL 1	CELL 2	CELL 3	CELL 4	CELL 5	CELL 6	CELL 7	CELL 8	CELL 9
RESIDENCE									
CELL 1	91.	16.	6.	174.	97.	6.	85.	30.	41.
CELL 2	26.	21.	1.	50.	23.	1.	21.	7.	10.
CELL 3	4.	1.	30.	12.	83.	5.	23.	26.	35.
CELL 4	35.	6.	3.	268.	53.	3.	84.	16.	22.
CELL 5	14.	2.	17.	38.	246.	18.	73.	91.	124.
CELL 6	10.	1.	11.	26.	201.	70.	49.	86.	422.
CELL 7	14.	2.	5.	68.	83.	5.	138.	26.	35.
CELL 8	5.	1.	5.	12.	97.	8.	24.	88.	93.
CELL 9	1.	0.	1.	2.	16.	5.	4.	11.	78.

TOTAL TRIPS	MEAN TRIP LENGTH	BETA
3740.	0.816	1.200

Run 2: For this run the employment in zone 4, $E(4)$, is changed from 650 to 950. This would simulate the effect of a new industry locating in zone 4.

From the output it can be seen that the increase in employment in cell 4 leads to an increase in the number of people who live in every cell and work in cell 4. This increase in the number of employees would be covered by people migrating into the town and also by a lessening of the unemployment rate. The latter would necessitate an adjustment of the labour participation ratio which has been omitted from this model for simplicity.

275

A RESIDENTIAL LOCATION MODEL

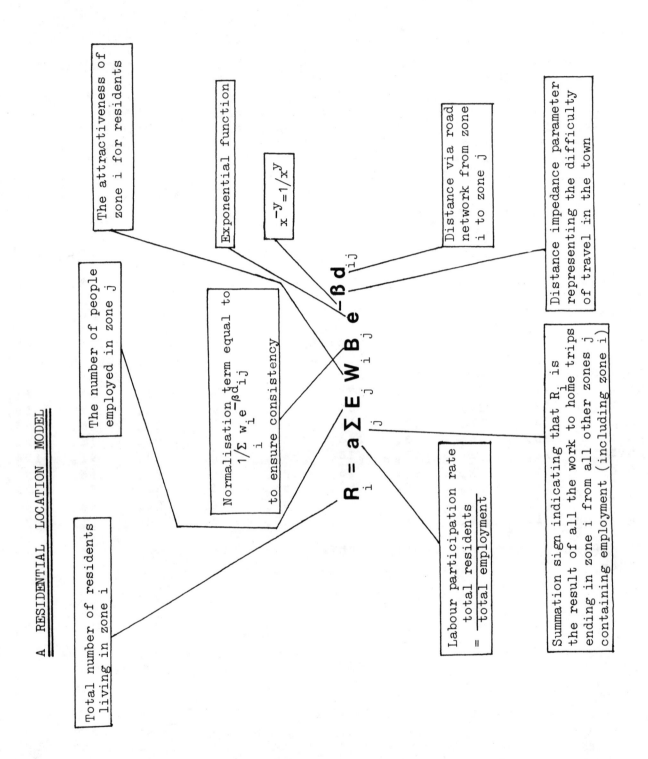

The attractiveness of zone i for residents

Exponential function

$x^{-y} = 1/x^y$

Distance via road network from zone i to zone j

Distance impedance parameter representing the difficulty of travel in the town

The number of people employed in zone j

Normalisation term equal to $1/\sum_i w_i e^{-\beta d_{ij}}$ to ensure consistency

Total number of residents living in zone i

Labour participation rate $= \dfrac{\text{total residents}}{\text{total employment}}$

Summation sign indicating that R_i is the result of all the work to home trips ending in zone i from all other zones j containing employment (including zone i)

$$R_i = a \sum_j W_j B_j e^{-\beta d_{ij}}$$

NO. OF RESIDENTS

1501.	443.	535.
1477.	1534.	2133.
978.	812.	282.

CHANGE IN RESIDENTS

192.	56.	13.
297.	41.	29.
75.	13.	2.

WORKPLACE

	CELL 1	CELL 2	CELL 3	CELL 4	CELL 5	CELL 6	CELL 7	CELL 8	CELL 9
RESIDENCE									
CELL 1	91.	16.	6.	254.	97.	6.	85.	30.	41.
CELL 2	26.	21.	1.	74.	23.	1.	21.	7.	10.
CELL 3	4.	1.	30.	17.	83.	5.	23.	26.	35.
CELL 4	35.	6.	3.	391.	53.	3.	84.	16.	22.
CELL 5	14.	2.	17.	55.	246.	18.	73.	91.	124.
CELL 6	10.	1.	11.	38.	201.	70.	49.	86.	422.
CELL 7	14.	2.	5.	100.	83.	5.	138.	26.	35.
CELL 8	5.	1.	5.	18.	97.	8.	24.	88.	93.
CELL 9	1.	0.	1.	3.	16.	5.	4.	11.	78.

TOTAL TRIPS	MEAN TRIP LENGTH	BETA
4040.	0.807	1.200

<u>Run 3</u>: For this run the intrinsic attractiveness of residential zone 4 is changed from 6 to 3. This simulates the effect of, say, condemning some of the housing in the zone due to its poor condition.

Looking at the resulting output one sees that the number of residents in zone 4 is about halved. These residents are then distributed fairly evenly over the other zones with more of them going into the adjacent zones than into the less accessible ones.

NO. OF RESIDENTS

1470.	435.	546.
690.	1564.	2169.
988.	828.	287.

CHANGE IN RESIDENTS

161.	48.	24.
-490.	71.	65.
85.	29.	7.

WORKPLACE

	CELL 1	CELL 2	CELL 3	CELL 4	CELL 5	CELL 6	CELL 7	CELL 8	CELL 9
RESIDENCE									
CELL 1	100.	17.	6.	219.	100.	6.	93.	30.	41.
CELL 2	29.	22.	1.	63.	24.	1.	22.	7.	10.
CELL 3	5.	1.	30.	15.	86.	5.	25.	26.	35.
CELL 4	19.	3.	2.	169.	27.	2.	46.	8.	11.
CELL 5	15.	2.	17.	48.	254.	18.	79.	93.	126.
CELL 6	10.	2.	12.	32.	207.	71.	54.	88.	428.
CELL 7	15.	2.	5.	86.	86.	5.	151.	26.	35.
CELL 8	5.	1.	6.	16.	100.	8.	26.	90.	94.
CELL 9	1.	0.	1.	3.	16.	5.	4.	11.	79.

TOTAL TRIPS	MEAN TRIP LENGTH	BETA
3740.	0.827	1.200

<u>Run 4</u>:   Here the travel impedance parameter β is decreased from 1.2 to 0.9.   Since it is a measure of people's unwillingness or inability to travel, this change corresponds to an increase in mobility.   This could be the result of increasing car ownership or the introduction of an improved public transport system, which would enable people to travel long distances more easily.

From the output one can see that the number of home to work trips that stay within the same zone has decreased.   These are the elements of the diagonal of the trip array.   It can also be seen that the other elements which decrease correspond to trips between adjacent zones.   There is a corresponding increase in the number of longer journeys in the town.

NO. OF RESIDENTS

1400.	484.	587.
1154.	1400.	2050.
892.	757.	250.

CHANGE IN RESIDENTS

91.	97.	65.
-26.	-93.	-54.
-11.	-42.	-30.

WORKPLACE

RESIDENCE	CELL 1	CELL 2	CELL 3	CELL 4	CELL 5	CELL 6	CELL 7	CELL 8	CELL 9
CELL 1	77.	16.	8.	170.	114.	9.	90.	39.	62.
CELL 2	27.	17.	2.	60.	35.	3.	27.	12.	19.
CELL 3	7.	1.	23.	19.	85.	7.	28.	29.	47.
CELL 4	35.	7.	5.	219.	68.	5.	83.	23.	37.
CELL 5	17.	3.	15.	48.	204.	18.	71.	80.	128.
CELL 6	15.	3.	13.	42.	203.	59.	61.	89.	370.
CELL 7	16.	3.	6.	71.	85.	7.	108.	29.	47.
CELL 8	6.	1.	6.	18.	89.	9.	27.	68.	90.
CELL 9	1.	0.	1.	4.	17.	4.	5.	11.	60.

TOTAL TRIPS	MEAN TRIP LENGTH	BETA
3740.	0.939	0.900

<u>Run 5</u>:   For this we have changed the distance between zones 2 and 5.   This corresponds to the effect of putting a new bridge across the river (the broken line on the map).   A new set of distances between the zones of the town has been computed.   This is the distance matrix in the file /INW/ACC2. Other than this the two data files are the same.

On looking at the output one sees that there is a large increase in the number of residents in cell 2.   In reality it would take time for this effect to come about and it would perhaps not be as pronounced as this. The model does, however, give an idea of where there is likely to be an increase in the demand for housing due to changes in the town.

```
        NO. OF RESIDENTS                         CHANGE IN RESIDENTS

   1246.      947.      479.              -63.       560.      -43.

   1140.     1375.     1947.              -40.      -118.     -157.

    849.      732.      260.              -54.       -67.      -20.
```

```
                                    WORKPLACE
            CELL 1 CELL 2 CELL 3 CELL 4 CELL 5 CELL 6 CELL 7 CELL 8 CELL 9
RESIDENCE
  CELL 1      91.     10.      6.    174.     86.      6.     81.     27.     39.
  CELL 2      26.     13.      9.     50.    139.      9.     41.     44.     63.
  CELL 3       4.      3.     27.     12.     72.      5.     22.     23.     33.
  CELL 4      35.      4.      3.    268.     46.      3.     80.     15.     21.
  CELL 5      14.      9.     15.     38.    214.     16.     69.     81.    116.
  CELL 6      10.      6.     10.     26.    174.     65.     47.     78.    396.
  CELL 7      14.      3.      5.     68.     72.      5.    132.     23.     33.
  CELL 8       5.      3.      5.     12.     84.      8.     23.     79.     87.
  CELL 9       1.      0.      1.      2.     14.      4.      4.     10.     73.
```

```
TOTAL TRIPS    MEAN TRIP LENGTH      BETA
   3740.           0.803           1.200
```

Description of the Data files

Line 1: If the number in line 1 is "0" then the trip array is printed. If it is any other number then the array is not printed.

Line 2: The first number "9" gives the number of cells in the town (this should not be changed). The second number gives the labour participation ratio, i.e. the ratio of the total population to the number of employed persons in the town.

Lines 3-11: This array gives the distance between cells, e.g. the fourth number across in line 5, "237", gives the road distance between cell 3 and cell 4.

Line 12: Blank.

Lines 13-15: Give the number of persons employed in each cell.

Line 16: Blank.

Lines 17-19: Give the intrinsic attractiveness for residence of each cell.

Line 20: Blank

Line 21:   Gives β the travel impedance parameter.

Data file /INW/ACC1

```
 1      0
 2      9    2.4
 3      15      79     211      70     132     213     113     182     242
 4      79      20     290     134     211     292     192     261     321
 5     211     290      20     237      87     168     166     137     197
 6      70     134     237      10     158     239      90     208     268
 7     132     211      87     158      15      81      87      50     110
 8     213     292     168     239      81      15     168     103      57
 9     113     192     166      90      87     168      15     137     197
10     182     261     137     298      50     103     137      10      92
11     242     321     197     268     110      57     197      92      15
12
13     200      50      80
14     650     900     120
15     500     380     860
16
17       8       5       4
18       6       5       9
19       4       3       1
20
21      1.20
```

Data file /INW/ACC2

```
 1      0
 2      9    2.4
 3      15      79     209      70     130     211     113     180     240
 4      79      20     130     134      51     132     130     101     161
 5     209     130      20     237      87     168     166     137     197
 6      70     134     237      10     158     239      90     208     268
 7     130      51      87     158      15      81      87      50     110
 8     211     132     168     239      81      15     168     103      57
 9     113     130     166      90      87     168      15     137     197
10     180     101     137     298      50     103     137      10      92
11     240     161     197     258     110      57     197      92      15
12
13     200      50      80
14     650     900     120
15     500     380     860
16
17       8       5       4
18       6       5       9
19       4       3       1
20
21      1.20
```

Outline of Instructions Needed to Change the Data Files

The first thing that must be typed is:

     EDIT /INW/ACC1

This makes the data file /INW/ACC1 ready for changing and the computer responds with:

     EDITOR READY

You then move to whatever line you wish to change (say line 14) by using the instruction:

     M14

The computer responds by printing the line you have moved to:

     14.
      650   900   120

If you want to change some number, i.e. you want to replace 650 by 950, you use the instruction:

     E/650/950/

The computer responds by printing the line with the changes made:

     14.
      950   900   120

This may be repeated if further changes are desired. To finish the editing type:

     W

The computer responds by typing:

     READY

You file the changed data by using the instruction:

     FILE I2

Finally to run the model with the new data you type:

     /INW/BRES(S5K D3 /INW/ORES)

The results should then be printed at the console.

AN URBAN MODEL AS AN EXPLORATIVE AND EDUCATIONAL TOOL

David Crowther

The aim of this lecture is to demonstrate the use of an urban model for explorative purposes. In this sense an urban model is analogous to a piece of laboratory equipment with which one can conduct experiments to determine how a particular town (or urban region) is likely to respond to changes of different kinds. Given this freedom to experiment it is possible to test not only specific planning proposals for their probable impact, but wider ranging and longer term urban strategies as well. Even though some of the strategies tested might not be capable of immediate implementation, explorations of this latter more hypothetical kind can perform a useful educational role in providing:

(i) An appreciation of the particular and possibly idiosyncratic ways in which the spatial structure of the town being studied is likely to behave in different circumstances. This is important since similar towns will tend to respond in dissimilar ways to the same kind of change according to their specific spatial organisation. By conducting a series of varied explorations it is thus possible to gain an understanding of how the spatial processes and cause and effect relationships influence each other in the case of the town under study. With this understanding one is in a better position to interpret and explain the model results – an important point when the consequences of a specific planning proposal are being tested and the results are to be used as the basis of a decision.

(ii) A knowledge of the possible benefits to be gained by directing change towards particular long term goals. For example, explorative studies might reveal that if a certain radical change were to be carried out it would have consequences unanimously accepted as beneficial. Even if such a change could not be implemented immediately, it is clear that the results of thoroughly exploring a wide range of alternative strategies would be useful for the formulation of long term objectives. In other words a model can be used to generate planning proposals as well as to test them.

In order to demonstrate the use of an urban model to generate proposals and to gain insights into the spatial behaviour of a particular town, a set of explorations is presented, using the LUBFS urban model and the town of Reading by way of example.

Once an experimental attitude has been adopted towards the use of a model there is an almost infinite range of possible explorations that can be carried out, but in order to keep within the practical limitations of a single lecture the results presented here are concerned with one topic only: the effects of changing the distribution of employment. The effects of changing other determinants of urban form, such as the distribution of developed land or the transportation network, are ignored. Even within this topic the number of possible explorations is very large; but with a high-speed computerised model the problem is not so much to produce results but to digest and interpret them. The results shown here are thus but the tip of an iceberg, and the insights that can be extracted from them are slight compared with what could be gained from a thorough and painstaking analysis of repeated model runs.

There are four explorations. In all four cases, the data inputs describing the existing (i.e. 1962) spatial structure of the town of Reading are taken as given, except for basic employment. In other words, of the three data inputs to the model (i.e. the zonal distributions of developed land, basic employment and the transportation network), the first and last are held constant, while the location of basic employment is allowed to change. The various ratios and parameters required by the model (e.g. the labour particulation rate and the beta calibration parameters) are also held constant. This allows one to explore the effects of different employment location strategies in isolation from other factors, so that all resulting change can be ascribed solely to this cause. This would not be the case if, for example, the effects of adding new employment in different places were tested, since the observed results could be ascribed partly to the shift in the pattern of employment location and partly to the arrival of new employees.

Within this set of four explorations, two contrasted strategies are investigated: the decentralisation of employment and the concentration of employment. The existing situation is taken as the basis for comparison, and the changes from the model results for 1962 data are output by the model for four runs. At one end of the scale all basic employment is considered to be evenly spread throughout the town, while at the other end of the scale all basic employment is considered to be in the central zone. In between, policies of more moderate dispersion and concentration are examined. In each case the outputs are expressed in terms of the resulting changes in the zonal distributions of total floorspace (for all uses), residential population and service employment, and in trip lengths. Certain evaluative measures of accessibilities and space standards are also output so that one can begin to judge whether the changes have good or bad consequences.

The results of the four explorative runs are presented on the following pages. The 1962 basic employment data and the input changes relevant to each exploration are shown first, together with a map of Reading specifying the zonal layout; this provides a key for reading the computer outputs. The results for each explorative run are presented as a double spread, those for the base year 1962 being placed first as the basis for comparison.

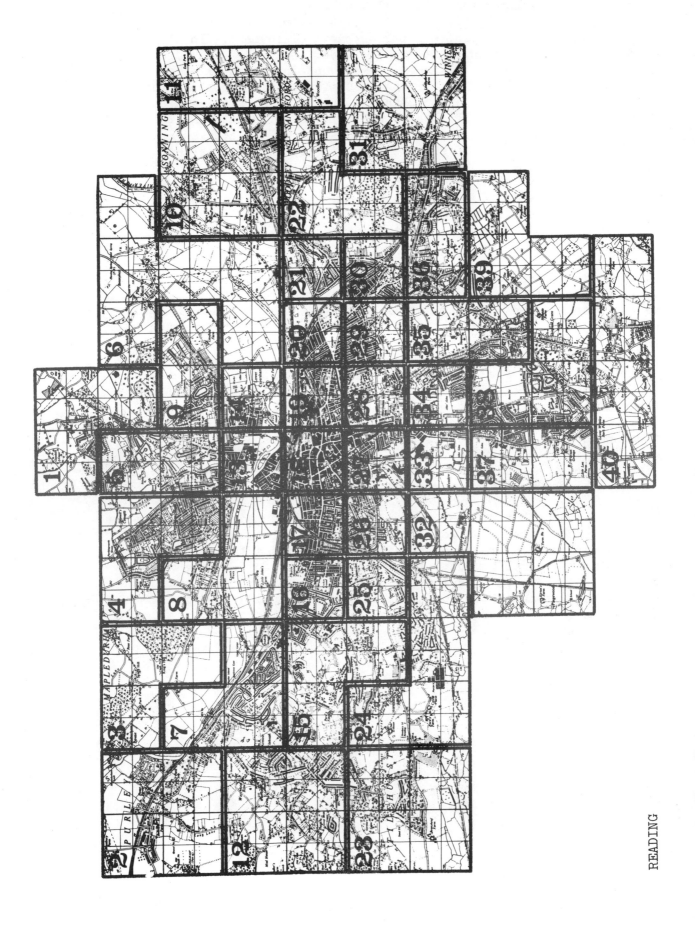

READING

DATA INPUTS FOR THE EXPLORATIONS - BASIC EMPLOYMENT

CELL	EXISTING SITUATION INPUT	DISPERSION				CONCENTRATION			
		EXTREME* INPUT	CHANGE	MODERATE INPUT	CHANGE	EXTREME INPUT	CHANGE	MODERATE INPUT	CHANGE
1	426	487	+61	426	0	0	-426	26	-400
2	133	1318	+1185	133	0	0	-133	133	0
3	0	0	0	0	0	0	0	0	0
4	4	1364	+1360	4	0	0	-4	4	0
5	135	1053	+918	1635	+1500	0	-135	135	0
6	10	22	+12	10	0	0	-10	10	0
7	841	1464	+623	1341	+500	0	-841	241	-600
8	1553	398	-1155	1553	0	0	-1553	2553	+1000
9	6	687	+681	6	0	0	-6	6	0
10	27	585	+558	27	0	0	-27	27	0
11	866	232	-634	866	0	0	-866	366	-500
12	36	2728	+2692	36	0	0	-36	36	0
13	1986	932	-1054	1986	0	0	-1986	2486	+500
14	208	388	+180	208	0	0	-208	1208	+1000
15	736	2107	+1371	1236	+500	0	-736	736	0
16	677	1021	+344	1677	+1000	0	-677	677	0
17	510	810	+300	1510	+1000	0	-510	2510	+2000
18	7608	976	-6632	2608	-5000	33294	+25686	7608	0
19	4318	632	-3686	2318	-2000	0	-4318	4318	0
20	965	554	-411	1465	+500	0	-965	965	0
21	570	521	-49	1070	+500	0	-570	570	0
22	869	1209	+340	869	0	0	-869	369	-500
23	73	1042	+969	73	0	0	-73	73	0
24	14	1119	+1105	14	0	0	-14	14	0
25	82	510	+428	582	+500	0	-82	82	0
26	142	532	+390	142	0	0	-142	642	+500
27	3108	821	-2287	2108	-1000	0	-3108	3608	+500
28	1400	621	-779	1400	0	0	-1400	1900	+500
29	31	621	+590	531	+500	0	-31	31	0
30	8	932	+924	8	0	0	-8	8	0
31	0	1452	+1452	0	0	0	0	0	0
32	28	66	+38	28	0	0	-28	28	0
33	2006	377	-1629	2006	0	0	-2006	506	-1500
34	87	532	+445	587	+500	0	-87	87	0
35	304	876	+572	304	0	0	-304	304	0
36	787	1442	+655	787	0	0	-787	287	-500
37	1896	676	-1220	2396	+500	0	-1896	396	-1500
38	212	1585	+1373	712	+500	0	-212	212	0
39	102	110	+8	102	0	0	-102	102	0
40	530	454	-76	530	0	0	-530	30	-500

* basic employment proportional to developed land in each zone

MODEL RESULTS - EXISTING EMPLOYMENT DISTRIBUTION

6 ITERATIONS

BETAS : STOCK = -0.462   RESIDENTIAL = -0.219   SERVICE = -0.362   (ALPHA = 1.400)
RATIOS: TOTFL/TOTEMP = 112.000   TOTRES/TOTEMP = 2.530   TOTSERV/TOTRES = 0.186   (SEFL/SE = 37.000)

CELL	TOTAL FLOORSPACE MODEL	CHANGE	RESIDENTIAL POPULATION MODEL	CHANGE	SERVICE EMPLOYMENT MODEL	CHANGE
1	57827.	-0.	993.	-0.	49.	0.
2	69841.	1.	947.	-0.	32.	0.
3	0.	0.	0.	0.	0.	-0.
4	212688.	0.	5129.	-0.	229.	-0.
5	205233.	-0.	5351.	-0.	273.	-0.
6	2286.	-0.	44.	-0.	0.	0.
7	182639.	-0.	3398.	-0.	294.	-0.
8	79503.	1.	1174.	-0.	252.	-0.
9	121607.	-0.	3166.	0.	109.	0.
10	67259.	-0.	1367.	-0.	37.	-0.
11	21240.	0.	0.	0.	28.	0.
12	190264.	1.	3046.	-0.	160.	-0.
13	300890.	-0.	7384.	-0.	1239.	-0.
14	124121.	0.	4020.	0.	198.	0.
15	349241.	-0.	7856.	-0.	811.	-0.
16	314898.	0.	9255.	-0.	1006.	-0.
17	346702.	1.	12046.	0.	1313.	-0.
18	503397.	-0.	1101.	-0.	0773.	-0.
19	300221.	1.	3795.	-0.	2514.	-0.
20	195465.	1.	5651.	-0.	618.	-0.
21	132135.	-0.	3471.	-0.	249.	-0.
22	167064.	-0.	3088.	-0.	259.	-0.
23	57206.	0.	829.	-0.	25.	-0.
24	138390.	-0.	3058.	-0.	126.	-0.
25	134217.	0.	4113.	-0.	215.	0.
26	196023.	-0.	6839.	-0.	456.	-0.
27	398840.	0.	9092.	0.	3136.	-0.
28	269155.	-0.	7952.	-0.	1258.	-0.
29	204054.	-0.	6859.	0.	449.	-0.
30	185307.	-0.	4915.	-0.	289.	-0.
31	119714.	-0.	2063.	-0.	72.	-0.
32	7355.	1.	140.	-0.	2.	-0.
33	128748.	-1.	2093.	-0.	567.	-0.
34	153813.	-0.	4890.	0.	241.	-0.
35	202123.	-0.	5496.	-0.	403.	-0.
36	259472.	-0.	5821.	0.	595.	-0.
37	153999.	-0.	2873.	-0.	462.	-0.
38	290732.	-1.	7151.	-0.	478.	-0.
39	12365.	-0.	201.	-0.	7.	-0.
40	50009.	1.	714.	-0.	49.	-0.
TOTALS	6986040.	2.	157378.	-3.	29272.	-1.
DISPLACED		5.		7.		6.

TRIP DISTRIBUTION RESULTS

% TRIPS OF LENGTH (KM):	TRIPS TO WORK MODEL	CHANGE	TRIPS TO SERVICES MODEL	CHANGE
1	4.0	-0.0	5.5	0.0
2	17.0	-0.0	21.5	0.0
3	24.1	-0.0	25.8	0.0
4	19.8	-0.0	19.6	0.0
5	15.2	-0.0	14.2	0.0
6	8.8	-0.0	6.5	-0.0
7	6.0	-0.0	4.3	0.0
8	2.6	-0.0	1.5	0.0
9	1.4	-0.0	0.6	0.0
10	0.7	-0.0	0.2	0.0
10+	0.4		0.1	0.0
MEAN TRIP LENGTH	3.5	0.0	3.1	0.0

ACCESSIBILITY MEASURES

AVERAGE DISTANCE OF:

	X=25% SCORE (KM)	CHANGE (KM)	X=50% SCORE (KM)	CHANGE (KM)	X=75% SCORE (KM)	CHANGE (KM)
RESIDENTS TO X% EMPLOYEES =	2.88	0.00	3.41	-0.00	4.71	-0.00
SERVICES =	2.98	0.00	3.16	0.00	4.10	-0.00
EMPLOYEES TO X% RESIDENTS =	3.01	0.00	4.53	-0.00	5.77	0.00
EMPLOYEES =	2.00	0.00	2.60	0.00	3.90	0.00
SERVICES =	2.06	0.00	2.41	-0.00	3.38	0.00
SERVICES TO X% SERVICES =	1.75	-0.00	2.17	-0.00	3.16	-0.00

DENSITY & FLOORSPACE PER PERSON MEASURES

	LOW SCORE %	CHANGE %	MED SCORE %	CHANGE %	HIGH SCORE %	CHANGE %	WEIGHTED AV SCORE PPH OR SQM	CHANGE PP
% RESIDENTS AT 60-,90-,90+ PPH =	31.1	0.0	14.8	-0.0	54.1	-0.0	74.52	-0.00
% RESIDENTS AT 24-,36-,36+ SQM =	13.9	0.0	54.9	0.0	31.1	0.0	31.91	-0.00
% EMPLOYEES AT 60-,90-,90+ PPH =	8.7	-0.0	8.5	0.0	82.8	-0.0	88.70	-0.00
% EMPLOYEES AT 24-,36-,36+ SQM =	8.1	0.0	90.2	-0.0	1.7	0.0	31.57	0.00

MODEL RESULTS - TOTAL DISPERSION

6 ITERATIONS

BETAS :   STOCK = -0.462   RESIDENTIAL = -0.219   SERVICE = -0.362   (ALPHA = 1.400)
RATIOS :   TOTFL/TOTEMP = 112.000   TOTRES/TOTEMP = 2.530   TOTSERV/TOTRES = 0.186   (SEFL/SE = 37.000)

CELL	TOTAL FLOORSPACE		RESIDENTIAL POPULATION		SERVICE EMPLOYMENT	
	MODEL	CHANGE	MODEL	CHANGE	MODEL	CHANGE
1	53797.	-5420.	839.	-154.	67.	18.
2	181732.	84358.	3025.	2078.	350.	318.
3	0.	0.	0.	0.	0.	0.
4	209270.	-34877.	3852.	-1277.	568.	339.
5	184599.	-41910.	3776.	-1575.	525.	252.
6	2014.	-584.	30.	-14.	1.	1.
7	309711.	112803.	6894.	3496.	1145.	851.
8	69174.	10035.	1604.	430.	126.	-126.
9	106390.	-31025.	2113.	-1053.	221.	112.
10	72005.	-8251.	1187.	-180.	108.	71.
11	15284.	8856.	149.	149.	10.	-18.
12	551007.	298523.	10656.	7610.	2371.	2211.
13	232117.	-43626.	5674.	-1710.	1004.	-235.
14	90350.	-37951.	2343.	-1677.	227.	29.
15	530526.	149632.	11758.	3902.	3301.	2490.
16	310291.	-12413.	8147.	-1108.	1829.	823.
17	270404.	-86729.	7451.	-4595.	1696.	383.
18	360487.	-8359.	8956.	7855.	3249.	-7524.
19	185313.	-9933.	5127.	1332.	866.	-1648.
20	143175.	-42718.	3796.	-1855.	522.	-96.
21	106706.	-23989.	2516.	-955.	274.	25.
22	190263.	15430.	3464.	376.	496.	237.
23	142497.	62774.	2476.	1647.	258.	233.
24	202129.	38124.	4356.	1298.	574.	448.
25	139944.	-4176.	3929.	-184.	474.	259.
26	158120.	-46920.	4562.	-2277.	655.	199.
27	267200.	-74427.	7143.	-1949.	1734.	-1402.
28	187015.	-64009.	5166.	-2786.	913.	-345.
29	170175.	-47549.	4528.	-2331.	720.	271.
30	205523.	-1137.	4605.	-310.	763.	474.
31	176189.	22863.	2613.	550.	362.	290.
32	6053.	-2142.	93.	-47.	3.	1.
33	85644.	-1527.	2215.	122.	212.	-355.
34	115591.	-48540.	2848.	-2042.	323.	82.
35	194300.	-21092.	4520.	-976.	716.	313.
36	301599.	26971.	6280.	459.	1300.	705.
37	112699.	-19352.	2312.	-561.	253.	-209.
38	270760.	-51764.	5227.	-1924.	955.	477.
39	14834.	2303.	269.	68.	12.	5.
40	47461.	-667.	700.	-14.	56.	7.
TOTALS	6972345.	-13649.	157198.	-183.	29239.	-34.
DISPLACED	846319.		31553.		11958.	

TRIP DISTRIBUTION RESULTS

% TRIPS OF LENGTH (KM):	TRIPS TO WORK MODEL	CHANGE	TRIPS TO SERVICES MODEL	CHANGE
0 - 1	3.7	-0.3	6.4	0.9
1 - 2	13.0	-4.0	19.2	-2.3
2 - 3	19.6	-4.5	23.9	-1.9
3 - 4	16.9	-2.9	17.9	-1.7
4 - 5	14.7	-0.5	13.2	-1.0
5 - 6	10.2	1.4	7.7	1.2
6 - 7	8.6	2.6	5.6	1.3
7 - 8	5.6	3.0	3.1	1.6
8 - 9	3.7	2.3	1.7	1.1
9 - 10	2.0	1.3	0.8	0.6
10+	2.1	1.7	0.7	0.6
MEAN TRIP LENGTH	4.2	0.7	3.4	0.3

ACCESSIBILITY MEASURES

AVERAGE DISTANCE OF:	X=25% SCORE (KM)	CHANGE (KM)	X=50% SCORE (KM)	CHANGE (KM)	X=75% SCORE (KM)	CHANGE (KM)
RESIDENTS TO X% EMPLOYEES =	3.19	0.31	5.15	1.74	6.94	2.23
SERVICES =	2.99	0.01	4.51	1.35	6.46	2.36
RESIDENTS =	3.12	0.11	4.77	0.24	6.75	0.98
EMPLOYEES TO X% EMPLOYEES =	3.34	1.34	5.33	2.73	7.16	3.26
SERVICES =	3.18	1.12	4.73	2.32	6.72	3.34
SERVICES TO X% SERVICES =	2.77	1.02	4.35	2.18	6.27	3.11

DENSITY & FLOORSPACE PER PERSON MEASURES

	LOW SCORE %	CHANGE %	MED SCORE %	CHANGE %	HIGH SCORE %	CHANGE %	WEIGHTED AV SCORE PPH OR SQM PP	CHANGE PP
% RESIDENTS AT 60-,90-,90+ PPH =	31.0	-0.1	20.5	5.7	48.5	-5.6	74.90	0.38
% RESIDENTS AT 24-,36-,36+ SQM =	0.	-13.9	72.8	17.9	27.2	-3.9	32.47	0.56
% EMPLOYEES AT 60-,90-,90+ PPH =	11.0	2.3	53.3	44.8	35.7	-47.1	80.54	-8.16
% EMPLOYEES AT 24-,36-,36+ SQM =	0.5	-7.6	99.5	9.3	0.	-1.7	29.01	-2.56

MODEL RESULTS - TOTAL CONCENTRATION

6 ITERATIONS

				(ALPHA = 1.400)
BETAS :	STOCK = -0.462	RESIDENTIAL = -0.219	SERVICE = -0.362	(SEFL/SE = 37.000)
RATIOS :	TOTFL/TOTEMP = 112.000	TOTRES/TOTEMP = 2.530	TOTSERV/TOTRES = 0.186	

CELL	TOTAL FLOORSPACE MODEL	CHANGE	RESIDENTIAL POPULATION MODEL	CHANGE	SERVICE EMPLOYMENT MODEL	CHANGE
1	55233.	7305.	966.	-27.	10.	-39.
2	60107.	-6735.	683.	-264.	8.	-24.
3	0.	0.	0.	0.	0.	0.
4	232312.	19724.	4882.	-247.	100.	-129.
5	217772.	15638.	5009.	-342.	105.	-168.
6	2344.	258.	40.	-4.	0.	0.
7	175377.	12338.	3129.	-269.	66.	-228.
8	91644.	41741.	2236.	1062.	31.	-221.
9	132287.	10780.	2957.	-209.	47.	-62.
10	42969.	-23690.	612.	-755.	6.	-31.
11	7651.	6610.	75.	75.	0.	-28.
12	164477.	-24887.	2118.	-928.	46.	-114.
13	320760.	66570.	9287.	1903.	262.	-977.
14	152206.	32975.	4740.	720.	85.	-113.
15	339319.	7176.	6894.	-962.	228.	-591.
16	370281.	71103.	10941.	1686.	356.	-650.
17	460703.	122301.	16682.	4636.	570.	-743.
18	1701752.	516476.	0.	-1101.	25188.	14415.
19	331439.	150818.	11656.	7861.	324.	-2190.
20	181444.	8380.	5169.	-482.	117.	-501.
21	110460.	-8176.	2583.	-888.	44.	-205.
22	99142.	-47723.	1484.	-1604.	24.	-235.
23	49407.	-6199.	572.	-257.	7.	-18.
24	136027.	-2064.	2449.	-669.	46.	-80.
25	143852.	11535.	3832.	-281.	83.	-132.
26	212098.	19374.	6603.	-236.	169.	-287.
27	422290.	99650.	14592.	5500.	515.	-2621.
28	275881.	39226.	8092.	1040.	255.	-1003.
29	186386.	-16969.	5092.	-1767.	125.	-324.
30	132952.	-52155.	2571.	-2344.	55.	-234.
31	68211.	-51503.	785.	-1278.	10.	-62.
32	5684.	-972.	88.	-52.	0.	-2.
33	110218.	31771.	2996.	903.	52.	-515.
34	148116.	-3699.	3928.	-962.	76.	-165.
35	153227.	-41896.	3260.	-2236.	73.	-330.
36	172143.	-69129.	3056.	-2765.	72.	-523.
37	105480.	-9920.	2167.	-706.	35.	-427.
38	205649.	-80184.	3802.	-3349.	86.	-392.
39	7008.	-2959.	93.	-108.	1.	-6.
40	27405.	-10204.	356.	-358.	3.	-46.
TOTALS	7812724.	826686.	157378.	-3.	29272.	-1.
DISPLACED		459064.		25391.		14416.

TRIP DISTRIBUTION RESULTS

% TRIPS OF LENGTH (KM):	TRIPS TO WORK MODEL	CHANGE	TRIPS TO SERVICES MODEL	CHANGE
0 - 1	0.5	-3.5	1.5	-4.0
1 - 2	38.8	21.8	37.8	16.3
2 - 3	26.1	2.0	26.2	0.4
3 - 4	18.9	-0.9	18.6	-1.0
4 - 5	10.4	-4.8	10.3	-3.9
5 - 6	2.0	-6.8	2.3	-4.2
6 - 7	3.0	-3.4	2.9	-1.4
7 - 8	0.2	-2.4	0.3	-1.2
8 - 9	0.1	-1.3	0.1	-0.5
9 - 10	0.0	-0.7	0.0	-0.2
10+	0.0	-0.4	0.0	-0.1
MEAN TRIP LENGTH	2.6	-0.9	2.6	-0.5

ACCESSIBILITY MEASURES

AVERAGE DISTANCE OF:	X=25% SCORE (KM)	CHANGE (KM)	X=50% SCORE (KM)	CHANGE (KM)	X=75% SCORE (KM)	CHANGE (KM)
RESIDENTS TO X% EMPLOYEES =	2.65	-0.23	2.65	-0.76	2.65	-2.06
SERVICES =	2.65	-0.33	2.65	-0.51	2.65	-1.45
RESIDENTS =	2.64	-0.37	3.75	-0.78	4.84	-0.93
EMPLOYEES TO X% EMPLOYEES =	0.63	-1.37	0.63	-1.97	0.63	-3.27
SERVICES =	0.63	-1.43	0.63	-1.78	0.63	-2.75
SERVICES TO X% SERVICES =	0.77	-0.98	0.77	-1.40	0.77	-2.39

DENSITY & FLOORSPACE PER PERSON MEASURES

	LOW SCORE %	CHANGE %	MED SCORE %	CHANGE %	HIGH SCORE %	CHANGE %	WEIGHTED AV SCORE PPH OR SQM PP	CHANGE PP
% RESIDENTS AT 60-,90-,90+ PPH =	32.2	1.1	8.3	-6.5	59.6	5.5	74.23	-0.29
% RESIDENTS AT 24-,36-,36+ SQM =	0.	-13.9	59.6	4.7	40.4	9.3	37.39	5.48
% EMPLOYEES AT 60-,90-,90+ PPH =	1.5	-7.2	0.8	-7.7	97.7	14.9	94.07	5.37
% EMPLOYEES AT 24-,36-,36+ SQM =	0.	-8.1	93.5	3.3	6.5	4.8	25.65	-5.92

291

MODEL RESULTS - MODERATE DISPERSAL

6 ITERATIONS

BETAS :	STOCK = -0.462	RESIDENTIAL = -0.219	SERVICE = -0.362	(ALPHA = 1.400)
RATIOS :	TOTFL/TOTEMP = 112.000	TOTRES/TOTEMP = 2.530	TOTSERV/TOTRES = 0.186	(SEFL/SE = 37.000)

CELL	TOTAL FLOORSPACE MODEL	CHANGE	RESIDENTIAL POPULATION MODEL	CHANGE	SERVICE EMPLOYMENT MODEL	CHANGE
1	61639.	3812.	1076.	83.	61.	12.
2	81943.	12103.	1183.	236.	48.	16.
3	0.	0.	0.	0.	0.	0.
4	219953.	7265.	5259.	130.	288.	59.
5	219850.	-22883.	4363.	-988.	653.	388.
6	2213.	-73.	41.	-3.	0.	0.
7	210971.	15832.	3775.	377.	508.	214.
8	79433.	-69.	1122.	-52.	303.	51.
9	118471.	-3136.	3012.	-154.	125.	16.
10	68405.	1146.	1382.	15.	44.	7.
11	21406.	166.	0.	0.	33.	5.
12	227030.	36766.	3853.	807.	253.	93.
13	295967.	-4922.	6740.	-644.	1526.	287.
14	113895.	-10226.	3485.	-535.	216.	18.
15	396304.	34563.	8673.	817.	1340.	529.
16	332810.	-7088.	8131.	-1124.	1800.	794.
17	331295.	-40406.	8916.	-3130.	2144.	831.
18	491451.	33054.	10305.	9204.	6667.	-4706.
19	256740.	6519.	4927.	1132.	1768.	-746.
20	184597.	-23367.	4270.	-1381.	876.	258.
21	130285.	-14350.	2791.	-680.	389.	140.
22	169900.	2836.	3095.	7.	310.	51.
23	65860.	8654.	1009.	180.	36.	11.
24	149937.	11547.	3400.	342.	170.	44.
25	139376.	-7341.	3720.	-393.	388.	173.
26	188488.	-7535.	6366.	-473.	528.	72.
27	365979.	-7861.	8620.	-472.	3016.	-120.
28	247776.	-21379.	6500.	-1452.	1453.	195.
29	200116.	-16438.	5847.	-1012.	686.	237.
30	187859.	2552.	4908.	-7.	350.	61.
31	122329.	2615.	2100.	37.	86.	14.
32	7656.	301.	149.	9.	2.	0.
33	125498.	-3249.	1798.	-295.	678.	111.
34	154351.	-11963.	4255.	-635.	397.	156.
35	207023.	4900.	5562.	66.	499.	96.
36	265616.	6144.	5861.	40.	734.	139.
37	162768.	-3731.	2560.	-313.	680.	218.
38	312669.	9436.	7274.	123.	745.	267.
39	13201.	836.	222.	21.	9.	2.
40	54963.	4955.	827.	113.	61.	12.
TOTALS	6986024.	-14.	157378.	-3.	29272.	-1.
DISPLACED	206017.		13742.		5572.	

TRIP DISTRIBUTION RESULTS

% TRIPS OF LENGTH (KM):	TRIPS TO WORK MODEL	CHANGE	TRIPS TO SERVICES MODEL	CHANGE
0 - 1	5.3	-1.3	8.1	2.6
1 - 2	14.7	-2.3	19.6	-1.9
2 - 3	22.5	-1.6	24.7	-1.1
3 - 4	18.4	-1.4	18.2	-1.4
4 - 5	14.9	-0.3	13.6	-0.6
5 - 6	10.1	1.3	7.4	0.9
6 - 7	7.1	1.1	4.8	0.5
7 - 8	3.6	1.0	2.1	0.6
8 - 9	1.9	0.5	0.9	0.3
9 - 10	1.0	0.3	0.3	0.1
10+	0.5	0.1	0.2	0.1
MEAN TRIP LENGTH	3.7	0.2	3.2	0.0

ACCESSIBILITY MEASURES

	X=25%		X=50%		X=75%	
AVERAGE DISTANCE OF:	SCORE (KM)	CHANGE (KM)	SCORE (KM)	CHANGE (KM)	SCORE (KM)	CHANGE (KM)
RESIDENTS TO X% EMPLOYEES =	2.94	0.06	3.93	0.52	5.20	0.49
SERVICES =	2.97	-0.01	3.57	0.41	5.01	0.91
RESIDENTS =	2.97	-0.04	4.32	-0.21	5.83	0.66
EMPLOYEES TO X% EMPLOYEES =	2.61	0.61	3.64	1.04	4.85	0.95
SERVICES =	2.64	0.58	3.26	0.85	4.63	1.25
SERVICES TO X% SERVICES =	2.36	0.61	2.95	0.78	4.39	1.23

DENSITY & FLOORSPACE PER PERSON MEASURES

	LOW		MED		HIGH		WEIGHTED AV	
	SCORE %	CHANGE	SCORE %	CHANGE	SCORE %	CHANGE	SCORE PPH OR SQM PP	CHANGE
% RESIDENTS AT 60-,90-,90+ PPH =	33.2	2.1	13.5	-1.3	53.3	-0.8	74.55	0.03
% RESIDENTS AT 24-,36-,36+ SQM =	12.0	-1.9	54.8	-0.1	33.2	2.1	31.73	-0.18
% EMPLOYEES AT 60-,90-,90+ PPH =	10.4	1.7	14.4	5.9	75.2	-7.6	87.19	-1.51
% EMPLOYEES AT 24-,36-,36+ SQM =	4.4	-3.7	94.2	4.0	1.4	-0.3	30.82	-0.75

MODEL RESULTS - MODERATE CONCENTRATION

  6 ITERATIONS

BETAS :   STOCK = -0.462   RESIDENTIAL = -0.219   SERVICE = -0.362   (ALPHA = 1.400)
RATIOS : TOTFL/TOTEMP = 112.000   TOTRES/TOTEMP = 2.530   TOTSERV/TOTRES = 0.186   (SEFL/SE = 37.000)

CELL	TOTAL FLOORSPACE		RESIDENTIAL POPULATION		SERVICE EMPLOYMENT	
	MODEL	CHANGE	MODEL	CHANGE	MODEL	CHANGE
1	57909.	9382.	1234.	241.	27.	-22.
2	70864.	1024.	979.	32.	32.	0.
3	0.	0.	0.	0.	0.	0.
4	235166.	22478.	5906.	777.	262.	33.
5	224371.	19138.	6079.	728.	305.	32.
6	2347.	61.	45.	1.	0.	0.
7	189203.	21064.	4014.	-616.	227.	-67.
8	89115.	-12887.	658.	-516.	413.	161.
9	134619.	13012.	3623.	457.	122.	13.
10	58006.	-9253.	1114.	-253.	28.	-9.
11	11616.	2876.	49.	49.	9.	-19.
12	197708.	7444.	3237.	191.	168.	8.
13	334916.	21527.	8129.	745.	1510.	271.
14	138555.	-8555.	3573.	-447.	404.	206.
15	381069.	31828.	8900.	1044.	898.	87.
16	352284.	37386.	10875.	1620.	1138.	132.
17	388280.	-3421.	10637.	-1409.	2435.	1122.
18	610987.	27590.	3373.	2272.	10277.	-496.
19	306554.	6333.	4324.	529.	2364.	-150.
20	192418.	-3046.	5525.	-126.	558.	-60.
21	125733.	-6402.	3207.	-264.	216.	-33.
22	134857.	-19707.	2523.	-565.	137.	-122.
23	60193.	2987.	891.	62.	26.	1.
24	149755.	11365.	3400.	342.	139.	13.
25	147174.	12957.	4668.	555.	239.	24.
26	207302.	-1221.	6694.	-145.	600.	144.
27	402301.	-9039.	8539.	-553.	3213.	77.
28	270777.	-10878.	7305.	-647.	1346.	88.
29	195013.	-9041.	6405.	-454.	381.	-68.
30	163677.	-21630.	4109.	-806.	214.	-75.
31	94492.	-25222.	1485.	-578.	45.	-27.
32	6141.	-1214.	107.	-33.	1.	-1.
33	112665.	21418.	3172.	1079.	211.	-356.
34	141302.	-12512.	4334.	-556.	197.	-44.
35	178689.	-23434.	4588.	-900.	305.	-98.
36	219292.	-27680.	4924.	-897.	345.	-250.
37	117208.	-6592.	2737.	-136.	148.	-314.
38	233878.	-56855.	5296.	-1855.	314.	-164.
39	9750.	-2615.	133.	-68.	5.	-2.
40	34616.	-3693.	586.	-128.	12.	-37.
TOTALS	6980312.	-5028.	157378.	-3.	29272.	-1.
DISPLACED.	274899.		11343.		2414.	

TRIP DISTRIBUTION RESULTS

% TRIPS OF LENGTH (KM):	TRIPS TO WORK MODEL	CHANGE	TRIPS TO SERVICES MODEL	CHANGE
1	4.9	0.9	6.5	1.0
2	17.9	0.9	21.4	-0.1
3	24.3	0.2	25.8	0.0
4	20.7	0.9	19.7	0.1
5	14.9	-0.3	13.8	-0.4
6	8.4	-0.4	6.5	0.0
7	5.1	-0.9	4.1	-0.2
8	2.2	-0.4	1.4	-0.1
9	0.9	-0.5	0.5	-0.1
10	0.4	-0.3	0.2	0.0
10+	0.2	-0.2	0.1	
MEAN TRIP LENGTH	3.4	-0.2	3.1	-0.1

ACCESSIBILITY MEASURES

	X=25% SCORE (KM)	CHANGE (KM)	X=50% SCORE (KM)	CHANGE (KM)	X=75% SCORE (KM)	CHANGE (KM)
AVERAGE DISTANCE OF:						
RESIDENTS TO X% EMPLOYEES =	2.97	0.09	3.24	-0.17	4.23	-0.48
SERVICES =	2.97	-0.01	3.12	-0.04	4.11	0.01
RESIDENTS =	2.97	-0.04	4.43	-0.10	5.80	0.03
EMPLOYEES TO X% EMPLOYEES =	1.82	-0.18	2.30	-0.30	3.26	-0.64
SERVICES =	1.82	-0.24	2.25	-0.16	3.16	-0.22
SERVICES TO X% SERVICES =	1.68	-0.07	2.14	-0.03	3.09	-0.07

DENSITY & FLOORSPACE PER PERSON MEASURES

	LOW SCORE %	CHANGE %	MED SCORE %	CHANGE %	HIGH SCORE %	CHANGE %	WEIGHTED AV SCORE PPH OR SQM PP	CHANGE PPH OR SQM PP
% RESIDENTS AT 60-,90-,90+ PPH =	32.8	1.7	11.5	-3.3	55.6	1.5	73.98	-0.54
% RESIDENTS AT 24-,36-,36+ SQM =	17.1	3.2	50.1	-4.8	32.8	1.7	32.38	0.47
% EMPLOYEES AT 60-,90+,90+ PPH =	6.3	-2.4	5.4	-3.1	88.3	5.5	90.53	1.83
% EMPLOYEES AT 24-,36-,36+ SQM =	6.2	-1.9	92.7	2.5	1.1	-0.6	31.35	-0.22

Bibliography

ABRAMS, M. (1964). Changing needs of different age groups. In Communities and Social Change. London: National Council for Social Service.

ALEXANDER, C. (1964). Notes on the Synthesis of Form. Cambridge, Mass: Harvard University Press.

ALEXANDER, C. (1966). A city is not a tree. Design, Vol. 206, pp. 48-55.

ALONSO, W. (1964). Location and Land Use: Towards a Theory of Urban Rent. Cambridge, Mass: Harvard University Press.

ANGEL, S. and HYMAN, G. (1971). Urban Spatial Interaction. Working Paper No.69. London: Centre for Environmental Studies.

ANTHONY, J. and BAXTER, R. (1971). The First Stage in Disaggregating the Residential Sub-Model. Working Paper No. 58. Cambridge: LUBFS.

APPS, P. (1971). An Approach to Modelling Residential Demand. Ph.D. Dissertation, University of Cambridge. (See also Working Papers 59, 60 and 61 published by LUBFS.)

BARRAS, R. et al. (1971). An operational urban development model of Cheshire. Environment and Planning, Vol. 3, pp. 115-223.

BATTY, M. (1969). The impact of a new town: an application of the Garin-Lowry model. Journal of the Town Planning Institute, Vol. 55, No. 10, pp.428-35.

BATTY, M. (1972a). An experimental model of urban dynamics. Town Planning Review, Vol. 43, pp. 166-86.

BATTY, M. (1972b). Entropy and Spatial Geometry. Reading: Urban Systems Research Unit.

BATTY, M. (1972c). Recent developments in land use modelling. Urban Studies, Vol. 9, pp. 151-77.

BATTY, M. and MACKIE, S. (1972). The calibration of gravity, entropy and related models of spatial interaction. Environment and Planning, Vol. 4, pp.205-33.

BAXTER, R.S. (1971). Urban Systems: the Development of a Cordon Model. Working Paper No. 47. Cambridge: LUBFS.

BAXTER, R.S. (1972). Computers in Local Authorities. Technical Note A3. Cambridge: LUBFS.

BAXTER, R.S. and LLOYD, N. (1972). Computers in Land Area Measurement. Technical Note A4. Cambridge: LUBFS.

BLACK, S.M. (1972a). Overview Sweden. Newsletter of the British Urban and Regional Information Systems Association (December).

BLACK, S.M. (1972b). Urban data management: a Danish feasibility test. In Urban Data Management: Proceedings of the Second Annual European Symposium. London: Planning and Transportation Research and Computation Co. Ltd.

BOOTH, P. et al. (1970). Model of a Town: Cambridge. Working Paper No. 13. Cambridge: LUBFS.

BOYCE, D.E. and DAY, H.D. with McDONALD, C. (1969). Metropolitan Plan Evaluation Methodology. Philadelphia: Institute for Environmental Studies, University of Pennsylvania.

BOYCE, D.E. et al. (1971). An Interim Report on Procedures for Continuing Metropolitan Planning. Philadelphia: Institute of Environmental Studies, University of Pennsylvania.

BRIGHTON URBAN STRUCTURE PLAN (1971). Report on the Evaluation of Alternative Strategies. Brighton: West Sussex C.C., Brighton C.B.C., East Sussex C.C.

BROADBENT, T.A. (1969). Zone Size and Singly-Constrained Interaction Models. Working Note No. 132. London: Centre for Environmental Studies.

BUCHANAN, S. and Partners (1966). South Hampshire Study: Main Report. London: HMSO.

BUTLER, E.W. et al. (1969). Moving Behaviour and Residential Choice. Report No. 81. Highway Research Board.

CAREY, H.C. (1858). Principles of Social Science. Philadelphia: J. Lippincott.

CARROTHERS, G.A.P. (1956). An historical review of the gravity and potential concepts of human interaction. Journal of the American Institute of Planners, Vol. 22, pp.94-102.

CENTRE FOR ENVIRONMENTAL STUDIES (1972). The Management of Urban and Regional Research: Some Guidelines for Participants. Report of a Working Group. London: CES.

CHADWICK, G. (1971). A Systems View of Planning: Towards a Theory of the Urban and Regional Planning Process. Oxford: Pergamon.

CHAPIN, F.S. (1965). Urban Land Use Planning. Second Edition. Urbana, Illinois: University of Illinois Press.

CHEESMAN, R. (1971). A Context for New Town Design (Unpublished paper).

CHEESMAN, R. with LINDSAY, W. and PORZECANSKI, M. (1971). New Towns: the Data Bank, its Construction and Organisation. Working Paper No. 63. Cambridge: LUBFS.

CHORLEY, R. and KENNEDY, B. (1971). Physical Geography: a Systems Approach. London: Prentice Hall.

CHRISTALLER, W. (1933). Die Zentrallen Orte in Suddeutschland. Jena. (Translated by C. Baskinas: The Central Places of Southern Germany. Englewood Cliffs: Prentice-Hall)

CLARK, C. (1951). Urban population densities. Journal of the Royal Statistical Society, Series A, Vol. 114, pp.490-6.

COMPUTER PANEL OF LAMSAC (1972). The Use of High Level Languages. London: Local Authorities Management Services and Computer Committee.

CORDEY-HAYES, M. (1968). Retail Location Models. Working Paper No. 16. London: Centre for Environmental Studies.

CORDEY-HAYES, M. (1972a). Dynamic Frameworks for Spatial Models. Working Paper No. 76. London: Centre for Environmental Studies.

CORDEY-HAYES, M. (1972b). On the feasibility of simulating the relationship between regional imbalance and city growth. In Papers of the Regional Science Conference, London 1972 (in press).

COUNCIL FOR SCIENTIFIC POLICY (1968). Enquiry into the Flow of Candidates in Science and Technology into Higher Education (The Painton Report). London: HMSO.

COVENTRY-SOLIHULL-WARWICKSHIRE SUB-REGIONAL STUDY (1971a). A Strategy for the Sub-Region: the Report of the Sub-Regional Planning Study. Coventry C.C., Solihull C.B.C. and Warwickshire C.C.

COVENTRY-SOLIHULL-WARWICKSHIRE SUB-REGIONAL STUDY (1971b). Supplementary Report 4: Evaluation. Coventry C.C., Solihull C.B.C. and Warwickshire C.C.

COWIE, S.R. (1972). The spatial data processing project. In Urban Data Management: Proceedings of the Second Annual European Symposium. London: Planning and Transportation Research and Computation Co. Ltd.

CRIPPS, E.L. (1968). Proceedings of the Regional Studies Association Conference. Nottingham.

CRIPPS, E.L. and CATER, E.A. (1972). The empirical development of a disaggregated residential location model: some preliminary results. In Patterns and Processes in Urban and Regional Systems. Ed. A.G. Wilson. London: Pion.

CRIPPS, E.L. and FOOT, D.H.S. (1969). A land-use model for sub-regional planning. Regional Studies, Vol. 3, pp.243-68.

DENNIS, N. (1970). People and Planning: the Sociology of Housing in Sunderland. London: Faber and Faber.

DEPARTMENT OF THE ENVIRONMENT (forthcoming). Manual on Point Referencing Properties and Parcels of Land.

DONNISON, D.V. (1967). The Government of Housing. Harmondsworth: Penguin.

DUNN, E.S. (1954). The Location of Agricultural Production. Gainesville, Florida: University of Florida Press.

DUNN, J.R. and HEARLE, E.F.R. (1972). The Wichita Falls integrated municipal information system: prototype for cities. In Urban Data Management: Proceedings of the Second Annual European Symposium. London: Planning and Transportation Research and Computation Co. Ltd.

ECHENIQUE, M. (1968). Urban Systems: Towards an Explorative Model. Working Paper No. 7. Cambridge: LUBFS.

ECHENIQUE, M., CROWTHER, D. and LINDSAY, W. (1969a). Model of a Town: Reading. Working Paper No. 12. Cambridge: LUBFS.

ECHENIQUE, M., CROWTHER, D. and LINDSAY, W. (1969b). A Structural Comparison of Three Generations of New Towns. Working Paper No. 25. Cambridge: LUBFS.

ECHENIQUE, M., CROWTHER, D. and LINDSAY, W. (1969c). A spatial model of urban stock and activity. Regional Studies, Vol. 3, No. 3, pp.281-312.

ECHENIQUE, M. and DOMEYKO, J. (1970). A Model for Santiago Metropolitan Area. Working Paper No. 11. Cambridge: LUBFS.

EVANS, A. (1971). The calibration of trip distribution models with exponential or similar cost functions. Transportation Research, Vol. 5, pp.15-38.

FORRESTER, J.W. (1969). Urban Dynamics. Cambridge, Mass: MIT Press.

FRIEND, J.K. and JESSOP, W.N. (1969). Local Government and Strategic Choice: An Operational Research Approach to the Processes of Public Planning. London: Tavistock.

GAITS, G.M. (1971). Information needs for planning. In Proceedings of the First Annual Data Management Symposium, Bonn 1971.

GOLDNER, W. (1971). The Lowry-model heritage. Journal of the American Institute of Planners, Vol. 37, pp.100-110.

HAMILTON, H.R. et al. (1969). Systems Simulation for Regional Analysis. Cambridge, Mass: MIT Press.

HANSEN, W.G. (1959). How accessibility shapes land use. Journal of the American Institute of Planners, Vol. 25, .73-7.

HERBERT, J. and STEVENS, B. (1960). A model for the distribution of activity in residential areas. Journal of Regional Science, Vol. 2, pp.21-36.

HESSE, M. (1963). Models and Analogues in Science. London.

HUFF, D.L. (1962). Land Economics, Vol. 38, pp.64-66, Vol. 39, pp.81-89.

HYMAN, G. (1969). The calibration of trip distribution models. Environment and Planning, Vol. 1, pp.105-12.

IRVINE DEVELOPMENT CORPORATION (1971). Irvine: Master Plan Report.

JOHN MADIN DESIGN GROUP (1969). Telford. Development Proposals: Volume 1. Birmingham.

JOINT LOCAL AUTHORITY, SCOTTISH DEVELOPMENT DEPARTMENT and DEPARTMENT OF ENVIRONMENT STUDY TEAM (1972). General Information System for Planning. London: HMSO.

JONES, K. (1972). Which data base management system? A case study. In Urban Data Management: Proceedings of the Second Annual European Symposium. London: Planning and Transportation Research and Computation Co. Ltd.

LAKSHMANAN, T.R. and HANSEN, W.G. (1965). A retail market potential model. Journal of the American Institute of Planners, Vol. 31, pp.134-43.

LEICESTER and LEICESTERSHIRE SUB-REGIONAL PLANNING STUDY (1969). Volume I: Report and Recommendations. Volume II: Technical Appendices. Leicester City Council and Leicestershire County Council.

LICHFIELD, N. (1969). Cost-benefit analysis in urban expansion: a case study, Peterborough. Regional Studies, Vol. 3, pp.123-55.

LICHFIELD, N. (1970). Evaluation methodology of urban and regional plans: a review. Regional Studies, Vol. 4, pp.151-65.

LINDSAY, W. with CHEESMAN, R. and PORZECANSKI, M. (1971). New Towns: a Comparative Atlas. Working Paper No. 62. Cambridge: LUBFS.

LLEWELYN-DAVIES, WEEKS, FORESTIER-WALKER and BOR (1970a). The Plan for Milton Keynes: Report of Evidence Presented by the Consultants to the Milton Keynes Development Corporation. Two volumes, and technical supplements Nos. 1 to 9.

LLEWELYN-DAVIES, WEEKS, FORESTIER-WALKER and BOR (1970b). The Plan for Milton Keynes: Technical Supplement No. 5. Demographic Base Studies.

LONDON COUNTY COUNCIL (1961). The Planning of a New Town. London: LCC.

LOSCH, A. (1954). The Economics of Location. New Haven: Yale University Press.

LOWRY, I.S. (1964). A Model of Metropolis. Santa Monica, California: Rand Corporation.

LOWRY, I.S. (1966). Migration and Metropolitan Growth: Two Analytical Models. Institute of Government and Public Affairs, University of California.

LOWRY, I.S. (1967). Seven Models of Urban Development: a Structural Comparison. Santa Monica, California: Rand Corporation.

MASSER, I. (1970). A Test of Some Models for Predicting Inter-Metropolitan Movement of Population in England and Wales. University Working Paper No. 9. London: Centre for Environmental Studies.

MASSER, I. et al. (1971). Estimation of a growth allocation model for North-West England. Environment and Planning, Vol. 3, pp.451-63.

MASSEY, D.B. (1971). The Basic-Non-Basic Split. Working Paper No. 63. London: Centre for Environmental Studies.

MASSEY, D.B. and CORDEY-HAYES, M. (1971). The use of models in structure planning. Town Planning Review, Vol. 42, pp.28-44.

McLOUGHLIN, J.B. (1969). Urban and Regional Planning. London: Faber.

MEYERSON, H. and BANFIELD, E.C. (1955). Politics, Planning and the Public Interest: the Case of Public Housing in Chicago. Glencoe: The Free Press.

MINISTRY OF TOWN AND COUNTRY PLANNING, DEPARTMENT OF HEALTH FOR SCOTLAND (1946). Final Report of the New Towns Committee (Reith Committee). Cmd. 6876. London: HMSO.

NEW TOWNS ACT (1965). London: HMSO.

NOTTINGHAMSHIRE AND DERBYSHIRE SUB-REGIONAL STUDY (1969). Report. Nottinghamshire C.C., Nottinghamshire C.B.C., Derbyshire C.C. and Derby C.B.C.

OLSSON, G. (1965). Distance and human interaction: a migration study. Geografiska Annaler, Vol. 47B, pp.3-43.

OWENS, D. (1968). Estimates of the Proportion of Space Occupied by Roads and Footpaths in Towns. Report LR 154. Crowthorne: Road Research Laboratory.

PEARSON, D. (1970a). Monitoring and evaluation: planners' feedback. Official Architecture and Planning, Vol. 33, pp.769-71.

PEARSON, D. (1970b). The Plan for Milton Keynes. Technical Supplement No. 4: Notes on Monitoring and Evaluation. Milton Keynes Development Corporation.

PLANNING AND TRANSPORTATION RESEARCH AND COMPUTATION CO. LTD. (1972). Urban Data Management: Proceedings of the Second Annual European Symposium. London: PTRC.

PORZECANSKI, M. with CHEESMAN, R. and LINDSAY, W. (1971). New Towns: the Evolution of Planning Criteria. Working Paper No. 64. Cambridge: LUBFS.

RAVENSTEIN, E.G. (1885). The laws of migration. Journal of the Royal Statistical Society, Vol. 48, 1885 and Vol. 52, 1889.

REILLY, W.J. (1931). Laws of Retail Gravitation. New York: Knickerbocker Press.

ROBINSON, I.M., WOLFE, H.B. and BARRINGER, R.L. (1965). A simulation model for renewal programming. Journal of the American Institute of Planners (May).

ROBINSON, J. (1962). Economic Philosophy. Watts. Pelican Edition (1967).

SALOMONSSON, O. (1969). Data banking systems for urban planning. In Information and Urban Planning: Conference Proceedings. Information Paper No. 8, Vol. 2. London: Centre for Environmental Studies.

SCHNEIDER, M. (1968). Access and land development. In Urban Development Models Ed. G. Hemmens. Special Report No. 97. Washington D.C.: Highway Research Board.

SCOTTISH DEVELOPMENT DEPARTMENT and MINISTRY OF HOUSING AND LOCAL GOVERNMENT (1971). Information Needs of the New Planning System.

SENIOR, M. and WILSON, A.G. (1972). Disaggregated Residential Location Models: Some Tests and Further Theoretical Developments. Working Paper No. 22. Department of Geography, University of Leeds.

SHANKLAND, COX and ASSOCIATES (1966). Expansion of Ipswich: Designation Proposals. London: HMSO.

SHANKLAND, COX and ASSOCIATES (1968). Ipswich Draft Basic Plan. London: HMSO.

SIMON, H.A. (1969). The Sciences of the Artificial. Cambridge, Mass: MIT Press.

SOROKIN, P.A. (1928). Contemporary Sociological Theories. New York: Harpers.

STEELEY, G. (1970). The evaluation process. In Papers from the Seminar on the Process of the Notts.–Derbys. Sub-Regional Study. Information Paper No. 11. London: Centre for Environmental Studies.

STEVENS, B.H. (1967). Location theory and programming models: the von Thunen case. Regional Science Association Papers, Vol. 21, pp.19–34.

STEVENSON, J. (1971). Evaluation of structure plans: lessons from the West Midlands Study. In Some Papers from the CES–RTPI Conference on Structure Plan Preparation. Conference Paper No. 5. London: Centre for Environmental Studies.

TAYLOR, D.R.F. (1972). Bibliography on Computer Mapping. Exchange Bibliography No. 239. Monticello, Illinois: Council of Planning Librarians.

THORBURN, A. (1970). The decision oriented framework for the study. In Papers from the Seminar on the Process of the Notts./Derbys. Sub-Regional Study. Information Paper No.11. London: Centre for Environmental Studies.

TOWN PLANNING INSTITUTE/PLANNING AND TRANSPORTATION RESEARCH CO. LTD. (1968). Urban Data Management: Proceedings of Conference at University College, London.

UNESCO/IGU (1972). Second Symposium on Geographic Information Systems. Ottowa, August 1972.

U.S. BUREAU OF CENSUS (1970). Census Use Study: The DIME Geocoding System. Report No. 4. Washington D.C.: The Bureau.

U.S. DEPARTMENT OF HOUSING AND URBAN DEVELOPMENT (1969). Request for Proposals No. 11-2-70 for Municipal Information Systems, 31 July 1969.

VON THUNEN, J.H. (1826). Der Isolierte Staat in Beziehung auf Landwirtschaft und Nationalokonomie. Hamburg.

WEBER, A. (1909). Uber den Standort der Industrien, I: Reine Theorie des Standorts. Tubingen.

WELLOR, B.S. and GRAFF, T.O. (1971). Geographic Aspects of Information Systems: Introduction and Selected Bibliography. Exchange Bibliography No. 239. Monticello, Illinois: Council of Planning Librarians.

WILLIS, J. (1968). <u>Population Growth and Movement</u>. Working Paper No. 12. London: Centre for Environmental Studies.

WILLIS, J. (1972). <u>Design Issues for Urban and Regional Information Systems</u>. Working Paper No. 71. London: Centre for Environmental Studies.

WILSON, A. (1967). A statistical theory of spatial distribution models. <u>Transportation Research</u>, Vol. 1, pp.253-69.

WILSON, A. (1970). <u>Entropy in Urban and Regional Modelling</u>. London: Pion.

WILSON, H. and WOMERSLEY, L. et al. (1969a). <u>Northampton Master Plan</u>. Northampton Borough Council and Northampton Development Corporation.

WILSON, H. and WOMERSLEY, L. et al. (1969b). <u>Teeside Survey and Plan: Final Report to the Steering Committee. Volume 1: Policies and Proposals</u>. London: HMSO.

WILSON, H. and WOMERSLEY, L. et al. (1971). <u>Teeside Survey and Plan: Final Report to the Steering Committee. Volume 2: Analysis</u>. London: HMSO.

ZIPF, G.K. (1946). The P_1P_2/D Hypothesis: on the intercity movement of persons. <u>American Sociological Review</u>, Vol. 11, pp.677-686.

List of contributors

Richard Barras	Centre for Environmental Studies, London.
Michael Batty	Urban Systems Research Unit, University of Reading.
Richard Baxter	Centre for Land Use and Built Form Studies, Cambridge.
Erlet Cater	Urban Systems Research Unit, University of Reading.
Robert Cheesman	Centre for Land Use and Built Form Studies, Cambridge.
Martyn Cordey-Hayes	Centre for Environmental Studies, London.
Stewart Cowie	Department of the Environment, London.
David Crowther	Centre for Land Use and Built Form Studies, Cambridge.
Chris Doubleday	Centre for Land Use and Built Form Studies, Cambridge.
Marcial Echenique	School of Architecture, University of Cambridge.
Tony Houghton	Local Government Operational Research Unit, Reading.
Walton Lindsay	Centre for Land Use and Built Form Studies, Cambridge.
Nigel Lloyd	Centre for Land Use and Built Form Studies, Cambridge.
Brian McLoughlin	Centre for Environmental Studies, London.
Lionel March	Centre for Land Use and Built Form Studies, Cambridge.
Jean Perraton	Centre for Land Use and Built Form Studies, Cambridge.
Catherine Stoneman	Centre for Land Use and Built Form Studies, Cambridge.
Ian Williams	Centre for Land Use and Built Form Studies, Cambridge.
Jeffrey Willis	Department of Civic Design, University of Liverpool.

List of participants

Mr. Aguero	University College School of Environmental Studies, London.
Mr. K. Alsop	Building Research Station, Watford
Mr. B. Anderson	More Og Romsdal District University, Molde, Norway.
Mr. H. Andersson	Nordplan, Stockholm, Sweden.
Mr. P. Ashworth	Department of Town Planning, Haringey
Mr. J. Bailey	County Planning Department, Hertford
Mr. J. Bates	Operation Research in Transport, London
Mr. A. Battinelli	Laboratorio di Elettronica Industrial, Padova, Italy
Mr. A. Beattie	Polytechnic of North London, London
Mr. P. Bell	County Planning Department, Winchester
Mr. S. Black	Institute for Centerplanlaegning, Gentofte, Denmark
Mr. J. Blake	Planning Department, Brent
Mr. W. Bock	Schwetzingen, Germany
Dr. W. Bordass	Robert Matthew Johnson-Marshall and Partners, London
Mr. M. Bradshaw	County Planning Department, Leicester
Professor P. Brenikov	Department of Town and Country Planning, University of Newcastle upon Tyne
Mr. von Breyman	University College School of Environmental Studies, London.
Mr. A. Carruthers	Public Works Department, Birmingham
Mr. R. Chadirji	Bagdad, Iraq
Mr. I. Challen	County Planning Department, Chester
Mr. U. Christiansen	Danish Building Research Institute, Copenhagen, Denmark
Mr. T. Cocks	Geneva, Switzerland
Mr. J. Coghill	Architecture and Planning Department, Glenrothes Development Corporation
Mr. A. Davies	County Planning Department, Bury St. Edmunds
Mr. A. Delloro	Politechnico di Milano, Milan, Italy
Mr. J. Dible	Scottish Development Department, Edinburgh
Mr. F. Dijkstra	Emepo, Utrecht, Netherlands
Mr. R. Dodwell	DOE, London
Mr. R. Donnison	Oxford Polytechnic, Oxford
Miss D. Drake	Central Lancashire Development Corporation, Preston
Mr. R. Eagland	County Planning Department, Northampton
Mr. W. Ewing	Cumbernauld Development Corporation, Cumbernauld
Mr. M. Fairhurst	Operational Research in Transport, London
Mr. S. Ferrer	London
Mr. P. Filipek	Livingstone Development Corporation, West Lothian
Mr. Forese	Politechnico di Milano, Milan, Italy
Mr. M. Ganzuvles	Planologisch Instituut, Nijmegen, Netherlands
Mr. K. Gasson	Pontllanfraith
Mr. I. van Genugten	Planologisch Instituut, Nigmegen, Netherlands
Mr. J. Gibbons	Scottish Development, Edinburgh
Mr. R. Gilbert	DOE, London
Mr. C. Gregory	County Planning Department, Bury St. Edmunds
Mr. C. Gupta	Auroville Centre for Environmental Studies, Pondicherry, India
Mr. S. Hammerton	Department of Civil Engineering, University of Leeds

Mr. J. Hebrard	Centre D'.Etudes Techniques de l'Equipment, Lille, France
Mr. M. Hennings	G.L.C. Department of Planning and Transportation, London
Mr. S. Hurrell	County Planning Department, Chester
Mr. D. Hutchinson	Planning Department, Derby
Mr. K. Jack	Sir John Burnett Tain and Partners, London
Mr. J. Johnson	Wivenhoe, Essex
Mr. D. Jones	County Planning Department, Dorchester
Mr. P. Kettle	University College School of Environmental Studies, London
Mr. H. Knikkink	Planologisch Institut, Nijmegen, Netherlands
Mr. B. Kopp	Institut fur Angewandte Mathematik II, Universitat Erlangen, Germany
Mr. P. Langley	DOE, London
Mr. N. Lewis	County Planning Department, Preston
Mr. G. Linden	Planologisch Institut, Nijmegen, Netherlands
Mr. R. MacTaggart	Department of Civil Engineering, University of Leeds
Mr. I. Masson	Ministerie van Openbare Werken, Brussels, Belgium
Mr. P. McMahon	County Planning Department, Reading
Mr. J. Miles	Department of Civil Engineering, University of Leeds
Mr. M. Oakley	Planning Department, Bristol
Mr. K. O'Sullivan	Applied Research of Cambridge, Cambridge
Mr. A. Pizzati	Laboratoria di Elettronica Industriale, Padova, Italy
Miss N. Poix	OREAP, Amiens, France
Dr. H. Raum	Institut fur Angewandte Mathematik, Erlangen, Germany
Miss M. Rees	DOE, Leeds
Mr. D. Regenboog	Empeo, Utrecht, Netherlands
Mr. F. Rensson	Empeo, Utrecht, Netherlands
Mr. L. Shapiro	Manchester
Mr. D. Scheer	Institut fur Angewandte Mathematic II, Universitat Erlangen, Germany
Mr. B. Schlaffenberg	Planning and Communication Department, Camden
Mr. E. Seymour	DOE, Manchester
Miss J. Smith	County Planning Department, Stirling
Mr. S. Smith	DOE, London
Mr. B. Stearn	County Planning Department, Winchester
Mr. K. Stromberg	Chalmers University of Technology, Gothenberg, Sweden
Mr. G. Taylor	Skelmersdale Development Corporation, Lancashire
Mr. F. Thomas	Scottish Development Department, Edinburgh
Mr. N. Thorne,	Peterborough Development Corporation, Peterborough
Mr. C. Thunhurst	Polytechnic of North London, London
Mr. J. Varley	DOE, Newcastle-upon-Tyne
Mrs. B. Webster	Institute for Local Government Studies, University of Birmingham
Mr. R. Wherry	Planning Department, Matlock
Miss M. White	Scottish Development Department, Edinburgh
Mr. P. Woodhead	Municipal Offices, Hammersmith
Mr. A. Woollatt,	County Planning Department, Nottingham
Mrs. E. Worsley	Town Planning Office, Reading
Mr. G. Zanteke	London

Index